John M. DeGrove

Land
Growth
&
Politics

 Planners Press
American Planning Association
Washington, D.C.   Chicago, Illinois

Contents

v

Acknowledgments

Collecting data, analyzing it, and writing this book have taken eight years—1976 to 1983. During that time, I have traveled to each of the states treated in the book at least twice, and in most instances more than that. In the course of those visits—and by mail and telephone—I have talked to hundreds of people, to each of whom I owe my deepest thanks and appreciation. Without their cooperation, I could never have obtained the below–the–surface information that I hope informs the analysis in an effective way. Of course, the interpretation of what I have been told and what I have read are exclusively my responsibility.

I want to single out one person in each state for the special help and support extended to me, including assistance in collecting data and in reading successive drafts of this book. To these people I owe a special debt of gratitude. They are Carole Whitesell, Hawaii Land Use Commission member and civic activist through the League of Women Voters; Jonathan Brownell, practicing attorney in Vermont, long active in land–use matters, and director of the Public Affairs Center at Dartmouth College; Mike Fischer, executive director, California State Coastal Commission; Jim May, author of an excellent master's degree thesis on Florida land–use law and, until recently, chief of the Bureau of Land and Water Management in Florida's land planning agency; Henry Richmond, executive director, Thousand Friends of Oregon; Gary Fisher, Land Use Commission planner and author of a detailed and very helpful analysis of the adoption of Colorado's land–use law; and finally, Jonathan Howes, director of the Center for Urban and Regional Studies, University of North Carolina at Chapel Hill. All of these people gave generously of their time and energies not just once but many times. They were always helpful, and always appropriately critical.

The efforts of a number of people in typing and editing the successive drafts of the book have been invaluable. These persons include Janet Adair, former research assistant and secretary for the Florida Atlantic University/Florida International University Joint Center for Environmental and Urban Problems; Ann Cannon and Linda Adams, Joint Center secretaries, who typed much of the book

viii

more than once; Irene Gordon, who edited the entire draft in its semi-final stages; Millie Carr, administrative assistant for the Joint Center, who was most helpful in organizing the overall effort; and to my wife, Gail, I owe appreciation for patience and support in this eight–year effort.

The Kettering Foundation supported, through a grant, the travel funds necessary for the collection of data in the early stages of this project. To the foundation go my thanks and appreciation.

1

Introduction

This book examines the public policy area of land and growth management by assessing in detail the political context in which seven states adopted laws covering such matters between 1961 and 1974. This detailed description and analysis of the development and implementation of these laws is cast within a comparative framework. But it is also the flesh and blood story of these programs, from the first stirrings of concern, through the political maneuvers in the legislatures, to the push and pull among various levels of government as the provisions have actually been carried out.

For each state, the assessment begins with the *issue context*, the emergence of problems and issues that were seen by groups and individuals to demand strong state action in the area of land and growth management. The next step in the assessment is the *politics of adoption*, describing the forces, both public and private, that are involved in opposing or supporting a strong state initiative to improve land and growth management. The *politics of implementation*, an analysis of the major political and policy developments during the period in which the new legislation was put into practice, is next. This part of the analysis describes the continuing roles of the legislature, the governor, and the major interest groups involved in this public policy area, as well as major efforts to strengthen or weaken the original legislation. The closing section, the *politics of the future*, focuses on the prospects, based on recent developments, for the continuance or strengthening of these state initiatives in land and growth management during the 1980s.

The decade of the 1960s moved land and growth management upward on the public policy agenda in the United States through major policy development at all three levels of government in our federal system.[1] This book will focus on new state actions beginning with Hawaii in 1961 and ending with North Carolina in 1974.

The concentration on the state provides a unique vantage point from which to view the unfolding of land and growth management as a major public policy issue. States occupy a leverage point in the federal system that is of special importance in this policy area. If they choose to exercise it, states have the ultimate power over local governments in land- and growth-management matters. However, most states have been content to delegate that power to local government. This book examines the political context in which seven states asserted or reasserted a more activist role in land and growth management.

The state laws and their implementation vary substantially, but they all involve state action well beyond that taken by most states. All feature the establishment of a policy framework, however limited, to guide new state initiatives. In some of the case study states, such as North Carolina and California, the policies apply only to coastal areas. In other states, for example, Florida, Vermont, and Colorado, policy initiatives apply throughout the state, but selectively to certain geographic areas or development actions. In other states, such as Oregon and Hawaii, policy initiatives are more comprehensive, affecting in one way or another almost all the land- and growth-management actions taken in that state. Thus a rough typology emerges in which the state actions can be categorized from weak to strong in terms of comprehensive coverage and the strength of the state policy framework as it affects the land- and growth-management decisionmaking process.

The assertion of a stronger role in land and growth management by the state has produced, and is still producing, important impacts in the land- and growth-management arena, including:

- The scope and nature of public policy decisions in land and growth management.
- The distribution of authority and responsibility for such decisions among federal, state, and local levels, with especially important impacts on state/local relations.
- The nature of the relationship between the private and public sectors in decisions affecting land and growth.
- The links being forged between planning and regulation, which are introducing a new realism into the planning process.
- The shaping of new interest group coalitions that are strengthening the support for a more active state role in land and growth management.

All of these forces are examined in the case studies that follow. Although each state represents a unique set of problems and a unique regulatory approach, common threads can be found which run through each experience. These are discussed in a comparative framework in chapter 9.

The Environmental Base of
Political Support

The major source of political support for what some have called the "new mood" in land and growth management flows directly from the environmental movement that emerged in the late 1950s and 1960s and reached a peak of strength in the early 1970s in this country. Although many contributing factors may be cited to explain the increasing interest in growth management at all levels of government in the United States, the most important source of support clearly has been the rising concern of Americans for their environment.

The environmental movement undergirds much of the increasing skepticism toward the assumed "goodness of growth" that characterized public and private attitudes throughout most of our history. This growing concern for the environment continues to provide much of the political strength to land- and growth-management policy initiatives. Environmental concerns as they evolved in the 1950s and 1960s were rooted in the belief that the degradation of our land, air, and water resources was reaching such serious levels as to constitute a major public policy problem. This basic perception has led to increasing sensitivity on the part of interest groups and individuals to the more-than-local impact of any federal, state, or local land- and growth-management decisions. Such problems as the chronic overloading of wastewater treatment plants, the inability to deal effectively with solid waste problems, and the seemingly heedless and wholesale destruction of our natural systems have combined to create a genuine sense of crisis, first among fairly narrowly defined environmental groups but more recently among a much broader cross section of the population.[2] Even progrowth advocates began to be swayed by the argument that environmental degradation from unwise development was a threat to the economic vitality of their community and state. The emergence of the environmental movement as a major force in the United States is illustrated not only by the success of these forces and their allies in pushing major new actions at the federal, state, and local levels, but is confirmed by public opinion surveys that have attempted to measure the public's attitude toward environmental matters.[3]

The policy response to the rising environmental concern, which carried environmental groups in a short time from being a small minority with little political power to a much broader base of strength and thus increased political power, was exemplified in new laws and other actions at the federal level. During the 1950s and continuing into the 1960s, while stopping short of enacting a general land use law, Congress did take a number of major actions that directly and indirectly were of great importance to land and growth management.[4] Some examples of important federal initiatives that had an impact on land and growth management included the Comprehensive Planning Assistance Grant Program (701), established by the Housing Act of 1954; the Rural Development Program;[5] and the 1972 Coastal Zone Management Act.[6] These represent direct efforts to produce desired land- and growth-management results at state and local levels through federal grant programs. Another approach may be seen in major regulatory programs that included the Federal Water Pollution Control Act as amended in 1972,[7] the Clean Air Act,[8] and the Noise Control Act.[9] All of this legislation, and many additional congressional efforts, constituted a major federal entry into the land- and growth-management policy area that had implications, among other important effects, for the allocation of power among levels of government in the federal system. The Coastal Zone Management Act (1972) may be thought of as a geographically specific federal land use law that has had far-reaching impacts on the behavior of coastal states in both planning and implementing programs for the management of their coastal areas.

Policy responses to the increasing concern about the negative impacts of growth have in some ways been more dramatic at the local than at either the federal or state level. Several approaches have been taken which tend to be associated with the names of particular cities in states across the nation. All of them have as a common goal the effort to manage or redirect growth in order to prevent a further degradation of the environment and more generally to protect the quality of life in the community. The *phased* or *staged growth technique* is associated with the town of Ramapo, New York; another version of this approach is found in Petaluma, California, a fast-growing community north of San Francisco. Other communities have taken different approaches, including Boca Raton, Florida, with its so-called 40,000 dwelling unit cap, a kind of population ceiling technique, and the Loudoun County, Virginia, approach which at one time was a blanket denial of all new development. These models have been followed by hundreds of other communities under severe population or economic growth pressures.[10]

Important legal and social questions are raised by these actions, to be sure, including whether a restriction on land use constitutes a taking of property rights and whether equity requires that landowners be compensated.[11] The record in our courts to date suggests that a growth-management effort that is carefully crafted and carried out in an even-handed way can and typically will be sustained in the courts. Social questions about growth-management efforts center on their exclusionary potential. Others point to the inclusionary policies that are part of some growth-management plans. The courts in most states have not been a major factor in negating growth-management efforts on equal protection or due process grounds. Again, a carefully crafted growth-management system that makes an even minimal effort toward providing low and moderate income housing has typically been enough to avoid adverse rulings. The issue is one that will be fought out largely in the political arena.

From this brief review of policy initiatives in land and growth management at all three levels of government in our federal system, one can see an emerging pattern in which the central thrust is not so much the loss of power by one level to another, but a general situation in which all three levels of government have expanded their policy initiatives. This book has as its focus an examination of the politics of these new initiatives in land and growth management at the state level, including the impact of these new state initiatives on both the federal and the local levels. In the seven case states, the focus will be on such questions as:

- What were the major groups in support of the initial legislative proposals?
- Who opposed them?
- What were the major arguments pro and con involving proposed legislation?
- Does the *politics of adoption* differ in important ways from the *politics of implementation*?
- Are the political forces in support of a stronger state role in land and growth management such that they can sustain and even expand these programs, or is support apt to peak and weaken?
- Are there patterns of support and opposition that can be identified in key states that would provide important clues to other states just entering this policy area?

We have used in-depth interviews—most quite candid—with participants and observers and the record provided by authors close to the scene to gain a greater understanding of these questions involved in the land- and growth-management policy initiatives undertaken by the states.

Other policy questions that emerged from the process of collecting and analyzing the data will also be analyzed. One of the more significant to the evolution of public policy in the land, water, and growth-management areas is the link between planning and regulation. The environmental programs of the 1950s and 1960s were largely federal and state efforts, the latter often induced by federal action, that were regulatory in nature, depending on case-by-case permitting for their implementation. As new problems of environmental degradation became clear, new regulatory programs with a new set of permit requirements emerged. These regulatory programs often had little or no connection to broader planning and management programs, even when the latter were concerned with the same land- and water-management issues. The regulatory programs tended to be narrowly focused in a policy sense, designed to block action in particular circumstances, but largely incapable of positive initiatives that indicated where and how things could be done, in addition to where and why something could not be done. For instance, water quality regulatory programs administered by a federal or state agency were equipped to say where a marina could not be located, but poorly equipped to say where one could or even should be placed.

One striking feature of a number of land- and growth-management programs examined in the pages that follow is that the development of a planning system has been linked to existing or new regulatory systems with the result that the effectiveness and efficiency of each is considerably enhanced. The quality of the California plan for the coast has clearly been improved by the experience gained in implementing a regulatory system while the plan was being developed. Much the same thing is happening in North Carolina. As the local land use plans are undergoing revisions, they are being enriched by the insights gained through the issuing of permits in areas of environmental concern. The land capability and development plan in Vermont is an important but incomplete example of a policy framework within which an extensive permitting process is carried forward.

One of the major complaints about environmental regulations and the attendant permitting systems is that they are marked by duplication, overlap, and needless delays for the private sector. The decade of the 1980s clearly will see continued efforts to consolidate and simplify permitting systems. At the same time, those cases where formerly discrete permitting programs are drawn into and made part of a comprehensive planning effort seems to hold much promise for furthering two major goals of the development community: timeliness and certainty. The decade of the 1980s can be the time when environmentalists shed their passion for ad hoc solutions in exchange for a new growth-management system that draws the regulatory process within the framework of a new kind of comprehensive plan. The new comprehensive plans of the 1980s should be characterized by policies clear enough and simple enough to drive the decisionmaking process and by an implementing mechanism adequate to assure compliance with those policies.

Florida has recognized the need for such an integrated policy framework, and Oregon is far along in implementing such a system for its mandated local government comprehensive plans. If the state functional agencies can be drawn smoothly into Oregon's land- and growth-management system, that state will lead all others in the 1980s in bringing regulatory and planning processes together. The significance of such a development to the further reshaping of the planning profession in the United States is hard to overestimate.

Another issue that will be examined is whether the reassertion of state responsibility for land and growth management has a significance beyond the policy area of land and growth management. This would be the case if the increased state activism leads to changes in the allocation of authority and responsibility of sufficient magnitude to be an important factor in the evolution of the federal system in the United States. To the extent that states become the central integrating force for federal, state, and local programs in the land- and growth-management area, their role in the federal system could be importantly enhanced.

This study has not attempted to carry out a scientific assessment of the new land- and growth-management programs. That is, this book does not try to answer the question: "What difference have these programs made?" In examining the politics of implementation, a considerable body of data on the substantive impacts of the legislation has been gathered and presented. However, the focus has been on the sustainment of political support, or the lack of such support, for the implementation effort. Systematic monitoring and evaluation efforts are needed to track the result of the land- and growth-management policy initiatives. The major purpose of this book is to document the political context of the development and implementation of seven state land- and growth-management systems. It is hoped that the descriptions of pitfalls and political struggles and innovative solutions will be useful to and used by elected and appointed officials, especially at the state and local levels. It should be of special interest to planners and public administrators concerned with land- and growth-management systems. Finally, it is our hope that this book will add to the realism of academic courses in law, public policy, and planning.

Hawaii Land-Use Districts

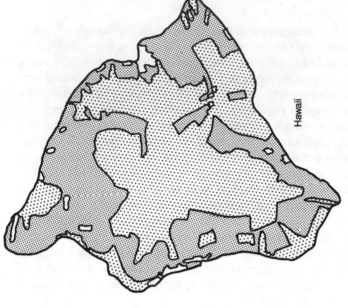

Hawaii

Oahu

Of Hawaii's eight major islands,
Oahu is the most urbanized, Hawaii one
of the least.

☐ Urban

▨ Agriculture

▨ Conservation

2

Hawaii:
First, Different, and Changing

The Issue Context

To understand why Hawaii was the first state to adopt a land use law involving the state in a major role, one must start with Hawaii's unique physical setting. While the Hawaiian chain includes more than 100 islands stretching across 1,700 miles of the Pacific Ocean, eight major islands form a 400-mile arc at the southeastern end of the Hawaiian archipelago and comprise more than 99 percent of the state's land area.[1]

Hawaii is by far the largest island, followed by Maui, Oahu, Kauai, Molokai, Lanai, Niihau, and Kahoolaue. The original Polynesians who came to Hawaii called it the "Big Island," a name still used by most long-term residents. Maui was the center of the whaling trade and the home of most of the Calvinist missionaries whose descendants were to have such an impact on the land-holding patterns of Hawaii. By 1970, this small collection of eight islands had grown to a population of 769,913 persons, some 80 percent of whom lived on Oahu, whose major city of Honolulu represented the island to most foreigners. The ethnic mix of the Hawaiian population is rich, varied, and still changing. Native Hawaiian and descendants of immigrants from Japan, China, the Philippines, Portugal, and the mainland U.S. are represented in significant numbers.[2] In the 1960s, the proportion of the population made up of Haoles (caucasians) increased from 32 to 39 percent. During the period 1970–75, the annual growth rate was about 2.3 percent with a decline to 1.3 percent in the recession years of 1974–75. Growth from 1930 to 1960 was concentrated in Oahu (Honolulu), but the trend in the 1970s shifted, with the neighbor islands as a group growing faster than Oahu.[3] By 1980, the total population was 965,000, showing a 25.3 percent increase since 1970.

The finite limits of the land available for residential, agricultural, commercial, and other uses is everywhere visible to residents of the islands. As one assessment put it, "Almost one half of Hawaii's total land area is within five miles of the shoreline and most development is found in this area. There is no point in the state more than 29 miles from the ocean." While there is a total of 750 miles of general shoreline, there are only 185 miles of sandy beaches.[4] Surely such a setting has had some influence on the special interest Hawaiians have taken in the way in which land is to be used and conserved.

The pattern of landownership in Hawaii had a substantial impact on the adoption of the state's land use law in 1961. The original Polynesian settlers seemed to survive very nicely with a kind of benevolent monarchy in which land was technically owned by the king or queen, but, in fact, was used freely by the members of the family units that made up the population. Two factors changed this easy going and apparently functional system. First, a Polynesian king managed to conquer most of the islands and in 1810 unified control over most of the area. At about the same time, the Calvinist missionaries made their appearance on the scene and began to introduce the notion of private property rights. By the time the monarchy was overthrown in 1890, over half of the land that was in private hands in Hawaii was owned by small groups of "Haoles," westerners who were typically descendants of the Calvinist missionaries. This laid the basis for the highly concentrated pattern of landownership and control that still characterizes the islands. Hawaii's coastal zone management application to the federal government noted that in 1969 only a small percent of the land was owned by small private landowners:

> In 1969 major private owners (with holdings of 5,000 acres or more) controlled an estimated 45.2 percent of the total (slightly over 4 million acres) land area in the state. State agencies, including the Department of Hawaiian Home Lands, owned 38.7 percent of the total. The federal government owned 9.8 percent. . . . The counties owned about 0.1 percent. . . . Only 6.2 percent . . . . was owned by small private landowners.[5]

The concentration of land ownership was one factor that expedited the establishment of a prosperous agricultural economy featuring sugar and pineapple production. The other factor was a discovery of a dependable water supply in the form of an underground reservoir lying underneath the dry Ewa plain on Oahu. By the end of the 1950s, just before the 1961 land use law was passed, only about 5 percent of the islands' land was in holdings of less than 1,000 acres. Just seven landholders controlled about one third of the land, with just 72 major landholders owning about 47 percent of the land.[6]

Perhaps only in Florida have drastic changes in a state's political setting had as much influence on the adoption of a land use law as such changes had in Hawaii. Hawaii's new political era arrived in 1955, when the Republicans were ousted from the state house of representatives by a coalition of unions and Japanese-Americans. Many of the Japanese-Americans were veterans of World War II, had taken full advantage of their federal educational benefits, and had emerged as the new dominant political force in Hawaii. The political setting thus shifted abruptly and drastically from control by conservative Republicans to a situation in which young, reformist, energetic Democrats, overwhelmingly Japanese in their ethnic background, came to power determined to bring in a whole range of reform legislation in Hawaii.

The land use law adopted in 1961 was just one of those major reform efforts, and at the time it was not uniformly viewed as the most important. The immediate problems that spurred the passage of the law involved the rising tendency in the 1950s for developers to buy tracts of land, especially on the big island of Hawaii, and chop them up into small lots for sale in fly-by-night subdivision land sales operations. This movement, if allowed to spread, was seen as a serious threat to agriculture, as one planner recalled.[7] The threat was even more immediate because the pineapple and sugar industries were under considerable financial pressure and thus vulnerable to raids by land speculators who were more than willing to buy prime agricultural land at a low price, divide it up into lots, and put it on the market. Another source stressed the determination of the young Japanese-American politicians to "get the old 'big five' oligarchy under control," a reference to the large companies that controlled huge tracts of land in the islands. This source stressed the fact that the 1958–65 period was one of innovation in the legislature for Hawaii, an "era of growth, reform, and intellectual ferment, all with considerable zeal and determination."[8]

An important part of the determination to break up the control of the big five was to bring the land into more productive use, according to the mayor of Maui, Elmer Cravalho, who in 1961 was the speaker of the house of representatives. He commented that the large landowners "in effect banked all the land with a low utilization rate and a low revenue generation rate. The idea was to get a sophisticated land classification plan and then tax on the highest and best use and make it unfeasible for the 'big five' to just squat on the land."[9]

Ray Suefuji, long involved in planning and land use controls in the islands, pointed to another contributing factor that is of special interest in the light of subsequent conflicts over the implementation of the land use law—the irresponsibility, as he saw it, of counties in managing land use. In his opinion, the counties had shown this lack of responsibility by approving the premature subdivision of agricultural land for land sales schemes. At that time, tourism had not become a major factor in the economy of Hawaii, and agriculture and forestry were the foundation. Any threat to their survival was seen as something that had to be dealt with in a forceful way. Suefuji also pointed out that the future economic prosperity of Hawaii lay in preserving forest lands for recharging vital water storage areas.[10]

A former chairman of the Land Use Commission confirmed that a major reason for a land use law was the "scattered development that was threatening agricultural land." He went on to say that the conservation or environmental factor was not a primary force, but that the few conservationists around saw their opportunity and supported the legislation.[11]

In summing up why Hawaii acted at such an early point in passing a strong state land use law, one can see a combination of forces including the political turnover which saw young reform-minded Americans of Japanese ancestry and their allies replace old-line conservative Republicans, first in the house and subsequently in the governor's chair and in the senate. This new political lineup was anxious to see Hawaii prosper economically, and the invasion of agricultural land by premature subdivision development was seen as a strong threat to that prosperity. Thus the movement for a land use law was not in any sense antigrowth or antieconomic development. On the contrary, it was based on the desire to promote and enhance the economic prosperity of the islands. The fact that this was so must be constantly kept in mind when the implementation record of the law is evaluated. Environmental concerns have, in fact, subsequently made themselves felt in Hawaii, but this concern has often expressed itself through additional legislation, and many environmentalists are hostile toward and suspicious of the work of the Land Use Commission. We turn now to a closer look at the politics of adoption of Hawaii's act 187, the land use law approved in 1961.

The Politics of Adoption

The movement to establish some sort of state planning process and to address both general planning and land use planning questions had its beginning in Hawaii well before 1961. In 1957, the territorial legislature passed three major pieces of legislation relevant to these purposes. One act created the Land Study Bureau at the University of Hawaii to classify all lands in the territory according to natural characteristics and productivity, with a view toward using such data to determine appropriate land uses.[12] A second act (act 234) established Hawaii's forest and water reserve zones and authorized the Territorial Board of Commissioners of Agriculture and Forestry (which later became the Department of Land and Natural Resources) to regulate and administer such reserves; elsewhere in the territory, counties were given all other zoning powers.[13] A third law, act 150, established a territorial planning office (which later became the state planning office), charged with the responsibility of preparing a long-range comprehensive plan to guide Hawaii's future development.[14]

Ironically given this early start, the effort to develop an effective and forceful state planning effort in Hawaii has been a frustrating and difficult process down to the present time. The first general plan was, in fact, developed in 1961, but had little impact beyond contributing to the adoption of the land use law. The plan, which recommended that much of the counties' zoning power be transferred to the state, was never adopted by the legislature. A second general plan, developed in 1967, "crumbled in the face of opposition from provincial island politicians, small landowners, and land speculators."[15]

The law that was introduced into the 1961 session of the Hawaii legislature and enacted on July 11, 1961 was for its time a bold and far-reaching effort in state involvement in land use. Certainly no state to that point had taken action that could be compared to it. What the law did in essense was to establish an independent Land Use Commission, appointed by the governor and confirmed by the senate, which was given the authority to divide all of Hawaii into three land use classes: urban, conservation, and agriculture. The major policy thrust of the act was clear in the findings and declaration of purpose that was included in the legislation:

> Inadequate controls have caused many of Hawaii's limited and valuable lands to be used for purposes that may have a short-term gain to a few but result in a long-term loss to the income and growth potential of our economy. . . . Scattered subdivisions with expensive yet reduced public services; the shifting of prime agricultural lands into nonrevenue producing residential uses when other lands are available that could serve adequately the urban needs; failure to utilize fully multiple-purpose lands; these are evidences of the need for public concern and action.
>
> Therefore, the legislature finds that in order to preserve, protect, and encourage the development of the lands in the state for those uses to which they are best suited for the public welfare . . . *the power to zone shall be exercised by the state.* . . .[16]

This declaration of purpose is a clarion call for the assumption of state responsibility for two major elements of land use control that lie at the heart not only of the Hawaii effort but almost all later efforts at state entry into the land use field. These two major elements were the protection of prime agricultural, open space, recreation, and other such lands on the one hand, and some kind of urban containment policy to force urban development into relatively compact and contiguous land areas on the other.

Unlike the experience of most other such efforts examined in this study, the proposed legislation was not highly controversial and escaped major compromises or changes in its passage through the legislature. Thomas Gill, a prominent attorney and later an unsuccessful candidate for governor in 1970 and 1974, played a major role in drafting the legislation. Governor Quinn, the first governor after statehood was approved in 1959, and the legislative leadership supported the legislation. Testimony conflicts somewhat over whether the "big five" supported or opposed the legislation. They may have perceived it as less radical than plans for breaking up the old estates being proposed by some political forces in the state. The best assessment seems to be that they saw the bill's passage as inevitable and stayed in the background, working only to make sure that tax benefits tied to the law were adopted. Elmer Cravalho, then speaker of the house of representatives, recalled that the only serious threat to the bill came from some of the old "power figures" in the senate who "were not eager for change." As Cravalho remembered it, the big plantation owners, big business, and a lot of "natives" opposed the legislation.[17] A long-time planner recalled that: "It was really a race to see who could get credit for the bill."[18] He and other observers agreed that the counties had been relatively ineffective in their opposition.

According to one assessment, the legislation was part and parcel of a "powerful wave of reform inherent in the new alliance of the have-nots [Japanese-Americans and their allies] and a genuine interest in responsive government in general and land use planning in particular shared by Governor Quinn and the legislative leadership." There was, in fact, little public argument over whether there should be a land use law, or even over the concept of zoning Hawaii, that is, placing all of the state into one of the three land classifications.[19] The legislature defused the most sensitive issue—the drawing of the boundary lines—by simply providing a process by which the Land Use Commission could carry out this function at a future time. This assessment gives considerable credit for ultimate passage to Elmer Cravalho, renowned throughout Hawaii for his political skill. It was his idea to link the land-classification approach to reduced taxation for agricultural use, "a move that made it irresistible to agriculture interests."[20]

Unlike the passage of land use bills on the mainland during the 1970s, environmentalists were not active proponents of Hawaii's 1961 law. The protection of the environment in the sense that it is understood today was not the major motivating force in passing the legislation. The prime motivating force was the fear that agriculture, especially the pineapple and sugar plantations, would be wiped out by careless and unplanned urban development.

Provisions of Act 187 and Subsequent Amendments

The original law[21] set up three land categories, which were referred to as districts. (See Figure 2.1.) The urban district included land that was already in urban use, plus lands that would be needed for foreseeable urban growth.[22] The agriculture district was aimed at giving "the greatest possible protection . . . to those lands with a high capacity for intensive cultivation,"[23] but could include lands not used for or not suited for agriculture if such lands were adjacent to or surrounded by agricultural land. Permitted uses were developed later by the Land Use Commission and included a wide variety of agricultural-related activities. A minimum lot size of one acre was added by a 1969 amendment to the agricultural district.[24]

The conservation district was to consist of previously established forest and water reserve zones. Subsequent Land Use Commission regulations allowed the inclusion of lands which did not fit into

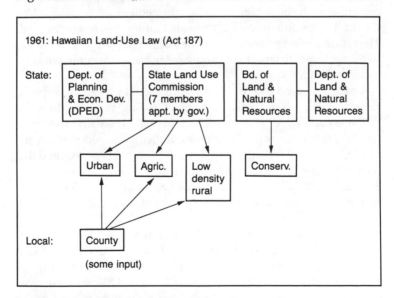

Figure 2-1. **HAWAII: Land-Use Regulation**

other categories. A rural district was added in 1963 at the insistence of the neighbor islands, to permit low density residential lots.[25] None of the land on Oahu has been classified as rural.

The Land Use Commission consisted of seven members appointed by the governor, with senate approval, and two ex officio voting members: the directors of the Department of Planning and Economic Development and the Department of Land and Natural Resources. The commission was provided with a small staff to carry out its duties, and appeals from its decisions were to go directly to the circuit court.

In drawing the original boundaries of the land districts, the commission was required to hold hearings in each county, establish land use district regulations and rules of practice and procedure, and set the district boundaries. The tax department was charged with taking the commission's classification of land into consideration in making property tax assessments.[26]

In order to change district boundaries, two different procedures were provided for in the original legislation. First, the Land Use Commission was to review all district boundaries and regulations once every five years. In addition, the commission could make changes in district boundaries at any time in response to a petition and after a public hearing. An extraordinary majority of six affirmative votes was required. Petitions could be put forward by either a landowner or lessee, or any county or state agency, including the commission itself. A citizen could not petition for a change in a district designation unless he or she had a direct interest in the land. The commission was required in the law to refer proposed changes to the appropriate county planning commission for comments and recommendations.[27]

A particular land use could also be changed by receiving a special permit which amounted to a kind of zoning variance from the purpose authorized in its particular district. Originally, seekers of special permits in agriculture or rural districts could petition the Land Use Commission directly, but a 1963 amendment required that the petition be first approved by the county planning commission. The Land Use Commission then could either approve, deny—or as authorized in the early 1970s—approve the special permit with conditions.[28]

The regulation of conservation land was provided for in an entirely different way. Act 187 authorized the Land Use Commission to place lands in the conservation district, but its authority stopped there. The Department (and Board) of Land and Natural Resources was given the sole authority to decide on the uses of land in the conservation district. This approach to regulating land use in the conservation areas, consisting of about half of the 4 million acres in the entire state of Hawaii, has had a profound impact on the implementation of the land use law, which will be examined in detail later.[29]

The Politics of Implementation

An Overview

Assessing the implementation record of Hawaii's state land use effort is a more challenging task than assessing any other state in the study. This is not only because Hawaii was almost a decade ahead of other states in taking a land use initiative. It is also because new values and forces have evolved that have imposed additional objectives on the law and the Land Use Commission. The most compelling illustration of this change has been the emergence of the environmental movement in Hawaii.

During the late 1960s and early 1970s, among Hawaiians concerned with protecting the environment, there was a rising tide of dissatisfaction and alarm at the ever increasing growth pressures on the finite territory of the islands. These environmentalists expected the land use law and the Land Use Commission to meet a range of environmental- and growth-management goals that went far beyond the law's original intent. When these new goals were not met, the commission tended to get the blame, whether fairly or unfairly. In any case, the dissatisfaction of the late 1960s and early 1970s led not only to a substantial revision of the land use law in 1975, but to additional overtly environmental legislation that was adopted in the early 1970s. These new initiatives have become part of a general attempt to link adequate planning with an effective regulatory program. The major topics addressed in this assessment will be:

- An evaluation of the Land Use Commission itself, its organization, funding, procedures and regulations, and political dimensions.
- The performance record of the Land Use Commission, evaluated in terms of major time periods and in terms of the four major land classification categories authorized in the law.
- An assessment of the increasing tensions between the state government and counties in the planning and land use area.
- An assessment of the land use effort in relationship to the increasing environmental concerns in Hawaii.
- A description of the development of Hawaii's coastal zone management program.
- A critique of citizen participation in the Hawaii land and growth management effort.

• An overall assessment of the strengths and weaknesses of the implementation effort.

The Land Use Commission: Organizational, Funding, Procedural, and Political Dimensions

An excellent assessment of the political context of the early years of the commission can be found in Myers, *Zoning Hawaii*, where she notes that:

> The first two years after passage of act 187 were chaos. This was the crucial period when the interim boundaries were in place and the permanent boundaries were under study. It was also a time of intense political and economic activity in the new state. The governor appointed a . . . commission, but his fellow Republicans in the senate refused to confirm the group. Developers and major landholders began to realize the implications of what had been done and tried to have the law repealed.[30]

Two close students of the evolution of the Land Use Commission also recalled that a political crisis occurred in the early life of the commission over the question of adding the rural zone to the classification system. As they remembered it: "In 1963 the neighbor islands said 'We'll kill the law if you don't give us a rural district.'" The root of this controversy seemed to flow from small farmers, many of them Oriental, who wanted to divide their already fairly small holdings so that they could leave them to their sons.[31]

Myers went on to note that after Governor John Burns' victory in 1963 and his installation as Hawaii's first Democratic governor, many established groups expected a far-reaching invasion of what they considered their best interests, but she noted that it soon became clear in the actions of the Land Use Commission that this would not be the case.[32]

There was a general consensus on the part of Land Use Commission members that the funding and staffing of the commission were from the first woefully inadequate and have remained so to the present day. The first chairman, Myron Thompson, recalled that: "We didn't get support from the legislature, and that was partly deliberate."[33] The initial appropriation was for $50,000. A later commission chairman, Eddie Tangen, noted that: "A problem from the very first was that the funds came to the Land Use Commission through the Department of Planning and Economic Development. They were pretty skimpy; at no time has there been adequate staff to really do the kinds of things that need to be done in the way of basic research and understanding the problems so that we can know more about what we're doing."[34] In a related comment, Carol Whitesell, one of the few commissioners with a strong commitment to environmental values, pointed out that the commission staff lacked the capacity to prepare and keep updated a data base by which to guide commission decisions, nor could it carry out special studies of long-range problems such as water resources and an evaluation of regional growth patterns.[35] She also noted that the commission's small staff had been almost totally preoccupied before 1975 with the analysis of individual petitions, and after 1975 with procedural and legal work associated with the new quasi-judicial approach. In neither period was the commission in a position to undertake the data collection and analysis and the special studies that would have allowed the drawing or redrawing of the district boundaries on really firm substantive grounds.[36]

The assumption seems to have been that the staff work needed by the commission would largely be supplied by the Department of Planning and Economic Development. This kind of arrangement, one that is followed in North Carolina and to some extent in Vermont, usually results in a weak and incomplete data base from which to make land use decisions. In contrast, the approach of providing adequate staff support directly to a special land use commission or other such body seems to work more effectively.[37]

The present head of the Department of Planning and Economic Development recognized the problem when he took that job: "I saw right away that there wasn't enough solid substance to the work product being done by the Land Use Commission." He expressed confidence that the department, acting within the framework of new plans and policies and a revised procedure for state government input to the Land Use Commission, would correct this deficiency.[38]

Policy/Political Context, 1969–72
In the period 1969–72, alterations were made both by rule and in the law that had a fairly substantial impact—or potential impact—on the work of the commission, especially with regard to the policy/political context of that work. One was the commission's adoption of an incremental development rule in 1969. This rule stipulated that only land which could be developed within a five-year period would be reclassified, and no further reclassification of land would be granted until the first development was substantially complete. If the proposed development was not carried out within the five-year time limit, the Land Use Commission could move to revoke the original reclassification.[39]

The other significant change, made in spite of county objections, was the 1972 amendment to the land use law which clearly authorized the commission to require certain conditions as a part of the approval of a land reclassification request. The amendment allowed the commission "to assure substantial compliance with representations made by the petitioner in seeking a boundary change."[40]

If used consistently, the incremental development approach and the imposition of permit conditions could move the Land Use Commission from a limited role of redrawing district boundaries to a direct and potentially major role in land and growth management in Hawaii. The potential impact of this change has been largely overlooked, except by Daniel R. Mandelker.[41] The commission, using these tools, could carry out a deliberate policy objective of articulating a kind of staged-growth approach. Other staged-growth policies would include a requirement that all the needed public services be completely in place at the time of the development, including land dedicated for such things as parks, school sites, public rights of way, and others.

Mandelker's assessment of these new powers, written in 1976, suggested that the commission had begun to take "a more active role in the regulation of land development when exercising its boundary approval powers." But Whitesell later held that these policies had been used rarely, and in the case of the incremental development rule not at all since 1975.[42] Nevertheless, the policy potential is there for important growth management initiatives if the commission chooses to use it.[43]

One very significant area in which the commission articulated a deliberate policy in growth management involved the requirement that as a condition of a boundary change approval, the applicant make provision for a number of low or moderate income housing units. Land Use Commission Chairman Eddie Tangen was especially active in persuading petitioners to accept such conditions. Since his retirement from the commission in 1978, this policy tool has been virtually abandoned.[44] This approach has also been used on the mainland United States, for example, in the development of regional impact approval process in Florida, and as one of Oregon's legally binding goals for growth management. The approach has the potential, assuming its constitutional adequacy, to overcome the charge that land- and growth-management policies exacerbate the problem of meeting low and moderate income housing needs. The approach has had a major policy impact only in Oregon.

Genesis of 1975 Legislation
The pressure for further changes in the land use law arose from the increasing dissatisfaction with the work of the Land Use Commission. One focus of discontent was the conclusion of the 1969

boundary review that land conversions from agriculture to urban had not been excessive. Myers described how "a newly aroused citizenry claimed otherwise and charged that the rezonings occurred without adequate public participation and, in some instances, illegally."[45] It was during this period that the leading environmental organization today in Hawaii, Life of the Land, came into being. In its frequent legal, press, and other attacks on the commission, Life of the Land charged that in many land use reclassifications notification had been inadequate and cited many other procedural inadequacies.

Part of the dissatisfaction arose because the Land Use Commission was being asked to accomplish goals for which the law had never been designed. Part of the citizen frustration seems to have stemmed from very real inadequacies in the commission's own procedures. Part of the pressure for change had to do with the political ferment of the time, in which growth management was being made a major political issue in 1970 campaigns for the U.S. Senate (by Tony Hodges) and for governor (by Thomas Gill).[46]

A particular source of discontent was the alleged development of bias by the Land Use Commission. One of the persistent charges of opponents was that at best the persons appointed to the commission were indifferent to good land and growth management, and at worst they were the tools of special interests. It is impossible to sort out the rights or wrongs of these charges. Perhaps what can be said is that the commission seems to have been as much a victim of the changing values being articulated by activist groups, as it was guilty of active bias in favor of development and other special interests. There undoubtedly was some of the latter, but the heart of the issue goes back to the changing policy context since the land use law was adopted. The law was passed originally out of an overriding concern for the economic prosperity of Hawaiian agriculture. The political coalition that was then the "new guard" in Hawaiian politics was made up of young and reform-minded politicians—mainly Japanese-Americans; business and commercial groups interested in developing Hawaii; and labor, especially the International Longshoremen's and Warehousemen's Union. For the Japanese-Americans, politics was a way up the status as well as economic ladder. Labor, of course, was interested in prosperity, economic expansion, and jobs. It is unrealistic to think that a land use law spawned in such a political milieu and a commission appointed by a governor who headed this particular political group would be anything other than dedicated to promoting the economic expansion and prosperity of Hawaii.

Friends and critics alike agreed that the commission had been strongly concerned with protecting agricultural land from the point of view of promoting economic prosperity for Hawaii. The question of whether the commission was authorized to or willing to attempt to protect agricultural land for urban growth management motives raised a whole new issue.

The actual appointments to the commission seem to have been predominantly from the ranks of strong political supporters of first Governor Burns and then Governor Ariyoshi: representatives of the business, commercial, and union sectors. An early chairman of the Land Use Commission, Myron "Pinky" Thompson, left that position to become an administrative aide to Governor Burns and since has become one of the five trustees of the Bishop Estate, one of Hawaii's big five land trusts. A long-term member of the Land Use Commission and chairman until 1978, Eddie Tangen, who some would say ran the commission with an "iron hand," was also a leading International Longshoresmen's and Warehousemen's Union member. He told the author that he came to the legislative sessions to represent the union and at the same time to try to look out for the Land Use Commission. Tangen's strong personal commitment to providing housing for low and moderate income people, while commendable to those concerned with this issue, did not necessarily endear him to environmentally oriented growth-management advocates. In 1977, only two of the members could be thought of as strongly representing a growth management and environmental point of view in making land use decisions. By the early 80s, several members of the commission seemed sensitive to environmental values, but the economic development thrust was illustrated by three appointments to the commission in early 1982. Carol Whitesell could not be reappointed because of the two-term limit, and the commission lost its strongest environmental member. She was replaced by a banker, and the other two appointments were a United Airlines employee and a leader of a native Hawaiian community group.[47]

It seems fair to say that the background of the typical commissioner has tended to make him or her more interested in growth, development, jobs, and housing than in land use in a growth-management or environmental sense. In making this assessment, it is not meant nor is it necessary to attribute good or evil motives to any individual commissioner. The point of the assessment is that the political context from which the Land Use Commission was chosen and operated was not one that made the environment a top policy objective. On the contrary, the political context made jobs, economic development, and growth the predominant values. One might even say that the young and progressive Japanese-American politicians

who under the leadership of Governor Burns gained control of the
Hawaii legislature and executive branch in the late 1950s and early
1960s had matured and become more establishment-oriented in the
ensuing years, even to the point of becoming the Hawaii counterparts of the "good old boys" of southern mainland politics.

In any event, the political context out of which the Land Use
Commission operated, and to some extent still operates today,
destined it to come into conflict with the passionate advocates of
environmental protection and related growth-management objectives. One mitigating factor that may prove to be of major importance is the genuine and firm commitment on the part of Governor
George Ariyoshi's administration to establish some kind of reasonable and viable growth-management system for the islands. There is
no question that Ariyoshi is sincere in his concern with the
potentially negative impacts of unbridled growth on Hawaii. It is
conceivable that the Ariyoshi administration will ultimately make
common cause with the land use and environmental groups to
pursue a stronger course of managed growth for Hawaii. However,
from the governor's point of view, there are political complexities
and dangers along such a path. The political organization with
which Ariyoshi is associated is a direct descendant of the coalition
that was put together to overthrow the Republicans in the late 1950s
and early 1960s, and unions remain a major bulwark, not only the
ILWU but also the union representing government employees in
Hawaii. To walk a line between economic prosperity and environmental protection will be at least as demanding and delicate in
Hawaii as it has proved to be in a number of other states. This point is
illustrated by the difficulties encountered in 1975 and subsequent
years, in attempting to legislate a strong state planning policy
framework for Hawaii's land- and growth-management system, to
which we now turn.[48]

The groundwork for this attempt was the commission's 1974
review carried out by a firm of planning consultants, a distinguished
legal consultant with extensive experience in the land use area, and
additional specialized consultants. Unlike the 1969 review, which
was focused solely on the adequacy of the districting effort by the
commission, the consultants engaged in the 1974 review were given
a broad mandate to assess how the commission's procedures,
approach to its work, and its involvement in policy development
might better be structured.

The report discussed the implications of a state supreme court
ruling, handed down in the midst of the 1974 boundary review,
which had created something of an administrative crisis for the
commission. The court's action in the *Town* case required the

commission to adopt quasi-judicial procedures, at least in all cases in which boundaries were challenged by adjacent landowners.[49] Although the commission's legal consultant argued that its proceedings were primarily rulemaking and should not become quasi-judicial, he recommended that the issue be settled one way or the other by the upcoming legislative session in 1975.

The commission's legal consultant drew up for the legislature's consideration a series of fundamental changes in the 1961 legislation—in effect, repealing the old law—that would have patterned the Hawaii land use law more along the lines of the critical areas approach used in the Florida legislation, drawn largely from the American Law Institute's Model State Land Development Code. These amendments would have had the effect of substantially strengthening the role of the state vis-à-vis local governments in the land use control system in Hawaii.

Although supported by Governor Burns, the timing of such changes could not have been worse. The public attitude toward the Land Use Commission was reaching a low point, and a combination of environmentalists, local government advocates, and others were in no mood to see the hand of the commission strengthened in any way. The mayors of the several counties came to Honolulu to fight the proposed change in the legislature. One observer recalled that about the only people for the bill were the Department of Planning and Economic Development, the legal consultant, and the commission itself.[50] The far-reaching proposals in the bill never had a serious chance of passing in the legislature, but they did have the effect of further mobilizing counties against state efforts to capture any additional control over land- and growth-management decisions in Hawaii.

The 1975 legislative session did respond to the *Town* ruling by mandating a quasi-judicial approach in Land Use Commission proceedings having to do with amending district boundaries. The legislature also established interim guidelines within which the commission was mandated to carry out its responsibilities, particularly with regard to approving proposed boundary changes. These substantive changes were part of a major bill establishing a state planning policy for Hawaii.

The legislature favored the quasi-judicial approach because the previous informal procedures had "proved inadequate and unworkable" and unable to reconcile hostile and conflicting points of view.[51] The legislature also reconstituted the Land Use Commission as a nine-member body without ex-officio members and abolished the requirement for five-year reviews.[52]

The interim guidelines included in the new legislation substantially tightened the criteria for making district boundary changes.[53] Several guidelines reinforced the urban containment policy, requiring, for example, adequate public services and facilities, or the ability to provide them at reasonable costs to the petitioner, in lands to be placed in the urban district.[54] Preference was also to be given to amendment petitions providing for permanent employment or contributing to a balanced housing supply for all economic and social groups.[55]

The legislature also strengthened and clarified the matter of conditions and their enforceability. The commission was specifically authorized to impose conditions necessary to uphold the intent and spirit of the law and its policies and criteria, or to assure substantial compliance with the representations made by the petitioner in seeking a boundary change. It was mandated that "such conditions, if any, shall run with the land and be recorded in the Bureau of Conveyances."[56] This forceful restatement of the 1972 amendment supports the ability of the commission to engage in detailed stipulations as to the development of land in the process of approving land-classification changes. The law required that any boundary changes be consistent with the interim policies and criteria or with any state plan enacted by the legislature, in which case the plan would supersede the interim guidelines.[57]

By linking the land use crieria not only to the interim guidelines provided in the law itself, but also to a future state plan, the Hawaii legislature was attempting to meet the extensive criticism of policymaking by the Land Use Commission. Many critics expected that the work of the commission would become a largely automatic process in which it simply carried out and applied policies and criteria in quasi-judicial proceedings that would involve very little judgment or policymaking on its own part. By clearly linking land use decisions to the anticipated state plan, the 1975 legislature may also have been responding to criticism of a general plan developed by the Department of Planning and Economic Development in 1967. The 1967 plan simply described a planning process and provided no clear-cut policy guidance. Its connection to land use was summed up in a statement that "The state land use plan may be identified at any moment with the district boundaries established under provisions of the Land Use Law." As a League of Women Voters of Hawaii analysis of planning in Hawaii noted: "This statement shows confusion about the difference between planning, and its tool, zoning, which is the short-range process of land use control based on long-range planning."[58]

It can be argued, and in the view of this author accurately, that such a "slot machine" approach to the work of the commission was naive in the extreme. In the first place, it was doubtful that the policies and criteria spelled out in the eventual state plan would be specific enough to convert the Land Use Commission to simply an automatic policy application body. This view has subsequently been supported by the experience under the state plan Hawaii adopted in 1978 and by similar experience in other states. Second, the language in the new law itself allowed the commission considerable flexibility. For example, in requiring that the commission adhere to the interim guidelines, the act added the phrase "except when the Land Use Commission finds that an injustice or inequity will result." Furthermore, the interim guidelines themselves clearly anticipated a considerable amount of judgment on the part of the commission, through such phrases as "reasonably necessary," "adequate public services," "maximum use," and a number of others. The language in the law clearly indicates that under the interim guidance policy— and it seems reasonable to assume under criteria developed in the state plan—the Land Use Commission was not expected to turn into a kind of robot applying policy automatically and without the need for judgment in petitions brought before it.

To say that the commission will continue to make policy judgments is not to say that the 1975 act and accompanying planning legislation did not bring about far-reaching changes in the way the commission operates. Among other things, the composition of the commission was altered by dropping the directors of the departments of Planning and Economic Development and Land and Natural Resources as members of the commission. Thus the commission became a 9-member body with a requirement that there be one member from each county and five members named at large. Members continued to receive no salary and were not required to have any special qualifications.[59] It remains to be seen whether the move to a quasi-judicial approach will prove to be a benefit or a detriment to making sound land- and growth-management decisions. It must be pointed out that another alternative was available to the legislature. By simply tightening the commission's quasi-legislative procedures, the legislature could have met most of the objections, without going to what some view as the extreme of the formalities involved in quasi-judicial hearings.[60]

Reaction to the quasi-judicial format was mixed. The abrupt shift in procedures in the middle of a complex boundary review inevitably caused confusion, with the result that the activities of the commission were to some extent justly subject to criticism. In recalling the events of those troubled times, the commission's general counsel noted that: "Developers as a matter of fact saw the quasi-judicial approach as a thing to benefit them. Life of the Land suddenly decided that they were opposed to going quasi-judicial because they interpreted it as an attempt to cut off their rights to state their case."[61] McConnell added: "I tried to sell environmental groups on the fact that this kind of quasi-judicial approach was needed to keep things in the open. The big problem is that it does, or at least it can, overcomplicate things so that you get all bogged down in procedural matters and you really don't or can't get around to a sensible consideration of the substance of the issues."

Another participant recalled that the court decision requiring quasi-judicial procedures for contested cases, coming as it did in the midst of the 1974 review, "was really a mess, and so we got a lot of attack on procedural defects." In the legislature, the commission decided to support the move to a quasi-judicial approach, in part to head off another bill which was designed to give the legislature the final word on all land use decisions.[62] In the view of this long-time observer and practitioner in the affairs of the Land Use Commission, the quasi-judicial format had both positive and negative aspects. On the positive side, "Everything is on the record, it is a formalized process, and everybody has to say why they are voting the way they are voting, and that's good." On the other hand, he echoed the general counsel's comments by noting the tendency to get bogged down in "procedural minutia." He expressed the hope that part of this problem would be cured by the adoption of a state plan that would give a clearer legislative policy framework.[63]

If it is true that the quasi-judicial format has overformalized and overproceduralized the work of the commission at the expense of a careful consideration of substantive issues, the 1975 law also brought about other procedural changes that have had a positive impact on the adequacy of the substantive considerations of boundary changes. The law created a land use division in the Department of Planning and Economic Development with responsibility for coordinating the state's position on a boundary change application. After receiving the comments of relevant agencies, the division had the responsibility to prepare and present the administration's unified position to the commission. A typical proposal would go to the same set of state agencies, including the departments of Health, Agriculture, Transportation, Natural Resources, and the Office of Environmental Quality Control.

An assistant to the governor noted that this was very different from how things were done in the pre-1975 period, when departments tended to "do their own thing" in testimony before the Land Use Commission and in fact often presented conflicting positions, He noted that it was still possible for the state to have more than one position, but the governor would have to sign off on such a division

if it should happen.[64] All the departments typically involved in the
state's response to a reclassification petition are headed by persons
appointed by the governor. Thus, in contrast to a state, such as
Florida, where many department heads are elected, the governor of
Hawaii has potentially a very strong role—for better or worse—in
developing land- and growth-management policy.

In the case of Governor Ariyoshi, persons close to him were in
unanimous agreement about his strong and increasing interest in
the whole question of land and growth management. As an
illustration, the governor's special assistant cited the case of the
Waiahole and Waikane Valleys, on the windward side of Oahu, an
area of small farms where agriculture had been long established.
The valleys came under heavy development pressure in the 1970s,
and indeed developers managed to buy the development rights to
land in both valleys. As a result of the governor's effort to prevent
their conversion from agriculture to urban use, the state purchased
Waiahole Valley and the Land Use Commission denied an urban
classification for Waikane Valley.[65] Another example of the governor's interest involved the so-called West Beach project on Oahu, in
which the state opposed a proposal to convert sugar cane land to use
as urban-resort-residential land to include eight hotels, golf courses,
and commercial facilities.

More recently, the Ariyoshi administration, through the Department of Planning and Economic Development, objected to the
development of a marina and related hotels and housing facilities at
Ewa Beach involving the conversion of agricultural land. The Land
Use Commission approved the district change from agricultural to
urban partly on the grounds that the land involved was marginal for
agriculture. The state and the county joined in opposing the project
in an appeal to the courts that succeeded in overturning the
commission action. The state and county objections included a lack
of sufficient infrastructure and the fact that most of the project was
not coastal dependent, thus violating an important policy in Hawaii's coastal management program.[66] The point here is not to
attempt to judge the right or wrong of these cases, but to illustrate
the governor's strong and specific interest in key land use decisions,
particularly involving the conversion of agricultural land to urban
uses.[67]

In making the 1975 changes, the legislature apparently expected
the new land use division to begin to give the commission the kind
of full and complete background information and data analysis that
would be needed for evaluating district boundary change requests
from a strong factual and analytical position. Yet, experience has

shown this not to be the case. The land use division itself is not heavily staffed, and it has a major task in simply attempting to coordinate the state's position on major classification cases. Many persons in civic, legislative, and executive circles in Hawaii seemed to feel that with the 1975 interim guidelines in place and with the policy framework of the anticipated state plan, the commission really would not need very much data gathering or data analysis in making its decisions, nor would it be involved in any major way in policymaking. As noted earlier, this expectation was and is unrealistic. The kinds of fairly general statements that must be made in such planning documents cannot provide specific criteria for decisions of agencies such as the Land Use Commission.

If the legislature had adopted a plan that was so specific as to remove most of the discretion from the decisions of the commission, it would have created a decisionmaking framework far too rigid and inflexible to meet what are often rapidly changing demands and needs of an effective land- and growth-management system. The fact is that both under the interim guidelines, and under the state plan adopted in 1978, the Land Use Commission will still need strong sustained staff support for substantive study of the issues involved in the land reclassification proposals that come before it. This kind of support has not been available to the commission to this date. It will come, if at all, either through a substantial expansion of the commission's own staff, or through a greatly expanded support from the land use division in the Department of Planning and Economic Development. A question can be raised as to whether a lay member, part-time unpaid commission can possibly give the time and attention to the petitions that come before it that are needed to assure wise decisions. Unless a clear state policy framework greatly reduces the burden of the commissioners, and there is no evidence that this has happened, not only will Hawaii need to consider additional staff support for the commission, but also may come to a serious consideration of full-time paid status for commissioners.

The commission meets once or twice a month, often for two to three days. It must meet in the county that is the location of the petition(s) before it. In 1980 it met 36 times, heard 24 petitions, and held 29 public hearings. Its operating budget of about $200,000 per year is often insufficient to cover such a schedule, and it receives supplementary funds from the Department of Planning and Economic Development. The 1975 law, in mandating contested case (quasi-judicial) procedures, also required parties to the proceedings to be the county involved in the petition, and the state Department of Planning and Economic Development. District boundary changes continued to require an extraordinary vote of six of the nine members. Before 1975 the commission's staff analyzed petitions and made recommendations to the staff, but since then that does not occur. The burden of mastering the facts of the case and reaching a decision falls squarely on the commissioners, a process that is very demanding, since formal hearings tend to produce voluminous records. All this leaves the commission no time to do anything but react to petitions on a case-by-case basis. It has not been able to devote time and energy to analyzing comprehensive studies of the cumulative impact of case-by-case decisions that would in turn place those decisions in a more certain policy framework. Even if the commission had the time for thoughtful deliberation on the cumulative impact of its work, it does not have the staff to prepare the necessary background studies to make such deliberations productive. Thus the capacity of the commission to make a greater contribution to overall growth management system for Hawaii is severely limited by time and a lack of staff support.[68]

Assessing the Performance of the Land Use Commission's Work: The Evaluation Dilemma

Any attempt to make a definitive evaluation of how effectively the 1961 land use law has met its goals is likely to achieve at best only partial success. It is difficult in the extreme to determine whether the law has made a substantial difference in protecting agricultural lands and hence Hawaii's agriculture, or in meeting the interrelated goal of containing urban development in reasonably compact areas. A review of various assessments suggest that there are both positive and negative forces at work in terms of the two major goals of the act; that there are gaps, deficiencies, and limitations in what the Land Use Commission has done, and indeed what it can do, in achieving the goals; and that overall one's judgment of the law's effectiveness depends at least in part on the value framework that one brings to the assessment.

The first point that should be made is that it is not sufficient to simply "work with the numbers," counting the acreage shifted from one land category to another. The numbers are important, of course, and we will be dealing with them. But it is far more important to assess the long-range impacts—positive or negative—implicit in key decisions. Some land reclassifications may set the state on policy paths that will either eventually undermine the law or lead to its effective long-run implementation. It is this kind of evaluation that is complicated by the overlap, fragmentation, and uncertainty as to exactly who is responsible for what in implementing the law.

One way to organize the assessment of the commission's work—and the one we begin with—is by the major time periods involved. This is a convenient approach, because it can make use of the results of the in-depth assessments in the commission's two five-year reviews. The three periods might be termed (1) the formative period: 1961–69, (2) the critical testing period: 1969–74, and (3) the period of adjustment: 1974 to the present time. This chronological assessment will be followed by a qualitative assessment of the implementation effort.

Assessing the Implementation by Major Time Periods

For the formative period 1961–69, the best data base is the first five-year review in 1969, carried out by Eckbo, Dean, Austin and Williams, commission consultants. The consultants concluded, as quoted in Myers, that "The processes the land use law has established have undoubtedly had a guiding effect on the location of new urban areas and a restraining effect on wasteful land use practices."[69] The consultants noted that only a little over 1,600 acres of land had been rezoned to the urban classification category. Of a total of 128 applications for boundary changes, the commission had approved 94 in whole or part, but only about 2,600 acres of prime agriculture land were actually reclassified.

The range of data marshaled by the consultants were extensive, and their evaluation certainly seems to have been thorough. Their cheerful conclusion about the work of the commission up to that date was tempered by a concern for the future that has proved to be prophetic. The consultants' fear was focused on the strong economic and population growth pressures coming to bear on the islands, which had already resulted in extensive pending requests for reclassifying other land categories to urban uses. The consultants saw these growth pressures as a threat to the integrity of the land use effort. They raised the key issue of whether the Land Use Commission would be able to carry out the major goals of the act without some clearer and more forceful policy framework that would allow it to hold fast to the goals of the act in the face of rising pressures for wholesale shifts of land to the urban category.[70]

Based on his analysis of agricultural to urban reclassifications, Mandelker noted that, although the Land Use Commission did seem to have a development bias, the amount of land that was actually converted from prime agriculture to urban in the formative period seemed to be very modest. However, Mandelker described the possible domino effect of the limited shifts from agricultural to urban uses, particularly at the Mililani New Town site in the Central Valley area of Oahu. This area, which contains some of the best agricultural lands in all the islands, also represented tempting development possibilities. The conclusion one can reach from Mandelker's detailed case study is that the political pressures for conversion were very strong, and without a clearer and stronger policy framework, and a resolution of some of the conflicts, overlaps, and contradictions among the various actors in setting land and growth policy in Hawaii, prospects for a continued effective adherence to the basic goals of the land use law did not seem bright.[71] Nevertheless, on balance the commission appears to have done a creditable job in the face of substantial handicaps in adhering to the goals of the act during the 1961–69 period.

The critical testing period, from 1969 to 1974, was again assessed by a team of consultants. Out of a total of 133,438 acres proposed for boundary changes during this period, some 66,670 acres were actually reclassified. In the critical agriculture to urban category, over 13,000 acres were requested to be shifted, with just under 5,000 acres approved. On the other hand, over 8,000 acres had been proposed for conversion from urban to agriculture, of which almost 3,400 acres had been approved. One reading of these statistics can be that fewer than 2,000 acres of net conversion had occurred from agriculture to urban. The commission in its own report on the five-year review, published in February 1975, noted that: "On a statewide basis, the commission considered a total of 133,438 acres proposed for changes in the four land use districts and reclassified 66,670 acres. Of the total reclassified, 5,436 acres were changed from agriculture and conservation to urban, and 4,056 acres were changed from the urban classification to agriculture or conservation. Therefore, the net addition to the urban district classification throughout the state during the 1974 boundary review was approximately 1,380 acres."[72]

Myers concluded that the land reclassifications covered in the 1974 boundary review were, on the whole, "less accommodating to growth than in the past."[73] The Honolulu Star Bulletin called the decisions a "reasonable compromise." The editorial noted that Governor George Ariyoshi had "challenged the assumption that the state commission is developer-oriented." The editorial quoted the governor as saying that "He [had] shared the developer domination impression of the commission when he became lieutenant governor, but that he felt that commissioners had changed during the last two years." The editorial concluded that the work of the commission in its five-year boundary decisions bore out Ariyoshi's view. The *Honolulu Star Bulletin* was especially pleased that the commission had rejected a petition to reclassify the almost 1,400 acres of land in the Waiahole and Waikane Valleys.[74]

It may well be that the most significant positive evaluation that can be made for the entire period covering the commission's work from 1961 to 1974 is that it did, albeit slowly, begin to develop in its reclassification decisions some policies that aimed at achieving the objectives of the law. The incremental approval approach, the attachment of conditions that would be monitored and enforced by the commission, these and other policy initiatives by the commission are potentially far more important than the quantitative data on how much land was being shifted from one area to another. As noted earlier, however, the growth policy capacity of these tools remains largely a potential rather than a reality.

The third major time period from 1975 to the present was marked by the passage—already noted—of major new legislation aimed at placing the work of the commission within a much clearer policy framework. The 1975 law also attempted to solve the fragmentation and overlap problem by establishing the land use division to coordinate state agency positions on land use issues. Finally, the law placed all of the agencies concerned with land use in Hawaii firmly within the framework of policies stated in a state plan. The concept is sound, but its implementation has been difficult.

The state plan was adopted by the 1978 legislature after extended hearings, discussions, and debate, especially in the house.[75] Contrary to the legislative mandate, the draft plan prepared by the Department of Planning and Economic Development did not include land use guidelines to replace the interim guidelines adopted in 1975. The state plan is comprehensive and short, and it follows that it is of necessity somewhat general rather than highly detailed or specific.[76] Yet, there are many goals, policies, and priorities that relate to land and growth management that are sufficiently specific to be directive in an important way for the commission, state agencies, and the four city-counties in Hawaii. Part 3 of the plan provides priority directions, the policies with the greatest potential impact on land and growth management. Brief summaries of these policies follow.

State Plan, Section 104: Population Growth and Distribution Implementing Actions. This section calls for (1) a carrying capacity approach to provide for the desired levels of growth in each geographical area; (2) the rehabilitation of appropriate urban areas; (3) directing urban growth primarily to existing urban areas; (4) directing urban growth away from areas where other important benefits are present, such as protection of valuable agricultural land; (5) the preservation of "greenbelts" through a variety of techniques; (6) the identification of critical environmental areas where urban growth should be excluded; and (7) the encouragement of new industrial development in existing and planned urban areas. All of this has the cumulative policy thrust of directing growth toward compact urban centers, and so far as possible existing urban centers, with the related policy of protecting agricultural lands, open space, and critical environmental areas. This section contains a number of the Ariyoshi administration's growth-management policies.

State Plan, Section 105, Hawaii's Land Resources.   This section sets out three priority actions for the use of Hawaii's resources:

- The preservation and improvement of shoreline open spaces and scenic resources.
- The wise use of Hawaii's limited land resources in order to insure the protection of the environment and the availability of the shoreline, conservation lands, and other limited resources for future generations.
- The accommodation of urban growth in existing urban areas while maintaining agricultural lands in agricultural designation.[77]

While the policies outlined here are general, they do have a clear and consistent direction that supports and reinforces the 1961 land use law and subsequent amendment goals of compact development and protecting important agricultural lands, clearly two sides of the same coin in Hawaii. While a set of policy guidelines specifically for the Land Use Commission was not adopted in 1978, the interim guidelines were extended until 1980.

Part 2 of the act mandated the preparation of state functional plans starting from the basis of county general and development plans, which dealt with all the policies and objectives necessary for the coordinated development of each county and areas within each county. County plans were required to be in conformance with the state plan by January 1982, and the state legislature was charged with the responsibility of adopting functional plans prepared by the agencies. The true significance of the state plan generally for Hawaii and specifically for the commission depends heavily on the implementing mechanism provided for in the laws.

Act 100, in setting the Hawaii state plan, established a policy council consisting of 18 voting members: the 4 county planning directors, 9 public members, and 5 of the 13 state agency members, depending on the issue before the council. The executive director of the Land Use Commission was included as a state agency member. The policy council was to be chaired by the director of the Department of Planning and Economic Development and staffed by that department.

The policy council was given the awesome task of assuring that the goals, policies, objectives, and priorities for the state plan were reflected in all state and county plans and programs. In addition to being consistent with the state plan, the functional plans and county plans were required to be consistent with each other. Where conflicts arise that cannot be resolved by the policy council, the issue goes to the legislature for resolution. Thus the ultimate answer as to whether this planning system will achieve its goal rests with the legislature. Hawaii's leading newspaper, the *Honolulu Star Bulletin*, refused to accept the conventional wisdom in 1978 that the plan was "mere words." The editorial's conclusion was that "It seems to us a significant base point from which to try to direct and shape Hawaii's future. It is one that can be revised as experience develops."[78]

The state plan spoke directly to the role of the Land Use Commission in several of its sections. For example, Section 52–D stated:

> The decisions made by the Land Use Commission shall be in conformance with the overall theme, goals, objectives, policies, and priority directions contained within this chapter, and the state functional plans adopted pursuant to this chapter. The rules and regulations adopted by the Land Use Commission to govern land use decisionmaking shall be in conformance with the provisions of this chapter.

The need to give added policy guidance to the Land Use Commission was recognized in the attempt to pass a land use guidance law (house bill 733) in the 1978 and succeeding sessions of the legislature. The bill reconfirmed the right of the commission to impose and enforce conditions and an incremental development system in connection with reclassification petitions and spelled out new statewide land use guidance policies that were much more detailed than the interim policies they were designed to replace. The approval of the proposed land use guidance policies clearly would strengthen the capacity of the commission to apply a consistent policy framework to its boundary reclassification decisions, thus putting it in a stronger position to resist pressures for inappropriate conversion of agricultural lands to urban uses.

From the perspective of one commissioner, the Department of Planning and Economic Development did not at first put a high priority on passing the land use guidance law, perhaps on the assumption that the state plan and subsequent state agency functional plans would give sufficient guidance to the commission. A strong push to pass the law was made in 1981, with strong support from the Ariyoshi administration and certain members of the legislature. The bill seemed on its way to sure passage, but was sidetracked at the last minute. It remains an important unfinished item on the agenda for completing Hawaii's land- and growth-management system, especially in view of the continued failure by the legislature to pass state functional plans.[79]

Qualitative Assessment of the Implementation Effort

The second approach to assessing the experience with the land use law in Hawaii involves a qualitative assessment of the implementation effort. No attempt will be made here to repeat the numbers game involving how much land has moved in gross or net terms from one category to another. That has either been covered earlier or more throughly by other persons who have assessed Hawaii's land use implementation experience. Instead, the focus will be on some of the policy and interagency overlap and fragmentation issues that are fundamental to the future evolution of the land- and growth-management effort in Hawaii.

The Agricultural-Urban Lands Interface

When the land use law was passed, agriculture was the mainstay of Hawaii's economy. The effort to implement the law has been substantially complicated by the decline in the importance of agriculture, and the emergence of tourism as a major new economic component. The major factor in the decline of agriculture seems to have been the increasing foreign competition for the pineapple and sugar industries, competition that seemed for a time to threaten the demise of these traditionally major agricultural enterprises in the islands. The declining profitability of Hawaiian agriculture simply contributed to the heavy pressures to convert agricultural land to urban use.[80]

Opinion is divided on whether there is a viable economic future for agriculture in the islands. However, all observers would agree that there are some very real problems that have to be overcome if agriculture is going to continue on a scale comparable with the past. Myron Thompson, one of the trustees of the Bishop Estate (the only one of the big five land trusts in Hawaii in which the entire proceeds of the trust are devoted to the education of native Hawaiians), reflected in a lengthy conversation on some of the difficult economic problems encountered in the effort to keep land in agriculture. He pointed out that the Bishop Estate got only about 12 percent of its income from the 98 percent of its holdings that are in conservation and agricultural land. In striking contrast, the estate received 33 percent of its income from its tiny percentage (1.6) of residential land, and some 55 percent of its income from the infinitesimal percentage (0.004) of its holdings in commercial land. The total income for the trust in 1977 was set at between $16 and 17 million.

Thompson, himself a former commission chairman, said that he and his fellow Bishop Estate trustees felt that the "land use law is too strict and discourages capital investment." Although he felt that it was proper that the state assert a strong interest in land and in seeing that land was used wisely in Hawaii, he was concerned about the lack of a strategy that would strike a reasonable balance between protecting agricultural land on the one hand and allowing a reasonable amount of capital investment in Hawaii on the other. When pressed as to whether agricultural land would simply be more or less eaten up by commercial or residential developments over the long haul, Thompson stated that he did not think that would happen, or at least it would not happen if the proper state policies were enunciated. In Thompson's view, the proper state policies involved "more incentives and promotion and not so much regulation. The idea of agriculture parks is good. The state will need to put up the front end money for new ventures, for instance, in the area of aqua-culture."[81]

Other persons interviewed also stressed the crucial role of the state if agriculture is to remain a major component of the economy of Hawaii. Part of the problem is to prevent the backdoor conversion of agricultural land to estate-type subdivisions, by means of a land use law provision allowing one residential unit per acre in the agricultural zone. The legislature apparently had in mind a farm dwelling, but the provision provides a loophole. Mayor Cravalho of Maui noted that in the agricultural zone on Maui, even though that county had increased the minimum lot size from one to two acres, it was still possible to "divide property into two-acre pieces and build a residence on that and that really defeats the purpose of preserving the agriculture land." He stated that if he could, he would like to see the minimum lot size increased to five or even ten acres, but left the implication that the politics of that kind of expansion would be virtually impossible.[82]

The county of Maui under Cravalho's leadership has been a leader in the attempt to develop agriculture parks as one way to deal with the problem of preserving agricultural land use in Hawaii. Under such a system, the land is leased to farmers at a modest annual rental. He noted that Maui had, in fact, gotten a start by acquiring 500 acres of such land on Maui, and that there was a need for 1,500 acres more that the state should control so that it would be used for agriculture in perpetuity. He noted that the council had voted $.5 million to begin the project and that he would get the additional funds in the budget in 1978. He went on to say that on the island of Molokai, the first phase of an agriculture park would be completed in May 1977 involving 6,700 acres.[83]

While it is true that Governor Ariyoshi, some of the mayors of the counties, and others are attempting to promote agriculture parks as one way of keeping agriculture viable in Hawaii, even the most ambitious efforts along these lines could not begin to encompass the many thousands of acres of land that are typically leased by the big five landowners to pineapple and sugar operations. One of the people interviewed was Fred Trotter, an executive of the Campbell Estate. Trotter is the grandson of the man who discovered the secret that made Oahu's agriculture possible—water. It was his ancestor who conceived the idea that there was water in a huge underground aquifer capped by the mountains, and that it could be withdrawn for irrigation. He noted that Campbell's lands—the largest piece of agricultural land on Oahu—have been in agriculture since 1890.

To Trotter—and to several others interviewed—water is still the key to either agricultural or urban development in Hawaii. He went on to say that in effect the state is now asserting control over water, and that, therefore, this is a critical growth-management tool for the future. Trotter commented that when the land use law was adopted, the big companies took the view that the state could not tell them what to do with their lands, but faced with the realities of trying to preserve agriculture, he felt that many were now more friendly toward land use controls. He reported that because agriculture is still the Campbell Estate's big revenue producer, the estate had put its industrial park on coral lands at the edge of the sea, and was proposing a new town on the same kind of marginal land on Oahu. Bartholomew and Associates, consultants hired by the estate in 1953 to plan the use of its land, have consistently recommended that all industrial and urban development be on marginal lands.

The Campbell Estate has dedicated all of its agricultural land under a state law which allows a property tax break of 50 percent if the land is dedicated for agricultural use for a 20-year period. This raises the issue of yet another critical tool for preserving agriculture in the future of Hawaii. A 50 percent reduction in property taxes certainly could mean the difference between an economically viable operation and one that could not survive in an economic sense. It would also be one way for the state to provide a kind of compensation for forcing landowners to keep their land in agriculture.[84] The use value taxation and dedication law gives agricultural land a tax break even if a contract is not made to dedicate the land to agriculture for a time certain, though the tax break is greater if such a dedication is made. As in other states, the use value taxation approach will not work unless married to strong land use controls that prevent through regulation conversion of agricultural land to urban use.

The Campbell Estate is also using the agriculture park approach on its north island holdings, where small agricultural users have access to the land of a defunct 3,500 acre plantation. Trotter described the project as a kind of experiment station and cited some very interesting aqua-culture developments. He noted that the estate was in the process of leasing the whole enterprise to the state so that the tenants would continue to be helped.[85]

In attempting to hold agricultural land for farm use, the state has to deal with some very tough dilemmas, especially with regard to whether to approve shifting land to an urban category. While the preservation of agricultural land is a prime goal, an equally important goal is a strong and healthy economy, with unemployment held as low as possible. This goal calls for jobs, and a major way to create jobs has been to make land available for the development of tourist or resort centers. A related—and controversial—question is whether attempts to keep land in agriculture conflicts with the need for a balanced housing supply. In any case, the Land Use Commission has had to make tough tradeoffs among legitimate but often conflicting values.

A 1971 study by the League of Women Voters illustrates the cross-pressures that have buffeted the commission.[86] The league noted that the most severe agricultural to urban conversion pressures had occurred on Oahu which contained 200,000 acres or about 28 percent of prime agricultural land in the islands. The league's analysis for the period 1964–68 concluded that approved conversions had not been excessive, but conversion pressures seemed to be building more and more strongly. At the same time, the league noted a growing countermovement among citizens and groups in Hawaii to "reinforce the law's clear call to save this basic resource— prime agricultural land—from development."

A 1971 bill calling for a two-year moratorium on rezoning prime agricultural land passed the house but did not pass the senate. Also in April 1971, Governor Burns asked the commission to delay major rezoning until completion of the state's open space study.

The league study highlighted the conflicting policy pressures:

We have many pressing needs for land. Do we need to re-examine the goal of protecting agricultural land in the light of these needs? What about the uncertain economic prospects of sugar, pineapple, and other agricultural products? What are the scenic, environmental, and open space values of agricultural lands? What are we willing to pay for these values?[87]

These are the kinds of policy issues that need careful, continuing, and in-depth study by the commission, and it is a continuing weakness that the commission itself has never had, nor has it ever received from other state agencies, the kind of staff support that would allow these sorts of in-depth policy evaluations.

The protection of agricultural land was the major factor in bringing about the adoption of Hawaii's land use law in 1961, and it has taken on new importance in the late 1970s and early 1980s. The adoption of the Hawaii state plan in 1978 coincided with a revision of the Hawaii state constitution which added to that document an important statement concerning agricultural land:

The State shall conserve and protect agricultural lands, promote diversified agriculture, increase agricultural self-sufficiency and assure the availability of agriculturally suitable lands. The legislature shall provide standards and criteria to accomplish the foregoing.

Lands identified by the State as important agricultural lands needed to fulfill the purpose above shall not be reclassified by the State or rezoned by its political subdivisions without meeting the standards and criteria established by the legislature and approved by a two-thirds vote of the body responsible for the reclassification or rezoning action.[88]

Surely few if any state constitutions contain such strong language aimed at protecting agricultural land, nor more specific directions to the legislature to implement the constitutional intent. The major vehicles for such implementation would be the state functional plan for agriculture, the statutory guidelines for the Land Use Commission embodied in the proposed Land Use Guidance Law, a special agricultural law aimed at meeting the constitutional mandate, or all three. In spite of repeated efforts to secure legislative passage of one or more of the three proposed laws during every legislative session since 1978, none has been enacted into law.

The functional plan for agriculture has shared the fate of the 11 other agency functional plans in failing to be approved by the legislature, even though functional plans are to be adopted by concurrent resolution. As such the plans will be an "expression of legislative policy" and will not "be interpreted as law or statutory mandate."[89] The first set of functional plans proposed in 1979 were very long and detailed and proved too much for the legislature to handle. The second try at the 1980 session took about two thirds of the text and data and placed it in a support document, leaving about 80 pages of text. Even this simplified version of the agriculture and other functional plans proved too complex for the legislature to handle. In 1981 the supporting document was expanded and the functional plans themselves reduced to thin volumes of some 30 pages. Brevity did not necessarily bring success, since neither the 1981 or 1982 sessions of the legislature succeeded in adopting any of the state agency functional plans.

One reason the plans have had rough going in the legislature is the fear by counties that the plans will restrict and constrain their land use and zoning powers. The state plan provides that county general plans and development plans be used in preparing state functional plans. Once adopted, these state plans must be used by the counties as guidelines in formulating their own plans. Just what the term *guidelines* means is not clear. Counties fear that it will erode their hard won authority in the land use area. They point to the fact that the Land Use Commission must conform its decisions to the state plan and functional plans but must only "take cognizance" of county plans as indicative of their unequal position in the system.[90]

When the state functional plans failed to pass the 1982 legislative session, the governor, who had strongly supported their passage, announced his intention to implement the plans by executive order to the extent allowed by law.[91] While most of the general substance of the functional plans can be supported by existing state law, this approach may weaken the position of the state in negotiating with the counties the exact meaning of the word *guidelines*.

A review of the proposed state agriculture plan and the supporting technical reference document reveals much about the weaknesses to date in the efforts to protect important agricultural land in Hawaii. Hawaii's six major islands contain a little over 4 million acres of land, of which about 1.9 million acres have been placed in the agricultural district. About the same amount of land is in the conservation district; with the urban district, a much smaller third at 152,000 acres; and the rural district, a very small 9,000 acres. The Land Study Bureau of the University of Hawaii conducted agricultural land classification studies from 1965–72 that rated agricultural land from Class A (best) to Class E, based generally on crop yield. About 5 percent of Hawaii's agricultural land was classed as A or B (prime) or some 200,000 acres. A recently developed land-classification system attempts to identify "agricultural lands of importance to Hawaii" (ALIH) uses categories of prime, unique, and other important agricultural land. Prime lands under this system exceed 300,000 acres, and when the three categories are combined, they total almost 1 million acres. The need for an appropriate land-classification system is tied to the fact that "an adequate data base for decisionmaking on the use of agriculture land resources is lacking." The state agricultural plan recommended a series of specific proposals for preparing and updating an agricultural land data base for Hawaii.[92] On the basis of the available data, it was concluded that "suitable land is not available for agricultural industries to expand or otherwise improve and modernize their operations."[93]

A 1977–78 study by the Hawaii Institute for Management and Analysis in Government located in the Department of Budget and Finance, noted that from 1962–77, the Land Use Commission approved the shift of 36,500 acres of land from the agricultural to the urban district. From 1977 through late 1980, another 4,000 acres were shifted from the agricultural to the urban district, with a sharp increase in the percent of prime agricultural land involved. Of much more importance than the numbers was the critique by HIMAG on how the commission did its job:

1. There has been a lack of consistency between the commission's decisions and plans and policies governing the direction and location of new urban growth.
2. Commission decisions redistricting agricultural land have been, avoidably in many cases, inconsistent with state policy objectives regarding agriculture.
3. Commission decisions have been unnecessarily *ad hoc* rather than geographically and temporally comprehensive within the reasonable limits implied by the land use law.
4. The commission is permitted to exercise undue discretion in its decisionmaking due to insufficient policy and procedural guidance from the land use law.[94]

The Department of Agriculture, through its functional plan, expressed great concern at the continued loss of prime, unique, and important agricultural land, predicted a shortage of such land in the future and made three key recommendations to strengthen the protection of agricultural land in Hawaii:

1. Propose amendment to the state land use law to provide standards and criteria to conserve and protect important agricultural lands.
2. Encourage the inclusion of important agricultural lands in county general plans and development plans, pursuant to the state agriculture plan.
3. In implementing the state land use law and county zoning ordinances, important agricultural lands shall be classified in the state agricultural district and shall be zoned for agricultural

use, except where substantial injustice or inequity will result, or where overriding public interest exists.[95]

These studies and recommendations point up the weakness of Hawaii's land use law to protect agricultural land and include important proposals to improve the system in that regard. Attempts to pass a special law in response to the 1978 constitutional mandate have not been successful. A bill that received serious consideration in the 1982 Hawaii legislature but which did not pass—S.B. No. 2434-82, would have established an independent study commission charged with: (a) consideration of alternative agricultural goals for Hawaii, (b) development of alternative definitions of "important agricultural lands," and (c) development of an agricultural land classification system. Even this seemingly sensible beginning failed to pass the senate.

Hawaii finds itself 21 years after the passage of a land use law primarily aimed at protecting agricultural land struggling to put in place additional policy and implementation tools to do the job. Unless new laws to guide the Land Use Commission and other actors can be put in place, rural sprawl in the form of agricultural subdivisions and the inappropriate reclassification of land from the agriculture to the urban district seems likely to continue.

The Special Issue of Housing. The relationship of an adequate housing supply to the implementation of Hawaii's land use law has been a subject of continuing debate. Both Myers and Mandelker point to Hawaii's innovative and progressive housing authority that makes it possible for the state to become a participant in the housing issue much more effectively than in most states on the mainland.[96] Furthermore, the argument that agricultural land must be converted to help meet housing needs can be countered by the fact that much of the land already zoned urban is unused, and that on every island the amount of land already zoned urban, if fully developed, would be sufficient to meet urban residential needs of the state for the foreseeable future.

An excellent analysis in the commission's second five-year review concluded that Hawaii's residential market did not require great quantities of land, and that "Inflation in the housing market does not appear to stem from heavy demand." This assessment argued that the spiraling costs of housing did not appear to flow from any lack of residential land. In mid-1971, the city and county of Honolulu had almost 10,000 acres of unimproved residentially zoned land with a capacity of over 60,000 units. The problem, in common with other states, was how to arrange for this land to be developed prior to any further conversion of agriculture lands to urban use. Partly due to the trend to large site development, the pressure to develop at the fringe was intense and showed no signs of yielding to the logic that ample land already zoned urban was ready for development.

Land speculation appears to have been a major factor in the escalating costs of housing. In Hawaii, development rights to land are sold separately from the fee title itself. Such rights are often sold many times on the same piece of property, typically at constantly increasing costs. The League of Women Voters traced transactions involving a tract of Bishop Estate land above Pearl Harbor, on which development rights were acquired in 1959. Three transactions later, the purchase price had jumped from $4.8 million for 12,000 acres in 1967 to $20 million for 11,000 acres in 1969. The result—a 1971 offering of expensive two-bedroom homes. To the league, the lessons were obvious: "Delay in making land available for use, and higher costs of houses when development finally takes place."[97]

Two bills were introduced into the Hawaii legislature in early 1971 to avoid this type of cumulative cost increase from the resale of development rights. One would have provided for a Vermont-like capital gains tax on land when it received urban zoning, the proceeds to be used to help provide the required public services. A land bank proposal was also introduced which would have authorized the state or county to buy land in places undergoing growth pressures and release it for development as needed "at prices consistent with social and economic objectives."[98] Neither proposal was approved.

Hawaii does, in fact, have one of the nation's more innovative state housing authorities, one that was designed to alleviate low and moderate income housing problems on the islands. The state can intervene in the housing market directly, and since 1977 counties have had similar housing powers.[99] As described by Mandelker, funds from state bond issues can be used for direct grant-type subsidies to low and moderate income home buyers and the subsidies can be recaptured through buy-back provisions "unique to the Hawaiian law." Homeowners who have purchased homes under the subsidy program and wish to resell must first offer their houses to the housing authority at the original price plus improvements and interest. The law also includes housing rent allowances. The Hawaii housing authority can go into joint ventures with the private sector, use land banking approaches, and employ other techniques.[100]

Governor Ariyoshi has taken a strong interest in the active implementation of the law. According to his special assistant, the $125 million loan fund established by a bond issue had increased to $200 million by 1977, and some 5,000 housing units had been put in place. He noted that the effort was somewhat dormant for a while, but that he had made it a high priority item in his administration.[101]

Mayor Cravalho reported that some 400 to 700 single-family units had been built on Maui under a special program in which the county put up front money in order to get favorable interest rates. Under another special program for renters, when the accumulated rent reached an adequate sum, it could be converted to a downpayment toward purchasing the dwelling. Cravalho noted that "We get the plantation people to make land available at below market cost, set rules for who can and who can't get the lots, and include a buy-back provision for seven to ten years at a fixed inflation rate." He noted that there was very little turnover in this kind of housing, and that far from hurting the private sector, it actually helped it.[102]

It seems clear that the high cost of housing in Hawaii is due at least in part to a housing market unique to the islands. It is also clear that developers and others have attempted to use the shortage of low and moderate income housing as the rationale for the conversion of land from agriculture to urban use. Yet, there is little or no evidence that making such reclassifications has any positive impact on low and moderate income housing needs. The need, if it is to be met at all, will be met through state and county government policies that put a high priority on providing low and moderate income housing. To a considerable extent, Hawaii has done this. If strong land- and growth-management controls do have a potential negative impact on a balanced housing supply, Hawaii appears to have better tools than almost any other state in the nation for alleviating this impact through aggressive and innovative state and local initiatives. Furthermore, there seems to be more public support for these innovations in Hawaii than in many mainland states.

The Conservation District and the Land Use Law.   The implementation of Hawaii's Land Use Law in the conservation district deserves special attention because of the tremendous potential for undermining the purposes of the law inherent in the way in which it is administered in this particular area. Of the 4 million acres of land in Hawaii, almost half lie within the conservation district. Of this amount, about half may be classified as forest and water reserve land; most of it is owned by the state. A substantial amount of the remaining conservation land is owned by private interests, and a very small amount is owned by the federal government, counties, and others.

The conservation district became the subject of continuing controversy and dissatisfaction in Hawaii because once the district boundaries are set by the Land Use Commission, another state agency—the Department of Land and Natural Resources—and its six-member board—has complete power over what land uses occur on such lands. The failure of the Department of Land and Natural Resources to develop any kind of overall land use plan for the conservation district brought about a series of sharp attacks in the late 1960s and early 1970s on the department's issuance of permits for urban uses, intensive agricultural uses, and even commercial and industrial uses. The department, under its "regulation 4," originally estalished just two subzones in the conservation district, an RW (restricted watershed) subzone, and a GU (general use) subzone. The permitted uses in the general subzone covered virtually the full range of natural resources and urban-oriented uses, including resorts, hotels, restaurants, target ranges, country clubs, scenic attractions, playgrounds and athletic fields, golf courses, camps, and small boat harbors and docks.[103] The potential for activity that can and sometimes has been in direct conflict with the basic purposes of the land use law was great. In 1972, when the League of Women Voters was studying the issue, there were complaints that the board permitted uses in the conservation district that were not in accord with the overall land- and growth-management policies. Although the department is not required by law to solicit the recommendations of any government agency, its planning office does distribute permit applications and other pertinent material widely. The department has noted that its feedback from this distribution is very limited.[104]

The first two subzones established in the conservation district were either extremely specialized or so general as to give very little guidance to the department. Furthermore, there was no adequate land use inventory of the land in the district, or any basic land use plan. The League of Women Voters study found that "a basic planning framework, a strong departmental coordination, and adequate program control are generally absent." Permit applications increased from an average of 20 a year in the 1964–69 period to 63 in 1970, 86 applications in 1971, and 80 applications in the January-May period in 1972 alone.[105]

In 1977, a long-time chairman of the Land Use Commission expressed the view that the responsibility of permitting uses in the conservation district should be taken over by the commission, with most of the actual permitting work being done by the county. He reported that counties were very unhappy about the way things had worked out in the conservation district, and in his view with good reason. He noted that counties were vastly strengthening their capacity in the planning area, but in a county such as Hawaii, over 50 percent of the land was not under county control because it was in the conservation district.[106] Another commission member noted that there was no real monitoring or follow-up on what amounted to conservation land zoning by the Department of Land and Natural Resources. This observor pointed out that: "Citizen groups have tried to get them (the Department of Land and Natural Resources) to develop an extensive classification program for years, and they still haven't done it."[107] The league study cited the example of the building of Keahole Airport within the conservation district on the big island: "This constitutes a rezoning from conservation to urban, not only because the use is of an urban type, but also because pressure for an urban area around the airport will no doubt follow."[108]

The solution seems, at last, to be evolving. Regulation 4 has been revised, a functional plan for conservation is being prepared under the state plan, and the Department of Land and Natural Resources has established a new enforcement division. The new regulations and enforcement procedures for permitting uses in the conservation district were adopted by the Board of Land and Natural Resources in June 1978. Four subzones were established: (1) *protective*, for example, restricted watershed lands, important ecosystems, and historic or archaeological sites; (2) *limited*, for example, lands subject to flooding, erosion, landslides, volcanic activity, or tidal waves; (3) *resource*, for example, parklands, commercial timber lands, outdoor recreation, and all territorial waters not assigned to another zone; and (4) *general*, for example, land not "normally adaptable or presently needed for urban, rural, or agricultural use, and lands suitable for certain types of farming compatible with the physical environment." Section 6 of regulation 4 contained 15 land use conditions and guidelines for use by the board and the Department of Land and Natural Resources.

This action seems to meet the long-standing complaint over the absence of sufficient subclassifications and standards to assure adherence to sound land- and growth-management policies in permitting uses in the conservation zone.[109] If these measures are effective in bringing sound management practices to Hawaii's conservation lands, a major loophole in the state's land- and growth-management system will have been closed.

The rural category also holds the potential for undermining the effort to preserve prime agricultural land, but this has not happened to date. On the contrary, it has solved a critical political problem in allowing a limited number of essentially small farmers to further divide their landholdings.

**State/County Relations in Land
and Growth Management**

One of the most important factors in the effort to implement Hawaii's land use law has been the increasing importance of the county in both a technical sense with regard to planning and in a political sense with regard to land and growth management. In the pre-1961 era, counties by and large were very weak in the planning area. With the passage of the land use law, professional planners could make the point that "If counties didn't shape up," the state would take over control of land and growth management.[110]

Ray Suefuji, former planning director for Hawaii County, recalled that in 1965 the county had zoning in only a few places. In his tenure as director, with the political support of the mayor and county council, the whole island was zoned, a strong subdivision ordinance was added, and the planning director came to be a much more influential person in the land use and planning area. The planning structure included under his directorship a 9-member county planning commission, and a planning department of some 15 professionals for a county with a population of about 74,000.

In Suefuji's view, until about 1977, the state was preoccupied with growth and economic development, and it was the counties which were trying to implement good land use controls. Suefuji went on to note that "The state is trying to get stronger, and if they pursue that effort through the state planning council, they may succeed in setting a good clear framework for both states and counties, and that will be good."

The director of the Department of Planning and Economic Development, Hideto Kono, cited the effort to develop a coastal zone management plan for Hawaii as a good illustration of the emergence of the counties as a strong political force. He noted that, partly as a result of pressure from the federal government, the original coastal zone management legislation proposed by the administration to the 1977 legislature included a strong state oversight role. As he described it, "The counties didn't like it, they fought hard against it, and the legislature found it a very hot and tough issue to handle." Kono attempted to act as a catalyst to bring the county and state positions together. The negotiating sessions narrowed the differences down to the question of the boundaries and to the question of the guidelines. The legislature followed the counties on both issues, in that the law that passed did not contain clear enforceable guidelines that would control the counties, and the ultimate authority for setting boundaries beyond the minimum required 100 feet remained with the counties.[111] (A more detailed discussion of the coastal zone management program is provided in the next section.)

According to one commissioner, the counties resented bitterly the commission's attachment of substantial conditions on approvals of requests to change land from agriculture to urban use. Counties viewed this kind of condition setting as "an invasion of their legitimate prerogatives."[112] A long-time chairman of the commission noted that in his view state-county relationships had improved as counties had strengthened their capacity in the planning and land-management area. He noted that there was a continuing issue of just where the county's responsibility stopped and where the state's responsibility started. His comment was that "My philosophy is that the state has an interest in land use that the Land Use Commission must protect."[113] The point of view of the counties on the issue was well expressed by Mayor Cravalho. After commenting that he felt the land use law had worked very well, at least for Maui, the mayor noted that his position—and that of the county of Maui—was that the state should set the broad guidelines and let the counties carry out the implementation within that framework. He felt it was necessary for the state to lean heavily on county input in developing the guidelines, but he also felt it proper that the state should monitor the implementation efforts of the counties, and "hold us accountable."[114] Three of Maui County's professional planning staff members were in agreement on the need for "a statewide overview that involved some guidance, but beyond this things should be left to the county." However, a fear was expressed that "the state will try to direct and control our growth, no matter what we might want." Thus, "if the state developed a population dispersion policy, they might want to put more resort facilities on Maui than we want."[115]

A member of the Honolulu county council noted that in Hawaii, in contrast to Florida, the legislature is a relatively weak, part-time group that in his view did not really follow through on important matters. He contrasted this lack of legislative follow-through with county councils which meet all year round and worked from day-to-day, and thus could see the results of what they were trying to accomplish.[116] Honolulu planning director, Bob Way, noted that he was very concerned that in developing the proposed state plan, the state "will try to take over some of our authority." He expressed skepticism, in contrast to other persons interviewed, that the state would really take the existing county plans as their starting point. As he saw it, the state was ignoring the counties and starting from the top and working its way down. In that kind of situation, he saw conflict as inevitable. Based on their success in the coastal zone

management area, he thought the counties would win.[117] Honolulu
council member, George Akahane, noted that in the tourist planning area, the state plan had used the county plans as a starting
point. But he expressed the fear that in the general plan as a whole
the state would go the same way it had on the coastal management
effort and try to take over things that they should not have control
of.[118]

The brief analysis of state and county actors in the planning, land
use, and general growth-management areas in Hawaii presents a
not unusual picture of continuing stress and strain in attempting to
develop a satisfactory working relationship. The situation is in one
way much simpler in Hawaii than on the mainland, since there is a
state government which is at least theoretically integrated under a
strong executive, and just four counties. Nevertheless, intense
intergovernmental tensions have arisen and have caused sometimes
bitter disputes between the state and local governments. Yet, one
comes away with the feeling that there is a general consensus at both
levels, in the abstract at least, that the state has the duty and
responsibility to set a general planning and land- and growth-
management-policy framework from which the counties will then
carry out most of the direct implementation of the land- and growth-
management effort. The difficulty comes in Hawaii, as it does in
many other states, when the planning framework with its guidelines moves into the implementation phase and hard decisions must
be made about the allocation of authority and responsibility among
levels of government. Furthermore, in Hawaii, as in other states, the
state has had difficulty in "getting its act together." Even though
Hawaii has a strong executive who appoints all major department
heads, there have been problems getting departments to work
together in their policy and implementation actions so as to further
the goal of effective land and growth management.

Many people in Hawaii at both the state and local levels are placing
great faith and hope in the development of the state plan to set the
framework which will guide both state agencies and counties in
furthering growth management and other goals for the islands.
Whether or not this approach will prove to be the solution to some of
the key areas of conflict remains to be seen. Should the development
of the state plan prove something less than a cure-all, there are
alternate policies that can be pursued. Consultants Eckbo, Dean,
Austin, and Williams have suggested two such possible approaches.
One would be to give the county a clear role in determining
permitted uses in the conservation district. This would involve a
system similar to that with which the counties deal with the state on
changes in the agricultural and rural districts. Under this proposal,

special permits would have to be approved by the county before being considered by the Board of Land and Natural Resources. Such a proposal would go far toward correcting what has been one of the most difficult and potentially divisive areas in the effort to implement the Land Use Act.

The consultants also proposed that the state plan be used to resolve the "confusion about the relationship of the land use law to the general plans of the county." While the Land Use Commission is charged with considering a county's general plan, it is not required to follow that plan. On the other hand, while the commission may approve a shift of land into the urban classification, the county is not mandated to grant the appropriate urban zoning.[119] Certainly there are policies and administrative mechanisms in the state plan to clarify the appropriate roles of the Land Use Commission and the counties in land and growth management. The question is one of political will, especially in the legislature, to resolve the conflicts that surely will arise.

State-county tensions have continued into the 1980s. As noted earlier, efforts to adopt state functional plans have been defeated in the legislature partly by county fears that the functional plans would restrict unduly local authority in the land- and growth-management area. The continuing uncertainty over how much monitoring and enforcement authority the state has in carrying out Hawaii's coastal management program is another example. Continued county fears of a Land Use Commission acting under clearer legislatively enacted standards remain, as illustrated by the half joking, half serious comment by a county planner that "Each year before the legislature meets planners from the four counties get together to discuss what they want or don't want from the session—they always get around to discussing if not proposing the abolishment of the Land Use Commission."[120]

Planning and Managing the Coast

One half of Hawaii's total land area is within five miles of the shoreline, and it is here that the great bulk of development has taken place, and where the future development pressures will be. These coastal areas include wetlands, reef flats, coral reefs, and other such areas that have been subjected to severe growth pressures, and a substantial amount of damage has already been done.[121]

Hawaii's concern with protecting its shoreline began in 1970 with the passage of a shoreline setback law which established a 40-foot strip extending inward from the upper wash of the waves, an area in which construction and other operations were generally prohibited except by special approval. In 1973, the legislature enacted a law

authorizing the Department of Planning and Economic Development to prepare a coastal plan for Hawaii, and in two years passed
the Shoreline Protection Act, which established interim guidelines
to be followed pending adoption of a federally approved coastal
planning and management program. This act set up special management areas (SMAs) which were to extend at least 100 feet inland
from the shoreline vegetation or debris line. Any development
within that line which exceeded $25,000 or which otherwise would
effect the shoreline in a significant way required a county permit.
Thus, in this first major effort to manage the coast, counties
managed to become the key implementation authority.[122] The state
government prepared and presented to the 1977 legislature a coastal
planning and management bill that the counties saw as placing most
of the controlling power in the hands of the state. The bruising battle
between the state government on the one hand and counties on the
other has been described. Although some compromises were struck
in the passage of act 188, the key victories in this struggle for power
were won by the counties.

The 1977 act highlighted seven major goals: furthering coastal
recreational opportunities for the public; protecting and restoring
historic resources; protecting and restoring scenic and open space
resources; protecting "valuable coastal ecosystems; providing for
both public and private development in the coastal zone to support
the state's economy; protecting against coastal hazards; and improving the development review process, communication, and public
participation in the management of coastal resources and hazards."[123]

The act contained a significant policy statement on the state/
county division of responsibility and authority: "The legislature
further finds that Hawaii's environment is both undermanaged and
overregulated; that new regulatory mechanisms must not be added
on to, but rather combined with, the existing systems; and that the
counties have shown their ability and willingness to play a con-
structive role in coastal zone management by their actions" in
implementing the 1975 Shoreline Protection Act.[124] Furthermore,
both the boundary issue and the prime responsibility for implementation issue were won by the counties. While the state was given the
authority to set boundaries for some purposes during the two-year
interim period before the new program would go fully into effect, in
essence the minimum 100 feet inland boundary was retained, and
the counties continued to be the central authority for issuing permits
within that boundary. Counties were authorized under the law to
extend the boundary inland further than 100 feet, subject to lead
agency review.[125] As lead agency, the Department of Planning and

Economic Development was required, in consultation with the counties and the general public, to prepare and present coastal policy guidelines to the 1978 legislative session.[126]

After the passage of the Hawaii Coastal Zone Management Act in 1977, the federal government approved Hawaii's coastal zone management program in September 1978. That action has enabled Hawaii to spend $3.8 million on its coastal program since 1978, about 80 percent of which has been federal funds.[127] An assessment of Hawaii's coastal management program reveals both strengths and weaknesses. On the negative side, the continuing uncertainty as to the authority of the state's lead agency for the program, the Department of Planning and Economic Development, has made it hard to fix accountability for the program. The guidelines called for in the 1977 law that might have clarified that question have never been adopted by the legislature. The most recent review of Hawaii's coastal program by the federal office of Coastal Zone Management was sharply critical of the Department of Planning and Economic Development for its "passive role in networked agency decision-making processes that involve significant coastal resources or pose significant coastal management related issues."[128] Strengthening DPED's monitoring and enforcement program has been a prime goal of the federal Office of Coastal Zone Management. OCZM reached agreement with DPED to "fully implement" its monitoring and enforcement program and to develop a guide to "identify coastal concerns and define what constitutes pattern of compliance and noncompliance . . . which the DPED will use to ensure compliance with the HCZMP. . . . " Perhaps of most importance to the ultimate success of the program, DPED agreed to seek an amendment to Hawaii's Coastal Zone law "clarifying networked agency reporting and analyzing obligations and clearly establishing the DPED's role in resolving conflicts, monitoring and enforcing compliance with the HCZMP, and improving Hawaii's permitting process."[129]

On the positive side, the Department of Land and Natural Resources' Division of Conservation and Resources Enforcement has developed a volunteer conservation officer program where carefully trained volunteers, some 86 in number, augment the enforcement capacity of regular conservation officers on weekends, at night, and at other special times.[130] The Board of Land and Natural Resources approved six additional natural area reserves, and had under consideration six additional recommended reserves.[131]

Furthermore, the Department of Planning and Economic Development took action in opposing petitions to the Land Use Commission for district boundary changes that would have violated the coastal goal of reserving coastal land for coastal dependent use.[132] Finally, DPED has developed a computer-based monitoring tool— H-PASS—to strengthen its monitoring and enforcement effort.[133]

Citizen Involvement

Citizen involvement in Hawaii's planning and growth-management initiatives has been surprisingly weak. Compared to California, Oregon, or Florida, there are no broad-based, strong environmental or other citizen groups that have a direct impact on the legislature and the executive branch, as well as on the behavior of local governments. The League of Women Voters has been the most active citizen group in taking a continuing interest in land and growth management in Hawaii and has conducted a number of excellent analyses of the implementation of the land use law and of the problem of linking land use to planning. The league seems to have been by far the strongest citizen group active in the area of providing a planning and policy framework for growth management.

The major environmental group in Hawaii, Life of the Land, has had an up and down history and has never enjoyed the broad base of support of, for example, the California Coastal Alliance. Life of the Land was formed in 1970 by Tony Hodges, a former air force pilot and land-development planner who had run unsuccessfully for the U.S. Senate on an environmental platform. His relatively impressive showing encouraged him to form the new environmental organization. Life of the Land flourished for a while in the general environmental ferment and activity in Hawaii in the early 1970s, which saw a Hawaii Environmental Protection Act, the beginnings of efforts to develop a strong coastal planning and management bill, and a law requiring environmental impact statements under some circumstances.

The tenuous base of support of Life of the Land, and perhaps for the environmental movement in Hawaii, is suggested by the fact that when the economy began to weaken, Life of the Land rapidly began to lose its support. When the unemployment rate rose in Hawaii and Life of the Land opposed projects that would provide jobs, it came under strong fire from union leaders. One newspaper article quoted the president of the state Federation of Labor as saying Hodges "wants us all to go back and live in grass shacks."[134] A community activist quoted in the same article described the group's public image as a "bunch of rich, long-haired Haoles who went around filing lawsuits against construction projects, putting people out of work, and being a general pain in the ass." Whatever the

cause, it is a fact that in the mid-1970s Life of the Land suffered a drastic decline and at one point was pretty much out of operation. However, in the late 1970s the group began to rebuild under new leadership.[135] In 1977, Life of the Land secured a VISTA grant which was used to expand the staff by about 10 persons, largely for the purpose of helping neighborhoods organize and making their impact felt on growth-management issues in Hawaii. One observer noted that the movement was taking root very well. The group seemed to be involved most actively in the planning and land use field, and in her view had opened up new citizen participation opportunities on Oahu.[136]

The League of Women Voters' interest also apparently peaked in the early 1970s when the league published several excellent studies analyzing the work of the Land Use Commission. Two of these studies looked specifically at the issue of citizen participation in Hawaii. The league noted that one real block to effective and meaningful participation was the prevailing view in Hawaii that "the present (early 1970s) commission is too much involved with and influenced by land development interests."[137] Several recommendations that had been made to correct the real or perceived undue influence of development interests on the commission were cited. One would have prohibited commissioners from being involved in land development for profit except for their own personal residence. A second proposal would have provided for a statutory broadening of the representation pattern of the commission. The commission at that time was described as having two agriculturalists, three businessmen, including a hotel manager and a land company executive, and one union executive. A third proposal was to enlarge the membership of the commission on the premise that it would then become more representative. A fourth would have included the county planning directors as ex-officio members.[138]

A more fundamental issue is the attitude Hawaii's executive and legislative branch has taken toward such citizen input into the decisionmaking process. One close observer and participant in land use matters in Hawaii expressed the view in 1977 that "the state government is very reluctant to allow real citizen participation, and this has been especially true of the Department of Planning and Economic Development. The reason is that they are afraid that they won't be able to control it."[139] However, two years later the same observer cited the passage of the 1975 Shoreline Protection Act as a prime example of successful citizen initiative. "The bill was initiated and put through by . . . a group of concerned citizens and groups who felt that both the counties and the state were doing a miserable job of managing the shoreline and its resources.[140] These activists

subsequently incorporated themselves as the Shoreline Protection Alliance. A participant noted that the Shoreline Protection Alliance demanded citizen participation in the development of the 1977 legislation, and that as a result the Department of Planning and Economic Development did set up a citizen group, the Coastal Zone Management Statewide Citizens Forum, which he described as somewhat developer and professional area oriented but which included representation from many environmental and citizen groups. The department also set up regional groups in each county. He reported that, in spite of the mixed background of the group, it ended up being surprisingly united in deciding on the general goals to be pursued.[141]

As he described the struggle over the permanent coastal law, the counties wanted a narrow coastal zone and so did the developers. The citizen group decided to support the counties on this issue, but to fight for making it easy for any citizen to bring suit to force compliance with the coastal program. He noted that the group's goals, objectives, and policies were adopted, and that the forum also won on the liberal appeals issue.[142] The advisory committee that participated in the preparation of the coastal program has been reorganized into a state advisory committee, and in response to the urging of the federal Office of Coastal Zone Management, its duties and responsibilities are being better focused.[143]

In general, citizens have had little involvement in the state planning process in Hawaii. The league study expressed the pessimistic view that "In general, citizens know little and under-stand less about state planning, its purpose, and what it does." The process in Hawaii as described in the early 1970s (and this writer did not find it to be substantially different in the late 1970s and early 1980s) was one in which the planning efforts went on largely inside government until a particular issue had reached the public hearing stage. According to the league study, one reason seemed to be the planning division's rather exclusive orientation toward its chief client, the governor, to provide him with staff assistance for developing and administering policy. Even completed plans were not widely distributed nor public discussion encouraged.[144]

However, gaining citizen participation early in the planning process is something that has been achieved in very few states. It is difficult, it requires the investment of substantial amounts of funds, it requires an almost unreasonable level of sustained interest by at least a cadre of citizens, and it requires a positive and even enthusiastic attitude on the part of the elected and appointed state and local officials. This combination of attitudes and forces is sufficiently rare that not even in public-spirited Oregon has citizen

participation reached its full potential. Hawaii is not greatly different from most other states where some movement is taking place either because of the environmental movement, the neighborhood government approach, or simply because some group or organization manages to impose itself on the decisionmaking process in an effective way. In Hawaii, the whole citizen participation effort is still relatively weak, but there are areas in which it seems to have a potential for gaining strength. One of these may be in connection with the implementation process under the state plan. The policy council has nine citizen members. In the preparation of state agency functional plans, the state plan mandates that the governor appoint an advisory committee which includes citizen members. A limiting factor here is that when the functional plans are adopted, the advisory committees will cease to function.

Summary Assessment of the Implementation Effort

There is no unequivocal answer to the central question of how well has Hawaii's land use law worked? A League of Women Voters' analysis of the 1964–68 period noted that scatterization had been largely brought to an end, speculative subdivision of new lands far beyond the need for new home sites had been greatly reduced, and prime agricultural and conservation district lands had been protected from urbanization by Land Use Commission denial of rezoning applications. But the league cited continuing concern about the transfer of agricultural lands, especially the most highly productive ones, into urban use; land speculation causing land prices to rise, while lands were withheld from use; and the lack of coordination between state and county planning and Land Use Commission decisions.[145]

In 1977, two members of the academic community in Hawaii made similar comments. While agreeing that there had been some unwise reclassifications, and that special interests had had some success in distorting the goals of the legislation, these observers felt that the law had made development a little more orderly than it otherwise would have been, and had slowed down the conversion of land use from agriculture to urban. These observers felt that the early implementation of the land use law had been "a mixed bag, just like the whole Burns administration. A lot of good and a lot of narrow special interest stuff."[146]

Perhaps a better question to ask is what factors have caused the law to work less well than it might have? The answer clearly is the persisting lack of a clear policy framework to guide the commission, the counties, and other state agency actors in the land- and growth-management process. This guidance is increasingly needed in

Hawaii as conflicting values make themselves felt. If these conflicts are not reconciled within the framework of a clear set of policies, there is a danger that they will undermine the objectives of protecting agricultural land and open space on the one hand, and assuring adequate but compact and closely guided urban development on the other.

The state seems no closer in the early 1980s to producing clearer guidelines and more specific standards to guide its land- and growth-management effort than it was when the land use law was revised in 1975. A kind of legislative paralysis seems to have set in, partly caused by county government belief that strengthening state standards and guidelines will weaken the counties as participants in the land- and growth-management system in Hawaii. The unfinished agenda in this area is long and important. It will require some kind of breakthrough in state-county relations before it can be completed. If the functional plans do not make it through the legislature; if coastal standards and guidelines are not strengthened; and if the Land Use Commission is not given new guidelines to replace the interim guidelines that expired in 1980, the land- and growth-management program in Hawaii is not likely to achieve its goals.

The Politics of the Future

The central issues that will dominate the political scene over the next few years seem to be the relationship between the state and the counties in Hawaii and the attempt to balance economic prosperity with environmental protection and growth management. The Hawaii legislature and Governor Ariyoshi's administration have tried to deal with these issues in a variety of ways. Vis-á-vis the counties, the state has attempted to expand and strengthen its role in land and growth management both through far-reaching amendments proposed to the land use law in 1975 and through its initial proposal in the coastal management area. In each case, the legislature refused to extend the state's power in relation to the counties. Hawaii's four counties, rarely united on any other issue, stood together and opposed vigorously in the legislative efforts to extend the state authority in the land use area.

The efforts to block expanded state authority were not completely successful, as witness the legislature's approval of the authority of the Land Use Commission to attach conditions to reclassification decisions, but even here county objections apparently have sharply limited the use of this authority. For the most part the political power of the counties, combined with other factors, have been enough to prevent a substantial extension of state power. The *politics of the future* in Hawaii seems to center on the need to strike some kind of bargain between the state and the counties that will result in enough state oversight to assure the effective implementation of policies and programs aimed at managing growth, while at the same time leaving the bulk of the day-to-day administration in the hands of the counties.

The question of managing growth has emerged as a major issue in Hawaii in the last few years, and it is an issue that goes beyond a small group of environmentalists concerned with limiting the growth of the islands because of environmental reasons. In the last several years, the Ariyoshi administration in general, and the governor himself in particular, have evidenced an increasing concern with the in-migration pressures on Hawaii. Discussions with a number of the governor's key staff people reveals the depth, the breadth, and the unquestioned sincerity of the administration's concern with this matter. One of his chief aides expressed the view that as a political issue, land use would get to be more and more important: "The mayor of Honolulu will run [in 1978] on a wide open, grow, grow basis next time, and he will attack the Ariyoshi administration on that basis, accusing us of being antigrowth in trying to stifle the development of Hawaii." The aide cited a number of critical land use decisions in 1977 in which the governor had taken a strong and aggressive stand to attempt to prevent the conversion of agricultural land to the urban category.[147]

Another member of the Ariyoshi administration, Dr. Hubert Kimura, has had the major responsibility for devising tactics and strategy to put a growth-management approach into place. He cited the governor's support of two pieces of legislation aimed at slowing down the flood of new residents to Hawaii: one proposing a one-year residency requirement for eligibility for welfare payments, and the other proposing a one-year residency requirement for eligibility for employment by the state or a county. The welfare bill did not pass the legislature, but the state job bill did, and the view was expressed that the welfare legislation would be reintroduced.

A key point was that Dr. Kimura was spending almost full time researching the whole question of growth management and devising a battery of growth-management tools that would form the basis for legislation for the 1978 or succeeding legislatures. One proposal, for example, would have required the Land Use Commission to develop performance standards and a point system for evaluating and acting on boundary amendment petitions. Dr. Kimura made clear that the overall goal was to limit growth, but he was also clear that no single approach would achieve that objective. He identified the issue of what may be the ultimate weapon for those in Hawaii who wish to control growth—water. The water supply in Hawaii is fixed, and a determined state government could limit population growth by refusing to convert water now used for agriculture to urban uses.[148] The Ariyoshi administration's commitment to growth management is perhaps best illustrated by the fact that in 1978 the administration did introduce the package of growth-management legislation, even though it failed to pass.[149]

The predictions about the 1978 gubernatorial primary were indeed fulfilled. When the state moved to indict Honolulu Mayor Fasi for campaign violations involving charges of soliciting a half million dollar gift in return for a $50 million urban renewal contract, Fasi "retaliated by announcing the next day he would be a Democratic candidate for governor in 1978." A widely distributed UPI article went on to note that Governor Ariyoshi had articulated "What now seems to be the chief issue in the gubernatorial campaign: How to manage Hawaii's growth." Governor Ariyoshi was pictured as stressing Hawaii's unique and limited land mass and resources and the need to limit growth in the interests of protecting the welfare of present residents and their descendants. As predicted, Fasi charged Ariyoshi with giving people a false sense of security by suggesting that growth could be limited when in fact it could not be. Fasi added: "I think it's hypocritical to tell people throughout the state, 'Hey, we're going to stop all growth,' and at the same time say, 'We're going to build job opportunities.'"[150]

In the primary election, Ariyoshi took the position that there was no contradiction between managing and even limiting growth in Hawaii and achieving economic prosperity, including jobs. Given the unique economic base of Hawaii, focused firmly on tourism as the number one industry, Ariyoshi was in a strong position to assert that growth management was compatible with economic prosperity and jobs, and even the key to the future economic prosperity of Hawaii. Although Fasi attacked the Ariyoshi administration as antijobs, antihousing, and antieconomic development, he lost the primary battle. Governor Ariyoshi went on to reelection by a comfortable majority in the fall 1978 election, again campaigning on the need for Hawaii to develop a strong growth-management system to prevent the state from being overrun by excessive growth. The election returns are evidence that, despite the general weakness of citizen lobbying groups, there is public support for rational management of Hawaii's growth.

The Hawaii state plan approved by the 1978 legislature contains policies and an administrative process that in theory can settle the issue of the relationship between the state and counties in Hawaii in the land- and growth-management area. The policy council set up by act 100 has the responsibility of assuring that both state agencies and counties conform their planning and implementation activities to the goals, objectives, and policies set forth in the plan. The weakness of the system may be in the provision that the final resolution of any dispute as to whether a state or county plan and/or its implementation is in conformance with the state plan must be settled in the legislative arena. Will decisions be forthcoming in a timely way, or will they be forthcoming at all? Through the 1982 session the legislature had not managed even the initial adoption of the functional plans. Obviously the politics of adoption of act 100 did not permit the lodging of final conflict resolution authority in the policy council. From the land- and growth-management perspective, there are unfinished agenda items that remain, some of which were noted earlier. In addition, the legislature has not adopted the comprehensive growth-management package of legislation proposed by the Ariyoshi administration. Yet a step of major importance was taken with the adoption of the Hawaii state plan. The effectiveness of land- and growth-management efforts in Hawaii will depend heavily on how successfully that law is implemented.

It remains to be seen whether a general plan can be developed that is specific enough to provide a framework that can integrate the activities of the state agencies and the counties, and at the same time survive in the legislature. Yet, some such policy framework will, it seems clear, be necessary if Hawaii is to carry out a land- and growth-management program that balances in some reasonable fashion the legitimate economic requirements of growth and the equally legitimate environmental requirements of protecting a fragile, finite, and precious island ecology.

There may be a unique opportunity for the public and private sector leadership in Hawaii to reach a viable compromise that would allow the implementation of the key objectives of Hawaii's original act 187: the preservation of agricultural land and the requirement that urban development be contained and limited in a compact development pattern. Much has been written about the difficulties inherent in the concentration of landownerships among a small group of landowners. Yet, this concentration may represent more of an opportunity than a disadvantage in attempting to put in place permanently an effective land- and growth-management system for the state. This point of view is argued persuasively by one of the chief officers of a large land trust. Speaking of the so-called big five, he noted that it is true that "We control the land," but it is just as true that "The state controls us." He expressed the view that the limited number of large landowners presented a rare opportunity for the political leadership of the state to sit down with these owners and hammer out some decisions on drawing permanent boundaries between the urban and agricultural uses. As he saw it, the time was ripe in Hawaii for a "major quid-pro-quo to firm up long-term agriculture in exchange for some urban zoning to stabilize the development pattern as well as agricultural uses into the long-term future."[151]

The fact is that the pressure for conversion of agricultural land to urban use has been building steadily in Hawaii, and the verdict on whether the Land Use Commission can resist those pressures is far from clear. It is extremely doubtful that the pressures can be resisted unless some fundamental policies are developed and enforced to avoid piecemeal conversion. The state plan will be a help, since it speaks clearly to the issue, but more detailed guidelines are needed. The alternative is to allow urban encroachment to gradually eat away at prime agricultural land, with population growth eventually supported by water made available by the conversion of agricultural land, and with the fragile island ecology severely damaged by the simple pressures of overuse.

Governor Ariyoshi ran for a third term as governor in the 1982 elections. The lieutenant governor, Jean King, opposed him in the Democratic primary. She has been increasingly critical of the Ariyoshi administration for failing to protect adequately the state's agricultural lands, and to promote self-sufficiency in agriculture for Hawaii.[152] As a candidate she was at least as supportive of a strong growth-management system for Hawaii as Governor Ariyoshi. The Republican candidate was a conservative state senator. As the incumbent, Ariyoshi continued his support of Hawaii's land- and growth-management system, always with an eye toward balancing growth-management and economic-development values. He defeated Lt. Governor King in the Democratic primary and went on to an easy reelection in the November general election.

The land- and growth-management objectives inherent in the original Hawaii land use law of 1961 may have been modified to some extent by the passage of time, but the fundamental proposition that agricultural land should be kept in agriculture and urban development should be confined to a relatively small amount of land in a compact and contiguous pattern is just as crucial for effective growth management in Hawaii today—indeed more crucial—than it was in 1961. Furthermore, these twin objectives are the central goals of almost every other state that is analyzed in this volume. Hawaii is significant for the remainder of the country, because it has been confronting these central issues for two decades. The history of the Hawaii effort is a mixed record of achievements and defeats, not a record of complete success or complete failure. Finally, it is a record that contains valuable lessons for those concerned with striking a reasonable balance between economic and environmental health that is the basis for a sound and stable growth-management system.

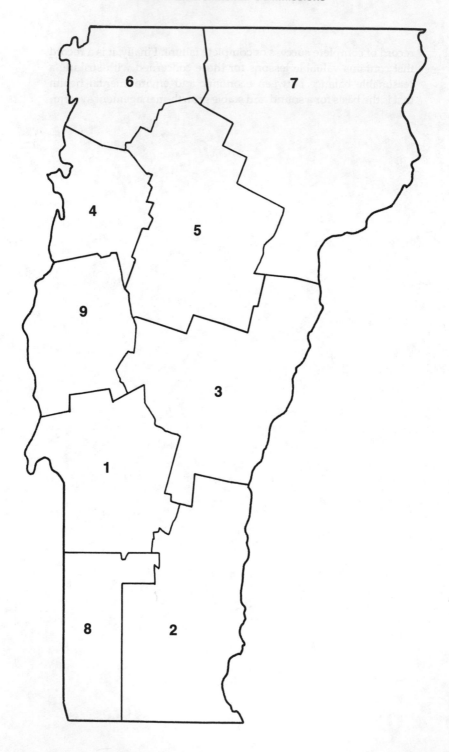

Vermont Environmental Commissions

3

Vermont: The Struggle to Meld Permitting and Planning

The Issue Context

Very few states have gone as far as Vermont in trying to impose substantial control over land and growth management from both the state and regional level. Perhaps more than in other states, the character of Vermont is important in understanding why the state passed a growth-management law in 1970, and why the follow-up action then envisioned has been difficult to achieve. Vermont is a small state both in terms of population and geographic area. From 1910 to 1960, its primary concern was the loss of population as many young people left the state in search of better employment opportunities. During this period, Vermont was relatively poor with relatively high taxes. During the 1960s, an abrupt change took place in which growth and its adverse impacts became the central issue, rather than negative growth and a weak economy. In 1960 most of Vermont's population, some 300,000 persons, lived in rural or small town areas. Vermont still has no officially designated standard metropolitan statistical area, although the state's largest city of Burlington is approaching that status.[1] Vermont's population in 1970 was 444,000. By 1980 it had grown to 511,000 for an increase of 15 percent. This is a relatively modest growth rate, but enough to sustain concern for the impacts of growth in the state.

In the 1960s, several factors brought a dramatic change in the growth picture in Vermont. The opening of an interstate highway made the state much more accessible to Boston and New York. Metropolitan New York, for example, became only a relatively short three-hour drive away. At the same time, riots in large cities probably caused an increasingly large number of people to consider returning to the more tranquil atmosphere of a state such as Vermont, especially now that it was within easy commuting distance. Finally, "Skiing changed from an esoteric sport to a winter mania."[2] With the ski industry and second home development (especially in southern Vermont) on the upswing, the nature of the state's economic base began to change. Dairying and lumbering declined in importance as tourism and second home development gained in strength. Although the increase in construction and population fed by these forces seemed welcome in their initial phases, they turned into a nightmare for many Vermont residents as the negative impacts of growth began to be apparent.

The nature of these impacts has been described in a number of studies of the Vermont growth-management experience: beautiful mountainsides scarred by unattractive development, development on steep slopes leading to severe erosion problems, and the conversion of crystal clear streams into open sewers. As one very close observer of the Vermont scene put it, Vermonters with a strong land conservation ethic and an equally strong small farm tradition became concerned that a lifestyle that they prized greatly would be ended forever by an influx of urban non-Graniteers.[3]

Such fears and anxieties had a great deal to do with providing a positive political setting in which a conservative state, historically dominated by the Republican party, could take far-reaching action in the land- and growth-management field. They could view such action mainly as an effort to prevent the destruction of Vermont by an influx of outsiders. The negative effects of the increased development were also felt in the pocketbooks of Vermont natives. The increased value of land meant that taxes rose rapidly, and that many Vermonters of low and moderate income found it increasingly difficult to cope with the rising tax costs.[4]

Although many projects contributed to the rising fears of a foreign inundation of Vermont, the one that is credited with being the catalyst was an International Paper Company proposal to build a very large development oriented to second homes and recreation in southern Vermont. Like much of Vermont, the area consisted of hilly slopes and thin soils where it is very difficult to accommodate such things as septic tanks, not to mention the roads needed to maintain and service such a development. The rising tide of concern with such a development proposal produced a sense of crisis in 1969 that led to far-reaching actions in the 1970 legislature.[5]

Before assessing those developments, we must look at Vermont's government structure, especially that of local government, to better understand why the state acted to take a state-regional control approach that largely bypassed local governments. In New England, the basic unit of local government is the town, which is not to be compared exactly to either an incorporated municipality or to counties in other parts of the country. In 237 organized towns in Vermont cover a large geographical area containing a relatively small number of people. One study puts their average size at 36 square miles but gives their average population as below 1,000 persons.[6] All of Vermont is organized into towns, with some minor exceptions growing out of extremely mountainous terrain and inaccurate surveys. There are, in addition, nine cities that are independent of the towns and possess a range of powers common to cities in the rest of the country. Vermont is also organized into nine regional planning councils that are controlled by the towns and as such are relatively weak. Counties exist in the state but have limited duties.

Little debate occurred over whether local governments were to be included as major actors in Vermont's initial growth-management effort. Apparently there was widespread agreement that neither the towns nor the newly organized regional planning councils were capable of meeting the problems. There was some sentiment for taking action that would gradually allow these towns or the regional planning councils to gain experience with new powers that had been granted to them under the administration of Governor Phillip H. Hoff. In retrospect, Hoff's initiatives in giving local governments new powers in the planning area assumed great importance for the long-run management of land in Vermont. Hoff, the state's first Democratic governor in over 100 years, sponsored legislation authorizing regional planning commissions and providing planning and zoning powers for local governments. One difficulty was that while this legislation included all of the standard elements of planning and regulatory powers for Vermont cities and towns, it also prohibited zoning or subdivision controls until a town adopted a comprehensive plan. Given the very limited experience of Vermont local government in this area, it probably would have been many years before very much could have been done by towns to regulate what was seen as in immediate growth-management crisis.[7]

With a sense of crisis firmly established, focused largely on a fear that Vermont's way of life, centered on rural and small-town areas with great environmental beauty, was about to be destroyed, decisions were made over a very short period of time that moved Vermont into the front ranks of states in the land- and growth-management area. The town officials, faced with what was to them a huge second home and recreation development, turned to a conservative Republican governor, Dean C. Davis, for help. As one close observer put it, the legislature at that time was "old in age, Republican, and conservative." However, these were the very people, often concentrated in the grange halls across Vermont, that during 1968 and 1969 began to feel that the new pressures for growth were going to destroy all that they loved most about Vermont. With the threatened 1,200-unit International Paper Company development, the whole concern seemed to crystalize, and the appeal to the governor to save a way of life was responded to with considerable enthusiasm and promptness.[8]

The Politics of Adoption

Laying the Groundwork

When Governor Dean Davis, described as a "highly respected old-line conservative Republican, heard the selectmen from southern Vermont describe the rash of development proposals facing them, he decided he had to do something about it. The governor seemed to hold strongly to the land conservation ethic that, to some at least, distinguishes Vermont from its neighbor state of New Hampshire.[9] The approach taken by the governor was to name a Commission on Environmental Control headed by a respected veteran state representative, Arthur Gibb. Governor Davis presented the Gibb Commission with the challenge of finding "how we can have economic growth . . . without destroying the secret of our success, our environment." This theme of balancing economic growth with protecting the natural systems of a state runs through the land- and growth-management initiatives in several of the states assessed in this volume. To overcome the natural conservative resistance to the management of growth in many of these states, it was argued that a failure to bring growth and development under some kind of reasonable control would result in a destruction of the very environmental assets on which the state's continued economic stability depended. This argument, which was made strongly in Vermont, has been repeated in a variety of forms in a number of other states.

Gibb occupied a central role in the legislature as a member of the House Natural Resources Committee and was also a resident of southern Vermont where many of the abuses were occurring. The commission was bipartisan and represented a broad cross section of interests and attitudes in Vermont, including businessmen, industrialists, developers, conservationists, and influential legislators."[10] Despite the variety of interests represented on the commission, the members reached a quick consensus that Vermont did indeed confront a true crisis in land and growth management and devoted themselves with enthusiasm to the governor's challenge. The group met every other week for about six months and came up with numerous recommendations, many of which were adopted by the 1970 Vermont legislature.

There seems to have been an almost unanimous consensus among the members that new authority had to be placed in the hands of the state to deal with the uncontrolled development.

However, little enthusiasm existed for putting any more power in the hands of the state's bureaucracy than absolutely necessary. For this reason, Vermont opted for a lay state board and lay citizen district commissions. The attitude of the Gibb Commission was reflected in one commissioner's comment that "with developers starting now to subdivide thousands of new acres of land, much of it on mountains and in areas where subdivision regulations are not in existence, towns cannot wait upon the completion of comprehensive plans in order to establish such regulation."[11]

The commission first recommended that immediate action be taken by having the commissioner of health put in place what were in effect subdivision regulations and strongly enforce those regulations while other controls could be adopted and implemented. On the primary problem of how to develop a land-regulation system for Vermont, the commission concluded that the proper approach would be to require a permit for all development of a certain size or number of units. The commission recommended that the criteria for granting such permits be based on a variety of factors such as the elevation of the land, the effects of development on local government, and the impact on the environment. These criteria were eventually spelled out in the act that was passed.

The Gibb Commission also made a strong recommendation to reorganize, simplify, and streamline environmental agencies in the state of Vermont. This recommendation was subsequently carried out by the legislature when it established a new environmental agency that pulled under its umbrella several former independent agencies. Finally, the commission, in what proved to be the most difficult proposal to implement, recommended that the growth of the state be guided in the future by "a comprehensive land use plan to be undertaken as soon as practical and completed within . . . one year."[12]

The Gibb Commission also recommended, and the legislature adopted, other environmental actions, such as regulations to control power transmission facilities, pesticides, and water. The commission's recommendations on open space preservation and flood plain zoning were not implemented by the 1970 legislature and have still not been approved. The fact is that the commission did a remarkable amount of work in a very short period of time, and in the Vermont tradition it operated on a financial shoestring. Virtually no funds were available to it, although the governor did assign a staff person to work with the commission.

Drafting the Legislation
Once the Gibb Commission had completed its report, the governor

acted promptly to get it in bill form in time to put it before the 1970 Vermont legislature. The drafting responsibility went to members of the governor's administration, and to Jonathan Brownell, an attorney who had served as an advisor to the Gibb Commission. The 1970 Vermont legislature was considered a "landowning legislature," and many feared that it would have little enthusiasm for bills that moved in the direction of regulating the use of land and protecting the environment. The fact that the legislation moved through the legislature with remarkable ease was seen as largely due to the very strong efforts of Governor Davis and his staff.[13] Governor Davis, for example, had one of his assistants systematically move about the state and obtain endorsement from all 14 of the Republican county committees before the legislature was convened.

In the legislature, the amount of opposition to the legislation was so small as to be virtually invisible. One close participant in the process noted that there was "hardly a dissenting vote," except for a couple of senator/dairy farmers who were concerned about giving the state too much authority over the district commissions. Furthermore, "the governor committed all his power for it. It was his top priority." There seemed to be virtually no organized opponent or proponent forces when the legislation was adopted in 1970.[14] Nevertheless, subsequent assessments suggest that a number of citizen-environmental organizations played a significant background role in getting the legislation through. It is perhaps typical of Vermont that these environmental groups were not affiliates of national organizations but were homegrown groups, such as the Environmental Planning Information Center of the Vermont Natural Resources Council.[15]

David Heeter, who has written the most detailed assessment of the Vermont land use law, has also noted that one of the reasons that act 250 attracted so little opposition was that other major land use control and environmental legislation was introduced into the legislature at the same time, and opponents had a difficult time deciding where to concentrate their opposition. For instance, the health department's emergency subdivision regulations were up for approval by the legislature in order for them to become permanent, and Heeter noted that they attracted much of the opposition. In view of the fact that Vermont has been held up as an example of one of the strongest state initiatives in the land- and growth-management area in the nation, it is interesting that much of the criticism of the legislation apparently came from environmentalists and local planners who viewed act 250 as too weak.

Heeter also noted that insofar as there was opposition to the passage of the Land Use Act of 1970, it was concentrated in the lower house. During floor consideration it did run into some opposition from a "coalition of conservative Republicans and some Democrats led by the [Democratic] minority leader, Thomas Salmon."[16] Ironically when Salmon later was elected governor, he became a leading advocate of environmental legislation and pressed for the adoption of the final stages of Vermont's land- and growth-management initiative. In 1970, however, he moved to limit the land use law's application to a pilot test area. Like other weakening amendments, Salmon's amendment failed, and the bill in the final vote in the house passed overwhelmingly. The legislation was much more warmly received in the senate, where its greatest danger was in having the session end without the bill coming up for a vote. Here again, Governor Davis's setting up the legislation as his number one priority saved it from dying on the calendar. The senate, in fact, added several amendments that strengthened the legislation, and it passed by a voice vote.[17]

As noted earlier, the 1970 legislature also established the Agency for Environmental Conservation, generally referred to as the environmental agency. The new agency was to coordinate the work of eight different departments or boards placed under it.[18] Other bills which were either new legislation or strengthened old legislation included the state's control over water pollution, the bringing of real estate transactions under the state's deceptive practices act, and the regulation of mobile home parks through state standards.

In assessing the *politics of adoption* in the 1970 Vermont legislature, one is struck again by the fact that a conservative Republican legislature added not only the land- and growth-regulation measure commonly known as act 250, but also a number of other strong environmental laws to the laws of the state. Even if one explains the easy passage of act 250 as due to the general feeling by natives of Vermont that "enemies from the outside" in the form of giant developers were moving in rapidly to rape the land, and that the "clear and present danger" had to be dealt with, one is left with the need to explain the passage of other environmental legislation that could not be tied so directly to the enemy from without. It seems reasonable to conclude that both factors—the feeling that Vermont had to be protected from outside forces and the growing support for environmental protection that in part reflected the national mood—were important in the quick and easy passage of act 250 and other environmental laws through the legislature.

Provisions of Act 250

The central core of the regulatory process established by act 250 was a permit requirement for virtually any development involving a greater than local impact. Specifically included were (*a*) all housing projects, including mobile homes, of 10 or more units; (*b*) commercial or industrial projects involving more than one acre in towns lacking land use regulations, or more than 10 acres if the town had such land use tools in place; (*c*) all state or municipal projects involving 10 or more acres; (*d*) all development at an elevation of 2,500 feet or higher; and (*e*) the sale of subdivided land where 10 or more lots were involved, and each lot was less than 10 acres.

Act 250, then, took aim at virtually all types of development in the state, with the exception of farming, logging or forestry products, and electric generation and transmission facilities. The logging-forestry exemption was a concession to those large-scale operations in the so-called Northeast kingdom area of Vermont, where growth pressures had not been substantial.[19]

The mechanism devised to implement this bold new approach for land and growth management was a unique blend of state and lay local responsibility that flowed from Vermont's history and political philosophy. The main state responsibility was lodged in a state environmental board consisting of nine members serving staggered four-year terms, appointed by the governor with the advice and consent of the senate. (See Figure 3-1.) Among other responsibilities, the environmental board would decide appeals of permit decisions. At the local level, existing units of local government were bypassed entirely, largely because they were typically ill equipped to take on such responsibilities; partly because the special brand of Vermont conservatism was more comfortable with giving responsibility for implementing the act to local nongovernmental officials.

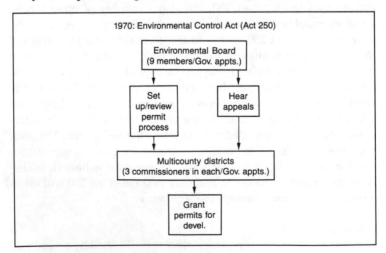

Figure 3-1. **Vermont: Land-Use Regulation**

The approach to achieving this local brand of control was to establish three-member district environmental commissions, made up of lay persons appointed by the governor, for two-year staggered terms to be the permitting authority. The districts themselves average about 35 towns and thus constitute in effect regional regulatory mechanisms roughly comparable to California's regional commissions. By their decisions on permit applications, the district environmental commissions carry out the great bulk of regulation of Vermont's land use under the law. While the proceedings are technically quasi-judicial, they have been conducted typically informally, and the emphasis from the very beginning has been on working out settlements with developers through negotiations. The state's interests in permit proceedings are represented by the environmental agency as well as by other state agencies that make an appearance. Other parties include towns and regional planning commissions, citizens groups, property owners, all of whom have standing under certain circumstances.

The heart of the permitting procedure involves measuring a proposed project against the legislative criteria. These criteria can cover a wide range of potentially detrimental impacts of development. An applicant must show that the project:

- Will not result in undue water or air pollution.
- Has sufficient water for its reasonably foreseeable needs.
- Will not cause an unreasonable burden on an existing water supply, if one is to be used.
- Will not cause unreasonable soil erosion or reduction in the ability of the land to hold water.
- Will not cause unreasonable congestion or unsafe conditions on highways or other transportation facilities.
- Will not cause an unreasonable burden on the ability of a municipality to provide educational service.
- Will not place an unreasonable burden on the ability of the local government to provide governmental services.
- Will not have an undue adverse effect on the scenic or natural beauty of the area, aesthetics, historic sites, or rare and irreplaceable natural areas.
- Is in conformance with statewide plans required by act 250.
- Is in conformance with any duly adopted local or regional plan or capital program.[20]

The chairman of the state environmental board over the life of the act has alternately been part-time or full-time. The board's only other professional staff is a full-time administrator, now called an executive officer. For housekeeping purposes only, the environmental board is under the Agency for Environmental Conservation. Thus, we see a system adopted in act 250 in which the process for regulating land in Vermont is strongly decentralized, though decentralized in a way which bypasses existing local governments.

The regulatory features of act 250 have been relatively non-controversial and seem to have worked surprisingly well. The same cannot be said for the additional provision in the law that a land use plan be developed in three stages according to rather loosely defined directions in the legislation. The assumption was that each stage would build on the other. The first stage was to be the interim land capability plan, which was adopted in 1972. This plan merely stated very general policies and involved maps which indicated some areas in Vermont that were unique or especially subject to environmental damage should they be developed, or were especially suited to certain uses such as agriculture or forestry. The provision in act 250 was that subsequent plans had to be consistent with this first interim land capability plan, and since there was no clear consensus in the legislature on what should be the ultimate form of a land use plan in Vermont, it, of necessity, had to be kept very general.[21]

It is around the next two planning components that the most controversy has evolved. After a political struggle, the second stage, the land capability and development plan was approved by the legislature in 1973 and included substantially more detail than the interim plan. The final step envisioned by act 250 was a Vermont land use plan, which has not yet been put on the books, and which continues to be the focus of attention from opponents and proponents alike.[22]

At one early stage of the Gibb Commission's considerations, it was recommended that the environmental board be empowered to draw up the land use plans mandated by act 250, and that the plans themselves be approved by the governor. This approach would not have required approval by the legislature. The Gibb Commission assumed that the state plans would be couched in broad overall terms. When proponents of more specific language in the state land use plan succeeded in getting some of their ideas into the act, including a requirement for mapped areas with permissible zones and densities, the legislature took the position that it would have to approve such plans. The controversy over whether the state land use plan does or does not involve state zoning has been a continuing and bitter one in Vermont and lies at the heart of the difficulties that have been encountered in adopting the plan.

The Politics of Implementation

Some Problems and Limitations

Assessing the implementation of Vermont's land use law is difficult in any complete sense. Although there has been more than a decade of experience in issuing permits under act 250, this is still a relatively short period for attempting to attribute impacts to the land use law. In addition, the intervening variable of the economic recession of 1973 and after had a major impact on growth and development in Vermont, as it did in other states. It is even difficult to try to assess the changing political context of the law's implementation, because most of the controversy has not involved the regulatory effort but has been focused instead on the attempts to put into place the planning process called for in act 250. In the assessment that follows, the implementation of the regulatory aspects of act 250 will be treated first.

Permit applications over the period 1970–79 totaled 3,413. Almost 90 percent of these were approved at the district commission level. Denials amounted to only 2.5 percent of total applications, and some 3 percent were appealed to the state environmental board. Only 15 applicants chose to exercise their option to take their case to the superior court, and 18 cases have gone to the state supreme court. In only one case was the district commission's decision overturned and the permit issued, albeit with six conditions.[23] Action on permits has been prompt, reflecting the relative informality of the procedures, and the efforts of the district environmental commissions to function as mediators among the parties. In the nine-month period, April 1 through December 31, 1978, 49 percent of the permits were issued within 30 days; 61 percent within 40 days, and 75 percent within 60 days.[24] Like the experience in most other states assessed in this study, the overwhelming percentage of the permits applied for in Vermont were approved. However, major applications have typically been approved with important and substantial conditions attached. Thus, the high approval rate does not mean that the regulatory process has not had major impact on development in the state.

From a political perspective, there is a widespread consensus that the local lay citizen approach embodied in the district environmental commissions is one of the outstanding strong points of the law. One close observer said that having fellow local citizens make the decisions about permits produces a wide spectrum of political support for the act. He cited the fact that act 250 does not come in for the kind of attack that the state's environmental agencies or even local or regional planning commissions are subjected to as they go about land use and environmental control activities, although the district commissions do much more controlling and regulating than the other agencies.[25]

Opinion is divided on whether the district commissions have enough staff to help them do their jobs adequately. In fact, they had originally only the assignment of two persons who gave them support on a regular basis. One was called an environmental coordinator, who was (and is) an employee of the state environmental agency assigned to the district commission, and the other was the district forester, who worked up the initial set of data with regard to a permit for each district commission. That source of staff support was later eliminated because of budget cuts. Thus, in neither case did the district hire or fire what limited staff it had. Some observers indicated that it is a source of political strength that the district commissions have virtually no staff of their own, but one regional planning commission executive director in Vermont felt strongly that the district commissions do not have the staff to do the job properly. He noted that there has been some movement to handle what he considers the greatest problem—the failure to do any consistent monitoring and enforcement of the important conditions that are attached to the act.[26]

Schyler Jackson, who has held top positions on both the environmental board and the environmental agency, noted that act 250 required the environmental agency to be of assistance to the district environmental commissions. During the initial period of implementation, the environmental board and the environmental agency worked together closely to develop the rules and regulations for the district commissions. However, stresses and strains soon developed, with some members of the environmental board feeling that the environmental agency did not really understand act 250, and the environmental agency feeling that the environmental board was being unreasonable and stiff-necked.[27]

The "Act 250 Interagency Review Committee," which is made up of state agencies that may be involved in permit applications, is supposed to be the source of comprehensive recommendations to the district environmental commissions. The "Act 250 Club" was originally created informally although it was later established by executive order of the governor in 1972. According to Heeter, the depth and general adequacy of the agency reviews tend to be very uneven, partly because the agencies have only a short time in which to consider the applications. Heeter noted: "The best the Act 250 Club can do with respect to many applications is to warn the district commissioners to further investigate suspected problems. The environmental agency then prepares a final position paper which contains its recommendations and any conflicting recommendations or caveats from the Act 250 Club or other agencies."[28] Heeter's conclusion was that the in-depth technical help available when district commissions have an unusually complex and difficult case was not adequate.

For a long while there was no record of a strong effort by the executive branch or in the legislature to achieve additional funding for the environmental board and the district commissions. The assumption was that the necessary technical support could come from existing state agencies. The district commissions received very little systematic and regular local government support in a technical sense. There has been some change, as more and more towns begin to undertake planning and land use regulation of their own, and as some regional planning councils strengthen their planning capacity and attempt to involve themselves more heavily in the act 250 permitting process.[29]

Staff support for act 250 has actually declined in recent years. The loss of the district forester meant that the district environmental commissions lost their only source of data and help in interpreting the facts. This forced them to rely on the parties for the facts involved in the permit applications. The current (1982) executive officer of the state environmental board is strongly supportive of finding a way to at least replace the district forester either through the environmental agency or by authorizing and providing funds for the district environmental commission to hire such a person. Such action would only bring the commissions back to where they were before they lost the services of the district forester.[30]

One frequent criticism is that there is considerable variation among district commissions with regard to treatment and application of the criteria to the projects brought before them. There has been some feeling that the environmental board should have issued more detailed regulations and criteria to assure more standard treatment of projects across the state. On the other hand, a considerable body of opinion holds that the flexibility and decentralization involved in the differing styles and approach by the individual district commissions had been a considerable source of strength in maintaining public support for the land use regulation effort. There is, in any event, apparently no data to support the proposition that there are major and fundamental differences in the way in which the district environmental commissions apply the criteria of the act.[31]

Heeter holds that "There is no question that some of the criteria in the capability and development plan are not being fully implemented." He noted that the environmental board had backed off from using its rule-making power in substantive matters, partly because of adverse reaction to its attempt to strengthen the regulations involving the criterion on aesthetics. That effort attracted widespread and unfavorable attention, and the board was forced to drop the effort. This occurred during the height of the efforts to adopt a land use plan, when tempers and passions were running high, and opponents were in no mood to accept any expansion of the environmental board's authority.[32]

With regard to what might be called the politics of bureaucracy, it is not easy to assess the degree to which state agencies managed to "get their act together" in supporting act 250. The Agency for Environmental Conservation has tried to coordinate the programs under its control in order to more effectively support the permitting process. For example, in 1970, it did establish regional offices coinciding more or less with the environmental district commission boundaries, with each office headed by a district environmental coordinator. This coordinator has the authority to act on many environmental agency matters at the regional level, although all act 250 applications acted on by the agency still must go to Montpelier.

A recent assessment held that the permit cases at each end of a "complex to simple" continuum are handled reasonably well. In really major complex cases, state actors are there, and regional and town forces often play an important role. In very minor cases, the limited staff support is not serious. For those permit applications in the middle range, the staff support for district commissions was seen as inadequate and more inadequate since the departure of the district forester.[33]

The rising frustration and hostility toward bureaucracy in general that has characterized the entire United States in the last few years certainly has been present in Vermont. Both the environmental board and the environmental agency have attempted to respond to this by taking actions to clarify and simplify both act 250 permitting matters and other permitting requirements that do not fall within the act 250 framework. For instance, the environmental board acted to empower district commissions to issue a permit for minor developments without holding a hearing if no party or adjoining owner requested one.[34] In addition, the environmental board has authorized its chairman to hold a prehearing conference if it will speed up the process of deciding on an application. Furthermore, it is now possible, upon agreement of all parties, to have a permit heard before one member of the board who acts as a hearing officer and makes the final decision.

The environmental board came under some criticism for not implementing a provision under which applicants could demonstrate their compliance with some of the criteria on the basis of having received a permit issued from another state agency or local government. Under a recently adopted rule, the board has provided that a "permit or certificate of compliance" by certain state agencies creates a rebuttable presumption that the criteria have been satisfied. Applicants with a very complex project are also allowed to present elements of their proposal in sequence, so that compliance with different criteria can be examined separately. Should a developer discover early on that his proposal fails to meet a particular criterion, this approach saves him the cost of needlessly working up the data for all the other criteria. And, finally, provision has now been made for a joint hearing between district commissions and the environmental board and any affected government agency should that be requested by such an agency or an interested party. All of this indicates that Vermont has made a very strong effort to respond to the criticism that a bureaucratic jungle of red tape needlessly stifles legitimate development in the implementation of land use regulations.[35]

The relationship between the district commission and local governments has been generally positive. District commissions have demonstrated their willingness to listen closely and respond to local opinions in application hearings. The participation not only of towns but also of regional planning commissions has steadily increased over time. According to the executive director of the Burlington area planning commission, his commission participates in prepermit discussions and has tried to be a catalyst in getting the towns and the developers together to work out differences and problems in the early stages of the application process.[36]

On balance it can be said that the permitting process under act 250 has worked quite well, but has some serious weaknesses that need to be addressed. The system of lay bodies, one board at the state level and seven to nine commissions at the local level, seems to have been successful in sustaining political support for some rather far-reaching restrictions and controls placed on development. It was repeatedly stated that the feeling that ordinary citizens, not state or local government bureaucrats, were making the decisions over what could or could not be done had a great deal to do with the acceptability of the process. The weaknesses involve assuring adequate staffing for the district environmental commissions, discussed earlier, and also assuring staff support for the state environmental board to allow even a minimal monitoring and enforcement effort. Given the standard practice of approving projects with important conditions attached, this is a matter of great importance. The executive officer of the state environmental board plans to launch a compliance and enforcement effort, relying heavily on computers, with the very limited staff available. Plans are to demonstrate the importance and potential of monitoring and enforcement with this in-house effort then to use it as the basis for seeking support for a full-time attorney to work on enforcement and eventually another staff person to work in the monitoring and enforcement area. These tentative plans for strengthening staff support seem modest even in a state famous for its suspicion of bureaucracy. They are also crucial to the long-run integrity of the law.[37]

The real controversy in Vermont has not centered around the permitting process under act 250. That process has never been seriously threatened with repeal or major weakening in the legislature, and, indeed, several legislative actions have strengthened the process. The controversy has centered on whether and how the state of Vermont should move from a case-by-case primarily reactive permitting procedure to a regulatory system within the context of a state plan.

The Politics of Implementing Vermont's Three-Step Planning Process

The seeds of continuing strong controversy were sown in the wording of act 250 that provided for the implementation over time of the three-step planning process described earlier. From the very first, controversy, confusion, misunderstanding, and interagency conflict have dominated the effort to implement the planning portion of Vermont's land use law. With the benefit of hindsight, the central question was whether the proposed land use plan would be a very broad policy statement to serve as a state framework in an advisory way only (the position of Representative Gibb) or whether it would be much more detailed and specific, in effect, amounting to a kind of statewide zoning. Conflict over this issue led to some bitter interagency and legislative battles, culminating in the failure in 1974, 1975 and 1976, to adopt stage three of the state land use plan.

Stage One: The Interim Plan

The development and approval of the first step, the interim plan, was relatively noncontroversial, but it did engender friction among state agencies over the content of the succeeding plans and the prime responsibility for their development. Act 250 directed the environmental board to adopt the three plans, but the board had no

professional capacity for planning. Its only staff member was an
executive secretary who was totally occupied with the development
of the permit review and appeals process. Heeter points out that an
agency that might have served as the professional staffing source,
the central planning office, had been dismantled under a 1970
reorganization, and most of its personnel dispersed among the line
agencies, with only a small core making up a state planning office in
the office of the governor.[38]

By the fall of 1970, the gathering of physical data on which to base
the first interim plan was underway, and a state planning team had
been formed under the leadership of the state planning office to
carry out the work and prepare the initial draft. A series of "county
capability maps" identified natural system characteristics such as
susceptibility to flooding, soil conditions detrimental to development, steepness of slope, and aquifer recharge areas. A kind of
critical area map pinpointed "certain unique and fragile areas which
could be jeopardized by anything other than low intensity development."[39]

When the environmental board reviewed the draft in June 1971,
the members were not entirely pleased with it. Before adopting the
plan, the board insisted on inserting some policies that it felt could
serve as guides in acting upon permit applications and made it clear
by contrast that the maps and text were not to be related to the
permitting process, but were for informational purposes only.
Governor Davis approved the plan on March 8, 1972, and it
subsequently was adopted by the legislature.

The board members felt that "the planning staff had let them
down and that the strongest feature of the interim plan was the
policies the board had added." On the other hand, "The planners
blamed the mixed reaction of the board members to the interim plan
on their failure to pay sufficient attention to the initial proposals
made earlier in the year and to maintain contact thereafter."[40] To
some extent, one might blame the controversy on a lack of clarity in
act 250 as to just what would be the content of the plans and who
would be responsible for developing them. In any event, well before
this, the focus of attention had shifted to stage two, the development and approval by the legislature of the Land Capability and
Development Plan.

Stage Two: The Land Capability
and Development Plan

It was during the effort to prepare and adopt the Land Capability
and Development Plan and the companion effort with regard to the
state land use plan that the relevant political forces at work in

Vermont were most clearly exposed. The twin efforts also brought into clear focus the rivalries and conflicts among the state government agencies involved. In particular it was the proposed land use plan that aroused the opposition of local governments and organized groups.

The planning team responsible for the Land Capability and Development Plan had a draft proposal ready by May 1972. During its preparation, the conflicting views of the state planning office and the environmental board became evident. The board wanted to be in the driver's seat. These lay members saw themselves as having the prime responsibility for producing a plan that would be couched in clear and simple terms that any citizen of Vermont could understand. Conversely, the planning office people tended to feel that the magnitude of the task and its complexity demanded that in effect the board play a reactive, rather than an initiating role.[41]

By late September 1972, the environmental board had made a crucial decision to move rapidly to develop not only the Land Capability and Development Plan but also the state land use plan. The planning staff responded to this call for double action, and two months later had put together a land capability and development plan and a somewhat hastily thrown together version of the state land use plan, including maps, and some basic concepts. At this point, another critical decision was made to mail the two plans to all households in the state prior to the public hearings that were to be held by the environmental board. There is virtually unanimous agreement that this mailing had a devastating impact. As Heeter described it, "The hearings on the newsprint plans were generally confused and often tumultuous." The hostile atmosphere was also affected by the health department's extension of its mandate to regulate subdivisions by including all developments of three or more lots or less than 10 acres, thus filling a gap in the original act 250 regulations. There was a very negative reaction to this action by developers and speculators, especially in the Northeast Kingdom area of Vermont. A new group called the Landowners Steering Committee was formed in the area to oppose the proposed health department action as well as any other further action on land use in Vermont.

The maps that were distributed were of very poor quality, and it was very difficult to interpret just what the different colors meant in terms of land use in any particular place. This occasioned a great deal of confusion and suspicion, as citizens all over the state began to try to see what the proposed state land use plan would do to their "very own" piece of land. While the hearings were beginning to reveal the breadth and depth of the hostile responses, proponents urged outgoing Governor Davis and Governor-elect Salmon to clarify what was actually being proposed in the two plans being circulated, and to try to get at least something through the upcoming session of the legislature.[42]

Jonathan Brownell, a private practicing attorney who had been deeply involved in the Vermont land use effort from the very beginning, felt that the proposed land use plan "was a wide and sweeping thing, and politically naive." At this point, he and an associate, Leonard U. Wilson, who was close to Governor-elect Salmon, tried unsuccessfully to persuade the chairman of the environmental board that the "planner's document" was not going to fly, and would cause the whole land and growth management effort in Vermont a great deal of trouble. Subsequently, Governor Davis and Governor-elect Salmon informally named Brownell and Wilson to work with the environmental board to do something about the zoning map and the more detailed material that had been mailed out.[43]

Since Brownell and Wilson were interested in clarifying and strengthening the Land Capability and Development Plan, they wanted to have stage three and the land use map put aside. Brownell recalled that "There was great public concern about the maps, the maps scared everybody to death, and there was a feeling that the central planning office was going to try to run the whole state.[44] Brownell feared that, without clearer rules and regulations in the second plan, a strong wave of resentment would threaten the broad base of support that had developed for a fairly strong land use control program.[45]

In Schyler Jackson's view, the source of the problem was an "unwise separation between authority and responsibility" for drafting and adopting the plans. Jackson, who had been the director of the environmental agency, became the chairman of the environmental board under incoming Governor Salmon. Jackson noted that the governor, through an executive order, gave the planning office the responsibility for developing the plan, but the environmental board still had the statutory responsibility for holding the hearings on the plan that the planning office had developed. As he saw it, the environmental board was forced to go public with a plan that they really did not want. In Jackson's opinion, the planning office people simply were not sensitive to the people's fear of what he called "arbitrary action in error." He was referring to the error-marred and confusing land use map distributed to every box holder in Vermont. When Vermonters tried to figure out the map, they "just went crazy."

Ultimately, Jackson pointed out, the map was withdrawn, but the effort to adopt a state land use plan never really recovered from the negative attitudes it engendered.[46]

Brownell and Wilson proceeded with the crash redrafting of stage two during the first three weeks of December 1972. As they had urged, the introduction of stage three, the state land use plan, was postponed on the grounds that it was not in good enough shape to be pursued in view of the intense opposition expressed at the hearings. During the redrafting, the whole thrust of stage two, the Land Capability and Development Plan, was changed from a statement of broad general policies that would eventually be developed by rule into criteria, to one in which the plan itself would involve more specific policies and criteria that would be presented to the legislature for adoption as an amendment or series of amendments to chapter 250.[47] During this redrafting process, there were three major actors involved—the environmental board, the planning office staff, and the Brownell-Wilson team. It is perhaps inevitable that tension, resentment, and even hostilities developed, setting the stage for bad feeling that carried over into the later attempts to adopt the state land use plan.[48]

The proposed Land Capability and Development Plan was introduced into the general assembly on January 3, 1973 with the hope that it could be treated as a joint resolution. When the speaker of the house chose instead to treat it as a regular bill, a month of valuable time had to be used converting the proposed plan from layman's language into bill form. A number of changes made during the bill drafting stage were resented by both the environmental board and the planning office, to the extent that some members of both agencies were unsure that the bill deserved any support at all. The point is not whether putting the plan into bill form weakened or strengthened it (one view is that it strengthened it), but that it further increased the bad feeling that had begun to surround the whole effort of moving the land- and growth-management system in Vermont through the successive planning stages.

A special house committee was appointed presumably to speed up the consideration of the plan. Instead, according to Heeter, hostile house members took the opportunity to try to discredit the plan, and only 4 of the 12 committee members voted for it. The house Natural Resources Committee, in an attempt to rescue the situation, redrafted the plan a number of times, and the confusion surrounding the whole thing was increased when a substitute bill was introduced that would have limited Vermont's planning and regulatory powers to certain critical areas and large scale development.

The landowners steering committee launched a strong attack on the Land Capability and Development Plan through the media across the state, and a counterattack was launched by a group called "Landowners for Act 250." It was not until the senate threatened to adopt the plan by resolution that the house moved off dead center. Ultimately, the plan redrafted by the Natural Resources Committee cleared the house by a very comfortable margin of 212 to 26.[49] There was a last minute hitch in the senate, but on the very last day of the session, the Land Capability and Development Plan was approved by voice vote of the members of the senate.[50]

The Land Capability and Development Plan was a considerably stronger and more detailed document than the interim plan. The series of amendments to the original act clarified and added to the criteria in a variety of ways. First, the changes expanded and added detail to act 250's environmental criteria, including new provisions regarding the polluting of public water supplies or an aquifer recharge area. Second, the changes would make it harder to use agriculture, forest, or mineral lands in a way that would interfere with these uses. In the case of prime agricultural land, it could be developed for anything other than agriculture only if that was the only way that the landowner could get a fair return on the value of the land. Whether or not this is a strengthening or a weakening provision, of course, depends on how it is interpreted.

The Land Capability and Development Plan also addressed the question of the relationship between act 250 and local governments in a more thorough way than had been the case before. Any action by the state would have to be consistent with an adopted local plan or capital budget unless following the local plan would have a substantial negative impact on surrounding towns or a substantial negative impact on an "overriding state interest." This can be interpreted to mean that towns can really do anything in the area of growth that they want to as long as the impact of that growth is confined within the borders of the town. Again, of course, the significance of this provision depends on how it is interpreted. How one interprets "overriding state interest" or "impact on a surrounding town" will go a long way in determining whether this provision could, in fact, weaken act 250, or whether it will simply provide an added incentive for local governments to get into the planning business.[51]

In what has been described by one observer as the "most important section of the capability and development plan," a provision was made requiring that the public service impacts of a development be considered in terms of the ability of a town or a region to provide those public services. Under the original act, the district environmental commission could attach conditions to ease any financial burden on towns caused by development, but could not deny a permit on those grounds alone. Under the amendment, assuming a town had a capital improvement program, the burden of proof as to the adequacy of public facilities becomes the responsibility of the developer. In effect, this provision provides a tool under which local governments could impose a staged growth approach on the development industry.[52]

In the process of adopting the Land Capability and Development Plan, some new insights into political attitudes and political possibilities had been revealed. The growing ability of opponents to organize and express opposition to any extension of the authority of the state to regulate land was clear. Confusion and conflict within the state government had contributed to a strong and building suspicion among many Vermont residents as to whether an effort to impose a strong statewide zoning scheme was underway. At the same time, a substantial amount of support for completing the planning process called for in the original act 250 remained in Vermont in general and in the legislature in particular.

Stage Three: The State Land Use Plan

Once the Land Capability and Development Plan was adopted, everyone agreed that a new land use plan would have to be put together quickly in order to present it to the 1974 legislative session. The environmental board reacted coolly to the initial concept presented by the planning office, which again included maps and detailed regulations by districts of the state's land. The board seems to have favored a very general framework plan, leaving the detailed plans, including mapping, to be done at the town and regional level. The planning office argued that the law required the detailed plans and pointed out that some two thirds of the state still had neither general town plans nor zoning and subdivision regulations. Despite the lack of agreement, the state planning office, with its mandate from the governor, moved forward in developing a land use plan that contained a number of major elements.

The plan as proposed contained a classification system whose principal elements included categories of urban, village, rural, natural resource, conservation, shoreline, or roadside. Each of these development categories contained assigned maximum densities, with rural, natural resource, and conservation lands subject to quite low density regulations. For instance, in rural lands the development would be restricted to one unit on 5 acres; on natural resource land, one unit on 25 acres; and conservation land, one unit on 100 acres. There was a special rule for shorelines and roadsides that provided for very large lots—200-feet frontage in the case of shorelines and 400-feet frontage in the case of roadsides.[53]

The proposal also called for local governments within a year to draw up plans for the development of land within their borders. On the bases of comments from adjoining towns, regional bodies, and state agencies, the secretary of development and community affairs would decide whether the town plans were consistent with the state land use plan. Under the proposal, the secretary's decision could be appealed to the environmental board, but if the board rejected the plan, the state was empowered to step in with its own plan which it could enforce.[54]

The environmental board responded in a fairly positive way to the planning office's proposed plan presented in August 1973 and even seemed to accept the inclusion of maps so long as the legislature had the opportunity to accept or reject them. However, at public hearings on the plan in October, the board announced its intention to rework the plan and hold a second round of hearings. Despite the governor's very negative reaction, the board proceeded with a redraft of the plan in which it made some substantial changes.[55] In general, the changes underlined the fundamental disagreement between the board and the planning office. The environmental board still tended to see a state land use plan as primarily a negative control document to prevent bad things from happening in areas that were particularly susceptible to environmental damage. The planning office, on the other hand, saw the plan as a much more positive approach in which intensive development would be encouraged in certain locations, and thus development more or less automatically discouraged in those areas where it was inappropriate.

At the urging of the planning office, the governor tried unsuccessfully to prevent a second round of hearings based on the revised plan. The hearings were, in fact, held, and once again brought the "antis" to the fore. A new opposition group, known as the Green Mountain Boys, came on the scene, whose leaders tried to mold it in the Ethan Allen tradition. Whereas the landowners steering committee had been largely a group representing large landowners, the Green Mountain Boys were supposed to represent the everyday, low to moderate income natives of Vermont, the so-called Woodchucks. The emergence of this new or at least better organized opposition to a state land use plan boded ill for success in the 1974 legislature.[56]

The timing for a major effort to adopt a comprehensive state land use plan could not have been worse. Economically, the winter of 1973–74 was very difficult for Vermont. There was not much snow to attract the skiers, there was an energy crisis, and the uncertainties about gas and heating oil all combined to make the usual spirited mid-winter recreation industry a near disaster. Furthermore, the construction industry was in a substantial slump. Under these circumstances, environmental protection, while it still was important to many Vermonters, simply did not have the high priority that it had enjoyed in earlier years. Furthermore, there was a growing feeling in Vermont that too much power was being concentrated in the state's environmental agency. Special shoreline and floodplain zoning bills that might have received favorable treatment in earlier legislatures went to a prompt death in the 1974 session. One newspaper expressed the view, as quoted in Healy and Rosenberg, that these bills were "victims of what boils down to more anti-bureaucratic sentiment than a disregard for the environment."[57]

In addition to unfortunate timing, there was still confusion over exactly what the proposed land use plan would entail. Local government interests had also had a change of heart. From being all too eager for help in 1970, local governments had gradually become increasingly interested in getting into the planning field and now resented having to do so within the framework of tight state controls. They began to complain that the land use plan was a piece of state dictation to local governments.

The land use plan was introduced into the legislature in January 1974, but the land classification maps did not appear until a month later. At that point, many Vermonters found out more than they apparently wanted to know about the real content of the plan. About half, indeed slightly more than half, of the state's entire area would fall into the natural resource classification or category where densities were limited to one unit per 25 acres. Another one third of the state was in the conservation category with a density limitation of one unit for each 100 acres. Thus nearly all of the future growth of the state would have to occur in some 20 percent of the area, and the great bulk of that was concentrated within the urbanized and adjacent town and village areas. However, the land use plan was not designed to choke off development—far from it. The plan, as reported in Healy and Rosenberg, "could accommodate an additional 1.7 million people, two and a half times its current population and far more than any foreseeable population projection." Further, there remained the persistent question of whether what was being proposed was not, in fact, state zoning.[58]

Governor Salmon had approved the land use plan on January 8, 1974, but apparently without enthusiasm.[59] The governor certainly would have been in an awkward position in refusing to accept the draft, since it came to him from a board almost all of whose members he had either appointed or reappointed. Furthermore, as a leading Republican legislator-dairy farmer pointed out, Salmon had been elected on a "liberal environmental platform" which included a clear pledge to complete the land use plan.[60]

Jonathan Brownell, who served as house counsel in 1974 during the time the land use bill was considered, noted that there were still bad feelings between the environmental board and the state planning office from the 1973 struggle over the Land Capability and Development Plan. The differences became very bitter, and "each side started appealing to individual legislators for support." In Brownell's view, the planning office had come up with "practically a zoning ordinance for the entire state," which they subsequently did produce, which had gotten the usual very negative reception. Brownell held that the planning office approach had "poisoned the well badly for this final element."[61]

As the 1974 legislative session began its deliberations, proponents of the land use plan were cautiously optimistic that at least some version of it or some parts of it would be approved. The initial approach was to have two bills prepared, one to apply the land use bill only to those developments subject to review under act 250, and another bill closely following the plan approved, however reluctantly, by the governor. After the house Natural Resources Committee approved the limited bill, the house decided not to take any further action until the environmental board adopted the necessary maps. The board, still unenthusiastic about the maps, finally did so, but they recommended that none of the mapped areas take immediate effect except those in the conservation area.[62]

Subsequent developments in the house revealed a growing feeling opposed to any state "takeover" of local land use and environmental responsibilities. When the legislature turned its back on a 1970 piece of legislation empowering the Agency for Environmental Conservation to control the use of certain shorelines, the Natural Resources Committee put the land use bill through several gradually weakening redrafting phases. The environmental board watched all this with some alarm, and apparently without notifying the governor, asked the legislature to return the plan to them so they could do further work on it. The governor, in the meantime, admitted that the poor handling of the plan had contributed greatly to the legislature's failing to adopt it, although he also accused the Republican leadership of "playing politics."[63] In any event, the session ended with the only action the creation of a special committee to study the bill and make recommendations for the 1975 session.

In the view of one Vermont legislative leader, Henry Carse, the insistence of the head of the planning office (who had been one of Salmon's campaign managers) on pushing hard for a complete land use plan "split the legislature wide open, at least split the house Natural Resources Committee wide open." For the committee's hearing on the bill, "They had to hire the biggest auditorium in Montpelier" to hold the busloads of people attending. As Carse saw it, the whole affair was orchestrated and spearheaded by "those folks up in the Northeast Kingdom." Carse noted that, although the unrest and opposition had spread to other areas, some of the strongest opposition in the legislature still came from lumber barons who controlled the Northeast Kingdom and managed to get them- selves elected to the legislature. In Carse's opinion, "They really were land speculators who didn't want any interference with their game." In any event, the chairman of the house Natural Resources Committee tried to carry the bill without success.[64]

When the 1974 legislative session failed to adopt a land use law, the governor announced his intention to try again and in the meantime was reelected. In the interim, the Special Joint Committee on Land Use Plans, including planners, legislators, citizens, and developers, tried to come to some new agreement on what might be done about a state land use plan. The house speaker also decided to reconstitute the whole Natural Resources Committee and try to get members on it with experience in the planning and zoning area. The reconstituted committee was still split on what to do about a land use plan, but both sides accepted Carse, a dairy farmer from the Burlington area, as the new chairman.[65]

In January 1975 the director of the state planning office made a presentation to the Natural Resources Committee that was essen- tially a rehash of the 1974 plan. When it received the same lukewarm response, the committee sought the views of Vermont's regional planning commissions and were shocked to learn that "there had never been any input from the towns or the regions into the third- stage plan. The state planning office dreamed it up out of thin air."[66] The committee also insisted that the state Department of Commu- nity Affairs be drawn into the process. It turned out that the community affairs people opposed any plan with at least the potential of allowing the state to "ram land use planning down the throats of the towns and regions within a strong state framework." Carse felt that the governor should have been seeking this type of feedback from the first.

After these consultations, a new bill was drawn up that was approved by the house Natural Resources Committee by a vote of 10 to 1, and passed the house on a close vote. Even one key legislator from the Northeast Kingdom supported it.[67] This version of the state land use plan set up a procedure under which there would be one map, not a town map on the one hand and a state map on the other. The bill did mandate that all towns develop a land use plan which would include a map. It did not, however, try to draw the map ahead of time and "thus scare everybody in Vermont half to death."[68]

Carse noted that the state planning officer and the chairman of the environmental board considered house bill 383 to be too weak. On the other hand, senate agricultural committee members considered the bill to be too strong. They reportedly were afraid that a property tax break for farmers would not be worked out along with the statewide land use plan, and that the farmers were going to get "taken to the cleaners." The state farm bureau, which had been in favor of a state land use plan, now reversed itself and came out against it, and the bill failed in the senate.[69] Representative Carse held the view that the most effective opponent in the Northeast Kingdom was the person who ran a newspaper in the town of Kirby, whom Carse considered to be unusually skillful in mounting opposition to issues in general and to the state land use plan in particular.[70]

A number of factors contributed to the ultimate failure to adopt a statewide land use plan in Vermont. Most of these came into focus during the ultimately successful effort to adopt the land capability and development plan. They included (1) a fear on the part of many residents and others in Vermont that what was being proposed was in fact a thinly disguised system of statewide zoning; (2) increasingly bitter infighting at the state level between the two key actors in attempts to draft a plan and get it to the legislature, that is the environmental board and the state planning office; (3) an increasing interest on the part of local government in land use planning, accompanied by a growing resistance to having that planning controlled in any detailed way by the state; (4) the gradually worsening climate for the adoption of any additional far-reaching land use or environmental legislation brought on by Vermont's share of the national economic decline as well as the particular problem arising in Vermont of a major negative impact on its recreation industry; and (5) the growing organized opposition which, while it was undoubtedly led by large developers, many of whom were from outside Vermont, certainly came to include many native sons who feared that their land was going to be controlled absolutely from the state level.

Act 250's Potential—A
Landmark Case

Although the 1973 Land Capability and Development Plan did provide a broader conceptual framework, act 250 itself and those supplementary amendments can be viewed as essentially a negative approach to regulating and managing growth. Certain criteria are laid down, against which proposed projects are measured and found worthy or at fault. Unlike the land use map, this system does not channel development into areas where it is desirable and keep it out of undesirable areas. Furthermore, only perhaps one third of the total development in the state is subject to the permitting process.

With the failure to adopt a land use plan in Vermont and the lack of support for such action in the forseeable future, there is an obvious need for a clearer state policy framework within which to carry out act 250. However, such a policy framework is, to some extent, imbedded in the Land Capability and Development Plan, particularly the requirement (criterion no. 9) that an applicant's project cannot be approved unless "It conforms to a duly adopted development plan, land use plan or land capability plan." With more and more towns adopting their own plans, there is an opportunity for a state-local cooperative effort guided by other relevant criteria, to move beyond a negative, case-by-case approach to a more positive approach which prevents growth in some areas, but encourages it in others.

A case in point is the Pyramid Company of Burlington's 1977 application to build a regional shopping mall in the town of Williston, Chittenden County, Vermont. The development would have been Vermont's first regional shopping mall, with two major department stores, 80 other shops, and 20 restaurants. Its proposed location was some six miles from Burlington's central business district. A project of such a size required a permit under act 250. The district environmental commission held prehearing conferences during the first half of August 1977; the formal hearings lasted through mid-October 1978 with hearings on 43 different days. The parties to the proceedings were the town of Williston, the Williston Planning Commission, the Chittenden County Regional Planning Commission, two other regional planning commissions, several state agencies appearing as a single party, three adjacent property owners, pro and con citizen groups, the city of Burlington, and other municipalities.[71]

The case was seen from the beginning as testing the constitutionality of act 250 and, by some at least, as testing the potential of act 250 as a positive growth-management tool. That potential is implicitly recognized in the summary of the decision denying the permit (in which the numbers refer to the criteria added to act 250 by the land capability and development plan):

The application is denied because the commission finds . . . , that the development does not satisfy the criteria enumerated in the act regarding the following matters: (5) highway congestion, (7) burden on ability of local governments to provide services, (9-G) private utility services, (9-H) costs of public services and facilities as compared with public benefits from a scattered development, (9-J) demands on public facilities and services, (9-K) jeopardizing or interference with the efficiency of existing services, and (10) conformance with the local and regional plan.

Criteria that call for compact rather than scattered development and that contain a mechanism for implementing the policy clearly can involve growth management in a positive sense. The findings of fact included the information that the mall would concentrate on one noncontiguous site, shopping space amounting to one third of all such space in Chittenden County.[72] Stated in its simplest terms, the commission found that the mall would have an adverse economic impact on Burlington that was not adequately balanced by its benefits.[73]

After waffling, the Williston Town Planning Commission had finally found that the mall would conform to the town's duly adopted plan, but the district environmental commission overruled this finding.[74] This decision has major implications for the future in using act 250 as a positive growth-management tool. The district environmental commission not only held that it was not legally bound by the Williston Town Planning Commission's finding on conformance with its plan, but also that act 250 gave regional plans binding legal status in view of criterion 10 of the act.[75]

The Pyramid case is a major policy as well as legal milestone for act 250. It has been described as the most important event in recent years regarding the law since "This is the first case which examines in detail the effect of criterion 9 and applies it in a case of very substantial complexity."[76] The point is that a number of the original criteria, with the added detail that came with the approval of the 1973 Land Capability and Development Plan, can be used as a growth-policy framework. One view is that the problem lies less in the law's inadequacies and more in the negative approach to permitting taken by the middle management level of Vermont's state bureaucracy in such agencies as transportation and fish and game than in inadequacies in the law.[77] An intensive middle management training program was seen as the best investment the state could make in developing the positive potential of act 250.[78]

The final act in the Pyramid case is yet to come. The developer has appealed the case to the superior court, and action is pending on a further appeal by the developer to the state supreme court as to whether fiscal and economic data can be admitted in evidence by the superior court. The disposition of the case should go far toward determining the constitutional status of act 250 and shed considerable light on its capacity as a positive growth management law.

The Politics of the Future

Certainly as a growth-management measure capable of directing growth into desired areas and preventing it in areas marginal or unsuitable, act 250 has yet to be fully utilized and probably cannot be so utilized without changes in the law. Growth management would enter the picture in a major way if a state land use plan were passed which could have a positive effect on the distribution pattern of population growth in Vermont or some other state policy framework emerged that would serve the same purpose.

Within the framework of its objectives, there is a broad consensus that act 250 has been successful. Observers and participants agree that while the law has not had a significant impact on the rate of growth in the state (the economic decline and poor snow winters caused a sharp drop-off in the growth rate shortly after the law was adopted), it has substantially improved the quality of the growth that has taken place in Vermont. The fact that developments must be planned and justified in their entirety has led to higher quality pretty much across the board in comparison to what was going on before the act was passed. This quality improvement, most would agree, has produced some increase in costs, although there is little hard data on this aspect of the matter.

In its impact on housing, act 250 has affected primarily units for recreational purposes as well as commercial and governmental uses. This being so, the notion that it has increased the cost of housing significantly for native Vermonters is at least questionable. So far as the attitude of developers goes, Brownell felt in 1976 that, "Large developers have been strongly supportive of the act because they feel that it protects their projects from undesirable development on adjoining lands, a particularly strong selling point when dealing with out-of-state buyers."[79] Reconfirming that assessment in 1980, he also reported that economic development during the 1976–80 period had been strong, partly because investors from outside the state had shed their initial caution about bringing capital into a state with a strong land– and growth–management law. Governor Richard Snelling was given credit for much of this improved attitude. He had been very active in assuring bankers and other private sector investors and developers that act 250 was not an antigrowth measure.[80]

A question that should be assessed is whether or not, at least in the near future, Vermont will complete the process specified in the 1970 legislation and adopt a statewide land use plan. Among those interviewed in Vermont there seemed little sentiment in favor of moving in any such direction, at least in the short run. The attitude of some was that while the statewide land use plan would certainly be highly desirable, the possibility of mobilizing the political support for it and getting it through the legislature did not look promising and probably was not worth pursuing in the immediate future. Others took the position that the statewide land use plan was not really necessary. Brownell's view was that "After the 1974 and 1975 failure to pass it, the best approach might be to just let things go along the way they are with phases I and II for a time." His view remained essentially the same in 1980, although he stressed the need for a state policy framework to guide the use of act 250 as a positive growth-management tool. If such a set of policies were called a state plan, not a state land use plan, the fear of state zoning might be quieted.[81]

It is interesting to consider whether act 250 would pass today if it were just coming before the Vermont legislature. Of course, that question cannot be answered in any definitive way, but it seems reasonable to presume that in spite of the changed economic conditions since 1970, there is still strong support for protecting a cherished way of life and environmental amenities in Vermont. If that is so, a carefully crafted set of growth policies might well pass the legislature, for many of the same reasons act 250 passed in 1970. It could and would be conceptualized as an effort by a small state to protect itself from the invasion by a horde of greedy large-scale developers from the outside intent on raping the landscape of the state and making off with the profits from that action.

There have, in fact, been no major efforts to repeal act 250. Indeed, while there can be some debate over this issue, on balance subsequent actions of the legislature, especially the passage of the Land Capability and Development Plan in 1973, have strengthened the act. While there are doubtless a handful of legislators from the Northeast Kingdom territory who would like to repeal the law, they have not been able to garner substantial support in the legislature. Actions by the 1982 session of the Vermont legislature with regard to act 250 give support to the proposition that there is hope for strengthening the law. One potentially important change involved the role of regional plans in the permitting process. While the law amended was Chapter 117, Title 24, local planning, it impacts directly on act 250 in its provisions. The change requires that *both* regional and local (town) plans must be looked at in considering a permit. If there is a conflict between the two plans, and if the project has regional impacts, the regional plan controls. This sets the stage for regional planning commissions to spell out in their plans what constitutes regional impacts and may prove the beginning of a stronger role for regional plans and regional commissions in the act 250 process.

The other change to act 250 approved by the house but not acted on by the senate involved an effort to close a loophole that is widely considered to be a major weakness in act 250—the "over 10 acre" rule. The original law provided that the sale of subdivided land would be covered where 10 or more lots were involved, and each lot was less than 10 acres. The potential for abuse in this rule by ducking over the 10-acre limit has long since turned into a reality, but efforts to amend the law have not been successful. Resistance to any change has been especially strong in the Northeast Kingdom area. Among other things, the provision has created a kind of false market in land in which "10 acres or more" becomes the standard "land available" newspaper ad in some sections of the state. Many people purchasing the 10 acres use only a small part of it, and all too often a large tract of important farmland is rendered useless for farming.

The problem is illustrated by a recent court decision upholding an action by the state environmental board. The property owner proposed to subdivide about 58 acres of a 140 acre tract of land into two acre lots, an act consistent with local zoning. The environmental board rejected the proposal, on the grounds that it needlessly converted 58 acres of prime agricultural land, and suggested instead that cluster development on a small part of the land would leave the rest available for agriculture. By upholding the board, the court may have opened the way for most if not all of the lot to be developed in tracts larger than 10 acres.[82] The proposal in the legislature was to remove the 10-acre limit, so that all land subdivided into 10 or more lots would be covered by act 250. The proposal passed the house by a two-to-one margin, and while it did not clear the senate, a determined effort will be made in the next session to close the loophole.

A number of improvements certainly could be made short of any further legislative activity, and some of these were being developed in the late 1970s. Forging a stronger partnership among towns, regional planning commissions, and the district environmental commissions might lead to a more thorough and effective review of applications, and at the same time bring about a more prompt disposition of the applications which would be welcomed by developers. Indeed, the question of the role of local government in land use planning in Vermont is crucial to any consideration of the future in land use matters in the state. Some local governments, probably largely through the impact of act 250, have begun to come of age in the land- and growth-management field in the last few years. Many of them have moved to strengthen their capacities, have developed town plans, and are determined to play a major role in growth management in the future. Should the leadership at the state level and supporters among citizen groups in Vermont decide to return to the effort to adopt a set of state growth policies, it will be absolutely necessary to begin that process by forging a strong and trusting partnership with Vermont's towns. Otherwise the fears and suspicions and uncertainties that so handicapped the efforts in the past will continue.

One can say in conclusion that the land and growth management carried out through act 250 in Vermont is alive and well and in no prospect of being weakened in the foreseeable future. Furthermore, the development of a growth-management system capable of directing and guiding the location of growth is emerging, though so far with only a very limited impact. One positive development could be to tie the state's capital outlay program to growth-management objectives in such a way as to achieve some control over the location and intensity of growth. The state planning office and other state agencies in Vermont seem to be concentrating much of their energies in that direction at the present time. At the same time, the district environmental commissions, in cooperation with willing towns, regional planning commissions, and state agencies, could use more fully the positive growth-management potential inbedded in the policies of act 250 and the 1973 amendments.

Fashioning act 250 as a positive growth-management tool is the challenge of the 1980s for Vermont. The case-by-case reactive approach that is the heart of any system that applies policies as permit applications are received falls short of directing growth to areas able to sustain it, and restricting growth in areas unsuitable for development. Vermont's act 250 shares with Florida's land use law the ability to say where development should not go and can improve the quality of development that does occur. But neither law functions within a clear and consistent set of state, regional, and local plans that have the force of law—a prerequisite for saying where growth should go. Until some kind of integrated policy framework is developed in Vermont, act 250 as a positive, proactive growth-management system must remain tentative and incomplete. New planning initiatives at the town and regional levels offer hope for the future. Continued support for act 250 in the legislature holds out hope that the permitting component of the act can be strengthened, and that the planning framework needed to complete the system can be developed. Another attempt to pass a state land use plan that involves more or less detailed maps seems unlikely to command support. A state policy plan that included a mandate to develop regional and town plans consistent with the state policy plan might gain support from key actors at the town, state, and citizen levels. A favorable sign for the future of act 250 is that in the present (1982) campaign for governor, both the leading candidates—Republican Governor Richard Snelling and the Democratic Lieutenant Governor are strongly supportive of act 250. Problems remain, but act 250 is alive and well, if still incomplete as a positive growth-management system.[83]

There remains the question of whether the experience of Vermont in its land- and growth-management efforts has any relevance for other sections of the country. It is easy to dismiss the Vermont experience as irrelevant because the state is so small and its situation supposedly unique. In the view of this writer, that is a mistaken assumption. An examination of the issues that have arisen in Vermont make it clear that they are much the same as the issues that arise in other states that attempt to move in the land- and growth-management field. Such questions as, "How much control over growth shall be exercised?" and, "At what level shall it be carried out?" are common to the growth-management efforts in every other state assessed in this volume. The role of local government, the question of striking a reasonable balance between professional bureaucracies and citizen input, the question of working out a control system that protects the values that need to be protected and yet allows reasonable development to take place in a reasonably prompt way, the question of whether and how to compensate landowners for extensive regulation—these and similar factors have all been part of the struggle in Vermont to successfully implement the 1970 law. Every one of them are equally important issues in other states. Finally, there is one area in which Vermont has experimented with more imagination than perhaps any other state in the Union, and that is in attempting to link taxation policies with land use controls.[84] The so-called capital gains tax and other initiatives, some of which have been approved by the legislature and some of which have not, are approaches that other states either have or will want to consider seriously as they move into the land- and growth-management arena.

4

Florida: Harmonizing Growth
and the Environment

The Issue Context

Historical Goals of Land and
Water Policies in Florida

Florida's land- and water-management policies must be understood
within the context of an historically poor, sparsely populated state
that was anxious to grow and develop by using the only resources
available to it for that purpose: land and water, of which Florida has
an ample supply. The federal government, under the Swamp and
Overflowed Lands Act of 1850, had given the state about 20 million
acres. But the southern part of the state from the time of statehood in
1845 to the opening of South Florida by railroads at the turn of the
century was considered to be virtually uninhabitable.

In order to open up sparsely populated areas to growth and
economic development, the new state used generous grants of land
to encourage railroad and canal companies to build rail and water
transportation routes.[1] After the Civil War, efforts to use land to spur
railroad and canal construction were resumed by the state's land
control agency, the Trustees of the Internal Improvement Fund.
Their overly generous grants of land and reckless issuance of bonds
brought the fund to the brink of bankruptcy by the early 1880s. The
trustees (the governor and elected department heads) solved the
problem by selling 4 million acres of land to Philadelphia indus-
trialist, Hamilton Disston, for $1 million. Disston also contracted
with the state to drain and reclaim land to the north and west of Lake
Okeechobee, with Disston to receive one acre of bonus land for
every acre he drained. This was the beginning of the effort to drain
the swampland in South Florida that was the dominant approach to
land and water management in the area until the late 1940s.[2]

By the turn of the century, substantial railroad construction had
been completed. This included Henry Flagler's East Coast Railroad
stretching from Jacksonville to Miami and Henry B. Plant's lines

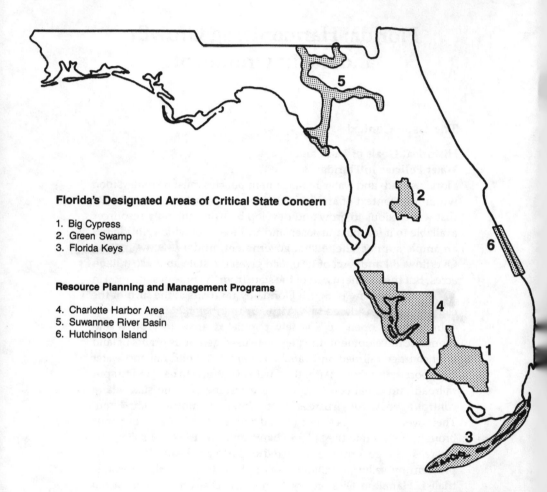

Florida's Designated Areas of Critical State Concern

1. Big Cypress
2. Green Swamp
3. Florida Keys

Resource Planning and Management Programs

4. Charlotte Harbor Area
5. Suwannee River Basin
6. Hutchinson Island

concentrated on Florida's west coast. But the cost in land grants had been high, upwards of 10 million acres, and the politics of the state turned from support of transportation to efforts to salvage the last large tract of land left from the Swamp Lands Act grant, some 3 million acres in the Everglades.

After a long legal battle, the state succeeded in establishing its right to the land in the face of claims by railroad and canal companies, and Governor Napoleon Bonaparte Broward promoted an elaborate drainage system of canals running from Lake Okeechobee southeasterly to the ocean. By the early 1920s, the basic network of drainage canals, still functioning in 1982, were in place, built by the state through the Everglades Drainage District. The 440 miles of canals opened up waterways from the headwaters of the Kissimmee River near Orlando south through Lake Okeechobee, westerly from the lake to Fort Myers, with canals from the south shore of the lake to the ocean at intervals from West Palm Beach to Miami.[3]

The unanticipated negative consequences of this ambitious effort to drain the entire Everglades for agriculture was clearly evident by the 1930s: overdrainage, saltwater intrusion into the freshwater aquifer that was the main municipal water supply for the lower east coast, the destruction of wildlife habitat, and the loss of organic soils through fires and a natural oxidation that occurred when the organic soils were exposed to air.

A severe dry period during the 1930s, followed by extensive flooding in 1947 and 1948, led to a joint federal-state-local project that fundamentally altered the approach to land and water management in South Florida and set the stage for far-reaching changes in the future. The effort to drain all of the 3 million acres in the Everglades was abandoned. About 800,000 acres south of Lake Okeechobee was designated for agriculture, but 1.3 million acres were set aside as water conservation areas in an attempt to maintain a better ecological balance in the area. In terms of land and water management, the new approach was a great advance over the original drainage scheme, and state policies have developed further in the direction of environmental sensitivity since then, though not without a great deal of political controversy. This brief historical setting is the background for examining the surge of growth in Florida after World War II, and the state's efforts to cope with that growth through land- and water-management initiatives.[4]

The Post-World War II
Population Surge

The fond dreams of business and political leaders of seeing Florida grow into a large state were not realized until after World War II. It was then that waves of newcomers, largely from the Northeast, Midwest, and other sections of the South, began to arrive in numbers that would satisfy the hearts of even the most ardent progrowth enthusiasts.

Population statistics make it clear that Florida has been in the midst of an explosive growth cycle since 1950. In the period 1950–76, when U.S. population grew by some 40 percent, Florida's population tripled, increasing from 2.8 million in 1950 to 8.5 million in 1976. This phenomenal rate of increase moved Florida from 20th to 8th in population rank among the states by 1976. By 1980, the population had increased to almost 9.8 million, and Florida ranked seventh in the nation in population. By the end of 1981, the population had exceeded 10 million and Florida was well on its way to a predicated population in 1990 of between 12 and 13 million, at which time it will rank fourth in the nation.[5] To put Florida's growth experience another way, net in-migration amounted to 1.6 million persons in the 1950s; 1.3 million persons in the 1960s; and more than 1.5 million persons in the first half of the 1970s. Since 1970, Florida has had a net in-migration rate that is three times as great as any other state in the nation.

Florida's growth in the 1980s is predicted to be twice that of the Sunbelt and three times the national average. This pattern of population growth means continued pressure on Florida's natural systems and ability to provide adequate infrastructure. Growth pressures will continue to focus on the South Florida coastal areas and on an urban corridor across Central Florida from Tampa Bay to the Daytona/Melbourne area. The three largest SMSAs—Miami, Tampa–St. Petersburg, and Ft. Lauderdale–Hollywood—will absorb more than 40 percent of the projected population growth for the 80s. These same areas already have substantial, often severe, growth-management problems. A land- and growth-management system of extraordinary capacity will be required to cope with the growth pressures that will dominate the rest of the century.[6]

The End of Florida's Love
Affair with Growth

Deep-rooted love affairs are always difficult to terminate, and Florida's love affair with growth has been no exception. By the mid- to late 1960s, the negative impacts of uncontrolled and indiscriminate growth on the scale Florida was experiencing began to be clearer and clearer: wet/dry cycles that brought periodic water crises, muck fires in South Florida, saltwater intrusion threatening freshwater supplies on both the east and west coasts, and extensive pollution of practically every river and stream and other water body in the peninsula. It cannot be said that all these negative impacts were new in the 1960s. Some problems had been evident as early as the 1930s; but by the 1960s a great many more people were around to observe problems of polluted water and loss of beach access. Furthermore, times were changing, and the late 1960s saw the emergence of the environmental movement as a major force in American politics.

To one observer, the sense of crisis that developed in the '60s and on to the '70s, "appeared in two forms—an immediate drought—and an increasing uneasiness over the implications of current and projected population growth."[7] By the early 1960s, Florida's love affair with growth was indeed strained. Nevertheless environmental groups had not yet gained their political muscle, and the prevailing attitude of political and civic leadership still was that "Growth is good." A series of horrible examples in the '60s and early '70s did much to strengthen the power and political experience of environmental groups and to broaden public support for some control on Florida's runaway growth.

The major environmental events that helped push Florida to the point of a new attitude and a new statutory and institutional framework for managing growth include: the effort to construct a barge canal across the northern end of the peninsula; threats to the water supply of Everglades National Park; the effort to build a major regional jetport in the Big Cypress Swamp in western Dade and eastern Collier counties; and the increasingly obvious abuses of the land sales craze in the '50s and '60s. Except for the Cross-State Barge Canal, all of these events occurred in the southern part of the state, where the environment was most fragile and where the growth pressures were the greatest.

The Barge Canal Struggle
The idea of constructing a ship or barge canal across the north Florida peninsula, using the St. Johns and Oklawaha rivers to connect the Atlantic with the Gulf, dates back to the first surveys authorized by President John Quincy Adams in 1826. Interest in the canal was renewed under Franklin D. Roosevelt's administration, and the state legislature in 1933 established a Florida Ship Canal Authority empowered to acquire the necessary right-of-way. Little work was done, but during World War II, the canal became part of the Corps of Engineers authorized (but unfunded) projects. Work on the canal did not get underway until 1964, fulfilling a 1960 campaign promise of John F. Kennedy to Floridians.

The Cross-State Barge Canal controversy was one of the resource controversies that allowed environmental groups to come of age politically in Florida and to discover that they had the ability to influence state politics. A small group of environmentalists—who at first hoped only that by forcing a new route for the canal they could save the beautiful springfed Oklawaha River—gradually increased in strength, formed the Florida Defenders for the Environment, made a liaison with the Environmental Defense Fund, undertook an environmental impact study of the project, and finally began to press vigorously to bring the canal project to an actual halt. The first construction phase had moved forward fairly rapidly, however, and by the time the group was able to prevail upon the Nixon administration to stop the project, some 20 miles of the lower reaches of the lovely Oklawaha River had been destroyed by the building of a dam.[8]

Water Supply for Everglades National Park

The struggle to guarantee an adequate water supply for Everglades National Park presents an even clearer case of environmental groups developing their political power in the face of a heated controversy. Efforts to establish Everglades National Park, the only biological national park in the United States, continued from the mid-1920s through the late 1950s. The long struggle to establish the park culminated in 1958 with a legislative bill establishing a park of about 1.3 million acres. The state of Florida provided $2 million for the purchase of the land and also contributed much of the land controlled by the Trustees of the Internal Improvement Fund to make up the area of the park.

The Everglades National Park receives most of its water through rainfall, but the sheet flow of water over land from north of the Tamiami Trail into the park plays a vital role in protecting the natural ecology of the area. This water is also in demand to recharge the Biscayne aquifer serving urban areas. The initial policy of the Central and Southern Florida Flood Control District and the U.S. Corps of Engineers was to release water for the park only when storage in the water conservation areas was at or near maximum capacity. The issue of water for the park was a classic conflict between protecting the urban water supply as against protecting the natural ecology of the park. In 1970 Congress provided the park's water guarantee that the National Park Service and environmentalists had been pressing for. The fund authorization for the Central and Southern Florida Flood Control project provided that when the enlargement of the Miami Canal was completed, the park would receive 315,000 acre feet of water annually, or 16.5 percent of total project deliveries, whichever was less. The park's cause had been pressed strongly by both Florida and national environmental groups, and their success was one more illustration of the growing political power of such groups both in the nation and in the state.[9]

The Jetport Issue

The struggle over whether and where to establish a major regional jetport in South Florida also contributed to the political education and strength of environmental groups. The Dade County Port Authority first began to seek a site to build a jetport in South Florida in the mid-1960s, and by 1967 had begun acquisition of a 39-square-mile site in the Big Cypress Swamp 45 miles west of Miami and six miles from Everglades National Park to the south. Plans for the facility were ambitious indeed. The original plan envisaged four to six giant runways, two of which would have been as long as 30,000 feet. Construction began in September 1968.

The chairman of the Central and Southern Florida Flood Control District, Robert W. Padrick, in effect blew the whistle on the project and attracted the attention of environmentalists and others to some of the potential threats. Padrick objected to the building of a road connecting Miami with the jetport that would cross "his" conservation area. He called on environmental groups in Florida and nationally to come to his assistance in defeating what he called an "abominable proposal." By the spring of 1969, a small Everglades coalition was formed in opposition to the construction on the site. It eventually grew to include some 21 environmental groups and two labor unions. A number of national political figures became embroiled in the controversy, as did Florida's Republican governor, Claude Kirk. At the urging of his environmental aide, Nat Reed, the governor abandoned his early commitment to the jetport site. The ensuing environmental impact statement concluded that the western arm of Everglades National Park depended on the diffuse movement of water overland through the Big Cypress to the swamps, and that while the jetport site itself would not have a major impact on that flow, the inevitable urban development it would spawn would, in fact, have a major negative impact.

The outcome of the struggle was that the Dade County Port Authority abandoned any plans to go beyond the training runway at the Big Cypress, and began a so far unsuccessful search for another site for the jetport. The defeat of the Big Cypress jetport was another victory for the environmental groups in Florida. Environmental "combat troops" had by now been trained in a series of environmentally oriented crises. What was needed was a timely environmental emergency to crystalize the general unease created by those crises and by the continued strong growth pressures being felt by the state. That major emergency—a severe drought in South Florida in 1970 and 1971—brought together all of the political and environmental forces concerned about the impacts of unchecked and indiscriminate growth on Florida's fragile environment.[10]

The 1971 Water Crisis

When the rains failed to come in 1970–71, the resulting water shortages were nothing new to South Florida. Water shortages had created a near crisis situation in the 1930s and again in the 1950s. The difference in 1970–71 was that the water crisis came amid rising general concern with the degradation of the environment in South Florida, and on the heels of other crises that seemed in the eyes of environmentalists and their increasingly large group of supporters to threaten the very values that had attracted many of them to move to Florida in the first place.

The water crisis itself, which began in late 1970 and stretched into the winter of 1971, has been described by a leading state senator and advocate of managed growth, who later was elected governor.[11] He noted "that a major portion of South Florida suffered from the most extensive drought in recent history. From June of 1970 through July 1971, rainfall in South Florida was almost 22 inches below normal— the lowest amount since 1911, when records were first kept. By May of 1971, Lake Okeechobee and the three water conservation areas were two and three feet below normal levels."

The extreme drought brought muck fires in the Everglades and the threat of saltwater intrusion into the Biscayne aquifer. The canals that had been cut from Lake Okeechobee through the coastal ridge to the ocean made the aquifer extremely vulnerable to salt water intrusion. The point was driven home as never before that indiscriminate drainage and headlong growth in South Florida had combined to produce an environmental crisis of truly major proportions. The response to this crisis brought about a coalition of political and environmental forces that thrust Florida from being among the least growth-management oriented states to becoming a state with advanced land- and water-management tools with which to attempt the management of growth.

Observers of the scene in 1971 all agree that it was the water crisis in South Florida, together with an almost equally serious water problem in the Tampa Bay area, that brought about this major policy initiative. As one leading developer/lobbyist and former Kirk administration official put it: "It was an idea whose time had come. We had fast growth and an apparent water shortage, some of which was real and some of which was not, and this 'water crisis' was the catalyst that produced the action."[12]

The governor's chief environmental aide in 1971 noted that the water crisis "focused the whole environmental concern and gave new force and a new broad base of support to those who wished to advance the cause of growth management in Florida."[13] An aide to the speaker of the house of representatives in 1971 pointed out that the water crisis came at a good time politically for achieving decisive action in growth management for the state. For the first time in the history of the state, both the speaker and the president of the senate were from South Florida. The water issue was the critical spur, but the whole issue of growth and the lack of any policy or administrative capacity to deal with that growth quickly moved center stage as the prime concern of the 1971 Governor's Conference on Water Management in South Florida.[14]

This conference was initiated on the suggestion of Bob Padrick, who had been appointed to the Water Management District Governing Board by Republican Governor Claude Kirk. Padrick directed his appeal for the conference to the new Democratic governor, Reubin Askew, who had come out of nowhere in Florida politics to capture the governorship in 1970. He had the reputation of a giant killer, of the young and progressive politician who would bring a new mood and a new viewpoint to Florida politics. Padrick's appeal fell on sympathetic ears, partly because Askew's staff was enthusiastic about attempting to assert the leadership of the Governor's Office in dealing with the problem. The governor's conference, convened in August 1971 in Miami Beach, turned out to be a pivotal event in Florida's efforts to manage land and water resources.

The 150 conference participants represented an amazing cross section of private and public sector citizens: developers, federal agency representatives, state and local government people, and environmentalists in some strength, balanced by people who feared going too far in managing Florida's phenomenal growth. The governor challenged the conference to " . . . build a peace in South Florida—a peace between the people and their place . . . between the natural environment and the manmade settlement . . . between the creek and the canal . . . between the works and needs of men and women . . . and the life of mankind itself." He noted that the work of the conference could " . . . well determine if the area is to continue as a leading resort and the nation's winter vegetable garden. Failure could make it instead the world's first and only desert which gets 60 inches of rainfall yearly." The governor declared that "It is time we stopped viewing our environment through prisms of profit, politics, geography, or local and personal pride." Striking a theme that was to characterize his leadership in the growth-management area throughout his administration, he warned that "A failure to find appropriate solutions to the effective management of growth would be disastrous to our economy as well as to our environment." The governor touched on the most sensitive subject of all and became the first statewide politician to openly question the automatic goodness of growth, when he asked: "Must there be a limit on South Florida's population?"[15]

The conference responded to the governor's challenge by producing a short but strongly worded set of findings and policy recommendations that went well beyond the original idea of addressing water problems for South Florida. The report to Governor Askew stated that " . . . an enforceable, comprehensive land and water use plan . . . must be designed to limit increases in population and machines, with their attendant demands on the water supply, to a level that will insure a quality environment. . . . "[16] The report went on to say that:

> There is a limit to the number of people which the South Florida basin can support and at the same time maintain a quality environment. The state and appropriate regional agencies must develop a comprehensive land and water use plan with enforcement machinery to limit population. This is especially crucial in the South Florida region.[17]

One could hardly imagine a blunter challenge to the traditional Florida concept that growth was inherently good and should be encouraged in every way possible. A new day had indeed come when a cross section of 150 citizens of the state could reach a majority concensus in a final session of the conference on such powerful language. The report proposed a comprehensive policy framework at the state and regional levels with the leadership role clearly being taken by the state of Florida. The policies were to be implemented by state and regional mechanisms with adequate powers to do the job.

By the conclusion of the governor's conference on September 24, 1971, Florida had entered a new era. Clearly the old and uncritical love affair with growth was over. For the first time in the history of the state, a governor had taken a key leadership role in raising the question of how, where, and to what degree the state should grow in the future. Florida had been wrenched from the old "Growth is good no matter what" approach into a new, uneasy, uncertain, but still powerful challenge to the necessary goodness of growth. The new movement would take time to mature. It would suffer setbacks in the face of economic crises and public mistrust of government, but one thing was certain—the new attitudes articulated by the water management conference ran deep and marked a permanent shift in Florida's approach to growth and development.

We turn now to the state's effort to take the conference's raw material, mix it with the new post-reapportionment politics in

Florida, join it to the new power of environmental groups in the state, cap it all with the strong leadership of the governor and key members of the legislature, and produce a viable growth-management framework for what seemed an endless and uninterrupted explosive growth for the state into the future.

The Politics of Adoption

Governor Askew promptly appointed a 15-member Task Force on Land Use to develop proposed legislation for carrying out the major recommendations of his Conference on Water Management in South Florida. The task force was made up of university faculty members, legislators, state agency representatives, people from regional agencies (two from water management districts and one from a regional planning council), and finally an architect active in the Florida chapter of the American Institute of Architects.

The intention was to draw in knowledgeable people who could make a major commitment of time, and who were deeply committed to coming up with a set of proposed laws that would implement the recommendations of the conference.[18]

The task force, organized by November 1971, had the full support of the governor. His chief environmental aide worked closely with the group and attended every task force meeting. Time pressures were severe; there was little time for floundering, for false starts, or for hesitation. From the first, the task force was concerned not with just land-management legislation, but with strengthening comprehensive planning at the state, local, and regional levels. The members also wished to give active support to an already drafted Water Resources Act that would complement anything done in the land management area.

Gilbert Finnell[19] persuaded the task force that the American Law Institute's Model State Land Development Code might well be the ideal solution for the state. The American Law Institute model appealed to the task force because it left most land use decisions to local governments, while providing a way to reflect any regional and state interests involved in those decisions. In addition, the ALI approach had passed the test of intense scrutiny by leading legal practitioners and scholars in the nation.[20] By late January 1972, the task force had prepared a draft of a land- and growth-management bill which followed closely article 7 of the American Law Institute's Model State Land Development Code (in its third draft form). The bill provided that the land regulation power should remain as close to those affected as possible, and the decisionmaking process should provide for a balanced consideration of all of the competing environmental, economic, and social factors.[21]

The task force, in spite of the very short time available to it, gave serious consideration to about 10 separate pieces of legislation, which it eventually narrowed to a prime legislative package of four bills for the 1972 session: (1) the Environmental Land and Water Management Act of 1972 (for the sake of brevity, we will at times refer to this as the Land Management Act, or shorter still, Chapter 380); (2) the Florida State Comprehensive Planning Act of 1972; (3) the Land Conservation Act of 1972; and (4) the Florida Water Resources Act of 1972. Probably very few people in the state at that time would have predicted that all four pieces of this landmark legislative package would pass the 1972 Florida legislature more or less intact. Before describing how the land-management legislation made its way through the Florida legislature in 1972, it is necessary to assess the impact of reapportionment and other forces that moved the state from the old guard politics of the past to a new, more progressive attitude that was crucial to the passage of the legislation.

The New Politics of Florida

Reapportionment in Florida, which was ordered by the federal district court after long years of unsuccessful efforts by the legislature to reapportion itself, brought with it stronger and more extensive political changes than perhaps in any state in the Union. This was partly because Florida had by the 1960s become the most malapportioned state in the United States. The population growth was concentrated heavily in South Florida, but the political power stayed firmly fixed in the hands of North Florida's political figures. The Florida of the 1950s and 1960s had a governmental structure that was a product of the past, fairly characterized as weak, fragmented, ineffectual, totally unsuited to face the problems of its explosive population growth.[22] In addition to reapportionment, the new Constitution of 1968 also strengthened the state government and for the first time in Florida's history gave a general grant of home rule power to both cities and counties. Without this new grant, it would have been very difficult to devise a land- and growth-management plan which leaned so heavily on local governments.[23]

New Land and Water Management
Initiatives: 1967–71

Reapportionment, the rising strength of the Republican party, and the increasing strength of environmental groups produced important land- and water-policy initiatives that set the stage for the 1972 growth-management effort. Between 1967 and 1971, several environmentally important laws were passed, including (among others): The Florida Air and Water Pollution Control Act (1967); the Coastal Construction setback line, aimed at protecting vital dunes and coastal vegetation; and the establishment of a Coastal Coordinating Council to develop a planning and management program for Florida's 11,000 miles of coastline.[24]

Republican Governor Claude Kirk (1966–70) and his chief environmental advisor, Nathaniel Reed, took a strong leadership role in these efforts, with Reed acting as an important link to the governor's office for the state's environmental groups, which were increasingly active during the period. One veteran observer of state politics said they "became strong almost overnight and became a potent force in the legislature."[25]

In a discussion of Governor Kirk's catalytic role in land and water management, his executive assistant recalled that Kirk was looking for good issues with which he could go after the power structure. Kirk proposed the Pollution Control Act and the relatively well-disciplined Republicans in the legislature played an important role in its passage. Reapportionment was an important factor, because it had given Florida "a new kind of legislature that was more urban, that was younger, and that was more Republican," and more accepting of growth management.[26]

Stormy Legislative Waters
Of the three key political actors in the 1972 legislature—Governor Askew, the speaker of the house, and the president of the senate— the first two were strongly committed to passage of land- and water-management legislation. The third, the president of the senate, had expressed concern at the impact of Florida's rapid growth, but his exact attitude toward the legislation was unknown. The governor made passage of the Environmental Land and Water Management Act a major objective in his opening remarks to the legislature. He warned that "Florida, like California, is in great danger of becoming a 'paradise lost,'" and that "it is not off-beat or alarmist to say that continued failure to control growth and development in this state will lead to economic as well as environmental disaster."[26]

House and senate sponsors of the legislative package agreed that the house would take the lead in regard to the Water Resources Act, the Comprehensive Planning Act, and another closely related bill— the Environmental Reorganization Act. The senate was to take responsibility for getting the keystone of the whole package, the Land Management Act, passed. Backers felt that if they could get the bill through the more conservative senate, house passage would be assured. Indeed, the speaker of the house promised supporters that, if the bill could be passed by the senate, the house would pass it even if it were "the last day of the legislature."[28]

The first hurdle was the Senate Natural Resources and Conservation Committee, whose chairman, a member of the governor's task force, was a cosponsor of the act. Two other members of the committee, Republican Senator Warren Henderson of the Tampa Bay area and Senator Bob Graham (the bill's chief sponsor and task force member), were fully committed to the legislation. The committee adopted several amendments that largely concerned the Area of Critical State Concern component of the legislation. In one critical change, the final decision as to whether to designate an Area of Critical State Concern was shifted away from a commission appointed by the governor and instead was given to the governor and the cabinet sitting as the Administrative Commission (the seven-member elected body that has historically been and remains so powerful in Florida politics). Sitting as the Land and Water Adjudicatory Commission, this body would also decide appeals of local government decisions on land use. The committee also eliminated interim controls that had been designed to forestall unwise development in Areas of Critical State Concern while rules and regulations were being developed.

Despite these important changes, the legislation emerged reasonably intact and was favorably reported by the committee in late February 1972. When the bill got to the Senate Ways and Means Committee, several fairly minor amendments were added, but when it came to a final vote, there was a tie and at that point, the bill failed. All of the splendid rhetoric by the governor and the speaker, the long hours of work by the task force, and the strong citizen input from the Governor's Conference seemed to have come to naught, at least as far as the land- and water-management legislation was concerned. However, there was hope a compromise could be worked out that would satisfy one of the senators who had voted against the bill—Jim Williams, a new senator from the Ocala area who had a reputation of honesty, independence, and informed and intelligent conservatism. In the subsequent struggle to get the bill out of the Senate Ways and Means Committee onto the floor of the senate and through the senate, Williams was to play a role of importance second only to the bill's chief sponsor, Senator Bob Graham.

In the week after the bill's rejection by the Senate Ways and Means Committee, Senator Graham and other advocates rewrote parts of the bill to attempt to meet the committee's concerns in general and Senator Williams' concerns in particular. The crucial compromise to

Senator Williams was that implementation of the environmentally oriented portion of the critical area designation process was made contingent on the passage and voter approval of the Land Conservation Act of 1972, providing $200 million worth of bonds to buy environmentally endangered land. Senator Williams had been concerned that in identifying Areas of Critical State Concern, areas would be found that could not be adequately protected through the regulatory process, but that, in the absence of funds to buy lands, the regulatory process would be stretched to unreasonable limits to achieve environmental protection.[28] In the ensuing November election some 70 percent of the voters of the state did approve the issuance of the bonds. Furthermore, as Senator Graham noted, "I think there is absolutely no question that had we not tied the two [pieces of legislation] together we would not have passed the environmentally endangered lands bond issue, so it worked out to be a happy result from what appeared initially to be an adverse situation."[30]

With the compromise struck, Graham and Williams both were now confident that they could get a favorable vote out of the ways and means committee, but this proved not to be the case. In fact, simply to get the legislation out of the committee and onto the floor of the senate, supporters had to accept an amendment that struck everything but the enacting clause and a provision to set up a study committee. Finally, on Monday, March 20, 1972, the bill did come to the senate floor late in the session with only 10 working days left. After one senator failed to gain approval for the study committee only amendment, Senator Williams and Graham moved a substitute amendment which consisted of the rewrite of the bill that had been done after its rejection by the ways and means committee.

When the legislation came before the senate again on March 27, 1972, there was some parliamentary maneuvering, but the Williams/Graham substitute amendment carried by a 27-to-16 vote, and the substantially intact bill was now before the Florida senate. The bill was brought to a vote on Tuesday, March 27, 1972, with only three days left in the regular session. The final vote in the senate was 31 to 13 in favor of the bill, but this relatively comfortable margin did not by any means reflect the closeness of the struggle. A series of hostile amendments had been narrowly defeated, one of them by a 19-19 tie vote.

The house kept its promise to act quickly—in the space of two days, the house leadership was ready to take the bill to the floor. The prompt action was largely the result of the fact that "There was a commitment and a resolve at the very top levels of leadership in the house that was conspicuously lacking in the senate, in the effort to get this bill passed."[31] When the bill came before the house for debate, the speaker took the unusual action of stepping down and strongly supporting the legislation. The complexity of the bill and the resulting need to explain it more fully to the house members resulted in delaying final action until the extended session made necessary by other problems. Over the weekend, an intensive effort was made out of the speaker's office to count the votes, to mobilize support, and to negotiate with key opposition figures so as to assure the passage of the legislation. On Monday, April 3, there was a special briefing session in the governor's conference room, at which Governor Askew, Senator Graham, Gilbert Finnell, and task force Chairman DeGrove explained the bill to a fairly large group of house members.

An agreement was reached with the house Republican leadership giving the legislature the power of approval over initial standards and guidelines for the Development of Regional Impact section. This agreement had the happy effect of solidifying house Republican support for the bill "and representative Don Reed, the house minority leader who ruled roughly one third of the house members who were Republican with a shrewd and more effective hand, then gave his strong support to the legislation." As Speaker Pettigrew put it, "I knew that as soon as we got the agreement worked out that we had it made."[32] The bill passed in the House of Representatives, 79 to 28, just one week after it had come over from the Senate. The Florida legislature, in one of the most critical actions in its history, had passed a law designed to bring Florida's runaway growth under some control and to try to balance social, economic, and environmental values so that the state could grow and develop without destroying its natural systems.

The bill passed, one assessment put it, because, "Strong leadership charted a pragmatic course as the bill went through the legislative maze, hammering out changes to make it more palatable to opponents. On key issues, implementation was delayed and differences buried in ambiguous language that moved resolution to another day."[33] Certainly Senator Graham's willingness to compromise was an important factor, but just as important was the fact that everyone involved in the process knew that the legislation had the governor's full support. The new politics of Florida had given the legislature a new breed of politician, Republican and Democrat, who worked together to back the legislation. Republicans were, in fact, a key element in the passage of the bill. The coalition that carried it in both the senate and the house consisted of aggressive urban Democrats and urban Republicans who were ready to face up to the need to better manage Florida's growth. The Republicans were well disciplined, especially in the house, and once the key house compromise was struck, supported the bill overwhelmingly.

Environmental groups were well organized during the session, and the Conservation 70s lobbyists worked persistently and effectively. The executive director of the Florida Audubon Society also made his presence felt throughout the session. In addition, Florida's League of Women Voters proved to be an unusually effective force in lobbying for the legislation. The league demonstrated its capacity, once it is geared up to support an issue, to bring powerful political support to it. Supporters also included the state chapter of the American Institute of Architects, and—a very critical source of backing—most of the state's metropolitan newspapers.

In general, the home builders opposed the Land Management Act strongly. Almost all developers also opposed the legislation, with one single and conspicuous exception: the Arvida Corporation. Elliott Messer, Arvida Corporation's Tallahassee attorney, was convinced that a rational and reasonable state framework would in the long run benefit legitimate developers, and he persuaded the Arvida Corporation to get behind the legislation. Its active and persistent support throughout the legislative effort did much to add credibility to the notion that the Land Management Act was not simply an effort to stop all growth in Florida. Agricultural groups took no active role since agricultural lands had been exempted in an early compromise on the measure.

Florida's cities and counties also took a neutral position. As the executive director of the League of Cities put it, "We didn't get too much involved in it one way or the other, but generally supported it."[34] As this veteran Tallahassee lobbyist recalled, counties also did not get heavily involved. So far as the cities were concerned, they anticipated that most Developments of Regional Impact would occur in the counties, so "It just wasn't a big deal with the cities, and they didn't really have it as a high priority item."[35]

In some ways the element of surprise—the mobilization of a powerful cadre of expertise to support the legislation—caught its opponents off guard and had much to do with the final passage of the legislation. Wade Hopping, the former Kirk administration official who had become one of the leading attorneys for Tallahassee developers, noted that, "The governor's office brought in experts such as Fred Bosselman [the task force consultant on the model code] and that caught the lobbyists unaware," and "The business community was just outgunned." From Hopping's point of view, a lot of new concepts with powerful and legitimate backing, such as the American Law Institute, were put before the legislature, and the opponents found it very difficult to argue effectively against what the proponents were saying.[36]

In looking back on the passage of the legislation, Governor Askew noted that, "The timing was right in terms of the environmental movement . . . and also you had Pettigrew as speaker of the house and Graham and Williams in the senate." He also gave special credit to Fred Bosselman and Gil Finnell for their crucial help in putting together a bill that was strong from a technical and legal point of view. Summing up his view of what happened in 1972, the governor said: "I don't think the act would have passed except in 1972. We had all the horses."[37]

The 1972 Florida legislature also passed other major legislative initiatives recommended to the governor by the task force: the Water Resources Act of 1972 (chapter 373, *Florida Statutes*); the state Comprehensive Planning Act of 1972 (chapter 23, *Florida Statutes*) and the Land Conservation Act of 1972 (chapter 250, *Florida Statutes*). Of these, the Water Resources Act has become a key element in the growth management picture in Florida, and the ultimate success of the effort to manage growth in the state depends just as heavily on its effective implementation as on the Land Management Act.[38]

The state Comprehensive Planning Act greatly strengthened the planning function in state government by creating a Division of State Planning in the Department of Administration. With the new responsibility being placed on the state's planning agency by the Land Management Act, it was necessary to strengthen this particular component of state government. The overwhelming approval by voters of the Land Conservation Act of 1972, and its constitutional amendment to allow the issuance of $200 million in bonds to buy environmentally endangered lands, turned out to be crucial to the full implementation of the Land Management Act. More than that, the vote demonstrated that there was widespread support by the citizens of Florida for environmental initiatives.

Initial Impressions of
the Land Management Act

Before examining the Land Management Act in detail, some general impressions and assessments of the bill are important. Friend and foe alike saw it as a major event in the history of Florida's government. Governor Askew noted some years later that "the Land Management Act is the most important piece of legislation passed in my 20 years in government."[39] The opponents were equally convinced of its significance. A key lobbyist for the Florida Association of Home Builders told a committee hearing that the measure was one of the more "far-reaching and devastating ever considered by the Florida legislature."[40] One key legislative aide in the house of representatives who later joined the private sector as a lobbyist for major developers commented that when chapter 380 passed, "The developer lobby couldn't believe it had happened."[41] The same can be said for many supporters of the legislation. On a less polemic note, Senator Graham stressed the underlying concepts of the law: the primacy of local governments, with the state acting only when land use decisions involve substantial regional or statewide impacts.

Provisions of Chapter 380

In two types of carefully and narrowly drawn categories, (Areas of Critical State Concern and Developments of Regional Impact), the state can reassert its authority over land use and reserve the right to overrule local governments whose land use decisions fail to take into consideration the more-than-local impacts of development projects.

Areas of Critical State Concern (section 5) are defined as geographical areas with special environmental, historical, archaeological, and other significance of regional or state importance. Any person or group in Florida can recommend an area for designation to the State Land Planning Agency. On recommendations deemed worthy of further study, the State Land Planning Agency determines whether there are sufficiently important state or regional interests to justify designating an Area of Critical State Concern. If so, the Agency's Bureau of Land and Water Management draws up criteria and standards for development in the area. The Land Planning Agency then recommends that the governor and the cabinet, sitting as the Administration Commission designate the Area of Critical Concern. If, after public hearings, the Administration Commission decides to designate, local governments have six months in which to develop land use regulations needed to protect the state-regional interests using the criteria and standards contained in the state designation. The local government's action must meet state approval and can be rejected with recommendations for needed changes. If local government(s) fail to act within the prescribed time, the state has six months in which to develop and gain Administration Commission approval of the special regulations. When developed they are then carried out by the local government or governments involved.

The law is very specific about the reasons for which an Area of Critical State Concern may be designated, and in view of the later legal controversy over the delegation of legislative authority, they are worth quoting in full. As the law states it:

An Area of Critical State Concern may be designated only for:

a. An area containing, or having a significant impact upon, environmental, historical, natural, or archaeological resources of regional or statewide importance.
b. An area significantly affected by, or having a significant effect upon, an existing or proposed major public facility or other area of major public investment.
c. A proposed area of major development potential, which may include a proposed site of a new community, designated in a state land development plan.[42]

The law provides that should a year pass with no regulations adopted either by the local government or by the state, the designation of the Area of Critical State Concern is to be terminated, and no additional critical area designation can be made for another 12 months.

The law gives the state a surprisingly strong monitoring role. The state is authorized to review and, if necessary, require modification of any local government regulatory action in a designated critical area.[43] It should be noted that the law restricted critical area designations in the first year of enactment to 500,000 acres and limited total designations in subsequent years to no more than 5 percent of the total land area of the state at any one time—about 1.8 million acres.[44]

Section 6 of the law, Development of Regional Impact (DRI), is designed to deal with projects such as large housing developments, jetports, power plants, mining operations, or large shopping centers which, "Because of [their] character, magnitude, or location, would have a substantial effect upon the health, safety, or welfare of citizens of more than one county." Its effective date was delayed to July 1, 1973, to allow time for the legislature to approve DRI standards and guidelines adopted by the Administrative Commission.[45] In preparing these standards and guidelines, the state planning agency was required to consult with the Environmental Land Management Study Committee established in the act. In adopting guidelines and standards (the act makes no clear distinction between the two terms), the Administration Commission was mandated to consider such factors as environmental pollution, traffic generation, employment impacts, site size, and the "unique qualities of the area."[46]

Unlike the designation of Areas of Critical State Concern, the execution of the DRI process depends heavily on the initiative and activity of both developers and local governments. Developers can request prompt information as to whether a project will fall within the framework of DRI regulations, or whether the developer has vested rights that would exclude the project from DRI coverage. The state land planning agency must respond to such requests within 30 days (later amended to 60 days) by issuing a "binding letter of interpretation with respect to the proposed development." This letter is binding not only on the state land planning agency but also on all state, regional, and local agencies as well as the developer. If the project comes under DRI coverage, the local government must then decide whether to issue a Development Order giving the greenlight to a Development of Regional Impact. There is minimal supervision and involvement in this process by the state land planning agency, but the regional planning agencies are given an active role.

When a local government is evaluating a proposed project, the designated regional agency is required to prepare and submit to the local government a report and recommendations on the regional impact of the proposed development. The statute requires that the regional agency consider whether:

a. The development will have a favorable or unfavorable impact on the environmental and natural resources of the region
b. The development will have a favorable or unfavorable impact on the economy of the regions
c. The development will efficiently use or unduly burden water, sewer, solid waste disposal, or other necessary public facilities
d. The development will efficiently use or unduly burden public transportation facilities
e. The development will favorably or adversely effect the ability of people to find adequate housing reasonably accessible to their places of employment, and
f. The development complies with such other criteria for determining regional impact as the regional planning agency shall deem as appropriate, including, but not limited to, the extent to which the development would create an additional demand for, or additional use of, energy, provided such criteria and related policies have been adopted by the regional planning council pursuant to s. 120.54.[46]

These factors go far beyond any narrow focus on environmental concerns. They constitute a broad mandate that regional agencies consider environmental, social, and economic factors and specifically that they consider the problem of adequate housing.

In considering the findings of the regional agency, local governments are further mandated to consider whether:

a. The development unreasonably interferes with the achievement of the objectives of an adopted state land development plan.
b. The development is consistent with the local land development regulations.
c. The development is consistent with the report and recommendations of the regional planning agency.[48]

The act makes it clear that the ultimate responsibility for DRI land use decisions rests with local governments, and the local governments are, in fact, free to ignore the regional council's assessment if they choose to do so. However, should they fail to consider the regional assessment in an adequate way, the act provides for an appeal to the Land and Water Adjudicatory Commission (The governor and the cabinet) and that the body has the authority to, in effect, force local governments to take into consideration regional impacts.

Within 45 days after a local government issues a Development Order, an appeal can be taken to the Adjudicatory Commission either by the owner or developer of the land, an appropriate regional planning agency, or the state land planning agency. The Adjudicatory Commission is required to give a decision on an appeal within 120 days, either denying permission to develop under the order, or granting permission to develop, but with additional conditions and restrictions. Such actions by the Adjudicatory Commission are subject to judicial review.[49]

The sequence of events just described is the sequence when proposed projects are in communities which have zoning or subdivision regulations. In communities without such regulations, a developer is required to notify the state planning agency and the local government of his intention to build a project. If no DRI or Critical Area regulations have been issued within 90 days, the developer can proceed with the project without regard to Chapter 380. This constituted a major loophole, since a majority of local jurisdictions at the time had no zoning or subdivision regulations. As discussed later, the 1975 Local Government Comprehensive Planning Act moved to rectify this weakness in the law.

Section 9 established the two-year Environmental Land Management Study Committee, to consist of 15 members, 9 appointed by the governor and 3 each by the president of the senate and the speaker of the house. The gubernatorial appointments were to include a broad cross section of private sector interests.[50] The Environmental Land Management Study Committee was given a very broad mandate. It was to present a report to the governor and the legislature not later than December 30, 1973, which would include any proposed legislative changes, drafts of model development ordinances to help local governments strengthen their land management process, and other matters involving analysis and comments on the relevant work and reports of other state agencies. The committee was also required to review and recommend "the current status and effectiveness of regional planning agencies with regard to land and water management,"[51] and it was also given a catch-all mandate to study almost anything else that it thought was appropriate to its general mission. An interim report to the governor was required by December 31, 1972, and to the legislature not later than March 15, 1973. The committee was given a key role in the initial implementation of chapter 380 by the provision that "prior to submitting any recommendation or issuing any rule under this chapter, the state land planning agency shall consult with and obtain the advice of the committee."[52]

Section 10 of the law represents the compromise, hammered out in the house of representatives to satisfy key developer lobbyists and some house members, to assure the role of the legislature in the development of the initial DRI standards and guidelines. At the time the law was adopted, any future standards and guidelines could have been adopted without reference back to the legislature, but this provision was changed in 1973 so that the legislature could assert its power to review also any future changes in the standards and guidelines.

The new law, even considering the increasing strength of environmental groups and the impact of reapportionment on the state, was a radical departure from past practice in Florida with regard to land and growth management. The fact that it passed the 1972 legislature was, in the eyes of proponents and opponents alike, a remarkable thing. Once passed, the next question was whether it would be properly implemented. Would adequate funds be appropriated? Would the forces that opposed the law be able to cripple it through amendment or through underfunding? Would there be adequate bureaucratic machinery at the state, regional, and local levels to protect state and regional interests and at the same time give fair and equitable treatment to developers who wished to carry out projects under the law? These and related questions are the heart of the considerations to which we now turn, the *Politics of Implementation* of Florida's land-management legislation.

The Politics of Implementation

Implementing Chapter 380:
The Context for the Analysis

There have now been 10 years within which to judge the implementation of Florida's Environmental Land and Water Management Law. In attempting to evaluate how effective the implementation process has been, it should be kept in mind that in part one's expectations shape the assessment. Thus, those die-hard environmentalists who expected the law to solve every aspect of Florida's environmental and growth problems have been disappointed. Developers, who feared that all growth would grind to a halt, have found their fears to be unfounded. Those who hoped to see some improvement in the quality of development carried out in the state have found much to approve of. In the following analysis, our prime concern is with the political forces that have aided or hindered the effective implementation of the law.

Assessing the implementation effort is complicated by the strongly decentralized nature of the process. Most of the responsibility still lies with the state's some 400 cities, 67 counties, and numerous special districts. These local governments are very uneven in their capacity and political willingness to undertake growth-management initiatives. The state law covers only a relatively small part of the total development process in the state, and thus has little or no impact on a large part of the development process.[53]

The following assessment will focus on:

a. Initial funding, and efforts to get the implementation process moving.
b. Amendments and new related laws adopted over the 1973–82 period.
c. The Area of Critical State Concern process.
d. The Development of Regional Impact process.
e. Key actors in the implementation process.
f. The complex intergovernmental relationships set up in the legislation and the strong and weak points of the emerging system.
g. A summary evaluation of the law.

Although the law passed in 1972, the full implementation of its major sections, the critical area designation and the DRI process, were delayed by provisions in the law. This delay proved to be a sound public policy decision. It provided time for gearing up and more carefully planning the implementation of a complex law involving the intermeshing of state, regional, and local governments.

**Staffing and Funding Patterns
in the Implementation Effort**
Legislative opponents of far-reaching new policy initiatives often attempt to limit the impact of these initiatives by influencing both the funding and staff levels of new agencies charged with putting the legislation into effect. In the case of the Land Management Act, the funding levels have not been so low as to seriously cripple the implementation of the law, but they have not been adequate to fully

use the policy initiatives embedded in this complex piece of legislation.

The Bureau of Land Planning (later to become the Bureau of Land and Water Management) in the Division of State Planning was given $150,000 in start-up funds to get the process underway. The Environmental Land Management Study Committee also received $150,000 in its supporting role in the process. Given the fact that the process was not fully implemented until July 1, 1973, these low figures are not out of reason. More serious was the failure to secure more adequate appropriations beginning in July 1973 and in subsequent years. For example, the new chief of the bureau asked for a $900,000 appropriation in the July 1973 to July 1974 period and received only $300,000. One careful review of the funding pattern cast strong doubt on the adequacy of the funding to give the state's role in the process professional credibility. The Bureau of Land Planning, with extensive responsibilities under the new law, had only 11 professionals as of 1976. Four professionals in the DRI section, and five professionals in the Areas of Critical State Concern section came under strong workload pressures with the designation of Critical Areas and a flood of DRI decisions in the early years of the law.[54] The head of the Bureau of Land and Water Management, Bob Rhodes, felt that the staff limitations in both sections of the bureau did place important limitations on the state's capacity to play its full role in both policy development and monitoring.[55] Another staff member felt that "from the start, the effort did not have enough staff."[56] The bureau could not develop the policy and monitoring that would allow the law's growth management possibilities to be fully exploited. For instance, lack of staff severely limited the bureau's efforts to influence the growth management process by working closely with developers, regional planning councils, and local governments.

Nevertheless, the start-up implementation effort overall can be judged a modest success. Much of the credit must go to the Environmental Land Management Study Committee, which not only helped to develop standards and guidelines, but also mobilized public support for the law. By the time the ELMS Committee, with strong private sector representation, had worked through the problems of developing reasonable DRI standards and guidelines to recommend to the Bureau of Land and Water Management, a powerful coalition of state agencies, key developer and home builder representatives (the head of one of the largest home building companies in the Tampa Bay Area and the president of one of the largest development corporations in South Florida), and environmentalists had united to support the adoption of the standards and guidelines in the legislature, and, in fact, these were adopted with relatively little controversy. The political effectiveness of the Environmental Land and Management Study Committee in the legislature was undoubtedly a major factor in getting the implementation effort off to a good start. The legislature did insist on approving any future changes in the standards and guidelines that might be made. In the light of the subsequent ruling by the Florida State Supreme Court, which took a very narrow view of the delegation of legislative authority in designating Areas of Critical State Concern, a key state planner has argued that this insistence by the legislature was "a blessing in disguise."[57]

Key Amendments and Related Legislation in the 1973–82 Period

Other legislative action since 1972 has been important in the process of implementing Florida's land management law. These legislative initiatives have taken the form of amendments to chapter 380, appropriations to support its implementation, and the adoption of new land or water management legislation that has had a direct bearing on the implementation of the Land Management Act. In a general way, all of these activities have been positive in terms of implementing the land-management legislation. A number of amendments have been aimed at adjusting the DRI process to fit more realistically the needs of developers, without reducing the ability of the law to achieve its goals. A critical element of the amendment process involved coalitions that developed to attempt to weaken or support the law. We will give special attention to the maturing of a new coalition of environmentalists, private sector groups, and local governments who joined forces to pass major legislation involving both the critical area and the DRI sections of the law. This coalition, which began with the Environmental Land Management Study Committee support in the 1973 legislature, came to its full flowering in major changes that were made in the 1979 and 1980 sessions of the Florida legislature.

The year 1974 was of major importance in the implementation history of the Land Management Act. First, very substantial funding was secured for the implementation process, the only year to date in which substantial funding increases have been granted. In addition, the time frame for regional agency review for Developments of Regional Impact was made far more realistic by extending it from 30 days to 50 days, and other changes in the time frame allowed a more in-depth review to take place. The injunctive action for enforcing the law, formerly limited to the state's attorneys, was expanded to include the State Land Planning Agency, cities, and counties. According to a key staff member of the State Land Planning Agency, this expanded injunction power gave the state an important bargaining tool in dealing with developers. He went on to say that although it had never been necessary to actually shut down a project, the authority to do so was important in assuring compliance with the provisions of Development Orders.[58]

If these amendments made 1974 a good year for the Land Management Act, part of the credit goes to the initiatives of the State Land Planning Agency in going to the development community to seek agreement on the kind of changes needed to make the law more effective and to enlist private sector support for both appropriations and needed amendments to the law. These efforts helped to strengthen the coalition between the private sector, environmentalists, and the state in assuring effective implementation of the law. The support for the implementation of the law was reflected in the appropriations for 1974. The Bureau of Land and Water Management asked for 10 new positions and actually got 11 positions. In addition, substantial funds, approximately $1 million, were appropriated for regional planning councils to help them carry out their review function under chapter 380. One important lesson from the 1974 experience was that it indicated that support for environmental, land management, and growth initiatives in Florida had not peaked in 1972.

In 1975, the only important amendment to chapter 380 involved adding energy demands as one of the factors that should be considered in assessing the regional impact of a project.[59] The following year was important mainly for a major effort by one large land developer to substantially weaken the DRI section by amendments that would have allowed piecemeal development of very large projects to avoid coming under the DRI process. Despite substantial legislative backing of the amendments, they did not get the full support of other developers, and at the last moment sufficient support for the existing law was martialed to defeat the proposed changes.

In 1977, extensive amendments were written into the DRI section of chapter 380. These changes grew out of the realities of the development process in Florida. In the first year of implementation, the construction industry was in a boom period. A great number of DRI projects were approved, many with a build-out period of 30 years, as the market was able to absorb the new units. In the 1974–75 recession, the construction industry in Florida virtually collapsed. When the revival began to make itself felt in 1977, many developers had Development Orders that were inappropriate for the 1977 market. The issue that arose was what criteria would guide the degree to which a developer could change a Development Order to make it useful in the new market without having to go back through the whole DRI process.

The Bureau of Land and Water Management, the development community, and to some extent environmentalists again negotiated intensely to strike a balance of interests that would satisfy the developers and at the same time protect the public interest. The resulting amendments included some very specific guidelines, under the general principle that if a proposed substantial change to a Development Order would result in *reduced* regional impact, the change would not divest the developer's right to complete the development.[60] Another closely related amendment held that if a proposed development is planned for development over an extended period of time, the developer may file an application for master development approval and agree to present subsequent increments of the development for preconstruction review.[61]

These two changes in 1977 attempted to meet head-on a strong claim by developers that without such alterations it simply was not realistic or practical to try to operate under the law. Although the changes did not end the criticism of the DRI process, they went a long way toward strengthening a dialogue between the development community and the state in making adjustments in the law that could be justified from the point of view of the public interest and at the same time make it more useable for the development community.

There were no substantial amendments in 1978, but a court ruling precipitated a legislative crisis that was not resolved until 1979–80. In November 1978 the state supreme court had declared unconstitutional the entire Area of Critical State Concern component of the law, thus upholding a First District Court of Appeals ruling that held both the Keys and Green Swamp Areas of Critical State Concern designations unconstitutional.[62] Governor Askew immediately called a special session of the legislature in order to bring about a temporary readoption of two Critical Area designations that otherwise would have lapsed because of the adverse court decision, but the task of permanently readopting the section was then left for the 1979 legislature. Later, newly elected Governor, Bob Graham, appointed a Task Force on Resource Management to look closely at the whole question of land- and water-management initiatives in the state. The Task Force was to recommend for legislative action in both 1979 and 1980 any changes that needed to be made to make the law more effective.

The immediate job faced by the governor's task force, whose membership again included a cross section of environmentalists, home builders and developers, and local government officials, was to tackle the entire Critical Area section of the law that had been declared unconstitutional. The court had ruled that delegating the authority to designate and write rules for Areas of Critical State Concern to an administrative agency was an unconstitutional delegation of legislative authority. The task force drafted proposed legislation that spelled out in more detail the criteria that would guide designations of Areas of Critical State Concern. The proposed changes also provided that new Critical Area designations would not go into effect until after they had been reviewed by a subsequent session of the state legislature.[63]

The legislative session of 1979 presented a clear test of the question: Could a major land- and growth-management initiative be passed in Florida in 1979, long after the initial fervor of the environmental movement was assumed to have died out? Many had considered 1972 to be a unique year, and thought it would not be possible ever again to pass strong land- and growth-management laws in Florida. The legislature's readoption of the Area of Critical State Concern component of the law, with provisions that were in some ways stronger than the original section, proved that there was still a strong political coalition in support of land and growth management in the state. The Florida State Association of Home-builders and the Florida State Association of County Commissioners joined environmental groups to give strong support to the proposed legislation. It passed with surprising ease, with the strong support of the home builders especially important in winning the approval of the key committee in the Florida Senate. In addition the Governor made reenactment of the Critical Area section a major part of his legislative program for the 1979 session and pushed very hard for its adoption.

The new Critical Area provision as approved by the legislature: (1) retained the authority for the executive branch to initiate and make Critical Area designations, but added an opportunity for the legislature to veto the action at its next session; (2) spelled out in more detail the criteria for designation that would guide the administrative process; (3) made mandatory the use of Resource Planning and Management Study Committees to attempt voluntary resolution of development problems before a formal critical area designation could be made; (4) provided that all future designations sunset three years after the adoption of acceptable land development regulations by local governments, and for even earlier dedesignation under certain circumstances; (5) established closer ties between Areas of Critical State Concern and the Environmentally Endangered Lands purchase program; (6) required that all local governments in Critical Areas conform their comprehensive plans to the ACSC Principles for Guiding Development; (7) provided that the City of Key West would be deleted from the Keys Critical Area designation on approval of the land use element of the city's comprehensive plan; and (8) provided that the entire Keys Critical Area designation would be ended July 1, 1982, subject to certain conditions being met.[64]

For the Land Management Act, 1980 was again a major year in the legislative arena. The previous year newly elected Governor Graham (the chief sponsor of Chapter 380 in 1972) had sent strong signals to legislative leaders that he did not wish to have the DRI section reconsidered by the 1979 legislature, on the grounds that his Task Force on Resource Management would bring forward comprehensive recommendations for changes in the law in 1980. Beginning in January 1979, the task force held hearings across the state and carried out an intensive study of the implementation of the DRI process. The Task Force recommended a number of small changes in the DRI process aimed at making it both more acceptable to the development community and also increasing its capacity to direct, guide, and manage growth in Florida.[65] The proposed changes received the same coalition support given the previous year to the Area of Critical State Concern changes. Home builders and developers, the environmental community, and local governments all joined to bring about approval of amendments to develop a clearer regional framework for DRI reviews by regional agencies and approval by local governments. To meet an almost universal complaint voiced in testimony before the Task Force, a prime objective was to assure that the regional review confined itself to regional matters and not concern itself with what were in effect local development decisions.[66]

In addition to these small changes in the DRI section of chapter 380, the 1980 legislature moved to strengthen regional councils by passing the Florida Regional Planning Council Act. One of the problems with regional assessments was that until 1980 the membership of regional planning councils consisted entirely of city and county elected officials. These elected officeholders found it difficult to develop and enforce a clear set of regional policies that inevitably at one time or another would disadvantage one local government or another.[67] The 1980 Regional Planning Council Act required that all regional planning councils in the state be reorganized under a new state general law; that such councils develop a set of regional standards within which DRI assessments would be made; and that the membership of the regional councils be composed of one third members appointed by the governor. The intent was to assure that state and regional interests not only in chapter 380 but also in other kinds of regional activities would be more adequately represented through the addition of gubernatorial appointments. The law was an important first step in strengthening regional planning councils.[68]

In assessing the several laws passed from 1973 to 1982 that directly or indirectly affected the implementation of the Land Management Act, it is clear that their collective impact was positive. Two disappointments were the failure to appropriate more funds for the state land planning agency and, until 1980, the failure to face the problem of strengthening regional planning councils. Sounder funding and further efforts to strengthen the regional planning councils were destined to be high on the agenda of the Graham administration during the first half of the 1980s.

Related Developments, 1973–80

Other events and legislation in the 1973–80 period also had an impact on growth management. The most significant are summarized in this section. The Governor's Conference on Water Management in South Florida had been so successful as a policy-initiating device that, in the fall of 1973, Governor Askew and his staff convened a follow-up conference entitled, "Florida 2000: Governor's Conference on Growth and the Environment." After three days of intensive effort, the conference issued a short but strong statement, recommending an assessment of the impact of Florida's tax policies on growth, adoption of a growth policy by the state legislature and a number of other actions aimed at supporting earlier efforts to develop a comprehensive growth management system for the state.[69]

The Environmental Land Management Study Committee, in its final report in 1974, had strongly recommended the adoption of legislation requiring a comprehensive plan in every county and city in Florida. This proposal was not enacted into law until the 1975 legislative session, with the passage of the Local Government Comprehensive Planning Act.[70] By the early 1980s, when all local governments are expected to have completed their plans and regulations, a major loophole in the Land Management Act of 1972 will have been closed. It will no longer be possible for developers to avoid the impact of the DRI process on the grounds that the local government has no land use regulations in place, assuming that the adopted comprehensive plans had an adequate implementation component.

Also in 1975, the legislature enacted the Environmental Reorganization Act, which put the responsibility for water quality and water quantity planning and management together for the first time and set

up a comprehensive set of five water management districts with strong
regulatory powers for the state.[71] In addition, a 1976 constitutional
amendment providing a common base of funding for the water
management districts was crucial to the eventual integration of Florida's
land and water planning and management.[72] As Governor Askew put
it, "The 1976 referendum which gave taxing power to water management districts on a uniform basis throughout the state was another key
tool being put on the line to manage our land and water resources."[73]
Another significant development was a 1977 act which authorized the
Department of Environmental Regulation to restore bodies of water
including the power to acquire lands. This law, the Water Resources
Restoration and Preservation Act of 1977, offers the potential for
undoing some of the extensive damage that has been done to Florida's
wetlands by indiscriminate dredging and filling.

Areas of Critical State Concern:
An Overview

There have been both positive and negative aspects in the implementation of chapter 380, section 5, Areas of Critical State Concern.
The fact that three rather large geographic areas have been declared
to be Areas of Critical State Concern demonstrates that this component of the Land Management Act had an important potential as a
growth-management tool. The Big Cypress Swamp was declared an
Area of Critical State Concern by a special law proposed by
Governor Askew and enacted by the 1973 legislature.[74] Although
section 5 was not used to initiate the designation, it was used in
setting the area's boundaries and regulations. The other two designations—the Green Swamp and the Florida Keys—were the successful culmination of the section 5 process. The Big Cypress Swamp
and the Green Swamp designations involved areas that were largely
undeveloped and ecologically valuable. The designation of the Keys
was a much more complex application of the Critical Area concept,
because it involved an already urbanized area, though one with
unique geographic and environmental characteristics. The Florida
Keys designation showed the relevance of the law beyond the
protection of largely undeveloped natural areas. The Keys designation was a success in that it tested anew the political will of the
governor and cabinet, sitting as the Administration Commission, to
designate a critical area in the face of strong opposition at the local
level. The implementation by local governments in the Keys of the
state standards resulting from the designation and the effectiveness
of the state's monitoring and enforcement function raises serious
questions about the adequacy of efforts by both levels of government that will be assessed below.

Many of the supporters of the original legislation had envisaged a much more aggressive and active use of the Critical Area process and had hoped to see a great many more areas under protection. These supporters probably underestimated the political firestorm that would occur each time a Critical Area designation was made. With every designation a major political event, there were great pressures to be selective and to hold Critical Area designations to only the most obviously necessary geographical areas. Further, the very limited staffing of the Land Planning agency made it unrealistic for it to assume all the complex tasks required for a designation except in a very few cases.

Finally, great potential still exists for the positive use of the Critical Area designation that has just begun to be appreciated. For example, efforts can be made to use the critical area approach in connection with the New Communities Act, a possibility mentioned in the original land management legislation. The State Land Planning Agency also can work with local communities and with regional and state agencies to try to solve critical problems without mounting a full-scale designation effort. The use of Resource Planning and Management Committees to achieve the goals of the Critical Area section of chapter 380 by informal efforts short of a formal designation had begun before the approach was mandated by the legislative reenactment of chapter 380.05 in 1979. The subsequent use of the Resource Planning and Management Committee approach is a development of major importance in Florida's growth-management system.

The following analysis examines the three major Critical Area designations, the implementation record after designation in those three areas, and the use of the Resource Planning and Management Committee technique in nondesignated areas and as a means of determining whether a designated area was ready to be dedesignated.

Areas of Critical State Concern:
The Designation Stage
The Big Cypress Area of Critical State Concern. The Big Cypress Conservation Act of 1973 not only designated the Big Cypress as an Area of Critical State Concern but also earmarked $40 million in state-matching funds toward the purchase of land within the proposed Big Cypress National Freshwater Reserve. The Division of State Planning, the State Land Planning Agency until 1979, was directed to come up with definite boundary and land development regulations for the state-protected area within 120 days after July 1, 1973. The state-protected area was to include the entire

national freshwater reserve (570,000 acres), "together with contiguous land and water areas ecologically linked to the Everglades
National Park, estuarine fisheries of South Florida, or the freshwater
aquifer of South Florida." The legislation also granted to the state the
power of eminent domain within the Big Cypress Area (an authority
not enjoyed by the state in any other environmentally endangered
area) and exempted the Big Cypress designation from the 5 percent
acreage limitation imposed in chapter 380.[75]

In its original assessment, the Division of State Planning included
over 1 million acres within the Critical Area boundary and developed fairly tough restrictions on development in four land classification categories. The proposed regulations were toughest on developments in Area 1 (frequently flooded mangrove swamps and
islands, coastal marshes, and freshwater sloughs). Less stringent
restrictions were recommended for the other categories but were
still fairly stringent for the urbanizing areas (Area 4).[76] In effect, the
Division of State Planning was attempting to include many of the
urban and urbanizing towns on the west coast in Collier County in
addition to the more primitive wilderness and agricultural lands of
Area 1.[77]

A storm of controversy broke out over the extent of the proposed
area and the detailed and stringent regulations. One observer
described the hearings in Collier County as follows:

> A road show of state planning officials took the boundaries and
> regulations to three public hearings. All were packed, tense, and hostile.
> At one point, state troopers were called to stand guard. "The people who
> live in the swamps don't want any kind of government," said one official
> who attended these meetings. There had been some local opposition to
> the federal purchase, and now state officials had to bear the brunt of that
> hostility as well as confusion between what lands would be purchased
> and what would be regulated. Conservationists were hooted down while
> officials listened to comments like, 'Some of us may have to sacrifice our
> lives to get rid of those who are destroying us, such as long-hairs,
> minority groups, one worlders, do-gooders, bird watchers, and so-called
> ecologists, and all the other draft-dodgers and get them off the backs of
> the people who are responsible for feeding them even if they don't
> deserve it.[78]

In the aftermath of the political battle, the boundaries were pulled in
to a total area of something over 800,000 acres, including the 570,000
acres in the federal purchase area, the Freshwater Reserve. Most of
this land had been classified as Area 1. The proposed regulations
were somewhat relaxed, but still involved sharp restrictions on
development.[79]

Although these drawn-in boundaries still proved to be highly
controversial, the governor and cabinet, acting as the Administration Commission, voted 6 to 1 to approve the Critical Area designa-

tion. The resulting political backlash included an almost successful attempt in the 1974 legislature to pull the Critical Area boundaries back to the 570,000 acres to be purchased by the federal government. This proposal at one time had the signatures of more than half of each house of the legislature. The steam was taken out of this movement when a straw vote held in Collier County in 1974 showed a 4-to-1 margin in favor of establishing the Critical Area designation for Collier County. Here was a case in which a vocal minority group was proven not to speak for all the people.[80]

The Green Swamp Area of Critical State Concern.   The process of nominating, investigating, and finally designating the Green Swamp as an Area of Critical State Concern covered a period of about a year, from the initiation of the study by the Division of State Planning in May 1973 to the Administration Commission's formal designation on July 16, 1974 of parts of the Green Swamp lying in Lake and Polk Counties as an Area of Critical State Concern. Perhaps even more than the Big Cypress case, this action by the cabinet was a key political test of the ability of the state to implement the Critical Areas section of the law. Local hostility was strong and unbroken. Environmental forces did not have the power or support in Lake and Polk counties that they had either in Collier County or later in the Florida Keys. Perhaps this is one reason that the designation vote by the Administration Commission was very close—4 to 3. As Governor Askew has put it: "The Green Swamp was the first general use of the Critical Areas section of the law, and if we had not been able to pass that designation, that is, get the votes in the cabinet, we would have lost a very major part of the bill simply through not being able to implement it. . . ."[81]

Heeding the lessons in the Big Cypress case, the Division of State Planning's Bureau of Land and Water Management went all out to document the case for the Critical Area designation in the Green Swamp area. The entire Green Swamp comprises about 800,000 acres lying roughly north and west of Orlando and stretching over toward Tampa. Many hydrologists and geologists consider it one of the state's most critical water recharge areas. It is vital to the Floridian Aquifer, supplying some 81 billion gallons of groundwater annually to that critical aquifer underlying most of the state.[82] The area was largely rural and agricultural, but it was coming under severe pressure from the development associated with Disney World, only a few miles from the southern edge of the Green Swamp.

The designated critical area totaled about 323,000 acres, about 15 percent of the land area in each of the two counties involved. The state's primary objectives involved protecting the swamp's water recharge capacities, guarding the area's natural flow of water, preventing the destruction of important wetlands, and protecting the flood detention areas of the Southwest Florida Water Management District. The regulatory guidelines had to do with site planning, site alterations, soils, groundwater, storm runoff, solid waste disposal, and other such matters.[83]

Neither Lake nor Polk county at the time of the Critical Area designation had a well-staffed planning or land regulation department. Their land use regulations were minimal or nonexistent. Furthermore, political hostility and resistance to the designation in the two counties were strong, and both counties failed to develop the regulations within the required six months. As a result, the regulations were developed by the Bureau of Land Planning, by then renamed the Bureau of Land and Water Management. These regulations were subsequently approved by the Administration Commission and put into effect on July 20, 1975.

The Florida Keys Area of Critical State Concern.   The Keys Area of Critical State Concern designation presented at once the most complex and most challenging use of the Critical Area designation to that point in the implementation of the law. As one assessment has put it:

> Many observers predicted that natural resource protection would be the effective limit of a critical areas program. Such a narrow view is understandable because in 1974 the concept of critical areas as a state land management technique was still being academically debated in most states; it was Florida that was breaking all the new ground in implementing the concept. The designation of the Florida Keys as the third critical area clearly showed that the program could deal with the infinitely more complex issues confronting a rapidly developing urban area.[84]

The Florida Keys comprises a low-lying chain of 97 islands of which 35 are linked with the mainland by what was formerly a railroad and now has been converted into an overseas highway. The existence of the road makes the area uniquely accessible to the rest of the nation, unlike the Hawaiian or Aleutian Island chains. Both the ease of access and the topography of the islands indicated that development on them required careful planning. The islands have a very low elevation—90 percent of the land area is 5 feet or less above mean sea level—and there have been recorded hurricane tides of 15 to 18 feet.[85] During the 1960s, the Keys' population grew 10 percent larger (from 48,000 to 52,000, and by 1980 the figure was 63,188. This is a fairly slow growth by South Florida standards. However, when one visualizes a long, very narrow, and environmentally sensitive strip of land stretching over 150 miles, with urbanization scattered along the entire stretch, the possibility for major problems becomes clear.

People in the Keys and elsewhere in Florida began years ago to worry about the impacts of uncontrolled and uncoordinated growth on the islands' fragile environment and about the vulnerability of the growing communities to storm damage and flooding. A 1935 hurricane that struck the middle Keys and killed over 400 people drew national attention to these risks. Extensive illegal dredge and fill operations had destroyed thousands of acres of valuable mangroves and other wetlands. Sewage treatment was primitive at best. For water, the islands depended on Dade County well fields to supplement an ancient desalinization plant constructed by the navy in Key West. The inadequacy of sewer and water facilities exacerbated the growth problems encountered as population pressures increased. The Keys Critical Area report summed up the damage from uncontrolled development:

> (1) Environmental degradation, (2) encroachment of incompatible land uses on essential resources and investment, (3) lack of phasing of development with the ability to provide public facilities and services to existing and proposed populations, and (4) a substantial amount of precommitted growth which will exacerbate all the other problems and dangers. The effects of these problems on the economic and physical structure of the area will be severe.[86]

In order to solve these increasingly severe problems in one of the nation's most beautiful but most fragile and endangered environments, the Bureau of Land and Water Management recommended to the Administration Commission a Critical Area designation which contained all of the island portion of the Keys, almost 70,000 acres of land. The primary principles for guiding development were focused on protecting the natural and aesthetic values of the Keys and on limiting development to a level that could be accommodated by the provision and expansion of public service facilities. The requirements illustrated clearly the Land Management Act's far-reaching mandate in asserting state controls over Areas of Critical State Concern. In by far the toughest requirement for guiding development that had been proposed since the initial Big Cypress proposal regulations, special zoning districts were mandated for environmentally sensitive areas including tidal mangrove communities. In an interesting further provision, local governments were to consider giving proposed development projects "density credit" as an incentive to preserve environmentally sensitive areas.[87]

A community impact assessment statement was required prior to the issuance of zoning or rezoning orders or site plan approvals for developments that exceeded fixed height or density limitations, so-called major developments.[88] The objective of the community impact statement was to enable local government officials to determine the proposed development's impact on the environment, natural resources, economy, the potential of the project to meet local or regional housing needs, and the project's potential impact on public facilities (water, sewers, solid waste disposal, and public transportation facilities).[89] Thus, one sees in the Keys Area of Critical State Concern designation the state's first effort to come to grip with an urbanizing area and to develop a state-regional-local growth-management partnership to protect legitimate regional and state interests in an area unique not only to the state of Florida but to the nation itself.

The political reaction to the designation and its implementation was complex and heated. Unlike the Green Swamp case, there was by no means solid opposition at the local level to the Critical Area designation. Public officials and citizens alike were divided, with a majority of elected officials expressing the view that a designation was not needed, but a minority strongly approving the designation. Citizens in the lower Keys generally opposed designation, while citizens in the middle and upper Keys strongly supported it. At the hearing at which the Administration Commission approved the designation, a highly vocal, overflow crowd of over 800 people seemed to be about equally divided pro and con. The final vote approving the designation—after a specially heated fight over the inclusion of Key West resulted in that city being left in—was 5 in favor and 2 against.[90]

Areas of Critical State Concern:
The Implementation Record

The *Big Cypress* designation was in place, and the Administration Commission had demonstrated that elected statewide officials could impose regulations that mandated on local elected officials a broad range of land- and growth-management controls. The next question was how effective the implementation process would be. Fortunately, as the straw poll demonstrated, the politics of growth management in Collier County was undergoing a rapid change at about the same time the implementation process began. Collier County's major problem in enforcing the new regulations was in the remote areas of the Big Cypress Swamp, with their many camps and temporary structures. For a time, one observer noted: "The county refused to monitor and enforce the regulations because they had inadequate money in their budget." Despite some complaints that the state should have had the chief responsibility, the county did begin a systematic effort to enforce the regulations, including using a helicopter to fly over the area on a regular basis.

In the beginning, the county also lacked technical expertise. According to the head of its planning and zoning department, 47 of the first 49 citations of individuals or companies for violations were thrown out on technical grounds. His staff and the county commissioners conferred with representatives of the attorney general's office to correct the situation. The county commission also began to use advisory groups to review all requests for oil exploration, a particularly controversial matter within the Area of Critical State Concern boundary. This official felt that after the initial rough start, the controls on oil exploration and other development were being strictly enforced: the digging of canals in the western part of the county had been almost entirely stopped, on-site retention of surface storm drainage was being required, and the zoning department was reviewing all permits for buildings and other structures within the Big Cypress Area of Critical State Concern for compliance.[91] His assessment indicated that most of the severe problems have been overcome and the implementation efforts in the Big Cypress Swamp Critical Area was going forward in a generally satisfactory way. A more recent assessment confirmed that few problems were occurring in the implementation of the Big Cypress designation, partly because the political climate in Collier County continued favorable to enforcement, and also because the planning staff was professionally competent and contained enough people to do the job. Furthermore, the amount of development activity in the designated area was very limited. The major problem that has emerged is the partitioning of agricultural land in such a way as to make it more likely to be a candidate for urban development, but since chapter 380 excludes agriculture that problem is left in the hands of the county unless or until actual development on such lands is attempted.[92]

The implementation record in the *Green Swamp* designation area has been characterized by the continued failure of the two counties involved to develop plans and implementing regulations of their own that conform to the critical area principles. Thus they have continued to be responsible for enforcing the regulations drafted by and put in place at the state level. The 1979 special legislative session redesignated the Green Swamp Area of Critical State Concern, and the regular session that year readopted section 5 (critical areas) of the Land Management Act. Part of that action provided for a lifting of the designation in the Green Swamp and the Florida Keys if and when three conditions were met:

1. Approval by the State Land Planning Agency of the local land

development regulations pursuant to sections 380.05(6) or 10, F.S.
2. Such regulations being effective for a period of 12 months.
3. Adoption or modification of the local government comprehensive plan to conform to the Principles for Guiding Development for the Florida Keys Area of Critical State Concern found in chapter 27 F-8, Florida Administrative Code (FAC).[93]

Some confusion about just what the legislative action required was cleared up by an attorney general's informal opinion that confirmed that all three conditions had to be met before the designation could be lifted. An argument had been made that dedesignation would be automatic on July 1, 1982, whether or not the conditions were met. Further, the opinion held that formal action by the Administration Commission was necessary before the designation could be lifted.[94]

The legislative action was prompted largely by proponents of the early lifting of the designation for both the Keys and the Green Swamp, but the impact of assuring that the conditions required before designation were met has set in motion a full scale review of the implementation record for Areas of Critical State Concern in the Green Swamp and the Keys. The use of the Resource Planning and Management Committee as the device for examining the implementation record was required in the statute. The Committee for the Green Swamp was established in September 1981 and charged by the governor with reviewing "land development regulations of Polk and Lake counties to determine whether they meet the requirements for repeal of the Critical Area designation," and to "address any additional problems which were not part of the original designation." In the event that the designation was lifted, "the Committee would then continue for a period to monitor development issues and local implementation of land development regulations."[95]

The Department of Community Affairs report in June 1982 to the governor and cabinet sitting as the Administration Commission regarding the Green Swamp Area of Critical State Concern noted that none of the local government's within the designation area had adopted regulations to conform to the critical area Principles for Guiding Development, and thus were not eligible for dedesignation. The level of development activity in the area has been very low, and where development orders have been issued, the two counties involved (Lake and Polk) have been responsible for conforming them to the state's Green Swamp Development Codes. In the meantime, the Green Swamp Resource Planning and Management Committee, staffed by the State Land Planning Agency through DCA's Bureau of Land and Water Management, is concentrating its initial efforts on assisting the two counties in developing and gaining approval for their own regulations that conform to critical area guidelines. DCA reported that "Lake County has amended its countywide zoning and subdivision regulations to reflect most of the Principles for Guiding Development found in chapter 27 F.S., FAC." Those regulations were approved by the State Land Planning Agency on October 29, 1981. The Resource Planning and Management Committee, through its technical advisory group, has determined that additional regulations involving site alterations in upland areas must be adopted and approved before the county is in conformance with the Principles for Guiding Development.[96]

Polk County "has adopted a surface water management ordinance aimed at protecting the county's wetland areas," but the ordinance is not fully in conformance with the Principles for Guiding Development, specifically with regard to protecting some flatwood and upland areas. The State Land Planning Agency, both directly and through the Resource Planning and Management Committee, committed itself to "work closely with Polk and Lake counties to insure that land development regulations consistent with the Green Swamp Principles for Guiding Development are adopted."[97] On the basis of these findings, the State Land Planning Agency reported to the Administration Commission "that Polk and Lake counties do not meet the requirement for repeal of the Area of Critical State Concern designation at this time. . . ." In turn, the governor and cabinet, sitting as the Administration Commission, approved a finding "that conditions for repeal of the Green Swamp Area of Critical State Concern have not been met pursuant to section 380.0551(3), Florida Statutes." Lifting of the designation does not seem imminent. The 12 months required for approved regulations to be in effect cannot begin until all necessary regulations are adopted by Lake and Polk counties and approved by the State Land Planning Agency. In the meantime, something has been added: a much more direct state presence in the area through the organization of the Green Swamp Resource Planning and Management Committee. The State Land Planning Agency's presence is greater, and a systematic monitoring of county development orders now seems much more likely if the Administration Commission's directive to the State Land Planning Agency to "vigorously enforce the existing standards" in the Keys carries over to the Green Swamp.

The Florida Keys Area of Critical State Concern offers at the same time the most disappointing and the most hopeful for the future experience in implementing a Critical State designation. The local governments in the Keys—Monroe County and four municipalities—missed the six month deadline requiring that the Administration Commission formally adopt the land development regulations. Subsequently all local governments in the Keys except the city of North Key Largo Beach, which had no residents and no development, did develop and were approved by the State Land Planning Agency. The city of Key West was removed from the Critical Area designation by action of the 1979 legislative session effective July 1, 1981.

According to state and regional officials, a major effort was made to assist the Keys local governments in drawing up their regulations. According to the local governments involved, the state and regional assistance was too little and too late. Perhaps one of the more important lessons to be learned from the implementation experience in the Keys is that chapter 380 does not provide an adequate framework, nor did the State Land Planning Agency have adequate resources to give local governments in the Keys the kind of assistance needed in developing and implementing regulations. State officials in general, and Governor Askew in particular, expressed a strong sense of responsibility for helping communities in the Keys and later succeeded in acquiring federal funds for such projects as rebuilding the deteriorating bridges on the overseas highway. Nevertheless, the kind of early on help needed for developing regulations and monitoring and overseeing their implementation simply was not forthcoming.[98]

The state's effectiveness can best be judged through the actual working of the monitoring process, in which the state had the responsibility for seeing that its critical area principles were followed. The state at first required that local governments send a copy of every Development Order of any kind for state review. Monroe County's planning director noted that after 400 Development Orders were approved without an appeal, the Division of State Planning "advised us that it would no longer be necessary to send Department Orders pertaining to single family and duplex units to them for review.[99] By 1978 more than 1,000 permits had been issued, and in the view of state and Monroe County officials, the initial problems of monitoring and enforcement seemed on the surface to be under control.

Not all observers took such a positive view. Some environmental groups feel that the state has been to lenient, and even lax, in ensuring enforcement of the regulations in the county. Leaders of some of these groups expressed frustration at not having been able to persuade the state to be tougher in seeing that the full letter and spirit of the development regulations were carried out. Many of these leaders felt the regulations were too lenient to begin with.[100]

Developments that stemmed from the actions of the Florida Courts and the subsequent action of the 1979 session of the Florida legislature to reenact section 5 of chapter 380 led to an in-depth review of the Keys implementation effort that raised serious questions about the capacity or willingness of the local governments in the Keys to implement their development regulations so as to conform to the State's Principles for Guiding Development. The reviews raised equally serious doubts about the capacity or willingness of the state, either through the State Land Planning Agency or otherwise, to monitor local government actions and where necessary take enforcement orders to the Land and Water Adjudicatory Commission so as to ensure conformance to state standards.

Water has long been an important constraint on growth in the Keys. The area has no potable fresh water supply of its own and must draw water from either: (a) the desalinization plant in Key West originally built for the navy, now virtually useless because of age; (b) brackish water drawn from the Floridian aquifer and made potable through the reverse osmosis process; and (c) water delivered to the Keys via wells located in South Dade County that draw water from the Biscayne aquifer that is carried to the Keys via a pipeline originally built by the navy. The replacement of that old and worn-out pipeline with a larger facility, including a major spur to provide water for the northern section of the Keys (the Upper Keys) caused great alarm to growth-management advocates, who feared that the availability of more water at lower costs would set off a wave of growth that would overwhelm the natural and manmade systems in the Keys. This alarm itself reflected a lack of confidence in the ability of the state or local governments to manage growth in the Keys so as to conform to the Principles for Guiding Development mandated by the critical area designation. At about the same time, the Resource Planning and Management Committee mandated by the 1979 legislature as the mechanism for determining whether the critical area designation of the Keys should be lifted began its work; a Florida Keys grand jury began an investigation of whether the regulations required by the critical area designation were being enforced; the State Land Planning Agency, in addition to staffing the Resource Planning and Management Committee, contracted with the South Florida Regional Planning Council for a three-part study of the effectiveness of the critical care implementation effort in the Keys; and finally the state university system approved a grant, at the request of the State Land Planning Agency, for a study of the economic, environmental, and public facility impacts of the critical area designation.

The appointment of the Keys Resource Planning and Management Committee (RPMC) and the work of the other groups evaluating the critical area implementation effort coincided with cries of alarm from the Audubon Society and other groups that the pipeline completion would set off a wave of uncontrolled growth that neither state nor local governments could manage. The environmental groups appeared before the governor and cabinet sitting as the Administration Commission in November 1981 and charged that a large number of developments in the Keys, especially in the Upper Keys, that did not conform to critical area principles or sensible growth-management policies, either had been or were about to be approved. The group held that monitoring and enforcement by the state had been virtually nonexistent. The response of the Administration Commission was to request that Monroe County not approve any more major developments in the upper Keys until the Resource Planning and Management Committee had completed its work. In response the county placed a 90-day moratorium on such approvals, with a possibility of extending the moratorium.[101]

Alarm about the apparent failure to manage the growth spurred by the pipeline replacement naturally raised serious questions about the effectiveness of the critical area designation. Those questions are being answered, and largely in a negative way, by the reports of the several groups assessing the effort, the most important of which to date have been the reports of the Florida Keys Resource Planning and Management Committee. Such committees have their minimal membership specified by statute.

> The committees shall include, but not be limited to, representation from each of the following: elected officials from the local governments within the area under study; the planning office of each of the local governments . . .; the state land planning agency; any other state agency . . . which the governor feels would be relevant . . .; and a water management district, if appropriate, and regional planning council all or part of whose jurisdiction lies within the area under study.[102]

The governor appoints the group, using an informal nominating process from the required participating interests, and names the chairman and vice chairman of the committee. In the case of the Keys committee, the chairman, Hugh Morgan, was a Key West lawyer, who has given the committee strong leadership.

Organized in August 1981, the Florida Keys Resource Planning and Management Committee delivered its first six-month report as required in February 1982. The report included the findings of a Technical Advisory Committee, which was appointed by the chairman of the parent committee at its first meeting. The Committee noted that its tasks, as assigned by the governor and reflecting the requirements of the statute, was to:

- *Task 1.* Review the land development regulations of Monroe County and the four municipalities and decide whether the

regulations, as they are now written, meet the requirements for repeal of the Area of Critical State Concern Designation.
- *Task 2*. Determine whether Monroe County and the four municipalities have implemented their land use regulations in a manner satisfactory to meet the requirements for repeal of the Area of Critical State Concern Designation.
- *Task 3*. Address any additional problems of state or regional significance which were not part of the original designation.

The "requirements for repeal" referred to were stipulated in chapter 380.05, and were noted earlier.

In summarizing its findings, drawn in large part from the work of its Technical Advisory Committee, the RPMC used the critical area principles and objectives as the standard of comparison and concluded that there were a number of "unsound policies and internal inconsistencies" in the comprehensive plans and land use control ordinances of the county and the four municipalities reviewed. Three problems identified that were common to all five jurisdictions were:

1. Proper land use planning cannot be effected without the implementation of a land use map.
2. To help assure permanency, all growth management and land use control ordinances should be referenced in the comprehensive plans.
3. Water quality programs are needed to determine the impact of surface water runoff and sewage wastewater on local water resources.[103]

The RPMC identified a number of issue areas for the county and the four municipalities, discussed the problem involved in each issue area, and made recommendations aimed at solving the problem. The data were drawn largely from the Technical Advisory Committee's work. The issue areas identified for the county or the cities ranged from fairly minor to fundamental and included such things as the adequacy of the Monroe County Shoreline Protection Ordinance, water quality monitoring, protection of tropical hardwood hammocks, strip commercial development, and many others, a total of 18 issues for Monroe County alone. Time after time major deficiencies were identified, perhaps best illustrated by the discussion and recommendation, adopted unanimously by the RPMC, regarding the Comprehensive Land Use Plan map. An excerpt from that discussion follows.

Discussion:
The Florida Keys Committee has found the Monroe County Comprehensive Plan generally deficient for failure to include specific guidelines and regulations into said plan. The Florida Keys Resource Planning and Management Committee also found that proper land use planning is

dependent upon the implementation of an adopted Land Use Map, which Monroe County has not accomplished. The present land use and growth control regulations (including the Comprehensive Plan) were therefore found not conducive to the proper enforcement of the critical area principles and objectives contained in Chapter 22F-8 and 22F-9, Florida Administrative Code.

Recommendation (Unanimous):
The Florida Keys Resource Planning and Management Committee recommends that Monroe County draft and implement land suitability map(s) showing vegetation communities, rare and endangered species habitats, existing developed areas including classes of development, and other natural and historic features based on available existing studies and inventories of the wildlife, sealife and vegetation of Monroe County.

Together with the land suitability map(s) there shall be drafted and implemented an overlay, or other suitable substitute land use map, which conforms with the approved comprehensive plan showing proposed land uses, including preservation, conservation, and development areas designating classes of development and use within said areas.

The map(s) shall encompass all of the area within the boundaries of Monroe County.

The Coastal Coordinating Council's Florida Keys Coastal Zone Management Study and other existing studies shall be used in developing said map(s). Conflict areas should be identified and resolved.

SOURCE: The Florida Keys Resource Planning and Management Committee. *Florida Keys Area of Critical State Concern: An Assessment of the Comprehensive Plans and Critical Area Regulations, with Recommendations.* Issue #18: Comprehensive Land Use Plan Map, p. 10, February 1982.

That such a critique could be possible seven years after the designation of the Florida Keys as an Area of Critical State Concern is a sad commentary on the inability and unwillingness of the local governments to adopt and enforce the regulations necessary to conform to the state standards. The critique also illustrates, with at least equal force, the unwillingness or inability of the state to carry out its monitoring and enforcement role in a manner calculated to protect the state's interest in sound development of the Keys. The findings of the RPMC seemed to confirm the charges of citizen groups in the Keys that the state had not been tough enough either in the original designation, or in the follow-up monitoring and enforcement of state standards.

The six-month report of the RPMC led to a recommendation by the State Land Planning Agency to the governor and cabinet sitting as the Administration Commission, that the critical area designation for Monroe County and the cities be continued because the conditions necessary for lifting the designation had not been met, namely that "the local government comprehensive plans [do not] conform to the Principles for Guiding Development as required in contingency 3."[104] The report then summarized the findings of the RPMC and its Technical Advisory Committee (TAC) and included a special recommendation regarding the city of Key West, which had been removed from the critical area boundary by a special provision of the 1979 law, effective July 1, 1981. It was noted that Key West was guilty of most of the deficiencies common to the other local governments in the Keys, including deficiencies in the comprehensive plan, in the implementing ordinances, and in their enforcement. It was recommended that, if these deficiencies were not corrected in a further monitoring period of six months, the city of Key West be redesignated as an Area of Critical State Concern.[105]

The Administration Commission acted on the recommendation of the State Land Planning Agency at its meeting June 29, 1982. The Commission accepted the report of the Resource Planning and Management Committee, reaffirmed its concern "about development which threatens the resources and services capability in the Florida Keys" and found that the conditions for repeal of the critical area designation for the Florida Keys had not been met. This action means that the critical area designation will continue indefinitely unless there is a positive action by the Administration Commission to remove one or more of the local governments in the Keys from the critical area boundaries. Furthermore, the stage has been set for the possible redesignation of Key West after further monitoring. The strong commitment of the governor and cabinet (Administration Commission) to making the critical area designation in the Keys effective is shown by the Commission's further instructions to the RPMC and the State Land Planning Agency (DVCA). The RPMC was asked to continue its work, and report to the commission by the end of January 1983 on:

1. Whether significant progress has been made in solving the area's problems since designation and address any additional problems of state or regional significance which were not part of the original designation.
2. Work with local governments to improve their ability to implement and administer the principles and standards for guiding development.
3. Determine whether the city of Key West is an Area of Critical State Concern.[105-A]

The instructions to the Department of Veterans and Community

Affairs (the state land planning agency) was even more pointed, and profoundly significant to the future integrity of the critical area process:

1. Assist the local governments in their efforts to implement the principles for guiding development.
2. Vigorously enforce the existing standards.
3. Report monthly the status of major development projects and the activities of the Resource Planning and Management Committee; and/or analyze it.
4. Analyze the report of the Committee and prepare recommendations to further improve the effectiveness of the Critical Area designation.[105-B]

The directive that the State Land Planning Agency "vigorously enforce the existing standards" involved in the critical area designation seemed a clear signal that the Commission was not satisfied with the State Land Planning Agency's performance in monitoring and enforcement. In fact, at the time of the report, only one development order had been appealed to the Land and Water Adjudicatory Commission, and it involved an historic preservation issue in Key West.[106] The directive that each major development order proposed in the Keys be reported to the Administration Commission on a monthly basis with an analysis of the order's impact on State Principles for Guiding Development in the Keys will force a more activist monitoring and enforcement role by the State Land Planning Agency, and sets the stage for appeals by that agency to the Land and Water Adjudicatory Commission if state standards are not met in local government actions.[107]

Two more reports added emphasis to the need to strengthen the monitoring and enforcement of Critical Area standards. The Final Report of the Grand Jury for the Sixteenth Judicial Circuit (Monroe County) for the fall term of 1981 devoted much of its time to the operation of the Monroe County Building, Planning, and Zoning Department. It was critical of the department for allowing development "without permits and inspections." The grand jury further concluded that the "Monroe County Building, Planning and Zoning Department is poorly organized, poorly administered, and that some employees in the department appear to be unqualified for the duties they are required to perform."[108]

The report noted further that the department was underfunded and understaffed and called on the county's elected officials to provide more funds even if it meant asking Monroe County citizens for more tax dollars for that particular purpose.[108] Finally, the grand jury noted that its work raised "the question of whether there is a working comprehensive development plan for Monroe County." The need for such a plan and map was endorsed as "essential to insure intelligent control of growth." The grand jury then called on its successor to "closely monitor progress of the Monroe County Building, Planning and Zoning Department and the development of a strong comprehensive development plan and map for Monroe County."[110]

The Keys RPMC issued its second report on June 18, 1982, detailing the results of its "assessment of local governments' implementation of land use regulations." The data collection was done by the RPMC's Technical Advisory Committee, which divided itself into four groups, each of which was responsible for examining one local government. Each group looked at the same three local government actions—major development approval, zoning actions, and plat approvals—and each used a common questionnnaire to insure comparable results. In some cases all local government actions were examined, while in others a sampling process was used. Data was also used that were collected by the South Florida Regional Planning Council under a contract with DVCA entitled *Local Implementation Issues and Recommendations,* which limited its analysis to Monroe County and the city of Key West.

The review of the implementation of land use regulations by the local governments in the Keys revealed at least as many errors of omission and commission as had the assessment of adequacy of the regulations to be implemented.[111] The extent of the problems involved in Monroe County's implementation of its land use regulations emerges from case reviews by the South Florida Regional Planning Council and the Technical Advisory Committee of major development, zoning, and plat ordinance actions.

Bay Hammock Community, a single family development of 33 quarter lots and a boat basin, revealed intrusion into a West Indian hardwood hammock, no adequate wastewater treatment requirement (in conflict with the county's services and utility element), and failure to adhere to the standards of the Shoreline Protection Ordinance. The Technical Advisory Committee noted: (1) Monroe County does not have specific water quality standards with which to evaluate the impacts of land use decisions; and (2) the action taken on this application of the Shoreline Protection Ordinance in allowing this 30 slip boat basin in the shoreline protection zone was inappropriate."[112]

The implementation shortcomings were both procedural and substantive, as illustrated by the Edwards Hotel/Key Largo Sheraton. The South Florida Regional Planning Council noted that "of all the major developments proposed in the Florida Keys during the

ACSC designation, the Edwards Hotel stands as a textbook example of land use mismanagement, illustrating a clear failure of existing regulations to provide the guidelines and standards necessary to conform to the principles of ASCS designation."[113] Without such standards a low density residential area was invaded by high density commercial activities, and unusually fine trees of a West Indian tropical hardwood hammock were destroyed. The Windley Key Station Planned Unit Development, approved by the Monroe County Zoning Board January 29, 1982, illustrated the procedural problem. After reviewing the project, the TAC stated that "Since specified procedures were not observed, neither Monroe County staff or the Department of Veterans and Community Affairs were able to ascertain whether the project, as approved, complied with Area of Critical State Concern standards."[114]

The sum and substance of these studies present a sad and sorry litany of insufficiently specific standards and guidelines; an inability of an understaffed and sometimes unqualified planning and zoning department to enforce standards that were in place; and a failure of either the zoning board or the county commission to take seriously the enforcement of standards, often ignoring good staff work where it existed. The situation was found to be bad across the board: major developments, zoning actions and plat approvals. This analysis has focused on Monroe County, since the great bulk of development in the Keys takes place in unincorporated areas. The situation was not materially different in the incorporated places.

The second report by the Resource Planning and Management Committee brought it all into focus under the heading of general recommendations at the end of the report:

1. We urge the governor and cabinet to take the steps necessary to assure that DVCA vigorously exercises the statutory powers under chapter 380 to bring appeals where the Area of Critical State Concern requirements are not met by local governments and where essential to seek injunctive relief as provided by statute. In the event that additional funding and personnnel are found to be necessary in order for DVCA to effectively meet its responsibility under chapter 380, we urge that such funding be sought as a high priority in the 1983 session of the Florida legislature (unanimously adopted).

2. It is recommended that the designation of Area of Critical State Concern be continued for Monroe County, Key Colony Beach and Layton and be reimposed for the city of Key West until the noted deficiencies, issues, and recommendations be substantially corrected, resolved or implemented and subsequent review by this or a successor committee confirms that such action has been taken. In this subsequent review, conformance with and implementation of the respective comprehensive plan should be confirmed (Attachment E, adopted, 11 to 4).

3. Because of the development pressure on Monroe County and the lack of planning tools, i.e., a land use map and a plan for the impact on

public services, we recommend that no further changes in zoning which result in higher density or major development projects be considered (adopted, 8 to 4 with 2 abstentions).[115]

The recommendations seem moderate in the light of the problems uncovered by the several evaluations of the implementation effort. There seemed little reason to wait six more months, as decided by the Administration Commission, to redesignate Key West as an ACSC. This would seem especially appropriate in light of the city's decision not to fill the city planner position vacated by resignation about June 1, 1982. The city's planning consultants were also dismissed, so that "without a fully functioning city planning unit, and/or a planning consultant, the actions necessary to implement the city comprehensive plan and to accomplish the incomplete portions of the ACSC regulations have come to a substantial halt."[116]

If local governments can be faulted for major deficiencies in implementing the Principles For Guiding Development involved in the Critical Area designation, the state must shoulder at least an equal blame. The recent monitoring and evaluation effort by the Keys RPMC, its Technical Advisory Committee, and the South Florida Regional Planning Council make it abundantly clear that local governments did not provide the professional planning and other resources to do the job. Development orders, major and otherwise, were approved by local governments and allowed to stand by the state that did not meet the Principles for Guiding Development. With the exception of one development order involving the Key West Historical District, no development order until 1982 had ever been appealed by the State Land Planning Agency. The question is why and the answer is complex. First, the Bureau of Land and Water Management, the action arm of the State Land Planning Agency, has never been staffed adequately to perform to the tasks that have been assigned to it. The bureau's last substantial increase in personnel was in 1974, when 11 new positions were added. In 1976, the total staff consisted of 22 persons; the figure had declined to 21 by 1982: 8 professionals in the DRI section; 8 in the critical area section, the bureau director, and 4 support staff. A major effort in 1981 to add 16 positions to the staff to: (a) bolster the Resource Planning and Management Committee approach; (b) strengthen the monitoring and enforcement effort; (c) carry the expanding burden of staff review of DRI binding letter requests; and (d) respond to the need to adapt chapter 380 to the needs of the coastal management program at first looked very promising, but state revenues tightened up and no positions were added. The ability of the bureau to staff the Keys RPMC has come mainly from a coastal management grant that allowed the addition of three professional staff and added secretarial support. Thus Florida joins a number of other states included in this book in failing to staff adequately the key state agency most responsible for the success of the program. The problem remains, although it is eased some by the availability of coastal management dollars. A tight money situation in Florida for the 1983 fiscal year makes prospects for expansion unlikely.[117]

The lack of staff, however, cannot explain or justify fully the failure of the state through the State Land Planning Agency and otherwise, to take a stronger hand in monitoring and enforcement. The assessment of local government actions over the 1981–82 period made it clear that local governments in the Keys had failed from the very beginning to adopt adequate comprehensive plans, and even where part of the plans were adequate failed to put in place regulations of sufficient specificity to assure conformance with state standards. Where specific standards were in place, they were often not enforced. Well over 1,000 development orders, both major and minor, were approved, with no indication that state standards were not being protected until the imminent completion of a new pipeline system for the Keys, including a spur line in the Upper Keys, brought growth management back into focus as a major policy issue.

Beginning in October 1981 the state Land Planning Agency stepped up its oversite efforts, perhaps motivated by the initial findings of the Keys RPMC, by sending a letter to the Monroe Building, Planning and Zoning Department director raising questions about the availability of services such as potable water and solid waste if pending major development orders were approved. The letter demanded that no development orders be approved unless and until "The county has developed a plan for services that can accommodate projected growth of the North Key Largo area." Such blunt and directive language was a first since the establishment of the critical area designation in 1975 and was followed by three additional letters in the next eight months that repeated the need for the county to complete an adequate plan for public services (January 19, 1982); notified Monroe County that the Administration Commission had asked that the Florida Keys Aquaduct Authority approve no additional connections to the North Key Largo spurline until the commission completed its review of whether the Keys Critical Area designation should continue, and calling on the county to suspend any further development order approvals until an acceptable plan for public approval was completed (January 20, 1982); and asked Monroe County not to approve four major developments scheduled for action by the Monroe County Zoning Board June 30, 1982, in view of the fact that "not . . . much progress has been made in formulating . . . [a] plan for public services for Upper Key Largo, June 22, 1982." The county was reminded that the governor and cabinet had called for no more development order approvals until the question of continuing the critical area designation could be settled and the state Land Planning Agency offered to organize "a joint planning effort between the county and the Bureau of Land and Water Management to address the needs of the Upper Key Largo area. . . . "[118]

This action by the State Land Planning Agency seems to set the stage for the appeal of one or more major development orders if the county does not respond to repeated warnings contained in the letters. The integrity of the process would seem to demand such an action if the county approved such orders without adequate standards that could be enforced through the development orders.

The clear inadequacy of the monitoring and enforcement function in the Keys by the state would have seemed to argue strongly for regional agency concurrent review of major development orders as allowed by chapter 380 in Areas of Critical State Concern. Such action by the State Land Planning Agency was never taken in the 1975–81 period, but by mid-1982 it appeared that the South Florida Regional Planning Council would be approved for such concurrent review.

Other Resource Planning and
Management Committee Studies

The oldest RPMC effort, begun before the approach was mandated by the legislature and continued after the 1979 legislation, was the Charlotte Harbor Resource Planning and Management Committee. The initial report on Charlotte Harbor was published in 1978, and the Charlotte Harbor Management Plan was adopted by the committee on June 5, 1982.[119] This report set forth a number of goals, objectives, and implementing actions that would be required of local governments if they were not to be designated as an Area of Critical State Concern. The directives were both procedural and substantive, the latter involving such things as floodplain regulation, control of stormwater runoff and drainage, wastewater treatment, wetlands protection, special controls for beaches and barrier islands, water supply, land development, site alteration, dredge and fill, restoration, and coastal flood plain protection. It was further provided that progress toward the goals should be monitored and assessed.[120]

Just before it dissolved, the Charlotte Harbor RPMC adopted a resolution spelling out what action would have to be taken by local governments to meet the growth-management needs of the area. The resolution held that:

> Each unit of local government in the Charlotte Harbor Study Area should formally adopt the Charlotte Harbor Management Plan's goals, objectives and local government implementing actions as major criteria to be used in making land use decisions. Formal adoption will be by incorporation of the Charlotte Harbor Management Plan within each local governments adopted comprehensive plan. All development orders entered by a unit of local government within the Charlotte Harbor Study Area would thus be required by chapter 163, Florida Statutes (F.S.) to be consistent with the Charlotte Harbor Management Plan.[121]

The resolution provided that such amendments be submitted to the appropriate regional planning council, the State Land Planning Agency, and any other agency "as provided by chapter 163 F.S." The resolution contained a powerful incentive for local governments to adopt the standards:

> It is the expressed desire of the Charlotte Harbor Resource Planning and Management Committee that the Department of Veterans and Community Affairs (DVCA) recommend to the Administration Commission designation as an Area of Critical State Concern all those local governments, within the three county area, which have not complied with section (1) . . . within six (6) months of the receipt of the model ordinance.[122]

The Regional Planning Council was given a major role as the agency responsible for reviewing plan amendments and implementing actions to determine whether a given local government should or should not be included in a critical area designation. DVCA was requested to prepare a model ordinance to guide local governments in complying with the resolution.[123] The six month period was complete by the end of July 1982, and indications were that of the three counties involved, Charlotte and Sarasota would meet the terms of the resolution, but it seemed doubtful that Lee County would succeed in doing so.[124] If not, the governor and cabinet (Administration Commission) may soon have an opportunity to make the first critical area designation since the Keys designation in 1975.

A number of things about the Charlotte Harbor Resource Planning and Management Committee are important in assessing the value of this technique. It supports the proposition that a committee made up of local elected and appointed officials, state and regional agency representatives, and citizen members can agree on tough standards and tough implementation mechanisms in a complex growth management situation. It also illustrates how regional agencies can be used in a much more important way in developing standards and monitoring their implementation. Two water management districts and the Southwest Florida Regional Planning

Council have played major roles in the effort to date. The effort also showed how state agencies can be drawn into the process in a more effective way, especially natural resource agencies such as the Departments of Environmental Regulation, Natural Resources, Game and Fish Commission, and Community Affairs. Finally, the effort has drawn the State Land Planning Agency into a strong leadership role, including, it would seem, a continuing monitoring and evaluation function.

The Suwannee River Resource Planning and Management Committee, organized in December 1980, reinforces the Charlotte Harbor experience in the use of the RPMC approach. The committee published the Suwannee River Management Plan on November 6, 1981. The formal, local government requirements, and the procedures, are much the same as for the Charlotte Harbor plan. Floodplain mapping and regulation is a major element in the plan. The Suwannee River Water Management District has played a key role in its development and bears major responsibility for the implementation effort. The Suwannee River Management Plan is not specific in recommending a critical area designation for local governments who do not take the actions recommended in the report. However, the State Land Planning Agency in mid-1982 reported that the model ordinance had been prepared, and indications were that all 11 counties would comply. For any that do not, the intent apparently is to recommend designation as a critical area to the Administration Commission. A monitoring and evaluation effort will be carried out through the Northeast Florida Regional Planning Council that will involve members of the Suwannee RPMC and its TAC, even though the committee has been disbanded. The State Land Planning Agency will continue to commit staff time to a monitoring effort leading toward a final determination on whether to recommend a designation to the Administration Commission.[125]

Developments of Regional Impact: An Evaluation
The state and local roles under the DRI section of chapter 380 contrasts importantly with those roles under the critical areas section of the law. In the case of critical areas, the initiative lies largely with the state. If the state is passive, if it does not aggressively pursue the designation of new critical areas, section 5 of the law will atrophy, and very little will happen. It is true, of course, that once a designation is made, the responsibility for the actual implementation of the new regulations falls on local government. Even here, however, Development Orders issued by a local government in an Area of Critical State Concern are subject to review by the State Land Planning Agency, and where local actions do not meet

the state standards, can be appealed to the Land and Water Adjudicatory Commission.

The critical area situation stands in sharp contrast to the DRI process, in which the state (through the Adjudicatory Commission) looks at only the relatively few DRI decisions that are appealed by the developer, regional planning council, or the State Land Planning Agency, the three parties with standing to appeal. The implementation of the DRI section of chapter 380 depends very largely on the initiative of developers in filing applications for development approval, and on local and regional governments in evaluating and acting on such applications. Thus, the DRI process has the potential for going forward in an effective and innovative way, even when the state takes a passive or even indifferent position. The DRI review effort, through its direct or indirect results, has the potential for helping shape the way in which local governments guide and manage their growth.

In the following section, we begin by reviewing Developments of Regional Impact in the first nine years of the program. We then describe some of the strengths and weaknesses of the process as seen by participants in it and assess the changes in how Developments of Regional Impact are identified. Some of the major policy thrusts are examined through brief case histories of actions of regional planning councils and local governments and the intensive negotiations within and among local governments, developers, and regional planning councils that may ensue. Such negotiations illustrate a major policy potential in the DRI process that has been largely overlooked.

The need for more effective monitoring of Developments of Regional Impact is also evaluated, particularly necessary in view of the extensive conditions typically attached to an approved Development Order, the spin-offs from the law in which some cities and counties have adopted "little DRI" processes of their own, and finally, the need to modify the standards and guidelines, with or without legislative action.

DRIs: A Statistical Review
A total of 338 applications involving Developments of Regional Impact were filed in the eight-year period from July 1, 1973 to June 30, 1981, and 42 more were filed by June 30, 1982.[126] Residential projects accounted for 187 of these applications through June 1981, involving proposals for more than 1 million housing units, most to be completed by the year 2000. Other major categories were regional shopping centers (37), phosphate mining projects (17), and major electrical transmission lines (15). Office parks (20), amusement and

recreational attractions (15), ports (16), petroleum storage (11), schools (4), airports (9), industrial plants (6), and finally hospitals (1) were other categories.[127]

More detailed analysis shows several important trends. First, there was a drastic decline in the number of DRI projects in each year of implementation until 1977–78, when the trend began to turn up again. From 142 DRIs filed in the first year, the figure dropped sharply to 62 in the second year; to 22 in the third year; to only 11 in the fourth year, 1976–77; and rose again to 23 in the fifth year.[128] By 1982, the figure increased to 42 (July 1, 1981 to June 30, 1982), bringing the total DRI count to 380. Although a variety of types of DRIs have been filed, the majority of the applications filed in the first five years of the program (202 out of 260) were for residential units or directly related projects such as office parks and shopping centers. Residential DRIs have dominated in every year. Of the 142 DRI applications in the first year of the program, 103 were for residential development. This figure dropped dramatically to 31 in 1974–75; 8 in 1975–76; and 3 in 1976–77; the trend finally started to turn back up in 1977–78 with 12 residential DRIs. The number of dwelling units involved in these DRI applications range from almost 700,000 units in the first year, 1973–74, to a still substantial number even at the low point in 1976–77 of 26,171 units.

The reason for the abnormally large number of DRIs in the first year of the program was that the DRI process came on line in the midst of one of Florida's most explosive construction booms. If the close to 1 million proposed dwelling units had been built, they would have accommodated 2.5 million more residents, assuming 2.5 persons per unit. Very shortly after the process got underway, however, the construction bubble burst, and there naturally was a drastic reduction in DRI applications. Furthermore, very few of the DRI projects that were approved in the first year of the program got underway before the building boom collapsed. The great majority of these projects lay dormant, and by 1978 were only beginning to be actually constructed in accordance with Development Orders issued five years earlier. The DRI data to 1978 show that DRI activity has fluctuated among major regions of the state, but in a composite sense most of the activity has occurred in the Tampa Bay, Southeast Florida, Orlando, and Jacksonville areas.[129]

The overwhelming majority of all DRI applications have been approved, with or without conditions, by local governments. Of 243 DRIs acted on in the period 1973–81, 9 percent were approved without conditions, 7 percent were subjected to outright denial, but most (84 percent) were approved with conditions attached. Outright denials declined after the first years; instead, proposals were usually approved but sometimes with conditions attached. Some extensive conditions were so difficult to meet that they amounted to a denial of the project. The practice of attaching conditions to DRI approvals increases the need for an effective monitoring process. Without monitoring to check on the status of sometimes major and important conditions, whose implementation may take one or two decades, there will be no assurance that the goals of the DRI section are ever carried out. This problem will be assessed in more detail.[130]

Another vital element of the implementation of the DRI process involved appeals. As noted earlier, the appropriate regional planning council, the State Land Planning Agency, or the developer filing an application for development approval has standing to appeal a local government's decision. From 1973 to 1981, 46 Development Orders were appealed. As of 1978, regional planning agencies initiated or were party to over half of the appeals, the State Land Planning Agency initiated or was a party to 25 percent, and developers initiated or were a party to 18 percent. In five cases, adjacent counties attempted to appeal DRIs but were subsequently rejected in court action as not having standing.[131] In just over half (24) of the 46 appeals, a negotiated settlement was reached; the Adjudicatory Commission dismissed the appeal but approved an amended Development Order. In two cases, the process has produced a dramatic illustration of the power of the state to overrule local government under the Land Management Act of 1972. In the Three Rivers case, the Adjudicatory Commission overturned a local government's approval of a major DRI and voided the Development Order,[132] and in another, the ESTEC Case, a county denial of a phosphate mining operation was overturned and the Development Order granted.

The question of standing to appeal a local government development order has become increasingly controversial as disputes arise over individual developments. As noted earlier, standing to appeal development orders to the Land and Water Adjudicatory Commission was sharply limited by the drafters of Chapter 380, and included only the developer or owner of the land, the State Land Planning Agency, and the Regional Planning Agency. All efforts to broaden standing by including adjacent local governments, individual citizens, or groups have been rejected.[133] As a result, there has developed a growing sentiment that an amendment to Chapter 380 to extend standing to appeal to adjacent local governments and certain citizens groups be enacted. Such a move would bring the Florida law in closer line with the model code's more liberal standing provisions. This will be one of the issues considered by the second Environmental Land Management Study Committee appointed by the governor in late 1982.

It is important in evaluating the ultimate impact of the DRI process to understand the widely differing approaches taken by the planning agencies to their role under the Land Management Act. The approaches vary from aggressive and forceful efforts to protect what are identified as regional and state values to a very passive approach in which the regional planning council sees itself as a facilitator or as a source of technical assistance, but not as having the power or responsibility to force local governments to comply fully with the intent of the law.

The appeals records of regional planning councils vary widely. The East Central Florida Regional Planning Council and the Southwest Florida Regional Planning Council each appealed only one DRI decision in the 1973–78 period. This low figure is not so surprising with regard to the Southwest Regional Planning Council, since relatively few DRI applications were filed in that period. It is much more significant with the East Central Regional Planning Council, since there have been many DRIs filed in that region (the Orlando area). The contrast between the Tampa Bay Regional Planning Council and the South Florida Regional Planning Council is even more striking. Each area has had a large number of DRIs filed, yet the Tampa Bay Regional Planning Council had filed only two appeals to 1978, while the South Florida Regional Planning Council had filed 17 appeals. Thus, we see that of the three Florida areas where development has been the strongest (Tampa Bay, Orlando, and southeast Florida), in only one, the southeast Florida area, has the regional planning council appealed on a regular basis. The significance of these contrasting attitudes comes into focus when one considers the critical importance of the negotiation process that has evolved between and among developers, local governments, and regional planning councils. Such successful negotiations exemplify the underlying potential of the DRI section of the law as a policy force in land and growth management.

The General Impact of the DRI Process: Negative and Positive Views from Friend and Foe.   As we said at the beginning of this section, no systematic body of data is available upon which to base a thoroughgoing evaluation of the DRI process. Collecting such data would require a massive effort extending over several years and costing a great deal of money, given the decentralized nature of the process itself. In the absence of solid data, we must rely on the perceptions of key participants to determine what impact the process has had to date and to provide some insight into our main concern—the political "health" of the process.

Most observers are agreed that at the minimum the DRI section of the law has brought about substantial improvements in the quality of development in cases that have been subjected to review. On balance, projects that have gone through the DRI process are better planned, more carefully thought through, and, in general, represent a higher quality development than would have otherwise been the case. One problem is that there has been no policy framework to guide the DRI process The 1978 state comprehensive plan did not provide that policy framework. In its 1980 report, the governor's Task Force on Resource Management called for the development of an integrated policy framework at the state and regional levels to guide, among other things, the DRI process.[134] However, some growth policies are emerging from the DRI process itself, especially in those areas where strong and aggressive regional planning councils are ready to appeal local government decisions that do not seem to take into consideration the more-than-local impacts of proposed developments.[135]

One major problem, to a lawyer/lobbyist for several major developers in the state, is that regional planning councils often intervene in what are really local matters with little regional impact and thus make a nightmare of the approval process for the legitimate developer.[136] This complaint has been echoed by many observers, including participants in the 1979–80 hearings of the governor's Task Force on Resource Management. His solution was the same as that recommended by the task force—a set of clear and binding state policies to be reflected in regional policies. Within a clear state framework, the DRI process could be truly used to factor in the regional and state impacts of local government decisions and not to impose regional council biases on the local decisionmaking process. Furthermore, this observer noted that a developer's right to appeal a Development Order to the Adjudicatory Commission was largely meaningless, because the politics of the situation were that those elected state officials would seldom overrule elected local officials in favor of the developer. It is true in only two cases has the Adjudicatory Commission made such a decision, although it has had several opportunities to do so.[137]

The environmental coordinator for a major developer, who had worked in the Division of State Planning and been responsible for the DRI process, has published articles critical of the degree to which the DRI process had become an adversary proceeding between regional agencies and the developer. He, too, noted that regional planning councils were often seen as focusing on local problems rather than truly regional issues, a problem aggravated by the lack of good regional data.[138]

In the implementation of section 6, the DRI section, a long-

standing argument centered on whether its standards and guidelines formed the only basis on which a project could be designated
as a DRI. One school of thought held that it was possible to draw
directly from the language of the act in order to either (1) apply DRI
status to a project that falls below the quantitative thresholds set
forth by rule or (2) to allow a project to be built even though it
exceeds these criteria. This question was resolved in a 1978 court
ruling in a suit between a major Florida developer and the State
Land Planning Agency.[139] In its opinion in favor of the state, the First
District Court of Appeals went beyond the issues raised by either
party to find that Rule 22F–2, with its quantitative thresholds, did
not reduce the division's responsibility "to a mechanical chore of
counting dwelling units or making other quantitative calculations."
The impact of the ruling is that identifying regional impacts allows a
qualitative judgment that can go beyond the quantitative criteria.
Armed with this ruling, the State Land Planning Agency has begun
to designate DRI projects that fall below the quantitative criteria and
to relieve projects of DRI status even though they exceed the
quantitative criteria.[140] This court decision has had the effect of
drastically increasing the workload of the Bureau of Land and Water
Management in processing binding letters, the process by which a
developer asks for a formal ruling on whether a particular project is
or is not a DRI. In the period from July 1, 1981 to June 3, 1982, 58
binding letters were processed. The trend is to rule that projects that
exceed the criteria are not DRIs, but there also have been cases
where projects that fall below quantitative thresholds have been
ruled to be DRIs.[141]

The issue of whether the standards and guidelines developed by
the first Environmental Land Management Study Committee in
1972–73 should be revised has been debated continually since the
original quantitative criteria were adopted. The governor's task force
in its final report recommended a comprehensive review of the
standards and guidelines as a top priority item for completion. The
legislature must act on any formal changes, but it is also true that the
present numbers can be ignored under the court ruling through the
binding letter process. A number of proposals have come forward to
develop new standards and guidelines applicable only to the coastal
zone, especially barrier islands, where the thresholds that trigger a
DRI would be lowered, or where designation could be made on the
basis of locational or environmental sensitivity criteria rather than
on numbers such as building units.

Two recent court cases have helped define the scope of the DRI
process, and both have been supportive of a broad definition and
strong implementation of Chapter 380. The *Estuary Properties* case[142]

involved a proposed 6,500 acre development in Lee County on the Southwest Florida coast. Over half of the area was made up of red and black mangroves, some 1,800 acres of which the developer proposed to destroy by dredging and filling. The Southwest Florida Regional Planning Council recommended denial of the project on the grounds that it would pollute the waters adjacent to the project, which in turn would damage commercial and sports fishing and the shellfishing industry. The Board of County Commissioners of Lee County accepted the DRI regional assessment and recommendations by the Planning Council and denied the Application for Development Approval. The developer appealed this action to the Land and Water Adjudicatory Commission and requested a *de novo* hearing. The Adjudicatory Commission upheld the hearing examiner recommendation that the appeal be denied. The developer then appealed that decision to the Florida First District Court of Appeal. The court ruled that the Adjudicatory Commission's action was an unconstitutional taking and remanded the case to the Adjudicatory Commission, requiring it to permit the development of the property unless Lee County was prepared to buy the property. The court ruled specifically that to restrict the developer from using the wetlands constituted a taking. This decision sent shock waves through the state. If upheld, it would have constituted a new and much stricter definition of what constituted a taking than had been applied in either the state or federal courts and would have virtually eliminated the ability of government to protect wetlands through regulation. Lee County and the Adjudicatory Commission appealed the decision to the state supreme court. That court addressed two key issues: (1) whether the Adjudicatory Commission had properly applied a balancing test in which the "interests of the state in protecting the health, safety, and welfare of the public" would be weighed "against the constitutionally protected private property interests of the landowner" and (2) whether denying the development was a taking. The supreme court held that a balancing test was, in fact, implied in Chapter 380 and was appropriate, but rejected the district court's conclusion that the Adjudicatory Commission had not properly applied the test in denying the developer's petition.

On the taking issue, the supreme court rejected the district court's ruling that denying the developer the right to build on the mangroves constituted a taking. The court held that "protection of environmentally sensitive areas and pollution prevention are legitimate concerns within the police power" and thus confirmed the right of government to protect environmentally sensitive areas such as wetlands without having to acquire the property. In so deciding, the court rejected the developer's claim that "no beneficial use of its property" would remain if the wetlands in question could not be developed. It further affirmed the proposition that "the owner of private property is not entitled to the highest and best use of his property if that use will create a public harm."

It was assumed by the drafters of Chapter 380 that where local governments failed to approve an application for development approval, the developer could and would where appropriate appeal such a decision to the Land and Water Adjudicatory Commission. Many have appealed, but only one has succeeded in reversing a county commission's denial. This occurred in the case of *Manatee County* v. *Estech General Chemicals Corporation*, 402 So. 2d 1251 (Fla. 2d DCA 1981). The developer, a phosphate mining company, was denied a Development Order by Manatee County in spite of a positive recommendation by the Manatee County Planning Commission. Fears of pollution of the Manatee River and Manatee Lake from the mining operation "slime pond" seemed uppermost in the minds of the county commission in rejecting the Application for Development Approval. The developer appealed the county denial to the Land and Water Adjudicatory Commission, which reversed the county action after a *de novo* hearing. The Adjudicatory Commission accepted the recommendation of the hearing officer that a Development Order be issued for the mining operation. Both the hearing officer and the Adjudicatory Commission itself added important new conditions to the Development Order, including the requirement for "a sand-clay mix in its slime pond at an additional expense of $7 million in order to reduce the harm which would result from a dam break." Manatee and Sarasota Counties filed petitions for review, and the Second District Court of Appeal heard the case and sustained the action of the Land and Water Adjudicatory Commission. While the case had a number of important aspects, its chief importance from our perspective was that it affirmed both the legal and political capacity of the Land and Water Adjudicatory Commission to overturn a local government in favor of a developer by issuing a Development Order of its own that the local government was bound to carry out.

The Intergovernmental Challenge.   Perhaps more than any other major land use initiative in the nation, Florida's land-management effort depends very heavily on an effective meshing of state, regional, and local government activities, with the state having only a sharply limited supervisory and monitoring role. At the time the Land Management Act was passed, local governments were ill-prepared to cope with land- and growth-management problems.

That situation has improved to some degree. A Florida League of Cities survey showed that in 1974 all cities in Florida with a population of 5,500 or more (113 cities) did at least have zoning ordinances. However, only 29 of Florida's 67 counties had zoning ordinances.[142]

A giant step toward correcting the weakness of local land use measures was taken in 1975 when the legislature passed the local Government Comprehensive Planning Act. According to the 1978 update of the Florida League of Cities survey, all Florida cities had met the July 1, 1976, deadline for designating a planning agency, though five cities chose to have the county assume the responsibility. As of 1978, 51 municipalities and 11 counties had submitted plans or elements of plans for review and comment to the Division of State Planning. The plan was required to include future land use, traffic, general sanitary sewer, solid waste, drainage and water, conservation of natural resources, recreation and open space, housing, intergovernmental relations, power plant siting, and a coastal zone element if the county or city were a coastal unit. By mid-1982, 419 of 461 cities and counties had adopted comprehensive plans that had been reviewed and commented on (approval not required) at the regional and state levels. Of the remaining 42 local governments, 38 had submitted plans for state review but had not finally adopted the plan at the local level. Only 3 of 67 counties had not adopted the plan, and all 3 were expected to be approved by January 1, 1983.[143]

With regard to the regional component of Florida's land- and growth-management initiative, the original legislation did not specify whether the regional agency in the DRI process should be existing or new regional planning councils, or some other regional unit. The act's chief sponsor and other supporters thought that a combination of regional planning councils and water management districts would be used. Instead, in every case, the Division of State Planning assigned the lead regional role to what were often newly assembled and poorly funded regional planning councils. Water management districts, in contrast, were, in the more populous areas of the state, established agencies with large staffs, but their expertise was confined to water resource planning and management. The South Florida Regional Planning Council found a practical solution: it contracted with what is now the South Florida Water Management District to carry out the regional review in the areas of water quantity, water quality, and certain vegetative areas. This approach worked so well that it was eventually extended as a contract requirement by the State Land Planning Agency to all regional planning councils in the state.[144] There is still a need for a better coordination of these efforts, and a need for a more thorough utilization of water management districts in both the DRI process and in the Critical Area designation process.

The role of the State Land Planning Agency, and especially its Bureau of Land and Water Management, in improving the intergovernmental dimensions of the state's land-management effort has been somewhat late in developing but seems to be gaining strength. The agency finally did develop a standard application form which was mandated on all regional planning councils. There still remains a need to better integrate the various state programs which come to bear on chapter 380. The need for a better policy framework to guide the growth-management process will be assessed later.

Case Studies.   Some insights into exactly how the DRI process is working can be gained through two brief case histories, both involving DRI projects on Florida's Gold Coast. In one case, the South Florida Regional Planning Council took an active lead, and in the other, a determined county played the lead role.[145] In the case involving the South Florida Regional Planning Council, one can begin to see some of the very real regional policy thrusts inherent in the Land Management Act if a determined regional planning agency is willing to push the regional authority to its utmost. It is also possible to see why local governments and developers alike have complained that regional planning councils, particularly the South Florida Regional Planning Council, have involved themselves at times in what is seen as local land use and other development issues.

At issue was a developer's 1975 application to the city of Homestead (Dade County) for permission to build a 3,175 acre residential, industrial, and commercial project with an 18-year build-out period that was to house almost 40,000 people. The South Florida Regional Planning Council voted to approve the project, subject to four major conditions. After holding a public hearing, the city of Homestead issued a Development Order. The regional planning council then voted to appeal the Development Order on the grounds that it did not reflect adequately the four conditions raised in its recommendations. One month later, after differences between the developer, the city of Homestead, and the regional planning council were resolved, the council voted unanimously to withdraw the appeal.

This brief sketch shows only the bare bones of a flesh and blood process that illustrates much about the capacities and limitations of the DRI procedure. Three of the four major regional conditions recommended by the South Florida Regional Planning Council were the result of the South Florida Water Management District's review. They included the possibility of saltwater intrusion into the freshwater aquifer, the adequacy of the supply of potable water for the project, and the adequacy of wastewater treatment and water supply service levels. Only the adequacy of access roads did not involve the water management district. The regional planning council was also concerned about the composition of low and moderate income housing in the project; and the possible imbalance between the revenues needed to provide new public services and the revenues to be generated by the proposed development. Some of the issues raised by the council are clearly regional in scope, but others seem more local in their nature, however critical they might be to the city and county.

When the decisionmaking process reached the hearing stage at the regional planning council level, the developer's arguments were typical of those made in many such hearings. They centered on the proposition that all problems did not need to be solved at the front end, that many of the issues would be dealt with at the appropriate time, or by the permitting process of other regional and state agencies, particularly those that were water related. It took almost daily, hard-nosed negotiations between the regional council's staff and attorney and the developer representatives to work out an acceptable revised Development Order. Neither Dade County nor the city of Homestead were actively involved in the negotiations.[146]

The experience in the Homestead case demonstrates the act's potential for the development of regional policy if a regional planning council chooses to assert its regional authority to the utmost and if it has a skilled staff and attorney.[147] The case also shows the crucial role of the water management district in producing the hard data on which tough conditions about regional impacts can be based. Furthermore, it illustrates the difficulty of drawing the line between genuinely regional issues and local issues in need of further attention by local government. This is an ongoing controversy which will probably never be solved until a clearer policy framework for regional assessment is established, and even then there will be frequent gray areas that come down to honest differences of opinion as to what is regional and what is not.

The Land Management Act can also be used by a determined county to develop and support broad growth management on its own initiative. The DRI case assessed here involved Broward County's lengthy controversy with the largest developer in South Florida, ironically, the only developer who supported the adoption of the Land Management Act in 1972. The Arvida Corporation proposed developing a project on 10,000 acres of land in the western part of the county, much of it low with severe drainage problems, with a proposed population of 90,000. The county denied the first application for development approval in April 1976 on the grounds that the county's land use plan had not been adopted, that the impact of the development on natural and manmade resources was not fully understood, that the site plan should include the entire 13,000 acres owned by the petitioner rather than the 10,000 acres under consideration, and that in general it was not necessarily good policy to convert to urban purposes land that could be used for agriculture.

In 1978, the county approved the Development Order, but with many substantial conditions and restrictions. The Development Order permitted the construction of up to 2,500 dwelling units on one part of the property, but at various stages of construction the developer was required to contribute land for elementary schools and a fire station, to construct a $150,000 fire station, and to take the responsibility for organizing a volunteer fire department. The developer also was required to provide low and moderate income housing in the county.[148]

Other important conditions were attached to the Development Order regarding water supply and sewage treatment, the provision of solid waste facilities, the protection of archaeological sites, the donation of $2 million for the acquisition of road rights-of-way and the construction of roads, and the development of a master plan for the entire project consistent with the Broward County Land Use Plan.[149] This review illustrates clearly use of the DRI process and the Development Order to exact very substantial commitments from developers, in effect in exchange for the Development Order. Many developers complain bitterly about this legal "blackmail," but typically negotiations are successful because a developer is eager above all to get on with construction.

The issuance of DRI approvals with important and substantial conditions attached to them requires a continuing monitoring to see that the public policies imbedded in those conditions are in fact carried out. Two studies concluded that the monitoring process needed substantial strengthening at both the regional and local levels.[150] In the Critical Areas section as well as the DRI section, Florida's land management law has not provided an adequate description of state, regional, and/or local responsibilities for assuring that public policies are applied over long periods of time as projects are built out. This is a problem that remains to be addressed more fully.[151]

Other Local Government Initiatives:
The Little DRI Process
Another way in which the coverage of the Land Management Act can be extended indirectly is when counties develop their own little

DRI process that picks up where chapter 380 leaves off. Dade County, which comprises 26 municipalities, is one of the better examples of this approach. When the county completed its new master plan, the county commissioners voted to develop a new governmental unit, the Dade County Development Impact Committee, to review and assess not only chapter 380 DRIs, but other large-scale developments that might duck under the very high thresholds of chapter 380. One of the people who fashioned this approach pointed out that, "it was apparent that a substantial number of proposals were being processed which fall just under the DRI thresholds and collectively represented a far greater impact on Dade County."[152] Furthermore, the county program took into account developments that might have a special countywide impact even though their size fell below even the county's lower thresholds. The county also imposed an interesting condition on itself: its development impact process would not be put into effect until the county government had assembled an information center that could provide the necessary data for the development impact statements required in the program.

As of mid-year 1977, when the little DRI process in Dade County had been in effect for two years, it was described as enjoying "a tremendous degree of success." Reportedly both developers and county government department heads were supportive of the procedure.[153] Other cities and counties in the state have adopted similar approaches, but there are no hard data on exactly how many and with what result. If such a trend does continue, one of the major deficiencies of the Land Management Act—its very limited coverage—would be corrected at least in part.

Summary of the Implementation
Record of the Land Management Act

Funding, Staffing, and Political Support.   Has the implementation effort received adequate funding and staffing as well as the policy and political support needed to fully use the Land Management Act? It is difficult to say. There is a considerable body of opinion that, after about 1974, a series of events and attitudes coalesced to lessen the intensity of leadership and support from the state level. These forces included a 1974–75 fiscal crisis brought on by the general recession, the legislature's growing hostility to alleged "lawmaking" by the executive branch, and a series of personnel changes that lessened the force of state leadership in state planning.

Responding to the question of whether the implementation effort did in fact go downhill after 1974, the man who had been the governor's key environmental aide during the law's adoption indicated that the budget-minded legislature probably had discouraged the Division of State Planning from "breaking new policy trails in the implementation effort."[154] Governor Askew himself noted that the recession eroded fiscal support for the implementation effort and that "in some ways a strong environmental support seemed to have faded somewhat." In the face of threats to attempt to repeal important sections of chapter 380, such as the Big Cypress Critical Area designation, the governor had to "let it be known that I would veto any such bill if it should pass." His consistent support of efforts to protect the 1972 initiatives allowed the implementation process at least to proceed without excessive concern that activities might result in a legislative effort to repeal the law. The governor noted that using the elected governor and cabinet to hear appeals and to develop Critical Area designations was rapidly outliving its usefulness and that an appointed board would be better. The governor stated: "The cabinet just doesn't have the time to do it, and it's unrealistic to expect that it ever will."[155]

Despite the governor's defense of chapter 380, it got a little lonely down in the trenches of the Bureau of Land and Water Management, where some key actors were eager to see the law more aggressively and more effectively implemented. According to one key staff member in the post-1974 period, the program suffered from "benign neglect from the governor's office." The staffer cited the reduction in funding for regional planning agencies, and the continued failure to get any added funding for new positions for the Bureau of Land and Water Management after 1974. The difficulty was that "we got no DOA support" (meaning the Department of Administration, in which the Division of State Planning was lodged). Also in 1974, the governor's environmental aide, who had served as a link between the governor's office and the Bureau of Land and Water Management, moved on to another job as head of the state's major environmental agency. From the point of view of key Land and Water Management staff members, added staffing would have allowed the state land planning agency to deal more positively with local governments and developers and to balance environmental, social, and economic equities while at the same time helping the development community with its concerns.

What then can be said about the related problems of governor's office support and adequate funding and staffing of the implementation effort? First, it must be said that Governor Askew in every public and private pronouncement throughout his term gave complete support to the full implementation of the Environmental Land and Water Management Act as well as other related growth-management legislation. In spite of a severe economic recession, the governor steadfastly maintained this support in the face of the strongest kind of criticism, much of it irrational and ill-founded, from certain parts of the private sector. Furthermore, the governor continued his strong initiative in adopting new legislation such as the water management district funding legislation in 1976, and his coastal zone management initiatives in 1977 and 1978. The governor also gave his full support to the implementation of the comprehensive planning requirement spelled out by the 1972 legislation.

What some of the governor's critics would have liked for him to do was involve himself in a more detailed way in the implementation effort by working more directly with the Division of State Planning and supporting it in more policy initiatives. Some of their frustration stemmed from an original feeling by a majority of the governor's 1972 Task Force on Resource Management that the planning effort should have been lodged directly in the governor's office to guarantee the governor's close and intimate relationship with the implementation effort. The governor did not agree with that approach, and there are those who feel that the result was that the program did in fact after 1974 not receive the direct attention of the governor to the degree needed to maximize the effectiveness of the law. On balance, Governor Askew must be given very high marks in the whole support of the land-, water-, and growth-management efforts over his entire administration. His style as the chief administrator, and the fact that the Division of State Planning was in an agency headed up by the lieutenant governor in whom the governor had every confidence, resulted in some feelings of frustration among those who would have wanted to see the governor engage more regularly in the implementation process. The question of whether the whole land- and growth-management effort would fare better if the planning function were lodged directly with the governor's office is one that will be tested in the 1980s, since Governor Bob Graham, shortly after assuming office in 1979, supported and the legislature approved a thoroughgoing reorganization of the agencies under his direction which has resulted in part of the planning function being moved to the governor's office and another part being moved to a state agency, the Department of Community Affairs.

Perhaps the most important question that can be asked about Florida's land- and growth-management effort is whether the intergovernmental requirements set out by the act, which assume the existence of a strong state framework, strong regional agencies, and equally strong local agencies, can be realized in sufficient degree to allow the act to be fully implemented. The weakness of all three levels have been discussed in this analysis, and it is clear that much remains to be done. Yet, it is also clear that Governor Graham is at least as interested as his predecessor was in trying to strengthen the capacity of the state at all three levels in both land and growth management and related areas. In this regard, the initial accomplishments by the 1979 and 1980 legislature are encouraging.

What can be said, finally is that Florida's Environmental Land and Water Management Act of 1972 is alive and reasonably well but suffers from major weaknesses in the monitoring and enforcement area. It survived a major threat of court action when the legislature reenacted a crucial portion of the law, and the present governor fully supports further development and implementation of Florida's pioneering land- and growth-management initiative. Issues that must be high on the agenda for the immediate future involve adequate funding, and a continued strengthening of an integrated state policy framework framing regional policies that are binding on local governments as they carry out their role in the land-management law. This integrated policy development is now underway at the direction of the governor and will be coming online for implementation by both the legislature and the executive branch in the next several years.

Knowledgeable political leaders in Florida are definitely turning their eyes to the future in terms of further strengthening Florida's land- and growth-management program. There is little concern that any major effort will be made to repeal any of the land- and water-management initiatives that were mounted in the early 1970s. The challenge now is to strengthen the land- and growth-management framework, which will involve further action at the local, regional, and state levels. In considering the politics of the future, former Governor Askew noted that the two pieces of legislation in most immediate need of further consideration were the strengthening of the coastal zone management law and the comprehensive planning effort. Askew was optimistic. As he put it, "We've turned the corner and support is going to increase rather than decrease." Askew did note several lurking dangers, including a probable effort to eat away in small pieces at the effectiveness of the legislation. He singled out especially the whole question of compensation, noting that, "The taking issue is a dangerous area that can really undermine your ability to carry out a good land and water management system." The governor stressed his view that extensive regulation in the public interest is proper, since "We are stewards of the land and we don't have a right to treat it badly."[156]

The 1978 gubernatorial and legislative elections in Florida were instructive with regard to the land and growth management. Growth management was not a major issue in the gubernatorial campaigns, nor was it featured in any of the legislative campaigns. The three leading Democratic candidates for governor were all committed, to one degree or another, to the land- and growth-management effort. The successful candidate was the leading legislative supporter of the Land Management Act in 1972, Senator Bob Graham. From the perspective of the politics of the future for land and growth management, the outcome was welcome indeed. Since assuming office Governor Graham has proven to be the strong leader for full and effective implementation of Florida's land-, water-, and growth-management initiatives that might have been expected of him, given his 12-year record as a member of the legislature. He took a strong leadership role in both the 1979 and 1980 sessions of the legislature as the Critical Area section of chapter 380 was readopted (1979) and the DRI section extensively amended in a way designed to strengthen its capacity for implementation (1980). Perhaps more important for the long run, the governor's Task Force on Resource Management has developed a policy blueprint for the future that would further strengthen the regional agency level, develop an integrated policy framework at the state, regional and local levels, and provide more adequate funding for land- and water-management implementation efforts, including the Land Management Act.

In looking beyond the political environment, one thing that stands out is that the growth pressures are back in Florida. The construction industry was well on its way to full recovery from the collapse of 1974 and 1975, and the worst of the economic slump in general seemed to be over for Florida. At first, the interest rate crisis of the early 1980s seemed hardly to dent the strength of the development industry, and any adverse impacts seem destined to be short term. When the high interest rates did not come down, the construction industry, especially home building, was hard hit, but even so, 42 Developments of Regional Impact were filed from July 1, 1981 to June 30, 1982. The energy crisis for the moment is history, and the state is again feeling all the pressures of growth, both positive and negative.

The Unfinished Agenda: A Planning/Policy Framework. Florida will grow to the nation's fourth largest state by 1990, to near 13 million persons. As the state faces the continuing of strong growth pressures, the question is whether the land- and growth-management system is sufficient to assure that the growth over the next decade and beyond will be environmentally sensitive, economically sound, and socially responsive to such needs as an adequate supply of low and moderate income housing. The answer to that question is no. The funding weaknesses for chapter 380 resulting in a totally inadequate monitoring and enforcement effort for the Land Management Act have been detailed earlier. An even more critical issue involves the lack of an integrated planning and policy framework that can assure that clear state policies frame regional policies and equally clear regional policies frame local government plans and policies.

The State Level.   Chapter 380, Florida's Environmental Land and Water Management Act, was never designed to be the sum total of Florida's land- and growth-management effort. The need for a state planning and policy framework within which chapter 380 and related laws such as chapter 373 (the Water Resources Act) could operate was recognized in the language of chapter 380 itself. The Florida State Comprehensive Planning Act of 1972 was supposed to provide the needed planning and policy framework. A decade later, with substantial sums of money and endless hours of work committed to the effort, success is still in the future. Yet, it is also clear that substantial progress has been made since the completion of the first effort in 1978. This multivolume effort contained much that was good, but no viable means of linking its plans and policies to other state agencies, much less regional and local governments, has yet been devised.

The governor's task force put the highest priority on the need to develop an integrated policy framework, and the Graham administration has responded by reorganizing the planning function in Florida by including it within an Office of Planning and Budgeting located within the Executive Office of the Governor. The whole effort was given a powerful boost when the task force recommendation that Comprehensive Regional Policy Plans be prepared and approved by the governor for consistency with relevant state plans and policies was approved by the 1980 legislature. That requirement cannot be carried out unless the state policies are sufficiently clear, brief, and well focused to provide a framework for review and approval of the regional policy plans. The state effort to develop such a set of "policy guides" produced initial drafts in functional areas that track roughly the elements that are being developed by regional planning councils in their preparation of policy plans. These drafts will be revised in the light of comments by interested parties, and public hearings will be held around the state for citizen input in 1983. The drafts have been prepared by the Planning and Evaluation Unit of the Office of Planning and Budgeting in concert with the relevant state agencies. A critical question is whether a set of sufficiently brief major policies will emerge from this effort that can and will assure the reflection of state interests in Regional Policy Plans.

The Regional Level.   The success of the state effort to produce Policy Guides that can frame the development of the Comprehensive Regional Policy Plans is crucial to that effort, but other things are needed, too. State funds have not been forthcoming to develop the plans, in spite of strong efforts to secure $1 million from the 1982 legislative session. Other funds may be found, but another strong push is needed to get funding from future legislative sessions. Carefully developed Regional Policy Plans are needed to give regional planning councils the framework within which to review Developments of Regional Impact and Development Orders in Areas of Critical State Concern. Such plans will also help prevent the intrusion of regional planning councils into matters that are local in nature. Finally, Comprehensive Regional Policy Plans can serve as the framework for a more meaningful review of Local Government Comprehensive Plans by regional planning councils to assure their consistency with regional and state policies.

The Local Level.   State and regional plans of high quality that reflect important state and regional values are important elements in Florida's growth-management system, but they will not be sufficient unless local government plans are adequate in both a qualitative and quantitative sense. Almost all of Florida's 461 local governments have now prepared comprehensive plans, but it is widely recognized that these plans vary greatly in quality. Furthermore, they have not been reviewed for consistency with regional and state plans that are themselves sufficiently clear and specific to be meaningful, because such plans are not yet complete. Florida will not have a comprehensive growth-management system that can cope with the growth pressures of the 1980s and 1990s unless and until qualitative standards are mandated for local government plans. The mandatory five year review of local plans would seem to be the logical time to change the system from "review and comment" by regional agencies to "review and approve."[157] If regional plans are in place that have been, in turn, approved at the state level, Florida will at last have an integrated policy framework from which to guide its growth. Anything less will not be enough to protect the state's natural systems and its quality of life. Such a system might encourage the development of "Little DRI" processes in additional counties. It would also make it easier for Florida to decentralize its coastal management effort largely to the local government level with regional/state review of local government plans to assure their consistency with state and regional policies. Developers and other private sector interests who feel that the present fragmented growth-management system works to their disadvantage might be more supportive.

In general, close and careful attention will have to be given to the role of local governments in the land- and growth-management process. There is a paradox in the heavy reliance the Florida system has placed on local governments. By doing so, the state automatically assumes responsibility for interacting more with local governments in the matter of land and growth management than would be the case if the state had chosen to act directly in implementing a land- and growth-management system. Thus, the intergovernmental approach automatically produces a situation of considerable tension between the state, regional, and local levels in which some of the classical problems of the federal system are brought into play. The question of how much authority should reside at each level, and how that authority should be carried out, and what degree of monitoring by the state or regional level should take place, are all questions that are being and will continue to be raised in Florida. These are questions that are raised in any state which uses the intergovernmental approach in its land- and growth-management initiatives. And they are perhaps the key questions that must be faced in developing a system that works effectively in meeting the goals and objectives of a land- and growth-management policy.

The development of Regional Comprehensive Policy Plans is vital to a more effective regional level in Florida's growth-management system, but more steps need to be taken. Careful consideration should be given to the relationship of regional planning councils with the state's existing water management districts. Some kind of partial merger between regional planning councils and water management districts might well be needed in order to put together an effective regional system that can fully exploit the policy potential of Florida's land and water legislation. The 1980 Regional Planning Council Law brought a number of changes needed, including more adequate state funding, and a broad structure that combines the ex officio city and county representation with gubernatorial appointments comprising one third of the council membership.[158] An independent regional and state view needed to have its presence felt on regional planning council boards, as had already been the case with water management districts. The 1980 Regional Planning Council Law also mandated the development of regional policy plans, discussed above in order to end the present case-by-case DRI reviews. The amendments to chapter 380.06(22) required the regional planning councils to submit lists of regional issues to be adopted by the State Land Planning Agency. Although not directly related by statute, both the regional policy plans and the lists of regional issues are being coordinated in their development. In the case of water management districts, further consideration may need to be given to the composition of those boards. Mandatory local government membership and a greater state share in regional planning council funding arrangements are still needed. The regional level is an important area which must be addressed further by future governors and legislatures in Florida in order to complete the land- and growth-management mechanism for the state, but the 1980 legislature made a good beginning.

The Politics of the Future

If Florida's land- and growth-management efforts are to be sustained and even strengthened during the decade of the 1980s, where will the political support come from? The homebuilder-developer-local government-environmental coalition that emerged in major legislative changes to Chapter 380 in 1979 and 1980 offers considerable promise for the future, but much needs to be done to strengthen the coalition. From the perspective of the developer, the priority need is a clear and directive state and regional policy framework to guide the actions of state, regional, and local agencies. This framework is a must, if the quid-pro-quos for developers' support—timeliness and certainty—are to be achieved. The 1980 legislature made a good beginning by mandating the development of regional policies, and the governor has strongly supported developing a state integrated policy framework for regional and ultimately local policies and plans. If these policies can be properly developed and put into practice, Florida's experiment in growth management will have been greatly strengthened.

The 1982 governor's race in Florida seems to have presented no threat to the state's land- and growth-management system. The incumbent governor, Bob Graham, ran for reelection and won easily with 66 percent of the vote. Florida thus was assured of 14 years of strong support for its program from the governor's chair under Askew and Graham. The effect of reapportionment and a move to single member districts is hard to predict, but many observers believe that it will strengthen support for effective growth management, especially in the senate. Others, it must be said, fear that legislators elected from single member districts will adopt parochial views that make it harder to reflect regional and state interests in growth management and in other areas. The primaries and November elections brought a number of new faces to the senate more friendly to growth management than those they replaced. Further-more, in the contest for president-designate of the senate, a person was chosen who also is likely to be strongly supportive of sustaining and even strengthening the state's growth-management system. The present senate leadership is less supportive, but the winds of change seem very likely to bring new support for growth manage-ment in the senate.

Both the governor and the speaker of the house lost no time in making it clear that growth management would be at the top of their policy agenda as Florida moves into the 1980s. The speaker named a Select Committee on Growth Management composed of most key committee chairs concerned with coping with growth. The governor named a new Environmental Land Management Study Committee (ELMS II) and made its first task the preparation of recommenda-tions to strengthen the monitoring and enforcement effort in both the critical area and Development of Regional Impact sections of Chapter 380. By late February 1983, strong recommendations for more dollars and personnel to strengthen monitoring and enforce-ment for critical areas had been developed, and similar recommen-dations for the DRI process were being considered. The governor's proposed budget released February 21, 1983, included over $700,000 in additional funds for the State Land Planning Agency in its critical area and DRI sections. The funds, if approved by the legislature, will add 13 positions to the Bureau of Land and Water Management and will be the first increase in staff and support dollars received by the State Land Planning Agency since 1974. Among other things, the funds will allow adequate staffing of field offices in the Florida Keys.

In response to a request by the Administration Commission, the Department of Community Affairs prepared an update report on the Florida Keys Area of Critical State Concern.[160] Based on that report, the department, acting as the State Land Planning Agency, made a number of important recommendations to the Administra-tion Commission, all of which were approved. These new initiatives included a directive to the State Land Planning Agency to prepare and adopt by rule under the Area of Critical State Concern designation a comprehensive land use map should Monroe County fail to do so; more vigorous enforcement of land use regulations through injunctive action against a delinquent county; allocation of funds to sustain the State Land Planning Agency's field office in the Florida Keys for two years; a directive that all state agencies evaluate their regulations as they applied to the Keys Critical Area Principles for Guiding Development; and a requirement that the Local Govern-ment Comprehensive Planning Act be amended to require that in Areas of Critical State Concern the Local Government Comprehensive Plan shall be approved by the state. These actions affirmed the determination by the State Land Planning Agency, acting in part at the direction of the Administrative Commission, to take a much more proactive role in the area of monitoring and enforcement. Strong support by the governor's office and what appears to be continued support in the legislature for effective implementation of Chapter 380 bodes well for the future in this component of Florida's growth-management system.

In January, 1983, a special group spearheaded by the House Select Growth Management Committee and the governor's office began to meet to hammer out legislative or other changes needed to strengthen the state's growth-management effort. The governor, the speaker of the house, key committee heads from both houses, and selected agency heads make up the group. One of its key concerns will be to develop a state and regional policy framework that can give more consistency and direction to the state's growth-management system and serve as the reference point for reviewing local government plans. Florida may be the only state in the nation whose leaders, as they face the challenges of the 80s and 90s, are more concerned with growth management—broadly defined—than any other one issue. Given that Florida is, and probably will remain, the fastest growing large state, that concern seems well founded.

5

California:
Planning and Managing the Coast

The Issue Context

The importance of the coast in the broad sweep of life in California is difficult to overestimate. Along the 1,100 miles of coastline are 15 counties, home to more than 13 million people, or 63 percent of the state's population. Within this area, two thirds of California's people are employed and about two thirds of the state's total economy is concentrated. Major industries such as manufacturing, energy development, international trade, recreation, tourism, and agriculture compete for the finite amount of space along the coast.

The coast includes some marked contrasts in development. In general, the northern coast is sparsely populated and has been losing population in recent years. Moving down toward San Francisco, development activity increases substantially and continues south of San Francisco (excepting Big Sur and San Luis Obispo Counties), intensifying to its highest level in the southern California coastal areas. California is similar to Florida in the importance of its coast for population, economic, and tourism/recreation functions. Thus, the conflicting demands for the use of the California coast have long been evident in that state.[1]

The first formal expression of concern by the California legislature involving the coast came in a joint legislative committee report published in 1931. The report recognized the importance of the coast for a wide variety of uses and noted that: "It is desirable that these land and water areas be so developed as to meet the needs of the people of all parts of the state, both now and in the future in an orderly manner." The Department of Natural Resources was ordered to make a full study of the problems and opportunities of the California coast and called for appropriating the then substantial sum of $5,000 to carry out that task.[2] In calling for more public beach ownership and increased public access to the coast, the report voiced a concern that continues to this day.

California Regional Commissions

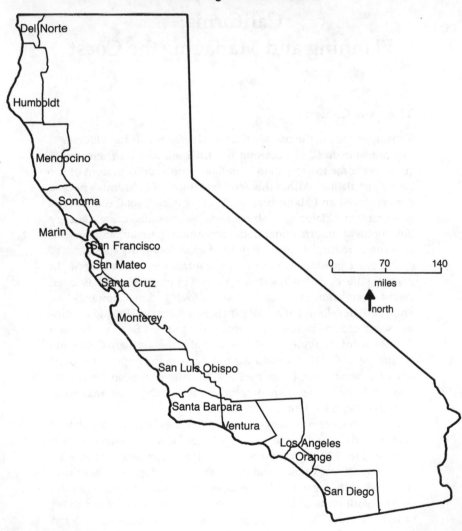

Del Norte

Humboldt

Mendocino

Sonoma

Marin

San Francisco

San Mateo

Santa Cruz

Monterey

San Luis Obispo

Santa Barbara

Ventura

Los Angeles

Orange

San Diego

0   70   140

miles

↑ north

In 1931, California had a population of over 5.5 million. Between
that time and 1964, the state underwent a growth explosion un-
paralleled in the history of the nation. By 1964, the population had
swelled to almost 18 million people, but during this period of
explosive growth little more was said about balancing the pressures
of growth with the need for environmental protection along the
coast. In 1964, California sponsored a conference on California and
the world ocean, which resulted in the creation of a governor's
Advisory Commission on Ocean Resources. Subsequent hearings
on coastline conservation led to the state's Marine Resources
Conservation and Development Act of 1967. However, the goal of
this landmark legislation was research and advice rather than
enforcement and control. It did direct the governor to begin work on
what was called a comprehensive ocean area plan. The governor
appointed such a commission made up of key state department
agency heads, a staff was organized, and some studies were
undertaken.[3]

An event of major importance occurred in 1965 when the California legislature established the San Francisco Bay Conservation and
Development Commission. The commision was first created as a
temporary body, mandated to begin a permitting program largely
aimed at controlling the indiscriminate filling of San Francisco Bay
but also charged with developing a plan for the Bay area. The plan
was presented to the legislature in 1969; the Bay Conservation and
Development Commission was made a permanent agency, and its
permitting authority was continued. The completed comprehensive
ocean area plan consisted mainly of an inventory of the California
coast and pointed up a number of old and new problems that
needed to be dealt with.[4]

Any attempt to catalog the full range of issues confronting the
citizens of California in their first attempt at managing the coast in a
more planned and environmentally sensitive manner would be
bound to omit some important areas. Almost every conflict and
problem that can be imagined along a coastal area were present in
one place or another, and since some 85 percent of the state's
population lived within an hour's drive of the coast, the steady and
sometimes dramatic degradation of the environment was clear for
many to see. Certainly the side effects of increased population—
urban sprawl and air and water pollution—were a major factor in
the rising concern for the coast. However, it was the buildings going
up and blocking public access to the beach that was probably the
most important factor in arousing the wrath of the public to the point
where decisive action was possible. The millions of Californians,
who expected to use the coast for recreation each year, were

increasingly finding the opportunity to do so limited and sometimes impossible. Furthermore, increasing notice was being taken of the destruction of marine life through dredging and filling (two thirds of the state's original wetlands had been destroyed), the erosion caused by indiscriminate building along the sand beaches, the ocean pollution from sewage outlets—these and many other problems were becoming increasingly evident in the 1960s and into the early 1970s in California.[5]

The increasing concern for the coast was deepened by a number of horror stories that soon attracted the attention of environmental groups and others concerned with the coast throughout the length and breadth of California. A major chain built one of its large motels directly on the Monterey beach; a major developer began to build a large residential project called Sea Ranch about 100 miles north of San Francisco that would have effectively blocked access to 10 miles of California beach. While local governments approved these projects, the citizens of California did not. Sea Ranch has become something of a symbol of both the need to protect the coast and the difficuty of resolving conflicts over coastal uses. Not until 1982 was the issue settled.

Many other large residential developments also were rapidly blocking off beach access, an access that Californians had come to think was theirs as a matter of right. The state's constitution seemed to support their views. In California, as in other states, the beach itself was public property, but in common with Florida and other states, access was the critical question. Public beaches to which the public has no access become, in fact if not in law, private beaches.[6]

Some of the problems contributing to the swelling tide of public concern for California's coast could have been solved by local governments. Cities and counties in California had long been delegated substantial powers in the area of land use. However, the environmental groups that had gained strength and numbers throughout the 1960s in California were virtually unanimous in feeling that local government had failed, and most thought failed miserably, to address the essential problems of conserving and protecting, rather than simply developing and exploiting, the California coast. To the environmentalists, the 53 cities and 15 counties (along with special interest groups, special districts, and state and federal agencies) seemed more concerned with instant returns for the tax base than with protecting the long-range environmental or even economic values of the coast. Coastal cities, counties, and some special districts, which relied on the property tax as the key prop for their financial base, were disinclined to heed the cries of environmentalists about the biological destruction of the coast. Environmentalists, on the other hand, became increasingly impatient with the failure of local government to face up to what they considered to be a crucial problem of protecting the coast for present and future generations. Positions became increasingly polarized, and charges and countercharges, many of them producing more heat than light, became very common.

Even if, by some miracle of foresight and political will, each individual local government had recognized and been willing to deal with all of the environmental implications of development proposals within its boundaries, many coastal problems would still have gone unsolved. They would have gone unsolved because there was no system in California's governmental structure for taking into account the more-than-local impacts of local development projects. Also, state agencies themselves were little inclined to consider how their own activities might be affecting California's coasts, even though concerns were being expressed for coastal protection and even coastal preservation. While the pressures for some kind of new state agency to concern itself exclusively with the coast would create yet another layer of government, its proponents saw it as the only way to bring order out of chaos and to assure that development decisions affecting the coast would be made at least reasonably coordinated.

By 1970 the environmental movement nationwide was reaching its peak, and certainly the same was true of California, where the coast became the primary focus of concern. The environmentalists wanted to have new rules and regulations to insure the full consideration of environmental as well as economic concerns in developing the coast and tried vigorously to pass a coastal management bill through the California legislature in 1970, 1971, and early 1972. When the bills all died in a conservative senate committee, in spite of apparent majority support in both houses of the California legislature, environmentalists forgot their differences, banded together in a new coalition, and took their case to the people of California. When 1972 drew to a close, a precedent-setting initiative had put California's first comprehensive coastal management legislation on the books.

The Politics of Adoption:
The Government versus the People

We will begin by reviewing briefly the attempts in 1971 and 1972, on the heels of the 1970 failure, to pass coastal zone management legislation. The 1970 elections seemed to hold much promise for the future of a coastal zone management bill in the 1971 legislature. The

Democrats—who were more sympathetic to the legislation—had won substantial control in the California assembly including the speakership. Democrats had also won—by one vote—control of the state senate. Shortly after the elections, the staff person for the California assembly's Natural Resources Committee contacted Janet Adams, a leading California conservationist, and proposed that plans be laid for a major effort to pass coastal legislation. Janet Adams had been active in the successful effort to pass the Bay Conservation and Development Commission legislation and had worked to elect Congressman Pete McCluskey, who later became Governor Brown's first secretary of resources.[7]

Adams quickly agreed to the proposal and called an organizational meeting in San Francisco that established the California Coastal Alliance as the key group responsible for directing and coordinating environmental support for coastal legislation. Harnessing the efforts of a large number of independent environmental groups proved to be no simple task. Many were fiercely independent and accustomed to taking strong noncompromising stands on environmental issues. Often competitive with each other, many environmentalists were suspicious of any efforts to pull them into an alliance which inevitably would involve some compromises and adjustments to individual group's goals. In spite of these difficulties, by March 1971 some 34 organizations had joined the Coastal Alliance. By this time, its drafting team had produced an outline for a coastal bill. California assemblyman, Alan Sieroty, who had sponsored the unsuccessful coastal bill in 1970, worked closely with the drafting team.

The legislative campaign to pass the 1971 bill began with a press conference organized by Assemblyman Sieroty and an impressive alignment of co-sponsors, including the powerful speaker of the California assembly, Robert Moretti. The proposed bill contained four key elements: (1) a thorough study of the coastal zone to determine "ecological planning principles and assumptions"; (2) preparation of a long-range coastal zone conservation plan; (3) an interim permit system for the coast; and (4) creation of a state coastal Conservation Commission and six regional coastal zone conservation commissions. This framework held up in a remarkably consistent way through succeeding legislative and initiative battles over the next two years.[8]

Assembly bill 1471 had the strong support of the Democratic leadership in the house (assembly), but it also had bipartisan support both in and outside the legislature. The campaign was organized by the California Coastal Alliance and was dubbed the "Save Our Coast" campaign. The alliance had produced a formidable mass of information to support its position that something had to be done to protect the California coast. More than 2,000 photographs of oil spills and other coastline disasters were widely circulated, as were literally millions of brochures and fact sheets.[9] The alliance was supported by more than 100 organizations with some 1,400 local chapters among them. Although this impressive array of support seemed adequate to success, the opposition was also well organized and determined.

In an effort to broaden its base of political support, the alliance legislative committee met for intensive negotiating sessions with local government organizations, including the California League of Cities, the California County Supervisors Association, real estate groups, large property owners, utilities, opposing unions, and others—always seeking compromises that would solidify support for the legislation. The city and county associations did support some form of coastal legislation, if local governments were given key responsibilities. However, to the disappointment and chagrin of the environmentalists—who felt in many instances that they were swallowing their principles by compromising—most opponents showed little interest in reaching any sort of compromise. In the eyes of one of the key leaders of the alliance, "The overconfident opposition threw away its opportunity to win through such compromises. It conceded not one obdurately held position and utterly failed to recognize that a legislative compromise would be in its own interests."[10]

With Speaker Moretti's solid support and the strong support of many other assembly members, the bill passed the assembly by a two-thirds margin. Despite this heartening victory, the battle was obviously far from over. The assembly-passed coastal bill was assigned to the senate Natural Resources Committee, where it failed once again. One version of why this committee consistently refused to pass the legislation was that a majority were "old guard-type" senators who were "bought, body and soul, by big oil, big developers, and other special interests."[11]

This 1971 defeat brought a different response than the one in 1970. In the interim, environmentalists had "put their act together" and were by no means prepared to accept what they considered a temporary setback. They immediately began preparing for another major effort in the 1972 California legislature and enlisted the support of a senior Republican senator from a coast district, Donald Grunski, as a sponsor for coastal legislation. It was while planning the 1972 legislative effort that Coastal Alliance leaders first began to talk among themselves about the possibility of going directly to the people in an initiative drive if the legislation was again defeated in the legislature. An initiative proposal was quietly drafted and held in the wings. Although the initiative option was no secret, there is little evidence that the opposition took this threat seriously. Some opponents later expressed strong regret that they had not supported the thoroughly compromised legislative bill and instead found themselves saddled with a much stronger version approved directly by the voters.[12]

The legislative effort in 1972 was essentially a rerun of the 1971 struggle. The assembly again passed the legislation easily by a large majority, but it again languished on the doorstep of the senate Natural Resources Committee in spite of Senator Grunski's sponsorship. By the middle of May 1972, all chances of the bill passing the legislature had ended, and the Coastal Alliance moved ahead with its efforts to go directly to the people to "save the coast." The defeat sent the Coastal Alliance and its allies to the people in no mood to compromise with an opposition that the alliance felt had by and large refused to cooperate with it.

In California, the voters' initiative has a long history of intense use. To qualify or place on the ballot a statutory initiative, a proposed action must receive the supporting signatures of not less than 5 percent of the state's electors. The California Coastal Alliance and its supporters faced the formidable task in May 1972 of securing over 400,000 signatures in a few short weeks. The task required collecting some 16,000 signatures a day for about 30 days, having them cleared through county headquarters, and checked and certified as acceptable. In an amazingly short period, with the dedicated efforts of an estimated 10,000 persons, signatures were filed with county clerks of 47 counties in California. This filing was done on June 9, 1972, and while 12 percent of the signatures were invalidated, on June 19, 1972 the alliance was notified by the secretary of state that the initiative had qualified with 418,000 valid signatures—18,000 to spare.[13]

The compromised versions of the earlier coastal law proposals had given local governments a strong role in implementing coastal legislation, but that was not true of the initiative provisions. Proposition 20, as it came to be called by its placement on the California ballot, was developed along the lines of the original bill drafted by the California Coastal Alliance. It provided for a state coastal commission and six regional commissions and included a mandate to develop a plan for the coast and carry out a permitting system in the interim period. Most of the compromises that the Coastal Alliance and its supporters had been willing to offer in an effort to get the bill through the legislature were abandoned.[14]

Proposition 20 was to be on the ballot in November. There was very little time to mount an effective campaign, but on the other hand the organization had already been put together, it had been tested in the fires of controversy, and it was ready to go. Several encouraging things happened to the effort very early. Key leaders in the California legislature, including the speaker of the assembly and the senate president pro tem endorsed proposition 20, and by August 1972 some 60 legislators had joined the bandwagon. This was unprecedented in California, since legislators as a rule kept carefully aloof from initiative campaigns. Members of California's congressional delegation and city and county officials, including candidates for office, began to make proposition 20 an element in their campaign or endorsed the proposition. The press began to rally in support of the effort and thus produced a very large amount of public exposure at no cost to supporters.[15]

All kinds of events were mounted to lend publicity and mobilize support for the campaign, including the "great coast bike ride" from San Francisco to San Diego, led by senate president pro-tem, James Mills. As this entourage rolled down the coast, it was joined at various points by large numbers of Californians and attracted a remarkable amount of favorable publicity. Support came from many quarters—from movie stars, from Dennis the Menace cartoon artist, Hank Ketchum, who donated two cartoons used effectively in the campaign, and from business groups in the form of both dollars and in-kind contributions. In Orange County, where a million votes were at stake, one young volunteer operating from her home put together a volunteer effort in which every voter in Orange County was called twice during the campaign. Cause and effect cannot be assigned with certainty, but in any event Orange County supported the initiative, though by a small margin.[16]

In terms of dollars, the Coastal Alliance put $145,000 into the campaign, and the Sierra Club, the strongest conservation group in California, put up $75,000. On the other side of the contribution fence, most of the many oil and land companies made substantial contributions to the effort to defeat the proposition. These efforts ranged from $50,000 each by two large land development corporations, to $35,000 by Standard Oil Company of California, to somewhat smaller contributions by other oil companies including Texaco, Mobil, and Gulf. Southern California Edison reported contributing $27,633, while General Electric provided $30,000 to the opposition campaign.[17]

One estimate had it that the opposition had over $1 million for buying media time. The leader of the Coastal Alliance campaign noted that "Oil companies, construction outfits, and developers, among others were pouring money into the campaign against the coastal initiative." This effort was counterbalanced at least in a small way by a Federal Communications Commission oral ruling that proposition 20 was a controversial issue of public importance and that radio and television stations had a responsibility for presenting both sides in a balanced manner. As limited as the ensuing media exposure was, it apparently was very effective.[18]

The foot-soldiers in the drive to collect signatures and support for the initiative were the members of the Coastal Alliance, which had grown from its original 8 organizations to more than 700 participating groups. *The Los Angeles Times* gave the initiative its strong backing, as did much of the other state media. While the California League of Cities opposed the effort by a vote of 124–74, many cities supported the initiative, including Los Angeles, San Diego, and Sacramento. Election day was a happy time for the exhausted supporters of Proposition 20, for it had carried by 800,000 votes—a healthy margin of 55 percent of the vote. One observer noted that the urban population really carried the day for Proposition 20. In Orange County the effort had done well to barely pass, and it lost badly in the smaller northern California coastal counties. For instance, it received only 17 percent of the vote in Del Norte County.[19]

Key Provisions of Proposition 20
The California Coastal Zone Conservation Act of 1972, put on the law books by the efforts of the citizens and electors of the state, involved the creation of a state California Coastal Conservation Commission and six regional commissions. These agencies were directed to do two important things during the life of the commission. First, the state commission and its regional arms were directed to prepare a long-term plan for the coast of California. In the interim, they were to operate a permitting system regulating development activity on the coast (a strip 1,000 yards wide measured from the three mile territorial limit). The state commission was established as a 12-member body made up of an equal number of public and local government members appointed by the governor, the speaker of the assembly, and the senate rules committee, and including a representative from each of the six regional commissions.[20] The public members on the regional commissions were appointed by the same state officials. The local officials who made up the other half of the membership were selected by cities, counties, and local organizations such as the Association of Bay Area Governments in the San Francisco region.[21]

Planning.   The California Coastal Zone Conservation Plan was the prime responsibility of the statewide commission, but cities and counties had some input into the process. The regional commissions were an important part of the state planning mandate.[22] The purpose of the plan was "to provide for maintenance, restoration, and enhancement of the quality of the coastal environment and for the orderly, balanced utilization and preservation, consistent with sound conservation principles, of all coastal zone resources."[23] The plan was mandated to contain elements that related to land use, transportation, conservation, recreation, public services, utilities, population density, and public access. For planning purposes, the area in the coastal zone was more extensive than that provided for in the permitting process. The planning boundary extended inland either to the highest elevation of the nearest coastal mountain range or five miles from the mean high tide line, whichever would be the lesser.[24]

The schedule for planning was tight. By August 1973, the commission was to publish objectives, guidelines, and criteria for collecting data and conducting studies. By February 1974, cities and counties were to submit their data and recommendations to the regional commissions. By August 1974 the regional commissions were to submit tentative recommendations to the state commission. Final comments to the state commission from the regional and local levels were due by April 1, 1975, with the plan to be adopted by the state commission by December 1975.[25] The task was a massive one, but, in fact, the coastal plan was developed on schedule.

Permitting. The new law provided that virtually no development would take place in the 1,000-yard coastal zone without a permit from the appropriate regional commission. The directive to the regional commissions was very broad and general, leaving them much leeway to decide whether or not to grant a permit. According to the law: "No permit shall be issued unless the regional commission has first found both of the following: (a) That the development will not have any substantial adverse environmental or ecological effect; (b) That the development is consistent with the findings and declarations set forth in Section 27001 and with the objectives set forth in Section 27302. The applicant shall have the burden of proof on all issues."[26] Some exclusions were provided for in the legislation, involving primarily built-up urban areas, but even in these areas no major changes could be made without a permit. A very broad appeal provision made it possible for environmental groups and invidivual citizens to appeal the granting or denial of permits by the regional commissions to the state commission. The planning and permitting mechanisms were to expire on the 91st day after the end of the 1976 legislative session, by which time it was assumed that new permanent legislation would be on the books.

The burden of proof was laid clearly on the permit applicant by the requirement that a majority vote of the total membership of the regional commission was required for approval of a permit.[27] Furthermore, the act made clear its special concern for some kinds of coastal activities by providing that a two-thirds vote be required for permits involving dredging and filling, for developments that would reduce public access to the water's edge, or developments that would reduce the size of any beach or area otherwise usable for public recreation.[28] The appeals provisions in proposition 20 carried the clear imprint of its environmental sponsors. Any person aggrieved by the approval or denial of a permit could appeal the regional commission action to the state commission. The state commission could refuse to hear the appeal if it decided that no important issue was raised by the appeal. The finest control system imaginable cannot accomplish very much unless it is given adequate financial resources. Understanding this, the framers of proposition 20 provided a total of $5 million to the state commission for both the planning and operational expenses of the state and regional commissions for the four-year life of these commissions.[29]

Local governments had been divided as to whether a state commission was required at all, although, of course, after the initiative was approved they had little choice in the matter. The League of California Cities recognized the need for some state involvement but had urged that most land use control responsibilities remain with local government. Many cities in California did in fact support proposition 20 as a mechanism by which they could gain some influence over land use decisions with more-than-local impacts.[30] Counties in California had taken the position that the job could be done by local government if the state were to set standards and goals and provide the necessary resources.[31]

The question of regional commissions also had been hotly debated when coastal legislation was under consideration. One strong argument for such commissions was the great diversity along the California coast. On the damp, cool, and sparsely populated northern coast, the economy has depended on timber, fishing, agriculture, and some tourism. In contrast, the dry southern coast is highly urbanized, heavily populated, and undergoing great growth pressures.[32] There was a feeling that regional commissions could best represent these diversities in terms of both planning and permitting in fragile environmental areas. At the same time, there was also a perceived need for uniformity, and proposition 20 looked to the state coastal commission to achieve this. The administration of the budgets for all seven commissions was placed in the hands of the state commission, which was charged with providing guidelines both in the planning and permitting areas to assure the needed common approach by the regional commissions. The final responsibility for adopting a coastal plan and for making annual progress reports to the governor and legislature was placed exclusively in the hands of the state commission.[33]

The Politics of Implementation

The Permitting Process Under
Proposition 20

The California Coastal Zone Conservation Act of 1972, the result of the Proposition 20 effort, was a model of brevity compared to its 1976 successor; its goals and policies, broad and general. In order to judge its effectiveness, we will first examine the record of the permitting system provided for in the 1972 act, and then the making of the required California coastal plan to be submitted to the 1976 California legislature.[34]

During the almost four-year period from the issuance of the first permits in early 1973 to the completion of legislation action on a new coastal law, almost 25,000 permit applications were acted on, and many issues were dealt with. While the permitting itself was not carried on within the framework of a well-developed plan, the regional commissions developed policies along the way that would be reflected in the California coastal plan (which was being prepared at the same time and by much the same staff responsible for the permitting effort). Our interest in the implementation process will focus on the kinds of issues that were raised, the approach taken by the state and regional commissions to these issues, and the reaction by key California groups, in terms of either building or weakening political support for a continued strong coastal planning and management program.

One detailed assessment of the permitting record identified a number of problems, each of which had implications for political support for the coastal zone effort. First, there was a failure to coordinate the activities of the regional bodies with each other and with the state commission in such matters as drawing boundaries and settling disputed cases, and no system was developed for treating state commission decisions as precedents for regional agencies. Second, there was no provision of authority for the state commission to call up appeals of regional actions. This led to a potential unevenness among the regions, with appeals dependent upon the alertness, capacity, and interests of individual citizens or citizen groups. Third, the substantial autonomy of regional commission staffs, where each regional commission appointed its own executive director, led to some fragmentation and hostility between state and regional staffs. The relative looseness of the approach could also be viewed as a source of strength insofar as regional differences were accommodated, and the charge of state domination of the process was somewhat minimized. Fourth, there was the potential danger that other state agencies might resent the invasion of the state coastal commission into their turf. In reality, both local governments and other state agencies were on balance helpful in the state and regional commissions' effort to get started in a very short timeframe (Proposition 20 took effect November 8, 1972, with permit requirements effective February 1, 1973.)[35] Fifth, there was a failure to develop a formalized working agreement with state agencies that would have simplified and expedited the management of the coastal zone. Only with the federal government's Army Corps of Engineers and the Association of Area Bay Governments (ABAG) were formal letters of understanding adopted to spell out the procedures where the jurisdictions of the two agencies overlapped. Sixth, there was a slow start in establishing a good working relationship with local government. This, of course, was a key to long-term sustained support for the planning and management activity in the coast. According to this evaluation, the relationships between the state and regional commissions and local governments improved over time, although some local units still viewed the act as an unwarranted invasion of home rule authority. In a general way, local government reactions ranged from "glad to have you" to grudging acceptance and an obvious wish that the whole effort would go away.[36]

Joe Petrillo, the man who headed up the permit section of the state coastal commission and served later as its general counsel, noted that the initial strategy of the commission was to deny almost all exemptions, but to deny very few, if any, permits, going instead with the attachment of conditions, far-reaching and large in number where necessary.[37] Petrillo recalled that he himself had gone directly to citizens to encourage them to organize as a counterbalance to special interests. He had set up a series of workshop training sessions to show small groups how to participate in regional commission hearings and how to appeal decisions. This unorthodox approach apparently had the support of the commission's executive director.[38] On the question of the quality of appointments to the regional commissions Petrillo indicated that a few of the initial appointments were so "weak" that they seemed even to be aimed at assuring that the act would not be strongly enforced. State commission appointments were seen as more sympathetic toward conservation and more sensitive to the environmental problems on the coast.[39]

One of the most significant of the initial operating decisions concerned the format of regional and state hearings. Although Petrillo was a lawyer, he argued against the imposition of a quasi-judicial format. He believed the stiffness and formality of such a hearing would not allow meaningful participation by ordinary citizens. After a tough battle, the attorney general's office agreed to a more informal approach. As a result of this crucial decision, Petrillo noted, coast watch groups were formed with a few people in each region who attended all regional commission meetings and were ready, willing, and able to institute appeals when that was called for. The Sierra Club, with his strong support and urging, hired two full-time persons (one in the north and one in the south) to do nothing but monitor the work of the regional coastal commissions.

Petrillo also noted that over the almost four-year period of permitting under proposition 20, some important political changes took place at the local government level up and down the coast. Both he and others interviewed felt that more and more often people sympathetic to proposition 20's environmental goals were being elected to city councils and county commissions. By 1975 at least three of the regional commissions were perceived as being more environmentally oriented than the state commission, largely because the local governments there were increasingly sensitive to such issues.[40]

Petrillo also pinpointed the close relationship between the permitting process and the planning effort being carried on concurrently by the state and regional commissions. Inevitably in the making of permit decisions some policy orientation began to evolve. He also noted the political impact of denying a really big development—the word got around that the commission meant business and that there was no point in bringing really bad projects in for permit approval. In his view, as citizens got more and more strongly involved in the permitting process, it was possible to sustain some important denials. By the end of the first year, the commission had gained confidence in its ability to come to grips with some of the toughest questions, even the question of whether or not to locate nuclear power plants on the coast.[41]

Overall, this key observer and participant felt that the permitting process did stop the worst abuses of large developments. However, the permitting staff came to realize that in order to deal with the cumulative effects of many small projects (which in the end could do as much damage to the coast as any single large undertaking) a planning approach was absolutely necessary. This experience with the limitations of the permitting process had a good deal to do with the kinds of recommendations developed by the coastal commission for the planning certification process in which local governments were to play a key role.[42]

A key environmental leader who had led the fight for proposition 20 indicated that she and other environmentalists found the eternal vigilance required to make the permitting process work was "tougher than any of us felt we could reasonably live with in the long run." The California Coastal Alliance and other groups did organize coast watch groups to monitor the work of the commissions and instructed them in "How to make a presentation, how to appeal, and other such instructions so that they didn't just go there as innocent lambs." She noted further that many of the leaders had learned the value of monitoring from their experience with the Bay Conservation and Development Commission. She conceded that one important conservation group got a little hysterical and filed a lot of appeals that really were not necessary. That situation was brought under control, and the process seemed to work effectively after that.[43]

The executive director of the North Central Regional Commission, Mike Fischer, expressed the view that the permitting process had "worked surprisingly well, considering all that might have gone wrong." He cited the successful effort to involve citizens heavily in the process. Perhaps the major weakness was problems with the lack of in-depth information on which to make decisions and an inability to apply a full range of facts to a particular geographical area.[44]

Sea Ranch, a project dating from the 1960s that helped fire citizen interest in protecting the coast, continued to resist all efforts at settlement until 1982. The state coastal commission set conditions on further development of lots involving beach access, scenic views, and septic tanks. The Sea Ranch Property Owners Association filed suit in 1977 claiming an inability as individual lot owners to meet the conditions. A three judge federal court ruled in 1981 in favor of the coastal commission, holding "that the commission's requirements for access are reasonable, proper and legally required."[45] In 1980, the legislature injected itself into the long-standing dispute by passing the Bane bill (assembly bill 2706) authorizing the payment of $500,000 to the Sea Ranch Association in exchange for accepting the public access and view protection conditions. The association at first rejected this settlement, but in the light of the federal district ruling it decided to reconsider its decision to appeal the court action and accept the settlement. Thus the issue after a decade was settled. Commission executive director, Mike Fischer, called the court decision "a major victory for the people of California and the nation who will not be denied access to the coast."[46] The case illustrated the capacity of the permitting system to achieve public policy goals, as well as how difficult and complex the process can be. Implementation of the beach access provisions is moving forward in a cooperative coastal commission-coastal conservancy effort, and the trimming of trees to restore ocean views will be done at a later time when the state coastal commission has funds available for the work.

With regard to relationships among the regional commissions and in turn with the state commission, one observer commented that it took two years for the coastal commissions to get together for a meeting, and when they did "it was pretty wild." He attributed this failure to achieve closer coordination largely to a state commission attitude that it was best not to get too involved with regional commissions. Regional representatives to the state commission were not viewed as delegates but as independent state commission members.[47]

One environmental leader assessed the overall implementation effort as "pretty good," though having only very broad policies to follow left the state commission "open to be very tough sometimes and not nearly tough enough at other times. They tend to give away things sometimes because they think maybe they'll lose them anyway." This characterization of the state commission's staff, and especially the executive director, as being too prone to make compromises to avoid sharp political controversies was repeated by a number of other observers.[48]

The permitting process was a controversial attention-getter. Douglas and Petrillo, in an article on the California coastal management program, analyzed 10,432 permits that were issued through December 1974. Of these, 9,997 permit applications had been approved, and only 453 had been denied. One thing suggested by these data was that proposition 20 did not bring construction to a halt on the coast. However, it is important to evelute these figures in the overall context. Most of these permits were for single family homes or other very small projects, often in areas which were already developed.[49] The permit conditions designed specifically to control density, appearance, and public access to the shoreline and generally to minimize adverse environmental effects were typically attached to large and controversial projects. Furthermore, the impact of the act cannot be fully judged without taking into consideration the fact that its very existence caused the modification of many projects before they came to the commissions for permits.

Many developers simply did not apply when it became clear that the plans they had made would in all likelihood be denied.[50]

The permit load at the regional commission level was extremely heavy, particularly in the urbanized areas. The South Coast Regional Commission (Los Angeles and Orange County), which had the heaviest workload, met 43 times to review permits in 1973, and meetings often ran from early morning until past midnight. Permits were required for almost any kind of activity by the private or government sector, including lot splits and subdivisions, waste discharges, removal of major vegetation, and other such matters. Some exemptions were included if certain conditions such as the dredging of existing navigation channels, improving single family residence at a cost less than $7,500, and other routine repair and maintenance activities were met. One assessment held that more flexibility for the commissions to exclude already built-up and stable areas from the permit process would have been helpful in reducing the high volume of permit applications and that approach was subsequently adopted.[51]

Experience showed that the 1,000-yard inland boundary for the permitting system was too restrictive in some places. On the other hand, the data for drawing the boundaries in a more sophisticated way simply were not available during the time frame needed to put the law before the public. Another important issue involved the grandfather provision of the act, which provided that developments undertaken prior to November 8, 1972 would not be subject to the permitting process. As elsewhere, the question of vested rights has been a difficult and perplexing one for the coastal commissions. The general rule followed was that a person who had actually started construction in reliance on a final government approval and had incurred liabilities through spending for labor and materials, had the right to complete that effort even though there was a subsequent change in the law. The grandfather clause in California has been the cause of a substantial portion of the vested rights litigation involved in proposition 20. On balance, most developers seem to have gone along with both the letter and spirit of the law, while others have pushed the limits of what constitutes a vested right to its ultimate extent.[52]

As those interviewed pointed out, the burden of proof is definitely on the applicants in the permitting process. Before a coastal commission could issue a permit, it had to make a positive finding that "development will not have any substantial adverse environmental or ecological effect" within the permitted area and that the development was consistent with the policies and objectives of the act. The requirement that development be consistent with the policies and objectives of the act meant that the regional commission had to consider a potential impact within the context of the overall coastal or planning area, thus broadening the implementation effort. For a permit to be issued, there had to be a positive vote by a majority of the full membership of the commission, not simply a majority of those present. An extraordinary vote of two thirds of the full membership was required in permits seeking permission to dredge and fill coastal waters, reduce the size of a beach or recreation area, put restrictions on public access to the shorelines, interfere with ocean views from the nearest highway, adversely affect water quality, fishery, or agricultural areas, or affect open waters heretofore free of visible structures.[53]

As noted earlier, the appeal procedure was very broad and gave access to appeal to virtually any interested citizen in the state. Through December 1974, of the 464 appeals that had been taken from regional commissions to the state commission, 156 permits were approved, 141 were denied, 22 claims of exemption were approved, 41 were denied, 54 appeals were withdrawn after filing, and 42 were determined to be without merit. In 161 cases, appeals were not heard at all on the grounds that they raised no substantial issue.

One way of evaluating the appeals process is to ask whether the state commission decisions on appeals tended to strengthen or weaken the implementation of the act. According to one assessment, based on appeals in just over one year, the state commission on the average was tougher in enforcing the objectives of the act than the regional commissions were. The state commission had upheld regional commission permits 49 times and reversed the regional action 30 times. The state commission approved permits which had been denied by the regional commissions in only 6 cases, and in 47 cases a regional denial had been upheld at the state level. Thus, it can be seen that the state commission very rarely overruled a regional commission's denial, but more often denied a permit after the regional body had granted it. It is fair to note that in a majority of the cases involved in this assessment, the state commission agreed with the regional commission, whether or not the action was positive or negative. However, the state commission, in upholding a regional commission's approval of a permit, often imposed additional conditions, often very important ones.[54] According to Douglas and Petrillo, "Many projects approved by a region which could have adverse environmental impacts or which are inconsistent with emerging Coastal Plan policies are not appealed because no individual or neighborhood group is directly affected." The solution proposed for this deficiency was to amend the law to give the state commission the authority to call up appeals when it felt it was necessary to do so.[55]

With regard to monitoring and enforcement after permits were approved, California's implementation record is like that in every other state analyzed in this volume: weak. Although observers generally agreed that the commission had at least the minimum funds required for planning and instituting the permitting process, Douglas and Petrillo argued persuasively that there were not nearly enough funds to put in place an adequate monitoring and enforcement system. As a result, student volunteers and citizen groups were relied on to patrol the coast for violations. In such a system, significant violations can be overlooked. As a general rule, cities and counties have not been of much assistance, although in some places an effective technique was worked out in which city and county building departments refused to issue permits unless the developers could show conformance with the conditions attached to a coastal permit. The attorney general's office, which was responsible for enforcing compliance when violations were discovered, was also underfunded for the task, although it was possible to secure some supplementary funds for the effort from the legislature. In fiscal 1973–74, $250,000 was secured; the next year, $420,000; and in 1975–76, $441,000 was allocated. However, these funds were for all the legal support needed by the coastal commission, not just for enforcement actions.[56]

Enforcement was also severely hampered by a number of lower court decisions that placed court costs and attorney's fees on the losing party in any suit brought to enjoin a violation of the act. These decisions apparently had a very negative impact on the enforcement process, since presumably the commissions themselves might be saddled with such costs when they brought action to deal with violations of the act. One suggested remedy was to fund citizen participation from public sources in view of the heavy reliance placed on citizens in enforcing the act. Such a proposal was made with regard to California's Energy Resources Conservation and Development Commission.[57]

Douglas and Petrillo have analyzed the major issues raised during the three-and-a half year period when the coastal commissions processed 18,000 applications and claims of exemption.[58] According to their analysis, the major issues involved: (a) local planning; (b) agricultural lands; (c) public access; (d) recreational opportunities; (e) industrial uses along the shore; (f) public agency projects affecting the coast; (g) wetlands; and finally, (h) policies emerging from the permitting process.

With regard to planning, the evidence indicated that the act has had a positive effect on stimulating effective land use planning in cities and counties in California. Conversely, the coastal commission came to accept the proposition that local governments could be the key to implementing the permanent coastal plan.[59] In connection with local planning, the commissions certainly were not hesitant in applying regulations to reduce the density of projects as permits came before them. This was done both in a direct manner and by reducing sewage capacity to serve a particular area. In other cases, the regional commissions or the state commissions ruled that a project could be built, but only if the proposed density was substantially reduced. For instance, a San Diego Regional Commission action approving a 380-unit condominium was modified in an appeal to the state commission by cutting the size of the project in half and pulling the development back some 300 feet from the water.[60] The state commission and some regional commissions also acted to protect older residential neighborhoods largely occupied by low and moderate income families. They denied a number of permits on the grounds that new high-cost housing would drive old tenants out of the area.[61]

Protecting the 3.5 million acres of land in agricultural use in California's coastal counties, about 340,000 acres of which were in coastal-related crops was an important issue for the program. Pressure from urban development had been steadily eroding coastal agricultural resources. One estimate was that 1 out of every 12 acres in the 1960s was converted from agricultural to other uses. Agricultural lands were singled out for special protection by the two thirds vote requirements in the coastal legislation passed in 1972. The state commission took a tough stance on applications for permits to subdivide farmland. For example, in one case, applicants wanted to divide a 1,000-acre parcel into 12 pieces. The commission limited the division to four parcels and before approving even this limited split required dedication of an open space easement over the entire acreage. The four-part division coincided with the amounts of land that past farm tenants had farmed successfully. Thus the land could not be divided into units too small to make farming economically viable, a move which would have set the stage for its conversion to other uses.[62]

The question of public access to the beach, which had spurred public support for coastal legislation in California, continued to be of vital importance in the permitting process under proposition 20.[63] Beach access was involved in an estimated one third of the controversial permit cases, and if one included such related issues as the requirement for additional parking and the legal access rules, the percentage was probably higher. Parking was an important concern to the commissions. The standard adopted by the state commission in certain areas was to require two parking spaces for each apartment along the coast, plus one guest parking space for every seven apartment units. The rule was not absolute, but it was the standard to which the commission repaired in attaching conditions to permits.

The role of the state commission in determining industrial uses along the coast can best be illustrated by its most controversial case, involving the expansion of the San Onofre nuclear generating plant on the San Diego County coast. The proposed project, at an estimated cost of $1.4 billion, would have involved the destruction of over 50 acres of unusual bluffs and canyons. A half mile of beach would have been lost, and great amounts of seawater would have been needed for the cooling system. The state commission staff concluded that a large area of coastal waters would be deprived of much of its marine life because of thermal pollution. The regional commission had approved the project, but on appeal to the state commission, it received a vote of only six in favor and five against. Since a two thirds majority was required for this type of project, the state commission's vote was in effect a denial.

No decision of the state coastal commission had aroused so much controversy. Governor Reagan, William Simon (then the national government's chief energy executive), chambers of commerce, and many other sources pleaded or demanded that the commission reverse its position. The state staff had recommended denial but had suggested several modifications that could have made the project at least marginally acceptable. The utility company had refused to consider such modifications, and the denial followed. The case went to court, but in the interim the applicant agreed to modify the project essentially along the lines suggested originally by the commission staff. The court remanded the case to the state commission, and the proposal as modified was subsequently approved. The extensive conditions attached were described as "the toughest imposed by any state on an AEC-approved nuclear power plant." In a general way, the conditions imposed reduced the damage to the bluff areas, narrowed substantially the amount of beach area lost, and in several other ways mitigated the negative environmental impact of the project.[64]

In permits involving public agencies, the commissions have taken some very interesting stands. In one key example, a regional commission had approved an Orange County waste water treatment system, but subject to water quality standards that were tougher than those set by the state Water Resources Control Board. In the ensuing appeal, the state commission upheld the tougher water quality restriction and imposed its own critical condition, which limited the capacity of the sewage treatment facility to serve a population of only 174,000 instead of the 230,000 as approved by the regional commission. The commission said that it was limiting the system's capacity so as to hold down population growth in the area, which would in turn mitigate already severe pollution problems. Although only a small portion of the project was in the permit area, the commisssion concluded that it could consider the development's impact outside the permit area.[65] These major policy issues that evolved during the permitting process are especially important, since many found their way into the coastal plan that was being prepared at the same time by the coastal commission. Thus, again we see the important link between planning and implementation.[65]

Proponents of proposition 20 had used horror stories of environmental abuses in order to push coastal legislation. By the same token, would-be home builders and developers came up with their own horror stories during the three-and-a-half years of implementation under proposition 20. Complaints about the difficulties of securing a permit to build something as simple as a single family home were fairly common. On a larger scale, *Business Week* for May 3, 1976, carried an article that detailed the frustrating experience of several companies, including California Edison with its San Onofre nuclear plant. Another example was AVCO Community Developers, Inc., which was attempting to develop a 7,000-acre coastal residential project. Its president alleged that delays in coastal commission permits were costing $13,000 a day. Exxon Company had applied for a coastal permit in 1974 for pipelines and an onshore processing plant to handle production of a new oil well in the Santa Barbara channel. Difficulties with the state coastal commission led Exxon to abandon its plans in favor of an offshore processing platform in federal waters. The company was reported to be suing the state, claiming that changes had added $21 million to the cost of the project.

Perhaps the most critical comment about the state commission came from law professors Donald Hagman and Gideon Kanner, who were quoted as having made the following statement in a brief to the California Supreme Court in 1975:

> A conspicuous exception is provided by the circus-like atmosphere of the Coastal Zone Conservation Commission which has been positively beserk in its arbitrary and inconsistent treatment of land use applicants, and whose proceedings consistently act out a grotesque parody of procedural due process. One suspects that the commission's temporary status and lack of any constituency to whom it is held accountable is responsible for this regretable state of affairs.[67]

The widespread criticism of alleged arbitrary and unreasonable action by coastal commissions was to have an impact on the 1976 struggle to adopt a new and permanent piece of coastal legislation. However, while there certainly must have been cases of arbitrary and even unreasonable decisions among the almost 25,000 permits that had been handled by early 1977, there seems to be little evidence of any systematic pattern of arbitrary and capricious behavior. Indeed, many environmentalists would argue that both the regional and state commissions had been too permissive, too ready to compromise, and had ended up approving all too much development along the coast. Since both development interests and environmentalists complain about the implementation of the act, one might conclude that a reasonable balance was struck.

The degree to which the permitting process brought into focus and forced regional and state commissioners to face up to fundamental policy issues that were in turn reflected in the permanent coastal plan is impressive. Perhaps the most important contribution made by the permitting process of proposition 20 was to keep the development of a permanent coastal plan closely in contact with reality. Commissioners came face to face every two weeks with countless issues with obvious policy implications.

The proper generalization seems to be that on balance the implementation process was carried out in a fair yet effective way, using *effective* to mean the protection of the coastal resources that were the primary focus of proposition 20. The patterns that developed certainly did not involve a no growth approach, but they did involve sharp limitations and new directions in what was developed on the coast, where it was developed, and how it was developed.[68]

The question of whether adequate funds were provided to carry out the functions of the coastal commissions can be answered "yes" or "no" depending on one's frame of reference. If one is talking only about the funds needed to carry out the permitting process and the planning function, there were sufficient funds, considering that the $5 million appropriated by the state was more than doubled by federal Office of Coastal Zone Management funds. Funds were probably more than adequate if one accepts the proposition that large and expensive data gathering efforts were not needed either to undergird the permitting process or to develop the coastal plan. Each of those assumptions, while subscribed to by a majority of the persons consulted in these interviews, is certainly subject to challenge. Some observers felt very strongly that the lack of accurate and reliable data, particularly in the area of economic impacts, was a major weakness in the implementation of the law.

There was unanimous agreement that there were not sufficient funds to carry out a systematic monitoring of the important conditions that were attached to almost every one of the major and controversial permits that came before the commissions. It was just as unanimously agreed that this constituted a major weakness in the implementation effort. Imposing conditions was the heart of the commission's control on what was happening to the coast in California. Yet, no reliable method was developed for checking on whether the conditions were being met.

The growing awareness of the monitoring and enforcement problem in California coincided with similar concern in other states which are trying to implement land use laws. Perhaps a major weakness of the implementation process in Vermont is the same inability to monitor and enforce the conditions attached to permits. In Florida, with regard to the Development of Regional Impact section of the law, neither state, regional, nor, in many cases, local agencies have any systematic effort underway to monitor what in effect are important conditions that are typically attached to Development Orders. The same is true in Florida regarding the monitoring and enforcement of state standards in Areas of Critical State Concern, especially in the Florida Keys. The major oversight in developing state initiatives in the land use field seems to have been the failure to provide for follow-up—to see that the major conditions attached to development projects are in fact carried out as the development unfolds on the ground.

Making the California Coastal Plan
The genesis of the California coastal plan was described by M. B. Lane, chairman of the California Coastal Zone Conservation Commission, in his transmittal letter to Governor Edmund G. Brown, Jr.:

> . . . The California Coastal Plan mandated by the Coastal Initiative (proposition 20) in 1972 . . . evolved through countless hours of public hearings, public review of draft proposals, and informational meetings—public participation in resource planning on a scale unmatched in California.[69]

The planning process got under way almost as early as the permitting process. By June 1973, the state commission had agreed on several important substantive areas to be included in the plan. The strategy called for the regional and state commissions to complete their simultaneous work on one element—for example, recreation and marine environment—before moving to a new element. The background research was done by the state commission staff to avoid duplication and unnecessary expense. In addition, each regional commission had a staff, and some used outside consultants on various aspects of their planning efforts. A maximum effort was made to get both ideas and data from a wide range of experts and ordinary citizens. By October 1973 the first hearings on plan elements got under way and were continued through the year 1974. The state commission consolidated the recommendations of the regional commissions, resolved any conflicts, and out of this process by early 1975 was ready to adopt a preliminary plan.

Some 19 public hearings and a much larger number of informal meetings were held on the preliminary plan in coastal communities in April and May of 1975, and one hearing was held in the inland portion of California. Out of this came the final plan, including the broad policies to guide the development of the coast and the implementation mechanisms to put those policies into place. Regional maps and texts were included in the plan and approved by the state commission.

The coastal plan did not abandon the environmental protection focus that had been so important in proposition 20, but it seems fair to say that it also put much more emphasis on the use of the coast and the ways in which it could be used without leading to environmental degradation. Its basic thrust is clear from the introductory statement: "The choice for California in 1976 is this: Shall the coast be abused, degraded, its remaining splendor eroded, or shall it be used intelligently, with its majesty and productivity protected for future generations?"[70]

The plan started from the premise that the California coast should be treated as a resource rather than simply as a commodity. It sought to achieve a balance where more than one of the competing uses had merit. However, the plan was highly restrictive in certain areas, such as the control of dredging and filling of coastal wetlands, protecting areas of unusual or natural historic value, and regulating activities that might involve substantial environmental damage or the loss of agricultural and forest lands.[71]

The core of the California coastal plan was titled "Findings and Policies." This section spelled out the basic goals of the plan, provided findings on the 11 major elements, and set out the policies for each of the elements.[72] Some of the findings of fact and the policies that grew from them were treated relatively briefly, as in the case of public access to the coast. For other issues, the discussion was quite detailed. For instance, in the area of geological hazards, the findings of fact included technical details related to earthquakes, tsunamis, landslides, and soil subsidence. Some of the policies were equally specific, detailing what could and could not be done in problem areas and setting the conditions that would have to be met if any development were to be allowed at all.[73] Perhaps the longest and most complex element in the entire plan was the one concerning energy and the coast. This element alone, including the findings of fact and policies, covered almost 50 pages in the coastal plan. It also in the end was one of the more controversial of the elements.[74]

Part III of the plan focused on how it would be implemented and laid out the general strategy of establishing a permanent state coastal commission, phasing out the regional commissions in not more than four years and lodging a very great part of the responsibility for making and implementing coastal plans with local governments. Part IV covered the actual application of the policies to geographic areas along the coast by regions. These descriptions involved both maps and text and for some places focused on specific projects in subregions, for example, the controversial Sea Ranch project in Sonoma County. The state commission refused to approve the project to its originally planned extent and proposed that the state purchase almost 300 acres to provide access to the beach and to protect coastal views.[75]

On the general question of buying coastal lands, the plan called for spending $180 million to acquire designated sites along the coast. The funding section also estimated that $1 million to $1.5 million would be needed to keep the state commission and six regional commission's permitting procedures in operation. This figure was projected to decline as local governments assumed more and more of the permitting responsibility. The California coastal plan also contemplated similar costs to maintain the planning functions of the state and regional commissions. In addition, it was estimated that support to local governments for their role in developing certifiable plans would be between $700,000 and $800,000 per year.

The funding section also included some innovative recommendations regarding in-lieu payments to local governments which suffered losses in their property tax base because of the implementation of the plan, and a recommendation to adopt an equalizing tax program modeled on the Minnesota Metropolitan Fiscal Disparities Act of 1971. Under this system, when development along the coast was concentrated in one area and prohibited in another, the tax revenues could be spread among all of the relevant local units of government rather than constituting a windfall for one local government.[76]

We turn now to the *politics of adoption* for the second time in this analysis of the California land- and growth-management experience. Once the California Coastal Plan was completed and submitted to the governor and legislature by the end of 1975, the task of carrying out the recommendations remained. There was no question that something would have to be done. Proposition 20 had called for the automatic self-destruct of the interim permitting mechanisms 91 days after the expiration of the 1976 legislative session. If no new legislation was adopted, there would be no coastal planning and management effort for California. Thus, there was an atmosphere of urgency and a feeling by friend and foe alike that action was necessary. This feeling, however, was not so strong as to prohibit a tense, sustained, and spirited battle, involving development and business interests, environmentalists, and state agencies and local governments who had a strong stake in the outcome of the proposed legislation.

The Politics of Adoption:
The California Coastal Act of 1976

The politics of land and growth management in California offers a unique opportunity to assess the effect of changing attitudes and conditions from the boom days of 1972 through an economic recession, an oil embargo, and the governmental crisis known as Watergate. Proposition 20 was adopted before any of these unsettling crises. Thus, the 1976 legislature's consideration of a permanent coastal program provides a chance to examine how the politics of adopting coastal legislation was affected by economic restrictions and by the cynicism toward bureaucracy that many saw as the legacy of Watergate. The confrontation would test the validity of the widespread view that legislators in California and elsewhere in the late 1970s would not be able to take the pioneering stands on coastal or other growth management legislation that had been possible in the heady days of the early 1970s.

The coastal legislation battlefield in 1976 was remarkably similar to the situation in 1970, 1971, and early 1972—when the California legislature had failed to pass a coastal management bill. Once more, there was strong support for the bill in the California assembly, including sponsorship by the speaker of the assembly, Leo McCarthy. Once more, despite substantial sentiment in the senate for a coastal bill, there was strong opposition in the senate Natural Resources and Wildlife Committee. Oil, utility, certain developer, and other business interests still enjoyed their greatest support in the senate, as did several state agencies that feared a permanent state coastal commission would invade their turf.

There were other significant factors that were quite different from 1970–72. Most importantly, attitudes had become far less polarized than they were in 1970–72, when environmental groups had tended to view their opponents as neanderthal—greedy, profit grabbers who would sacrifice any and every resource along the coast for the "quick buck"—and business and other private sector groups that had tended to view environmental groups as at least a lunatic fringe, if not communist inspired.

In order to move from such polarized positions, the environmentalists used an approach that was part olive branch, part threat. Janet Adams described how, about a year and a half after proposition 20 passed, she began to call up key opponents and say to them: "Look, we can get together. Environmentalists don't want to go the initiative route for permanent legislation unless we have to, but you ought to understand that we will if we have to." As a result of the positive response to these overtures, hostile attitudes began to soften little by little. One quite important change was the opening up of communications between environmental groups and the League of Cities. Meetings were also held with the big oil companies, with the Association of Port Authorities, and with other groups which had been key opponents in 1972.[77]

When the coastal bill was introduced in the legislature in 1976, the opposing sides were much more willing than in the past to sit down, discuss their differences, and try to arrive at a compromise. None of the major actors in 1976 seemed to want to go the initiative route again. Local governments were afraid that they might again be left out of the process, and private sector groups feared that the result would be a program completely unresponsive to the needs of development. Environmental groups were willing to give up the initiative not only because they were now much more comfortable working with local governments but also because they were not absolutely certain that another effort would win. Furthermore, the initiative involved a tremendous amount of time, effort and energy, and everyone seemed to be inclined to avoid that if at all possible.[78]

The first bill to implement the coastal plan, senate bill 1579, was sponsored by Senator Anthony C. Beilenson, who had a reputation for carrying through innovative and hard-to-pass legislation and was chairman of the powerful Finance Committee. Unfortunately, his announcement that he was running for Congress made him a lame duck, weakening his power base considerably. Futhermore, he did not have the time to pay close attention to the necessary negotiations and compromises, and his key staff person had too little experience in coastal issues to carry the ball effectively in his absence.[79]

There was a general agreement that the bill itself had many weaknesses. Friend and foe alike saw that it was much too long and detailed, attempting as it did to incorporate virtually all of the 162 policies that had been developed in the long, complex coastal plan. The immediate difficulty was that almost everyone in California, even ardent friends of coastal legislation, could find something in the legislation to dislike. Certainly it gave powerful ammunition to opponents who wished to point up examples of what a terrible thing passage would be. Nevertheless, the legislation did get out of the senate Natural Resources and Wildlife Committee, the historic graveyard of coastal zone legislation in California. The chairman of the committee, Senator John A. Nejedly, who was a proponent of coastal legislation, had worked with Senator Beilenson to iron out some of the problems with the bill. After seven hearings and various amendments, the committee passed the bill by a 5 to 4 vote.[80]

The next hurdle was the senate Finance Committee. Its failure there has been attributed in part to Beilenson's somewhat narrow and rigid view of what kind of coastal zone legislation was needed. According to this version of events, the bill's passage required a great amount of intense negotiation and compromise, and Beilenson "just wouldn't or couldn't do it." Nejedly declined to take the responsibility for working out all the compromise, and the bill died on a 7-to-6 vote. Senator David A. Roberti from the Los Angeles district, whose swing vote had been counted on for support, swung the "wrong" way. Roberti took the position that the poor people in his district were being badly served by the bill and that, in fact, it was "a rich man's bill."[81]

The executive director of the California Council for Environmental and Economic Balance considered the coastal plan itself a mess and the Beilenson bill an even bigger mess. A staff person for the senate Natural Resources Committee held that the major failing was the attempt to put the whole plan into the law, rather than just the framework from which a detailed plan could later be worked out at the administrative level.[82] This strategy had been considered early on but was abandoned for the Beilenson approach.

The defeat of the Beilenson bill sent a shock of dismay through the ranks of both advocates and opponents of the coastal management program. Despite its faults, many supporters had expected the bill to be passed by both the assembly and the senate. And opponents were afraid that failure to pass any legislation would risk the prospect of another initiative. In the search for a new approach, a young senator named Jerry Smith emerged as the new sponsor of the coastal bill. As one participant in the process put it, Senator Smith was "anointed by the powers that be as the president of the senate to pick up the pieces and try to put together a new coastal zone bill." Smith, perhaps anticipating the failure of the Beilenson bill, had a scenic highways bill which could be made the vehicle for the coastal legislation and thus avoid the procedural ban on introducing a new coastal bill that late in the session.

The Smith bill, senate bill 1277, was sent to the assembly and referred to the assembly Committee on Resources, Land Use, and Energy. This committee was chaired by Assemblyman Charles Warren, a strong advocate of coastal zone legislation and later chairman of the Council on Environmental Quality in Washington. During the July recess, Joe Petrillo, by then a key aide to Senator Smith, and a small group of other people familiar with the coastal zone history in California got together and drastically revised the Bielenson bill to simplify and shorten it for incorporation in the Smith bill.[83] Their experience and expertise allowed them to complete major revisions in a very short period of time. The result of this redrafting effort, preprint 19, was accepted by both Assemblyman Warren in the assembly and Senator Smith in the senate, and the stage was thus set for a new effort to pass permanent coastal legislation.[84]

When the legislature reconvened, proponents moved quickly in the Assembly to incorporate preprint 19 in the Smith vehicle and then to move the Smith bill out of the assembly Committee on Resources, Land Use, and Energy and the Fiscal Committee. The bill passed the whole assembly on Friday, August 13, by a 46-to-28 vote. As one participant put it, "We put it all the way through the assembly in just one week."[85] However, its passage through the assembly was not without controversy and sharp debate. Had it not been for the strong stand taken by Warren, and especially by the speaker of the assembly, Leo McCarthy, it is doubtful that the effort would have succeeded in time for final action by the 1976 California legislature. According to one observer, "McCarthy worked the bill all day and used his power to get the votes, particularly in the Ways and Means Committee."[86] In that committee and later on the assembly floor. McCarthy was credited with beating back some critical amendments, including one that would have added a compensation clause to the bill. The Republican leadership was pushing the compensation clause very hard and generally objecting to what they described as railroading the bill through the legislature. There were some very close votes, essentially along party lines, with McCarthy pretty much holding the Democratic majority.[87]

The battleground now shifted to the senate. The first hot fight was over whether the bill should be referred to the Natural Resources and Wildlife Committee which had passed the earlier Bielenson bill or to the Finance Committee which had killed it. The battle occurred in the Rules Committee, and for a time there was a deadlock. Finally, an agreement was hammered out by which the Rules Committee referred the bill to the Natural Resources and Wildlife Committee and recommended but did not absolutely require that it then go to the senate Finance Committee. Procoastal law forces considered this a victory. The Natural Resouces and Wildlife Committee voted 6-to-3 in favor of the bill and sent it directly to the floor of the senate with the recommendation that it be adopted, without amendments. Its supporters felt that if a conference committee with the assembly were required, time might well run out and the whole thing would be killed.[88]

With the bill on the senate floor, the central question was whether or not proponents could garner the 21 votes needed for its passage. All the compromises supposedly had been worked out, but a preliminary head count revealed only 17 (possibly 18) favorable votes. It was at this point that Governor Brown and his staff joined the fray, engaging in a series of tense negotiations with four senators described as representing labor. The house speaker, Leo McCarthy, also worked the senate floor trying to swing every possible vote. It all came down, however, to the several "labor senators." The governor and his staff, working in the senate chambers, moved back and forth between the environmental groups and representatives of labor and other interests either opposed to or unenthusiastic about a coastal bill. According to one description of the last minute maneuvering, senator Smith had confided only an hour before the final senate roll call, "We just don't have the votes." A compromise was finally worked out which allowed the governor to stroll dramatically to the very door of the senate chambers and announce that an agreement had been worked out and that the "labor senators" would swing their votes in favor of the legislation.[89] These four votes broke the logjam. Senator Smith immediately moved the bill, and it passed the senate by a 25-to-14 vote. The California legislature had finally managed to enact a permanent coastal management act.[90]

Behind this record of success lay an intense period of negotiations and compromise in which environmentalists, local government representatives, and private sector representatives negotiated in good faith to reach agreement on several key issues. It was clear to environmentalists that the coastal bill recommended by the coastal commission could not fly without substantial changes. Janet Adams and three of her colleagues handled the negotiations with oil companies, the port authorities, the California Association of Contractors, county and city groups, and others in working out the critical compromises that were necessary to get the needed support to pass the bill.[91]

Many business and development interests in California did agree that the natural systems of the coast needed some special protection during economic exploitation to prevent the long-range destruction of its resources. They responded to the arguments used repeatedly and convincingly by supporters of strong coastal legislation that to fail to protect the resources of the coast would ultimately kill an economic goose that laid many golden eggs. Many business and development interests began to abandon the notion that environmental protection and economic prosperity were opposing goals and to accept the argument that economic prosperity in the long run depended heavily on the reasonable protection of coastal resources.

Even with this basic agreement on the need for coastal protection, several compromises were essential to the bill's passage. Of these compromises, the decision to lodge prime implementation responsibility with local governments was seen as the most important. Another significant compromise was one involving ports. In effect, direct port responsibilities would be exempt from the permitting process but related functions, such as those involving real estate development, would not be exempted. After this compromise was worked out, port interests fulfilled their part of the bargain and supported the bill, bringing some key legislators on board. This outcome was useful in negotiating with the association of contractors, the oil companies, and the utilities, who decided they, too, might be able to reach an acceptable compromise with the environmental organizations. The ports agreement gave the environmental leadership the model to work with. In the end the association of contractors supported the coastal legislation, and the oil and utility companies said, in effect, "Well, I guess we won't fight it." Almost every important group with which negotiations were carried out came around either in support of the bill or assumed a neutral position.[92] The building trades people withheld their support until the last-minute compromise that was worked out with the "labor senators."

To almost all potential opponents of the bill, a very critical compromise involved the boundary of the coastal zone. Prior to 1976, the coastal zone boundary went inland to the highest elevation of the nearest mountain range. Within that boundary, the state had permit regulatory authority 1,000 yards from the mean high tide line and up coastal rivers to the extent of tidal influence. In the rest of the coastal zone beyond the 1,000 yard line, the state had only planning authority. After 1976, the agreed upon boundary compromise was to abandon a distinction between a planning area and a permit area and provide instead that the regulatory authority be extended to the entire coastal zone. That boundary was established by the legislature in 1976 and was supported with maps and considerable detail. The new coastal zone map goes up to five miles inland in certain rural areas. In the urban areas, the coastal zone boundary is sometimes only several blocks deep.

It is difficult to analyze the final compromise worked out by
Governor Brown with the labor-oriented senators. It involved six
agreements that were so imprecise that, even after they were
incorporated in legislation, there were disputes between labor and
supporters of the legislation as to exactly what had been meant.
Opponents later charged that they did not really mean anything at
all except that they had allowed the coastal legislation to "slip
through the legislature."[93]

Additional pieces of legislation that had a direct bearing on the
planning and management of the coastal zone deserve comment.
Assembly bill 3544, the California Coastal Conservancy Act, established a new agency to protect agricultural lands, promote the
restoration of degraded coastal areas, and promote the resource
enhancement of the coastal zone. The conservancy was authorized
to acquire a fee title, development rights, easements or other
interests in coastal lands. While no direct appropriation was provided for the coastal conservancy, $10 million was allocated to it as
part of a park bond issue that was in fact approved by the votes as
proposition 2 (the California Urban and Coastal Bond Act of 1976).
This act provided for $280 million in bonds for use by the state park
system and the Wildlife Conservation Board; grants to counties,
cities, and districts for land acquisition and development; and
monies for state water projects.[94] The Coastal Conservancy Act of
1976 has far-reaching potential for coastal management in California. The aim of the law was to carry out "a program of agricultural
protection, area restoration, and resource enhancement in the
coastal zone within the policies and guidelines of the Coastal Act."[95]
Assembly bill 2351, adopted by the 1978 legislative session, gave the
coastal conservancy more flexibility in acting to achieve its goals but
still did not give it additional funds.[96]

Assembly bill 44 provided various coastal land acquisition funds
and in addition provided an appropriation for the initial operation of
the coastal commission. Assembly bill 2133 provided funds for
coastal wetlands acquisition. Governor Brown signed all these bills,
though he reduced the acquisition funds by about $11 million out of a
total of $31.2 million. The governor justified his reduction on the
grounds that $110 million of Proposition 2 funds would be ear-
marked for coastal land purchases by the park system. The park
system was authorized to acquire coastal resources, especially in
urban areas, areas of environmental resources, and lands that would
give physical or visual access to the beach. Counting grants to local
governments, $150 million of the total $280 million was available for
use in protecting the coast.[97]

Major Groups For and Against the 1976 Coastal Law

Most observers agreed that the California Coastal Alliance continued to be the key influence in supporting the coastal legislation. Its
leaders assumed the responsibility of negotiating with the other side
to find common ground which could win new supporters for the
legislation. The Sierra Club, by far the strongest environmental
group in California, continued their vigorous support of the coastal
legislation. Its director was given credit for being a good negotiator
and playing an important role in passing the legislation. The
Planning and Conservation League, dedicated to passing sound
environmental legislation, also was active.[98] Most observers took the
position that attitudes did not divide neatly along party lines,
despite the example of the final vote in the California assembly. One
leading environmentalist noted that coastal management "cut
across party lines, and it wasn't clear liberal-conservative issue
either. We had a lot of conservatives in our camp."[99]

The issue of just how important the governor was in passing the
legislation is an interesting and complex one. Without question,
Brown favored coastal legislation throughout the attempts to pass
the law. However, many observers felt that the governor did not give
his full attention to the matter until after the Bielenson bill failed and
a crisis emerged. As one participant recalled:

> A lot of us tried to get the governor and his people to take some interest
> earlier, but they would not do it, and as a result nobody was in charge,
> and we kept warning them that the train was going to run off the track. In
> spite of that, they did not respond until in fact the train did run off the
> track.[100]

Part of the problem was, of course, that Governor Brown was
distracted by presidential ambitions that left little time for such
matters as a coastal bill for California. On the other hand, there
seems no question that the governor did enter the picture in a major
and important way during the latter stages when a new coastal bill
was put together, and certainly he was crucial to working out a
compromise with labor that finally allowed the legislation to pass the
Senate.

Some of the governor's executive agencies in California were
unenthusiastic about the legislation. One long-time holdout in the
executive area was the state's new energy commission, which took a
hard line position that the coastal commission should be out of the
power plant siting business entirely. The state energy commission
did succeed in being assigned prime responsibility for siting energy
facilities along the coast. However, the coastal commission kept an
important role through its capacity to designate areas unsuitable for
energy facilities under certain conditions and to comment on energy

sites proposed and ultimately selected by the energy commission.[101] The Department of Water Resources was rated as fairly positive toward a coastal bill, while the fish and game commission was opposed to allowing the coastal commission any role in its functions. The state lands commission had long been negative toward a coastal commission and remained in that posture during 1976. Some of these state agencies apparently used their influence in the senate to attempt to prevent passage of the legislation.[102]

According to one view, the secretary of the Department of Resources did not oppose the legislation but some of the constituent units in his agency did. This was important, because "These bureaucrats had a lot of friends in the senate."[10] The Forest Service also wanted changes to ensure that the coastal commission would not have anything to do with permitting in the logging field. There was a lot of negotiating with the agencies on just how the coastal commission would use its authority and mesh with the authority of other agencies, and the final legislation did contain a number of provisions to limit duplication and overlap of responsibilities and in general to keep the coastal commission from assuming responsibilities that could be satisfactorily carried out by other state agencies.[104]

Perhaps the most striking comment that can be made about the private sector forces, including oil, utilities and others, is that many of them did enter into good faith negotiation and achieved some changes in the coastal legislation that made it possible for them to either assume a neutral position or to support the legislation. The experience of Mike Peevey, the executive director of the California Council for Environmental and Economic Balance (CEEB), is perhaps illustrative. CEEB was a consortium of some 20 companies and 19 labor groups that was formed after passage of proposition 20. That law had sharpened the feeling that "The environmental pendulum was swinging too far and that something had to be done to restore the balance."[105] The group involved itself deeply in the implementation of proposition 20 and monitored the process, lobbied the legislature, met the coastal commission staffs at both the state and regional levels, and participated in reviewing the plan during its development. In the 1976 legislative session, Peevey commited himself to support coastal legislation if certain concessions were obtained. He adhered to this position despite considerable dissent within the rather loose-knit consortium. Some of his own members, when the compromises that had been demanded were in fact achieved, felt that they had been sucked into a kind of trap where they were then almost forced to support the bill.[106]

CEEB's executive director felt that the 1976 law was a major improvement over proposition 20 and that big developers like the

Irvine Company and big utilities like Southern California Edison all agreed on that. He supported the essential state role and the need to avoid overdevelopment on the coast, but also held that it was necessary to locate ocean-related business and industry along the coast. The negotiations over the bill went forward "without the rancor we have over a lot of issues in California." CEEB set up a special coastal program and hired a lobbyist to work full-time on it who had good ties both to the environmental and to the business communities. The key concession that made the bill acceptable to CEEB was the shift of authority and responsibility to local governments. Peevey confirmed that the willingness on both sides to compromise stemmed partly from the wish to avoid another initiative showdown. CEEB had good reason—its private poll indicated that if the issue came to another statewide proposition it probably would pass again.[107]

There was an interesting contrast between the position on the legislation taken by the California League of Cities and that taken by the California County Supervisors Association. The cities and counties both took an active part in negotiating to try to get a law that they could support, but in the end the League of Cities supported the legislation and the county organization did not. The county organization ended up focusing not on the policies but on the government powers and funding sections of the law, where the counties felt some success in getting a stronger role for local governments built into the legislation. Tim Leslie, the county association land use specialist, met with Janet Adams of the California Coastal Alliance and her allies a number of times and felt that they made great headway in coming to a meeting of minds. By way of contrast, he was quite bitter about the hearings conducted by the coastal commission on the California coastal plan on the grounds that no adequate opportunity to testify was provided.[108]

County governments did take strong exception to expanding the scope of the coastal zone and objected to the inclusion of agricultural land, which had not been a part of the coastal scheme under proposition 20. The basic position of the counties was that all that was needed was a state requirement that counties develop a coastal management element. A state agency that could second-guess the counties on the planning, zoning, and other land use regulations tools was seen as an excessive intrusion of the state into the counties' home rule authority.[109] After the legislation passed, the counties worried about the provisions for reimbursing local governments for their expenses in carrying out the requirements of the act. They feared that the dollars would be too little and too late and would have too many strings attached. A second concern involved the issue of just how the state commission would go about certifying the local government plans. Counties feared that without specific state standards that the state commission would simply carry on tough negotiations with each local government unit, to get just as much out of each of them as it possibly could.[110]

Provisions of the 1976 Law

We turn now to an assessment of the content of the California Coastal law (senate bill 1277) as passed by the legislature in August of 1976.[111] First, it can be said that in spite of the fact that the Beilenson bill was substantially rewritten to become the successful Smith bill, the basic framework and many of the policies in the coastal legislation in 1976 were as provided in the coastal plan. (See Figure 5-1.) Of the 162 policies proposed in the plan, 133 survived in whole or part. Furthermore, the basic management approach proposed in the coastal plan, shifting the key responsibility for making and implementing coastal plans to local governments, survived and, if anything, was strengthened by the legislature.

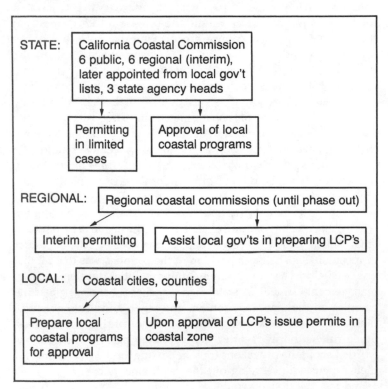

Figure 5-1. **California Coastal Act of 1976**

The act opened with a declaration that in order to promote the general welfare, it was necessary to protect the delicate ecological balance of the coast and to prevent its deterioration and destruction. From this strongly environmentally oriented statement, the bill quickly moved on to say that the legislature further found that it would be also necessary in some instances to locate some essential facilities (for example, energy production) on the coast, even though they might have adverse impacts on its environment. Such siting might sometimes be necessary to preserve inland as well as coastal resources and to promote "orderly economic development within the state."[112] Thus, the basic goals of the act reflected a firm commitment to environmental protection, but with a strong dash of balanced economic growth thrown in. The five basic goals were:

1. To protect, maintain, and, where feasible, enhance and restore the overall quality of the coastal zone environment and its natural and manmade resources.
2. Assure orderly, balanced utilization and conservation of coastal resources, taking into account the social and economic needs of the people of the state.
3. Maximize public access to and along the coast and maximize public recreational opportunities in the coastal zone consistent with sound resources, conservation principles and constitutionally protected rights of private property.
4. Assure priority for coastal-dependent development over other development along the coast.
5. Encourage state and local initiatives and cooperation in preparing procedures to implement coordinated planning and development for mutually beneficial uses, including educational uses, in the coastal zone.[113]

Chapter 4 of the law spelled out the creation, membership, and powers of the new state commission and the regional commissions which were to continue in operation for two more years. Members were to be appointed basically under the system devised for proposition 20. The act left it open to the state commission to decide whether a proposition 20 type regional commission would be reconstituted for the two-year period.[114] As noted later, the two-year interim period for regional commissions was later extended.

The problem of duplication and conflicts among the coastal commission and other state agencies was dealt with in Chapter 5. State agencies were directed to carry out their duties and responsibilities in conformity with the coastal legislation, and one section did specifically state that all local coastal programs should provide the basis upon which state functional plans for the coastal zone would be based. The state coastal commission was authorized to submit recommendations to encourage agencies dealing with energy, water, pollution, forestry, and other relevant areas to carry out their functions in a manner consistent with the act. If the agencies did not implement such recommendations they were required to explain their reasons to the legislature.[115]

Chapter 6 spelled out the implementation process through local coastal programs, including the procedures for approving and certifying local coastal programs. Chapter 7 spelled out the details for continuing the permitting process during the period that the local coastal programs were being developed and certified. If local governments chose not to perform this function, the regional commissions would continue to do so, though under the new policy framework. Chapter 7 also contained the procedures that would guide the permitting process after local coastal programs had been certified.[116]

The heart of the new legislation was the mandate that each local government in the coastal zone prepare a local coastal program. The content of each local program would be determined by the local government, but the act mandated that it be consistent with the policies of the act and state commission adopted procedures. The act specified that local programs would consist of a general land use plan, zoning ordinances, zoning district maps, and in certain areas other implementing actions. Components of local plans were to be submitted first to the regional commissions, but an appeal could be taken directly to the state commission.[117] It is rather curious that the requirements placed the regional commissions in a crucial role, since the act left it up to the state commission to decide whether a regional commission would be reconstituted during the period when local governments were preparing their plans.

Another important element in the legislation had to do with the designation of sensitive coastal resource areas. After consulting with local governments and regional commissions, the state commission was required to recommend to the legislature, no later than September 1, 1977, the designation of any sensitive coastal resource areas where the commission should consider additional measures to protect coastal resources and public access. These areas having a regional or statewide significance would be designated for not more than two years; if during that time the legislature did not designate the area by statute, the designation would not continue in force.[118]

On the matter of appeals, the legislation provided that prior to certification of a local coastal program, a coastal permit granted by a local government could be appealed by a regional commission executive director, any citizen wishing to appeal including the applicant, or any two state coastal commissioners. The appeal of regional commission permit actions would be taken in essentially the same way.[119] By providing that state commissioners could call up appeals, the law was broader than proposition 20. After the certification of local programs, local government permit decisions could be appealed to the state commission only under carefully defined circumstances, which depended on where coastal developments were located, whether developments were in a sensitive coastal resource area, whether a development conformed to the principal permitted use under the local coastal plan, and finally whether the development constituted a major public works project or major energy facility. The act specifically provided that a coastal permit could not be denied on the grounds that a portion of the proposed development outside the coastal zone would have adverse environmental impacts inside the coastal zone.[120]

The act provided for exempting improvements to existing single family dwellings; for maintenance dredging of existing navigation channels; for certain other maintenance and repair activities; any development found by a two-thirds vote of the commission to have no potential significant adverse effect on coastal resources or public coastal access; the installation and replacement of necessary utility connections; and carefully defined urban areas (a residential zone at least 50 percent developed at a density of four or more houses per acre or an industrial or commercial area at a similar stage of development).[121] The urban lands exemption had been the subject of some last minute compromises in the fight to get the legislation passed. The key compromise in effect mandated that if, on the request of a local government, the state Coastal Commission found that an area met the above density criteria, then further development would in effect be simply in-filling and would be excluded if it posed no significant adverse effect on coastal access and resources. Areas located near tide and submerged lands and areas adjacent to beaches or the mean high tide line could not be excluded. Exclusions were subject to coastal commission review and revocation on the basis of violations of the conditions of the exclusion.[122] From this brief introduction into the sum and substance of the 1976 coastal law, we turn now to an assessment of its implementation.

The Politics of Implementation: The California Coastal Zone Management Act of 1976

With the 1976 law presumably securely in place, the main task of the state, regional, and local governments involved in planning and managing California's coast in the next several years would be developing and carrying through to the certification stage local coastal programs. These local coastal programs (LCP) when pre-pared and approved by the regional and state coastal commissions, will become the central vehicle for planning and managing Califor-nia's coast. Thus, the success or failure of the new law rests on the initial and continuing quality of the local coastal programs.

The act directed regional and state coastal commissions to per-form dual tasks. First they would continue the permitting activity that they had been carrying on under the California Coastal Act of 1972, but within new interpretative guidelines drawn from the 1976 legislation. As part of this process, they were to devise interim guidelines for permitting activities until LCPs were certified. Their second, massive task was to provide regulations, guidelines, and assistance to local governments in preparing LCPs. At the termina-tion of the regional commissions, the LCPs would control develop-ment in the coast except in those areas where there was no certified local plan, in which case the state commission would directly control the development activity.

The state coastal commission tackled its responsibilities with vigor and dispatch. The commission distributed its initial draft of inter-pretative guidelines for coastal permits to local governments, state agencies, and others, on February 11, 1977.[123] A total of 11 hearings on the guidelines were set along the California coast beginning March 3, 1977, and ending March 29. Many of the guidelines were drawn from the California Coastal Plan of 1975. While the interim guide-lines were needed immediately to serve as the framework for per-mitting activities until local plans were certified, they also served the purpose of highlighting the key problems, issues, and opportuni-ties that local governments would need to consider in developing their own LCPs. The final interpretive guidelines were adopted by the California Coastal Commission May 3, 1977 and included only the general statewide guidelines and definitions. The specific guide-lines applying to particular geographic areas were not included.[124]

In the debate over the 1976 legislation, local governments had expressed concern about the possibility that the state coastal commission would be unwilling to produce specific and detailed criteria against which local governments could measure their LCP development and thus be reasonably assured that they would produce a document that would be certified at the state level. While proposition 20 was in effect, both its friends and foes had noted the tendency of the state coastal commission to keep criteria broad and general, leaving its options open for approving or denying permits on a case-by-case basis. Almost all observers felt that the time had come by 1976 for much more specific policies and guidelines as a framework for permitting activities.

There was a feeling among local governments that without specificity they would be put into a ball game in which they not only did not know the rules but also where the commission could alter the rules in an arbitrary and capricious manner. Despite the generality in the interim guidelines, it seems accurate to say that the commission subsequently moved strongly to lay this fear to rest. The 36 pages of regulations it issued on LCPs spelled out in considerable detail the procedural approach to be used by local governments in preparing and submitting their local coastal programs.[125] The commission also published a detailed *Local Coastal Program Manual*, prepared as a joint effort by the state coastal commission and the governor's Office of Planning and Research. The manual included a checklist of what should be contained in a local program with regard to a particular policy under consideration.

The process begins with the local governments identifying key issues and developing a work program, proceeds to an optional preliminary review by the regional or state commission, moves to the adoption of a land use plan including the final environmental impact review required by a separate California law, and finally proceeds to the development of the zoning districts and ordinances. By the end of 1977, nearly all of the 15 counties and 53 cities in the coastal zone had begun their efforts to develop a local coastal program. Three cities—Capitola and Marina in Monterey County and San Clemente in Orange County—had asked the state coastal commission to prepare plans for them.[126]

The coastal commission quickly moved to fulfill the commitment that local governments would receive substantial financial assistance in preparing the local coastal programs. Under the California law of 1976, at least 50 percent of all federal assistance received by the state of California to carry out its coastal program was required to be passed on to coastal cities and counties. The coastal commission's policy was to attempt from federal and state sources to pay for all the work required to meet the LCP requirements of the 1976 coastal law.[127] By January 1978, the commission had awarded 52 start-up grants totalling about $167,000 to help local governments identify issues and develop work plans for their programs. In addition, more than $200,000 had been allocated to nine local governments as part of a special pilot project. At this time, the commission was just beginning to receive substantial grant requests based on work programs completed by local governments.

By the end of July 1978, the first two LCPs certified by the commission, the Trinidad General Plan and the Aqua Hedionda Specific Plan, had been approved with substantial conditions.[128] By September 1978, the commission reported that more than half of the cities and counties in the coastal zone had passed through the preliminary stage and 35 local governments had land use plans under way, funded largely with federal grant money in which individual grants ranged in size from $12,000 to $170,000. The city of Los Angeles became the first local government in the coastal zone to apply for and receive permission to grant its own permits prior to the approval of the LCP.[129] A month later the state coastal commission reported that it had approved 34 of the 35 local government work programs.[130] The January-February 1979 issue of *Coastal News* reported that 62 of California's local governments along the coast had initiated the effort to complete local coastal programs. At this point the land use components of the Trinidad and Aqua Hedionda plans had been formally approved by the commission.[131]

Clearly, the initial implementation effort of the 1976 coastal law proceeded at a slower pace than might have been hoped for. Although the reasons are not easy to pinpoint, some are imbedded in a series of problems encountered along the way. Ironically, the same local governments who had feared that the state coastal commission's guidance would not be specific enough actually became increasingly apprehensive about the state's detailed requirements, particularly in connection with land use components in LCPs. If plans had to be so detailed as to go all the way to specific set backs on an individual lot basis, local governments believed they would lose absolutely necessary flexibility in carrying out the goals and policies of the state law. Some local governments found the state guidelines and manuals extremely helpful, while others found them too complex, too filled with jargon, and too difficult to interpret or understand.[132] The state coastal commission tended to take the view that without a great deal of specificity state goals and policies could not be enforced.

The argument over specificity has been defused substantially by the state coastal commission's new executive director, Mike Fischer, who gave the issue top priority and immediately directed his staff to work out new approaches for the so-called *Agua Hedionda* case. Fischer also asked the League of California Cities to suggest workable alternatives. From this exchange evolved a proposal to apply partial certification to an LCP, while further study could be made as to how the state interest in critical policy areas could best be protected.[133]

Under its new criteria, the state coastal commission focused on the most crucial state policies spelled out in the 1976 law. First priority was given to undeveloped land that was subject to strong growth pressure and the protection of vital natural resources. In already urbanized areas, the state criteria directed local coastal programs to focus on "beach access, parking and traffic congestion, visitor-serving uses, and low to moderate cost housing, usually in that order." Setback requirements and other aspects of development design were to be spelled out only in a very general way. Finally, it was decided that every effort should be made to minimize the collection of new data in order to avoid long delays in carrying out the program.[134]

While the preparation of local coastal programs was going forward, the permitting activities of the state and regional coastal commissions also were being carried out. During the January 1977–December 1979 period, almost 20,000 permits were acted on, ranging from 6,407 in the south coast region to 720 in the north central coast region. Of all permits applied for during this period, 96 percent were approved, but half of these were approved with conditions, some of major importance. Sixty percent of all permits during this period were for single family homes. More than 1,400 appeals were taken to the state commission, about evenly divided between permit applicants and other groups, organizations, or individuals. In more than 600 cases, the commission let the regional decision stand. Only 8 percent of all permit applications during the period were appealed to the state commission and only 2 percent went to public hearing at this level.[135]

From 1973 through 1979, over 40,000 permits were processed by state and regional commissions, of which 95 percent were approved, many with conditions.[136] The regulatory program clearly was successful in furthering the implementation of coastal policies and in bringing a clear sense of direction to the planning process. The point is well made in the following statement:

> California's coastal development control program while not a substitute for planning, has been an indispensible component of the planning process. In addition to providing an open forum in which to resolve current development conflicts, the process has brought planning down to earth. The intensity and give and take of permit decisions have provided the commissioners the hard experience on which to ground later decisions on local coastal land use plans. In fact, many permit actions are planning decisions in that they can set development and conservation patterns for entire areas. In other cases, permit decisions can preserve important planning options while additional information is being collected.[137]

Despite this positive view, there was also a steady flow of complaints about the permitting program, especially what critics called the "extortion style" conditions imposed in many cases. Some former supporters of the coastal legislation joined in the criticism of the commission's work at iterim hearings in the fall of 1978.[138]

These criticisms and the rising frustration with what was considered the excessively slow progress with local coastal programs contributed to a 1979 legislative crisis that for a time threatened the very existence of the coastal program. Bills were introduced to exclude all single-family homes from the coastal act and require payment for access conditions, delegate permit authority to local governments by 1981 whether or not LCPs were approved, and repeal coastal act policies related to housing. As many as 50 bills affecting the coastal program were introduced, most of them hostile to the commission. In response, the state coastal commission proposed legislation designed to eliminate unnecessary regulations. Support was marshalled by the senate's Natural Resources and Wildlife Committee and the assembly's Natural Resources, Land Use and Energy Committee. Supporters of the coastal program regrouped into California Coastal Alliance II, and the Sierra Club and Planning and Conservation League also made their presence felt.[139]

When the dust of the battle cleared, the 1979 legislative session had approved amendments "marking the first major reform of the act since its adoption in 1976." All the bills that would have seriously weakened the law died, most in committee. The commission's own bills for streamlining administrative procedures and boundary changes (aimed generally at eliminating areas from the coastal zone where no important coastal resources were present) passed. Assembly bill 643 contained the major revisions, including a requirement that the commission designate areas where single-family home construction would no longer require a permit if development would not harm scenic or environmentally sensitive resources, agricultural lands, or public access.[140] Commission staff estimated that this provision would reduce permits brought to the commission by as much as 30 percent. The commission moved with dispatch to implement the legislative mandate an on January 24, 1980, identified over 100,000 acres where single-family permits would no longer be required, primarily in the already developed areas of the coast.[141] Among other provisions of assembly bill 643, the commission was required to "review and simplify its regulations."[142] One other important piece of legislation (assembly bill 989) reaffirmed and strengthened the policy of "maximum public access" to the beach. Responsibility for improved access was transferred from the state Department of Parks and Recreation to the coastal commission and the coastal conservancy.[143]

One clear message that came from all sides in the 1979 legislative battles was "get the LCPs certified." By the end of 1979 only 11 coastal programs, including 2 port master plans, had been certified. Parts of 13 programs were being considered by regional or state commissions, and 20 draft programs were being reviewed at the local level. The year 1980 was to be the "year of the coast" in more ways than one in California. While there was general agreement that not all local coastal programs would be completed by July 1980, it was hoped—and seemed politically necessary if damaging amendments to the coastal act were to be avoided—that "A healthy majority of the total LCPs will meet this deadline . . . and most if not all the land use plans will be certified by that time."[144]

The regional and state coastal commissions made an all out effort, featuring both policy and fiscal initiatives, to come as close as possible to meeting the deadlines. The task was formidable. The first efforts to certify plans had exposed both process and substantive issues of major importance and difficulty. The question of specificity had been faced head on by the state coastal commission executive director, but it continued to be a difficult issue. Controversies over state and regional commission efforts to assure the reflection of state policies in areas such as wetlands, agriculture, and housing continued.

With all the difficulties, important progress was made. The commitment of fiscal resources to spur the program along was extensive. By the end of 1979 the state commission had earmarked more than $4.2 million in federal and state matching dollars in grants to local governments to prepare local coastal programs. An additional $3.2 million was earmarked to mid-1981. Out of this amount, an incentive fund of $800,000 was used to promote early completion of LCPs. A 1979 legislative action assured local governments of state reimbursement of all funds expended on local coastal program development costs not covered by coastal commission grants. The same law assured local governments that the state attorney general's office would represent them in litigation resulting from LCP implementation.[145] Grants were made to all of the coastal counties, ranging from $309,473 for Los Angeles County to $35,011 for San Francisco County. Twenty-four cities had received almost $1 million for preparation of land use plans by the end of 1979, and 15 cities had received $660,000 to prepare complete local coastal programs. The other 14 jurisdictions were either funding the work themselves, had asked the commission staff to do the work, or simply had not submitted a request for funds.[146]

At its April 1979 meeting, the state commission took a close look at its management of the local coastal program certification process and laid out a schedule to mid-1981 that would result in 80 percent of all LCPs being approved at that time. It was agreed to rely heavily on the regional commissions to do the bulk of the in-depth analysis of the LCPs, confining the state commission role to dealing with major unresolved issues. Finally, the commission committed itself to a constant monitoring role to assure compliance with the LCP certification schedule. By mid-1980, the certifications were roughly on schedule,[147] but since then progress has been slow. The March 1981 *Coastal News* issue predicted that one half of the 67 cities and counties in the coastal zone would be approved by the July 1, 1981 deadline, the date on which the regional commissions would be phased out. State commission chairman, Leonard Grote, defended the LCP completion record as remarkable when compared to the time required for local governments to prepare general plans mandated by state law—an average of 8 to 10 years. The general plans were seen as responding to a state law "which contains far fewer substantive and specific standards than does the Coastal Act."[148] By August 1981, the record of plan approvals was still far short of the 50 percent predicted the previous March: out of 67 cities and counties, 15 had fully approved LCPs; 16 additional local governments had approved land use plans, and all 4 port districts had approved master plans.[149] By November 1981, 19 total LUPs had been approved, as had 29 land use plans.[150] The figure in June 1982 showed 27 total LCPs approved, still less than the 50 percent predicted more than one year earlier.[151]

The legislature expressed its continuing frustration with the failure to complete the plan approval process by amending the coastal act to provide that cities and counties which had completed only the land use plan would be required to begin issuing coastal permits 120 days after such LUP approval. Local governments were allowed one 90-day extension before the permitting requirement went into effect. The coastal commission was required to adopt rules for public notice, hearings, and appeals to be followed by local governments, and supplementary funds were appropriated to cover the added costs to local governments for the early assumption of permitting authority. By July 1982, no local governments had chosen to assume early permit responsibility, and predictions were that few if any would, perhaps because most are nearing completion of the total LCP and wish to concentrate their energies on that task. Seventeen jurisdictions with approved LCPs had by July 1982 begun issuing coastal permits in all or part of their boundaries. The best estimate is that most LCPs will be approved by July 1983 except for a few hard core problem areas.[152]

During the 1977–80 period, the state coastal commission concerned itself with two other major policy issues: (1) the further elaboration of statewide interpretative guidelines in major policy areas and (2) planning for the role of the state (and possibly regional) commissions in the postcertification period. The commission published a public review draft titled "State Interpretative Guidelines for Wetlands and Other Environmentally Sensitive Habitat Areas" in December 1979. At its January 1980 meeting, the state commission adopted its interpretative guidelines for lower cost housing opportunities.[153] In reviewing its work through 1979, the state coastal commission cited beach access, housing, wetlands, compact urban development, and energy as major areas of coastal act policy where substantial accomplishments had been made.[154] In May 1980, the executive director, Mike Fischer, announced the findings of a task force on various short-, mid-, and long-range problems of the commission. That report concluded, among other things, that: a substantial number of LCPs would not be completed by July 1, 1981; and that the state commission workload post-July 1981 would be greater than it could handle if regional commissions were terminated as scheduled. The task force recommended that the operation of the regional commissions be extended one year.

The 1981 legislative session did not respond to requests that the life of the regional commissions be extended, at least until all LCPs were approved. The phase-out of the regional commissions presented the state coastal commission and its staff with a workload crisis that brought about a major reorganization of the commission's operations. For more than eight years the regional commissions had carried the brunt of the workload in planning for and regulating California's coast. In the year's immediately preceding their phase-out, regional commissions had decided on 5,000 to 7,000 permits each year, with fewer than 10 percent appealed to the state commission. The original assumption in the plan to end the regional commissions was that local governments would by then be issuing permits in the coastal zone, but by mid-1982 this was the case only for all or part of 17 cities and counties, about 20 percent of the total.

In an effort to cope with the situation, the state coastal commission established district offices that were the same as 5 of the former regional offices and retained as part of the state coastal commission most of the former regional commission staffs. The North Central office (north of San Francisco) was combined with the San Francisco state commission office. The public will continue to deal with much the same staff people at the same places as before. What will be lost will be the work of the 78 regional commissioners who had met frequently, at convenient locations, and for long hours to assure maximum citizen, local government, and interest group input into the decision-making process. The state commission announced plans to meet more frequently, perhaps as much as eight days per month. The workload on the state commission and its staff will ease as the LCPs are completed and local governments take over permitting responsibilities. In the meantime, long agendas, extensive use of administrative permits, and greater use of consent calendars seem inevitable. In a sense the change makes the state coastal commission staff's life simpler, since the directors of the regional commissions were named by those commissions. The view from the state level was that regional staff quality was uneven, a problem that was corrected in the general reorganization. What was lost was the high level of participation by local groups and citizens.[155]

The strong action of state coastal commission executive director, Mike Fischer, has helped considerably in easing the immediate intergovernmental tensions that have characterized the implementation of the law, but it is unlikely that such tensions can be ended in the system that has been adopted in California. The legislation created a classic federalism conflict situation. Local governments, jealously intent on guarding their home rule prerogatives, will resist as much as possible the imposition of meaningful state control over their local activities. The state, through the coastal commission, will just as consistently attempt to assert the state position as strongly as possible in order to assure the protection of state interests in the coastal zone. In a way, the direct state and regional permitting that characterized the 1972 law was less disruptive to local government home rule sensitivities than the new legislation. While it is true that local governments occupy the key role in implementing the 1976 law, it is also true that they must operate within state goals and policies as interpreted by the state coastal commission. It is a situation that is parallel to the intergovernmental tensions in the statewide land use system in Oregon, and similar to intergovernmental tensions that have developed in Florida, Hawaii, Colorado, and to a lesser degree in North Carolina and Vermont, in the implementation of land- and growth-management programs in those states.

Monitoring and Enforcement
A central question to be asked about the California coastal planning and management system is whether or not the effort to achieve important state goals and policies almost entirely through local government implementation can be made to work. The answer to that question, in turn, rests heavily on the quality and consistency of the monitoring and enforcement system that is put in place by the state coastal commission to assure that: (1) local government decisions are made in accord with approved LCPs (2) conditions attached to permits, whether issued by local governments or the state, are enforced, and (3) effective review of amendments to local

coastal plans is carried out so that LCPs continue to be consistent with state policies and standards.

California joins Oregon, Vermont, and Florida in having not developed a strong monitoring and enforcement program. The lack of such a program has been a major source of criticism of the California effort by the federal Office of Coastal Zone Management in its Section 312 evaluations, and these criticisms have been followed by grant conditions calling for the strengthening of monitoring and enforcement efforts. The difficulty of surviving repeated strong opposition to the program in the 1979 and 1981 sessions of the California legislature and the pressure to complete the LCP approval process, especially with the loss of the regional commissions, has made it hard for the coastal commission to give

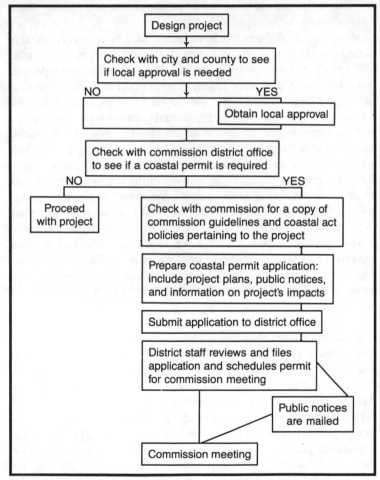

Figure 5.2. **The Coastal Permit Process After July 1, 1981**

time and energy to the monitoring and enforcement question, but by 1982 important progress was being made. (See Figure 5-2.)

In the face of criticism that local governments seemed to have no clear understanding of a monitoring or hearings appeal role for the state coastal commission, the development of a monitoring program was begun in 1981. The program when complete in 1982 will include "procedures for commission staff, guidance to local governments, regulations for hearings and appeals, and policies for the consistent processing of appeals." A staff member was assigned full-time to the management of the local monitoring program.[156] Unlike the Proposition 20 appeals procedure where citizens could bring appeals very easily to regional or state commissions, permits issued by local governments under LCPs can only be appealed on the grounds that the action violates the local coastal program. The commission itself, however, can call up appeals.

More than 50,000 permits have been issued by coastal regional or state commissions since 1973, first under proposition 20 and after 1976 under the new coastal law. While the great bulk of these permits were routine, many were highly controversial and approved only after the attachment of major conditions to the permit. Clearly the long-run effectiveness of the program depends on an effective and comprehensive permit condition monitoring system. As noted earlier in this chapter, there has to date been virtually no funds or time to develop such a system. As one critic put it, "Approximately 6,000 permits are issued each year with little follow-up monitoring to ensure compliance with permit conditions." A permit-enforcement system developed in the early 1980s marked an important beginning in protecting the long-run integrity of the California coastal program, but it will need to be strengthened as local governments take over the permitting process. Furthermore, enforcement of conditions under current law is a judicial matter, much more difficult than if the commission had the authority to enforce conditions administratively.[157]

State Agency Coordination

The problem of how to draw other state agencies into the California coastal program has been a challenge from early Proposition 20 days. The 1976 California Coastal Act required that state agencies have their development plans certified by the coastal commission for consistency with policies of the law. Some state agency relationships with the coastal commission are prescribed by other legislation, such as the partnership with the state coastal conservancy in developing and implementing a coastal access program (assembly bill 989). To implement that program, the two agencies have created a joint coastal access program. Funds for making accessways exacted as permit conditions available to the public and for acquiring new accessways come from federal coastal energy impact program and state sources. The importance of this program is indicated by the fact that almost 1,000 permits have been issued with access conditions since 1973. For a long while little was done to make these potential access points available to the public. Under the joint program, aggressive action is being taken to open up the access points.[158]

In an effort to improve state agency coordination with the coastal program, the coastal commission has sought the help of the Office of Planning and Research, a part of the governor's office, "to assist in resolving interagency conflicts . . . , and in identifying areas of duplication of effort among state agencies."[159] Involving the governor's office, as the experience of Oregon has shown, may be the only way to get the attention of state agencies who guard their turf with jealous attention. The 1976 coastal law mandated a coordinating role by the governor's Office of Planning and Research, but no funds were available to implement the mandate until 1981 when the state coastal commission provided it. The contract was for a one year period and expired in mid-1982.[160]

State agency coordination of another kind is necessary for successful application of the consistency provision of the federal coastal management law. Progress was reported in the 1980–81 period in coastal commission efforts to influence federal agency action, including the U.S. Navy and Army Corps of Engineers. The most dramatic consistency issue has involved the Federal Department of the Interior, where California has joined other West Coast states in objecting to DOI (Department of Interior) offshore oil leases in violation of state coastal programs. The state of California and the coastal commission brought suit in the U.S. District Court, which resulted in a ruling by the Court that Interior Secretary, James Watt, had violated the consistency provision of the federal Coastal Zone Management Act. As a result, Watt announced a two-year delay in leasing the four remaining basins in Lease Sale #53. The decision will be appealed by DOI. The coastal commission's aggressive efforts to force DOI conformance with federal consistency provisions has won it many friends in California—both Republican and Democrat, conservative and liberal.[161]

The 1981 Legislative Session
The last two sessions of the California legislature have seen strong efforts to abolish or weaken the coastal program. While the worst bills were not adopted in either session,[162] the 1981 legislature did

approve three bills which, while they could not be described as crippling to the program, certainly did weaken it to some extent. Senate bill 626 removed from commission jurisdiction one of its major coastal policy development efforts: affordable housing policies. Responsibility for implementing supposedly comparable policies was shifted to local governments within the coastal zone. Presumably the intent was not to kill the affordable housing effort, but to shift it to local governments to expedite the completion of the LCPs. Local governments who violated the policies could be taken to court. Several questions about just what the law means will be clarified in a future legislative session.[163]

The attack on the coastal commission's housing policy was orchestrated by a "heavy duty" corps of lobbyists from the California State Board of Realtors, the League of California Cities, and some parts of the California State Homebuilders Association, especially those who specialized in converting rental apartments in the coastal zone to condominiums. The coastal commission opposed the bill, but concentrated its efforts on assuring that the function would be continued, even if the responsibility were shifted from the state coastal commission. Even in that modest hope the commission was not successful, since loopholes in the bill make it unlikely that the successful commission policy of requiring a minimum of low and moderate income housing as a permit condition in the coastal zone will be continued except in those cities and counties that themselves favor such a policy and can stand the political heat of implementing it.[164] The development and enforcement of affordable housing policies was one of the more innovative, courageous, and successful efforts of the coastal commission. The change is a defeat for advocates of such housing policies. The new law will not, however, allow the modification or ending of affordable housing conditions in existing permits.

Assembly bill 385 contained a number of provisions making it easier to achieve LCP certification. Included was a provision that newly submitted LCPs would be reviewed for a finding of "no substantial issue," and if that proved to be the case, LCPs would be approved by a majority of the commissioners present, rather than a majority of the total commission membership. This bill also included authorization, noted elsewhere, for local governments to take over permitting duties upon approval of land use plans rather than complete coastal programs. The law did include a provision that in such circumstances all local government actions could be appealed to the state coastal commission. The law also expanded substantially types of developments that could be issued as administrative permits, requiring no hearings. Finally, senate bill 684 changed policies regarding the protection of agricultural land, permitting such conversion where consistent with the goal of concentrating development.[165] All of the amendments discussed earlier are weakening in their thrust. They do not go to the heart of the program, but they do raise danger signals for the future.

The 1981 legislative session also was not generous in providing the state coastal commission with funds for its operation. The commission requested slightly more than $11 million in its proposal to the governor, the governor recommended about $10.6 million, and the legislature appropriated $10,159,935. About 6.4 million was in state funds, and $3.7 million, in appropriated federal funds. A fiscal crisis was avoided when federal Office of Coastal Zone Management dollars were not eliminated, as had been feared. The importance of federal funds is illustrated by the fact that California has received since 1977 over $16 million for its federal coastal programs, of which about 10 percent went to the Bay Conservation and Development Commission.

The 1981–82 budget will force a slight reduction in the commission's staff—from 212 down to 198. The key point is that funds for the expanded responsibilities of the commission with the closing down of the regional commissions were not provided. The commission will have to do substantially more with almost a million dollars less than it requested. While the impact of the 1981–82 budget on program quality is hard to assess, it does not provide resources for a substantial expansion of the commission's monitoring and enforcement program.[166] The commissioner's director did note that the reduction in staff had been programed by the commission itself in light of the assumed completion of LCPs and the assumption of permitting authority by local governments. The slow pace of final LCP approval has put added pressure on the state coastal commission, at least for the next year or two. By mid-1982 the staff level was down to 171, with a scheduled commission initiated further reduction to about 140 positions by 1985. This smaller staff would concentrate on monitoring and enforcement, approval of all LCP amendments, processing or initiating appeals to the commission, public education efforts, and direct permitting in these special areas still under the direct jurisdiction of the commission.[167]

The Politics of the Future

In assessing the experience in those states analyzed in this book that took far-reaching land use actions in the 1970–74 period, the question is often asked as to whether the same land use initiatives could pass today in the light of the subsequent economic recession, energy crisis, and a general cooling of the fervor of the environmental movement. California, Oregon, and Florida are three states in which one can give at least a partial answer to that question. California and Florida are the most clear-cut examples where new land- and growth-management laws or major amendments were adopted following not only the economic recession and the energy crisis, but the general disillusionment with public bureaucracy that is sometimes associated with Watergate. In California, as we have seen, it was possible to develop a permanent coastal planning and management program in spite of these supposed handicaps. That program is not substantially different from what environmentalists were willing to agree to in 1972 if the legislation could have gotten past the California senate. In substance, the legislation is perhaps stronger in terms of its policies than the legislative proposals of the early 1970s, or at least it was until the 1981 session of the California legislature. The main reasons for this was the experience gained under the California Coastal Act of 1972 (proposition 20) with key problems and issues in the coastal zone. These problems had to be faced directly by the coastal commission and the regional commissions through the permitting process. It seems clear that the policies in the coastal plan drew heavily from that experience.

California certainly made a major change in 1976 by giving local governments the key responsibility for implementing the coastal zone management program. The central question now is whether the new approach will work. Another way to state that question is: "Are local governments sufficiently committed to including environmental as well as developmental considerations in their planning and management of the coast to assure a reasonable balance in the coastal zone?" Still another way of putting the question is whether the remaining state controls—in terms of certifying local programs, approving the changes in local coastal programs, monitoring and enforcement authorities and the limited appeals process—are extensive enough to assure that backsliding local governments, of which there are bound to be some among the 68 cities and counties in the California coastal zone, can be brought into line. A major determinent in answering this question will be the effectiveness of the monitoring and enforcement program in the postcertification period.

In posing questions to the persons interviewed in collecting data for this chapter, the question was consistently asked, "Will it work?" The answer almost always was a qualified "yes." Even the most ardent environmentalist seemed willing to undertake what he or she considered to be a somewhat risky experiment: that of placing a great deal of faith and trust in local governments to plan and manage

the California coast. Friend and foe alike of strong coastal management efforts expressed the view that the success or failure of the new
approach rested on the initial quality of the local coastal programs
and the ongoing efforts by local governments to make them work.
Those who have the most concern about whether local governments
will rise to the challenge find some comfort in the possibility of
increasing state controls if local governments do not adequately
carry out the goals and policies of the 1976 legislation.[168]

It seems clear that, for the foreseeable future, the politics of coastal
zone management in California will be dominated by the ongoing
development of state-local relationships, as well as by the relationship between the California Coastal Commission and other state
agencies. The key political question, however, will be whether or not
local governments will emerge as the permanent major custodians
of the welfare of the coast of California. The experiment is still in its
initial stages and certainly a number of years will be necessary to
bring in any kind of final verdict. A complicating variable in the form
of proposition 13 does not seem to have been as much a threat to the
program as at first feared. Of much greater seriousness is the
question of the future of federal funds. If there are no federal funds
in the program's future, the attitude of the governor and especially
the legislature toward the program will become even more important. In the meantime, California remains an important illustration
of moving from a heavy concentration on the state and regional level
in land use planning and implementation to a much reduced
dependence on the state level and a much heavier dependence on
the local level. It may be that in the end a reestablished reliance on
the regional level will be necessary to strike the right intergovernmental balance.

To conclude on a more overtly political note, the question can be
asked: Is the coastal act and programs associated with it likely to be
subjected again to the kind of political peril that was encountered in
the 1979 and 1981 sessions of the legislature? There is at present no
clear answer to the question. The state commission, under the
leadership of its executive director, has been preaching the gospel of
cooperation, partnership, and the need to pull together for a
common purpose: the protection and use of the California coast.
The new emphasis by the state commission on cooperation rather
than conflict is clearly more than just words. This approach should
serve the commission well in its effort both to be effective and to
survive politically. With 27 local coastal plans in place by mid-1982
and more about to be approved, California's adventure in state-local
cooperation to manage its 1,100 miles of coastline has reached a new
stage.

The 1982 session of the California legislature produced hope that the worst is over for the coastal commission. No further assaults on commission policies were mounted, and the general antibureaucracy rhetoric that dominated the 1981 session was muted. While an effort was made by one right-wing senator to "zero base" the budget and abolish the commission, there was no serious danger of that measure passing the legislature, in spite of the fact that it failed in committee on a 7–7 tie vote. The same group of lobbyists that had lead the attack on the commission's housing policy gave their support to winning approval of the commission's budget. For the moment at least, things look better on the political front. A complicating factor involved the 1982 governor's race in California. The Republican candidate campaigned on a platform that includes abolishing the coastal commission. The Democratic candidate was strongly supportive of the program. The Republican candidate won, but the prospects of his being able to carry out his pledge to abolish the state coastal program, including the commission, seem slim. Most observers feel that there is majority support in the legislature for continuing the program. A hostile governor, futhermore, is not an entirely new experience for the coastal program: Ronald Reagan as governor of California was not a strong supporter.[169]

A further encouraging note involves the apparent renewed interest in supporting the program by environmental groups. Such groups were not very helpful in the 1981 legislative fight over the commission's housing policy. The head of one powerful state environmental group expressed the view that the housing policy was "social engineering" and not a concern of that organization. In the 1982 session, environmental groups have taken a strong role in opposing efforts by a group of large landholders to have their wetlands excluded from the coastal zone. Such an issue is, of course, tailor made for even narrowly focused environmental groups.[170]

How well the local coastal plans actually will work is the crucial question for the 1980s. If they don't work in such a way as to manage the coast wisely and well, there may be another proposition 20 effort before the decade is over.

6

Oregon: A Blend of
State and Local Initiatives

The Issue Context

Oregon is attempting to develop a rational planning system in which legally binding state goals are the framework within which local governments, special districts, state agencies, and, to some extent, federal agencies must develop their own land use plans and activities. The process is a "top to bottom" and "bottom to top" effort which, in conceptual terms at least, is complete, rational, and comprehensive. No other state is attempting to put online a process that ties together so closely all levels of government in the broadly defined field of land use controls. It is important to understand why Oregon has taken such a potentially far-reaching action. There is considerable consensus that two factors were the most influential. First, Oregonians seemed to feel that the state enjoyed a special place in the world by virtue of its natural features and that these should be protected. The beauties of a wild and rugged coast, the pastoral valley stretching for a hundred miles between mountain ranges, and the rugged sagebrush and timber areas of eastern Oregon all were seen by many residents of the state as a precious and valuable heritage that made the state different from most other states.

The corollary factor was Oregonians' determination to avoid becoming another California. In its natural features, the Willamette Valley was all too similar to places such as the Santa Clara Valley and the San Fernando Valley in California, where uncontrolled development had turned a natural paradise into a polluted nightmare, at least in the eyes of many visiting Oregonians. There was a widespread fear in Oregon that somehow that tide of urban development would eventually wash over the Willamette Valley if the state did not take strong measures to guide, direct, and control the quality of this growth.

As a matter of fact, there was already evidence of problems developing in all three of the major geographic areas of Oregon: the coast, the Willamette Valley, and the eastern areas of sagebrush and timber. On the coast, there were scattered but very real development pressures. At least one participant felt that concern for the coast was the catalyst in the movement to bring development under control.[1] While not all observers could agree that the coast was the key, they all could agree that there were problems. In the view of another observer, the shabby development on Oregon's coast was symbolized by the Lincoln County area, near the center of Oregon's 400 miles of shoreline. Lincoln City "had become the paradigm for the reduction of this magnificence to a shambles of condominiums, high rises, amusement parks, industrial and municipal pollution, and shocking highway clutter." He noted that Senator Mark Hatfield had once dubbed that particular stretch of the Oregon coast as "the 20 miserable miles."[2] Oregon's Governor McCall stepped into this situation directly in the fall of 1972 when he ordered the Department of Environmental Quality and the state health division to stop all development in the area and to allow it to resume only where water and sewage facilities that could be certified as adequate were available. One journalist in Oregon, referring to Lincoln City's polluted streams, noted: "It's not nice to fool Mother Nature."[3]

Although a matter of concern, the Oregon coast was not under really severe growth pressures compared to many other coastal areas of the nation. Furthermore, the growth pressures certainly were more evident in Oregon's great central valley, where millions of acres of prime agricultural land were clearly tagged as future victims of urban sprawl. One fighter for better environmental management in Oregon felt that the very visible eating up of farmland in the Willamette Valley by urban encroachment was the key motivation for adopting a comprehensive land- and growth-management law in 1973. In the decade of the 1960s, farmland in the valley declined substantially—by some 34 percent. Clackamus County alone (in the Portland metropolitan area) had a loss of 10,000 valuable farm acres in one year.[4]

In his study of the Oregon Land Use Law, Charles E. Little assessed the growth-development pressures in the valley in his usual colorful fashion. Of the perhaps 7 million acres which make up the valley proper, a substantial part is forested slopes which Little saw not being prime targets for developers. The 2 million acres of flatland so attractive to developers also tended to be the prime agricultural land valued for food production. Thus a classic confrontation between urban sprawl and agricultural use that is so common in the rest of the country was clearly and forcefully focused in Oregon in the Willamette Valley. As Little put it: "Oregonians have reason to fear that Portland will ultimately merge with Salem, and Salem with Eugene to make one continuous conurbation, a nightmare of tract houses, clogged highways, factories, and commercial strips."[5]

If the coast and the valley were both important, Governor McCall saw eastern Oregon as also being in dire need of protection from the spoilers of the land. A study by Oregon's Department of Revenue in 1972 showed that about 160,000 acres of the state's dry rangeland deserts and plains lying east of the Cascade Mountain range had been subdivided into some 43,000 lots. Land sales, often fly-by-night schemes that were in fact illegal, threatened to do far-reaching environmental damage to a fragile landscape while duping outsiders into purchasing land that fell far short of the colorful brochures. In that dry and difficult area of Oregon, a lot with a view would often have no realistically available water, electric power, adequate roads, or almost any other amenity.[6] In addition to the gullible buyers, the fragile landscape was a silent victim. A member of Governor Stroub's administration offered other perspectives on Oregonians' willingness to support strong land use legislation. For example, protecting the beach and keeping it open to the public was a kind of glamour issue that crystalized public concern. Both the fishing and logging industries had declined as a result of too much stress on natural resources, and these economic side effects had brought some new converts into the environmental protection/land use camp.[7]

The leadership of Oregon's Governor Tom McCall was as important as any other one reason for the state's land- and growth-management initiative. Not only was Governor McCall one of the most colorful and effective phrasemakers of any of the governors of the 50 states, he was strongly committed to protecting Oregon from the kind of urban ravages that he had observed elsewhere, especially in California. In opening the 1973 legislative session, McCall noted:

> There is a shameless threat to our environment . . . and to the whole quality of life—[that threat] is the unfettered despoiling of the land. Sagebrush subdivisions, coastal 'condomania' and the ravenous rampage of suburbia in the Willamette Valley all threaten to mock Oregon's status as the environmental model for the Nation. We are in dire need of a state land use policy, new subdivision laws, and new standards for planning and zoning by cities and counties. The interest of Oregon for today and in the future must be protected from the grasping wastrels of the land.[8]

Oregon's reputation as a model in the environmental field was well founded. During the 1960s and early 1970s, the state had adopted a cluster of laws—the so-called B Bills—which mandated returnable bottles,[9] earmarked funds for bicycle paths,[10] issued bonds for pollution abatement,[11] reaffirmed the public's right and access to the beaches (not just to the mean high water line, but to the line of vegetation),[12] and finally removed billboards. Altogether, this legislation gave Oregon a legitimate claim to being the nation's leading state in terms of environmental awareness and commitment.[13]

Some important actions taken prior to 1973 were more directly tied to the subsequent land use legislation than the environmental actions just cited. For example, Oregon's passage of a scenic waterways bill by means of the initiative process may have brought home to politicians that the people were ready to move in the environmental/land use area, and that unless the legislators took action, the people would do so directly through the initiative process.[14] The use of the initiative in the land use area is one close tie between the Oregon experience and that in California. Senate bill 10, adopted in 1969, was a direct predecessor of the 1973 land use law.[15] Engendered by concern for agricultural land, this law mandated that all counties (and apparently all cities) in Oregon would have to develop land use controls, and that if they failed to do so, the governor had the power to step in and do it on behalf of local governments. Counties were having a very difficult time in attempting to move into this area, and, in effect, the Agriculture Committee's bill offered them a way to "get off the hook" through a state mandate to draw comprehensive land use plans.[16] The record of implementation under senate bill 10 was generally weak. Some local governments took some action, but even when they acted the focus on implementation was very limited. The "father" of Oregon's 1973 law felt that senate bill 10 "was a good start, but not good enough."[17]

The creation by the 1971 Oregon legislature of the Oregon Coastal Conservation and Development Commission provided a clear link to the coastal protection elements that eventually developed under senate bill 100. A 1969 effort to pass an estuarine protection bill through the Oregon legislature had failed, but by 1971 some local government officials on the coast apparently had begun to feel enough concern about growth pressures to support a new coastal commission.[18] Support for the commission was also buttressed by one of the earlier environmental groups concerned with the Oregon coast, the Oregon Shores Conservation Coalition.

Two other points should be made. First, environmentalists in Oregon, like their counterparts in other states assessed in this volume, viewed local governments as being very weak in either the will or the capacity to handle the land use problems developing in the state. Whether this view can be classed as a "bad rap" or an accurate assessment, local governments were not generally credited as having responded to senate bill 10. Second, the lack of adequate funding of senate bill 10 and the voluntary rather than mandatory character of the goals spelled out in it certainly troubled those who wanted to move more forcefully in the land use area in Oregon.

In moving to the *politics of adoption* in the next section, it is important to note that the time frame within which a major new land use law in Oregon was adopted was relatively short. From the time Senator Hector Macpherson decided to push for some kind of new land use legislation in 1971 to the passage of the legislation in 1973, Oregon was subjected to a kind of blitz, in which powerful forces allied themselves on both sides of the issue and a hard-fought series of compromises had to be worked out to obtain the bill's ultimate passage.

The Politics of Adoption

In one sense the groundwork for Oregon's 1973 land use law can be thought of as such legislative initiatives as senate bill 10. In a more immediate sense, the groundwork involved a key state senator elected to the legislature in 1971—a farmer, a local government official with experience in the planning field, and a person who had, along with some of his fellow agriculturalists, become increasingly convinced that something had to be done in Oregon to protect prime agricultural farmland. Hector Macpherson, however, had a broader vision than simply dealing with the loss of agricultural land to urban sprawl. His dream included creating a land use framework that would protect the state's land in all of its aspects. (See Figure 6-1.)

When elected to the legislature in 1971, he moved immediately to try to get legislative blessing for an interim study group that would consider the need for land use legislation and bring back a proposed bill to the 1973 session of the Oregon legislature. Although the 1969 and 1971 legislatures were generally friendly to environmental measures, Macpherson was not able to arouse much interest in his idea for an interim study group. In fact, he could not even get the support of the president of the senate, John Burns, a legislator from the Portland area. Nevertheless, Macpherson made it clear to all who would listen that he intended to put together some kind of group to study the problem of land use, and his suggestion was warmly received by the Oregon Environmental Council and by Bob Logan, director of the local government division in the governor's office. Macpherson also received some help from the legislative council in the matter of drafting and general research. The ad hoc group he got together to work on what ultimately became senate bill 100 included representatives from the city and county levels, some business people from the Portland area, and a number of persons with an environmental interest. Neither the Association of Oregon Industries (AOI) nor the Oregon State Homebuilders Association was at first convinced that broadranging action needed to be taken, but in spite of considerable skepticism the group managed in the period between the 1971 and 1973 sessions of the legislature to hammer out a general consensus on what they thought should be done in Oregon.

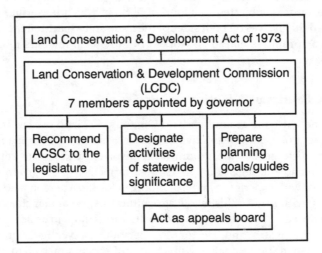

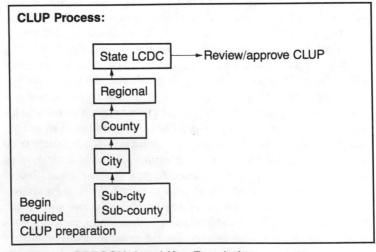

Figure 6-1. **OREGON: Land-Use Regulation**

The land use bill introduced into the 1973 legislature mandated that all cities and counties develop a comprehensive land use plan with a framework spelled out at the state level; provided that the local effort be integrated at the regional government level; and authorized a state agency to designate and permit areas of critical state concern and activities of statewide significance. As we shall see, the bill's final passage required major compromises in this system. The senate was closely divided in its attitude toward a land use bill, and the division was not particularly along partisan lines. The president of the senate, Jason Bae, was a moderate conservative from a conservative district on the coast whose position on the bill was uncertain. When the bill was introduced, the first question was not so much the effectiveness of external support groups, but whether or not the bill could be brought out of the senate Environmental and Land Use Committee, even though it had the support of the chairman, Ted Hallek. Altogether, there were only three votes in the committee, including Macpherson's, clearly in support of the legislation. The rest were described by Macpherson as "pretty conservative."

One of the committee members whose vote was doubtful was a coastal senator, Jack Ripper, whose opposition focused on the use of regional councils to integrate land use controls at the local level. Ripper's opposition, along with the strong opposition of the cities, counties, and others, led to the abandonment of that particular approach, in spite of the fact that it had the strong support of both Macpherson and the governor. As Macpherson saw it, integrating local land use controls from a regional perspective was the one thing that could be viewed as logical, yet would not sell. Once it became necessary to go all the way back to the local level, the only logical choice was counties, and this compromise in turn caused the legislation to lose the support of the cities.

The effort to reach enough compromises to get the bill through the legislature stalled at one point, and it looked as though the whole effort would fall apart. Senator Hallek despaired of the possibility of getting enough votes to get the bill out of the committee, much less through the entire senate. A determined Macpherson, however, persuaded Hallek to try the same approach that had worked so well during the interim period—an ad hoc committee. Governor McCall was involved in this decision and was instrumental in finding the key person to chair the ad hoc committee—L. B. Day. A former legislator, the former head of the state's Department of Environmental Quality, Day was at the time serving as the head of the Teamsters Union in the state of Oregon. A brusque, outspoken, but highly respected individual, he set to work with characteristic vigor and enthusiasm to hammer out a bill that could be passed. Day recalls his conclusion that: "If we can get the right people on the ad hoc committee, including some people from the counties, from the homebuilders association, from the governor's staff, from the Association of Oregon Industries, from the forest products industry, and others, I think we can hammer out a bill that will do it."

He succeeded in assembling such a group, but it went to work in what to many was an atmosphere of gloom and doom. However, they managed in ten days to redraft the bill. As Day recalled it:

> First, we maintained the idea that whatever passed had to have some place in it for the state level so that the state could step in when and if it was required to do so and see that proper action was taken at the local level. Second, we removed the mandated regional council authority. Third, the automatic authority for allowing the state land use agency provided for in the bill to establish and issue permits for critical areas was eliminated.

From Day's point of view, at least one of the compromises was clearly desirable—that of giving counties the responsibility for coordination at the local level. He noted that Oregon's 36 counties, in marked contrast to cities, had been generally supportive of land use planning. Another thing that Day brought to the land use legislation was a determination to write into the bill a very strong citizen participation element.[19]

When the redrafted bill was returned to the committee, there was some discussion as to whether the group had not far exceeded its mandate and made more changes that it really should have. Senator Hallek's explanation was simple: "Otherwise it wouldn't have been able to get four votes from within the committee." As it was, the new bill surprised everyone by being passed easily through committee, on a 6-to-1 vote.[20] Senator Burns cast the dissenting vote, noting: "I think we passed a paper tiger. . . . I think we've lobbied this bill to death." The bill was out of the senate committee, but it was far from being safe. On the one hand, it was feared that important backers of the bill would withdraw their support on the grounds cited by Senator Burns—that it had been made too weak by the work of the ad hoc committee. On the other hand, no one was sure how opponents would respond to the compromise. The passage of the bill in the senate turned out to be not as difficult as anticipated. An effort to remove the mandated goals and guidelines provision was beaten back, and the bill passed the senate by an 18-to-10 vote.

The next problem was to make certain that the bill was passed through the house in exactly the same form, in particular that it not be strengthened to such an extent that the senate would not accept it. Proponents of the legislation, with the strong support of the Oregon Environmental Council, urged the house leadership to pass the legislation exactly as it had been approved by the senate. One strong supporter of the legislation felt that the Oregon Environmental Council's decision to go along with not changing the bill in the house probably made the difference between passage and failure. He felt that if the group had taken a firm stand for strengthening the bill in the house, it would have succeeded, and that very success would have been the deathknell of the legislation.[21] Environmental groups generally maintained their support of the legislation, despite their disappointment at some of the changes. Their acceptance of "half a loaf" meant that what was still a trail-blazing experiment in land use planning and management could be carried out in Oregon.

The League of Cities opposed the legislation throughout, including its final compromised form. County coordination was as unwelcome to them as the initial regional proposals had been. Furthermore, the league was suspicious that the legislative oversight committee established by the bill might lead to legislative interference and undermine the home rule status of cities in Oregon.[22] According to one view, the League of Cities to some extent got "caught asleep at the switch" and was not really ready to press for what it wanted in the way of amendments. By the time the league got itself collected, the "train was so far down the track" that there was little or nothing it could do about it. By way of contrast, the county organization played a big part in working out the compromises and then strongly supported the legislation. A county representative was involved in the special (Day) ad hoc redrafting group, but the cities were conspicuous by their absence.[23]

In the lineup of groups for and against the bill, the timber industry is an especially interesting case. As a general rule, Weyerhauser was seen as favoring land use controls, while Georgia-Pacific was seen as opposing those controls, largely out of fear that the success of such controls in Oregon might spread to other states. In fact, Georgia-Pacific opposed senate bill 100, but a key Weyerhauser executive played a leading role in the Day committee's redrafting effort and subsequently supported the bill through to its passage. The Weyerhauser support illustrates how brilliant a strategy the ad hoc approach proved to be. It had the remarkable advantage of committing some of the strongest lobbyists in Oregon to support land use legislation. Once representatives of the Oregon Association of Industries, Weyerhauser, and the Oregon State Homebuilders Association agreed to serve on the ad hoc committee, they were caught up in the process and subsequently stood by their own work to support the legislation in the fight for adoption.

A representative of Georgia-Pacific felt that the Association of Oregon Industries got "snookered" into supporting the legislation. He noted that many members of the AOI as well as the farm bureau were greatly concerned that the legislation placed too much power in the hands of the state, represented a serious threat to private property rights, and was "being peddled too much as a panacea." In the end the Association of Oregon Industries "went along because we didn't think we could beat it." The opposition forces to the land use legislation were weakened by the fact that many of the most outspoken ones took such a violent and extreme stand that their effectiveness was severely limited.[24]

The Oregon State Homebuilders Association, according to its representative on the Day Committee, supported the legislation originally as a means of coping with no-growth advocates whom the association saw as especially strong in the Willamette Valley. The homebuilders association was especially supportive of the housing goal involved in the act, the mandate to provide public services to support needed development, and the development of an open planning process.[25] By contrast, in rural Washington County, the Oregon Rural Landowners Association recruited a statewide membership to fight the land use bill on the grounds that "If the concept contained in this proposal becomes law, it's only a matter of time until the state takes complete control over all rural land use and development."[26] The association continued its opposition throughout the session, stressing the pending state confiscation of private lands if the legislation were to pass. Coincident with the introduction of the legislation into the Oregon legislature, an "opposition group to the Macpherson bill" was formed in Clackamas County in the Portland metropolitan area. Its leader maintained that the bill would undermine the constitution and the bill of rights.[27]

Finally, it is interesting that the voting on senate bill 100 did not break along partisan political lines, but did break very sharply along geographical lines. The legislators from the Willamette Valley voted 5-to-1 in favor of the legislation, while the 30 legislators from the remainder of Oregon voted 2-to-1 against the legislation. As Little pointed out, this was more than simply an urban-rural split. It reflected the fact that heavy growth pressures that characterized the Willamette Valley were not yet as visible either on the coast or on the eastern Cascade side of the state. People in these sections of the state were and are very suspicious of state solutions to problems. To many of them, senate bill 100 seemed a hostile invasion by an alien power.[28]

When Hector Macpherson and his interim committee produced the first drafts of a proposed land use law for Oregon, the emphasis was on state-regional responsibilities, though a major role for local governments was also envisaged. In the end, when the dust of battle had settled and senate bill 100 became law effective October 5, 1973, Oregon's new land use initiative represented more of a state-local partnership than a state-dominated system. In this, the Oregon experience in the *politics of adoption* can be compared very closely to that in North Carolina.

Senate bill 100 authorized the establishment of a Land Conservation and Development Commission, composed of seven members appointed by the governor and confirmed by the senate, and a Land Conservation and Development Department, composed of a professional staff to serve the commission. The Land Conservation and Development Commission (LCDC) was charged with the duties of developing statewide goals and guidelines, model ordinances, an inventory of land use, the designation of activities of statewide significance, and the subsequent issuance of permits for such activities. It was also to review the comprehensive plans of local governments for conformance with the commission's goals, and to coordinate all state agency planning with the goals/guidelines process. The commission was specifically charged with promoting citizen participation.

Oregon's land use law relied heavily on enforcing state land use goals and objectives through carefully shaped local comprehensive plans. Until these plans were certified by the LCDC, the goals were to apply to specific local decisions. The commission was also authorized to recommend the designation of areas of critical state concern to the Oregon legislature, though in the legislative compromises worked out, its power to directly designate and permit such areas was eliminated. However, the law retained the commission's authority to take action in designating activities of statewide significance and to permit directly such activities as the siting of public transportation facilities, the planning and siting of public sewage systems, water supply systems, solid waste disposal sites and facilities, and public schools.

The role of local governments in the law that ultimately passed was very strong. Every county and city in Oregon, as well as the Columbia River Association of Governments (now the Metropolitan Service District) in the Portland metropolitan area,[29] must develop comprehensive plans consistent with state goals and guidelines. Conformance with state goals was mandatory, while the guidelines merely indicated to local governments how they *might* go about meeting the requirements of the act. The county, and in the case of the Portland metropolitan area, the Metropolitan Service District,[30] had the responsibility for reviewing the plans of special districts, cities, and state agencies within the boundaries of that county or regional agency and identifying any conflicts that might exist between those plans and the LCDC mandated goals. However, the task of bringing the local plans into line with the state goals was reserved to the state level through the Land Conservation and Development Commission.

Comprehensive plans (including zoning, subdivision, and other ordinances and regulations) are submitted to the commission, which has the authority and responsibility to analyze those plans and either approve ("acknowledge") them or require their modification. An initial mandate that the commission would itself produce the comprehensive plan if a city or county failed to act was repealed in a 1977 amendment. Instead, the state commission was authorized to issue an injunctive order requiring the local government to act. To force ultimate compliance, the commission must seek an order in the district court.[31] The law required local plans to be completed a year after the adoption of the goals and guidelines. However, added time could be provided, and has been provided, for cities and counties so long as they showed satisfactory progress toward meeting the requirements of the act.[32]

A very significant feature of the law was the provision of a bipartisan Joint Legislative Committee on Land Use which would act as a watchdog over the activities of state and local governments in carrying out the mandates of senate bill 100. The joint committee was to act as a liaison between the department and the legislature and to serve as a legislative policy review unit. Finally, the joint legislative committee was charged with solving a problem that has puzzled every state that has gone into the land- and growth-management field: whether and how to compensate for values reduced by land use regulations.[33]

Senate bill 100 also mandated the establishment of a state citizen involvement advisory committee which would be "broadly representative of geographic areas of the state and interests related to land use and land use decisions. . . . " The advisory committee was to help the commission devise a program allowing maximum public participation in the goals and guidelines process and would also review county citizen involvement plans mandated in another section of the act.[34]

Although one of the major compromises eliminated the integrating role of regional agencies, the new law did permit a considerable role for the regional level. As already noted, the integrative unit in the Portland area is a regional council rather than the three counties (Multnomah, Washington, and Clackamas counties) in that metropolitan area, which constitutes almost half of the total population of

Oregon.[35] Furthermore the law provides for the election of a regional planning agency if counties representing 51 percent of the population in their region request it. The commission is empowered to allow and oversee such an election. If a majority of the votes favor such action, then a regional unit to take over the integrating functions from counties can be formed. Furthermore, on the request of the county and cities where there is an existing regional council of governments, the council of governments can assume the county's planning role. In fact, several areas in Oregon have adopted this option, including the regional agency in Lane County (Eugene).[36]

The commission was given until January 1, 1975, to prepare the goals and guidelines. The broadness and force of the goals was set out in a special statement of legislative intent inserted into the *Senate Journal* in Oregon and reading as follows:

> To be precise, then, goals are intended to carry the full force of authority of the state to achieve the purposes expressed in the preamble and policy statement of this act. We make no effort to curb the limits to which goals may be applied, preferring to put faith in the process of citizen input, commission approval, and legislative review.[37]

Until the goals and guidelines were developed, all comprehensive plans and land use regulations were to conform to the goals set forth in the act's predecessor, senate bill 10. These ten goals served as the starting point for the commission's development of its own goals.[38]

The commission's authority merely to "review and recommend to the legislative assembly the designation of areas of critical state concern" was viewed by many at the time as a drastic downgrading of its authority in the original draft. However, in view of a Florida court ruling that a similar grant of power was an unconstitutional delegation of legislative authority, the Oregon compromise may have been a matter of wise foresight. What is certain is that the commission had not as of 1982 used even its reduced authority in this regard. In the section on activities of statewide significance, the law still contained a very strong potential power for the commission that could lead eventually to direct state permitting. As of 1982, the commission had not elected to move in that direction.[39]

The right to appeal is rather broad under the act. The county is assigned a lead role in carrying to the commission any action within its boundaries by a city, a special district, or a state agency that it considers to be in conflict with the commission's statewide planning goals. Appeals may also be filed by any city, special district, or state agency, as well as by citizens or groups of citizens "whose interests are substantially affected."[40]

Finally the legislature asserted its intention to keep close tabs on the implementation of the law. It required the land conservation and development department to report monthly to the joint legislative committee on the progress made by the department and commission, counties, and all other agencies involved in the act. The department was to issue a semiannual report to the legislature, incorporating any comments of the joint legislative committee.[41]

As this brief description makes clear, the law that came about through the determination and persistence of Hector Macpherson, Governor McCall, and a great many other Oregonians, is much more than a land use statute. In both substance and process, it represents a pioneering initiative in comprehensive planning and growth management. Many people and groups contributed to the adoption of the law, and most of them have continued their keen interest while the implementation process has moved forward. It is to that implementation process that we now turn our attention.

The Politics of Implementation

A decade has passed since the October 1973 date when Oregon's comprehensive planning and growth management law became effective. The effective date itself was delayed by an initiative petition effort that would have forced a vote by the people of Oregon before the law could have been put into effect. Although the petition effort failed by a substantial margin, it did cause a delay in getting the implementation effort underway.

In assessing the implementation record in Oregon, a number of factors must be considered. With a state level commission or board involved, the question arises as to the quality of leadership provided by that board. A related question is how quickly and effectively the staffing of the effort was carried out. Still another closely related question is whether there was timely, adequate funding both for the start-up effort and for the ongoing implementation of the act's provisions. Finally, it is necessary to assess the degree to which the law continued to receive support from the executive branch, the legislature, and interest groups. The other side of that coin is the degree to which opposition to the law continued and to what extent there were new sources or degrees of opposition.

On the matter of funding, action was delayed several months by the abortive petition effort. The 1973 legislature authorized funds but did not actually appropriate them. Fortunately, the Oregon legislature was in special session early in 1974, providing another opportunity. Governor McCall asked for a budget of almost $1.7 million for the land use program, but the more conservative legislature appropriated just over $600,000. Of this funding, about half was to be derived from state revenues and half from federal funds received by the state. Over the next several months, the commission also obtained $42,000 from Oregon's emergency board (a state agency empowered to make special appropriations when Oregon's biennial legislature is not in session), and a grant of $50,000 from the Northeast Regional Commission of the federal government.[42]

The first director of the commission felt that the start-up funds were far from enough and that the seven-number commission and a staff of only 18 people worked under "severely limited financial restraints." As he put it, "The Oregon legislature did what many legislative bodies do. It passed an innovative program and then sat back to let it be starved for funds.[43] Other commission members and observers did not stress the lack of initial funding, perhaps because the 1975 legislative session did fund the commission in a very substantial way. The commission did have what most states would regard as adequate start-up funds.

The quality of the membership on the commission appointed by Governor McCall was generally considered to be very good. The chairman was a veteran of both Oregon politics and land use and environmental efforts in the state—none other than L. B. Day, the head of the very effective ad hoc committee. Day was not a person about whom Oregonians had (or have) mild opinions. He was a self-confident, aggressive leader who moved forcefully to accomplish his objectives. The entire implementation effort was in many ways dominated by Day's personality from 1973 through to his resignation from the board in 1976. While there were mixed views on the matter—about Day's caustic tongue and abrasive approach to local governments, for example—the general consensus was that Day had succeeded in moving the implementation effort along. The executive director of Oregon's leading environmentally oriented watchdog agency gave Day credit for forcing decisions out of the commission, in keeping interest groups reasonably happy, and in drafting goals that the legislature found acceptable.[44] The father of Oregon's land use effort, Hector Macpherson, rated Day very highly in dealing with the public, but not so highly in handling local governments. He noted that Day had grown contemptuous of local governments, especially cities, during the working of senate bill 10, when he observed their reluctance and inability to respond to that mandate.[45]

A long-time participant in local governments held that Day and the commission tended to take the position that the commission was a "superagency in Oregon" and that this had not only hurt the commission with local government but also with other state agencies.[46] Day's own comment on local governments was: "We've had some problems with them and had to whip them into line." In his view, counties had been helpful but a lot of cities "would settle for a shithouse in the middle of the street for ten dollars."[47] Clearly, Day was a strong leader with strong opinions. On balance, he did a very good job in getting the implementation effort underway.

The matter of staffing adequacy was a continuing source of frustration for both commission members and close observers of the implementation effort. There were only two executive directors during the first five years of the commission's life—Arnold Cogan, who served for about one year, and Harold Brauner, who occupied the position until 1978. Each was judged to have strengths and weaknesses that, in fact, cause one to think that perhaps it would have been ideal to have had them both working for the commission. Cogan was universally credited as being a very capable planner in the technical sense of the word but not strong in working with the legislature and dealing with budget matters. Brauner, on the other hand, was credited with being very good in budget matters, very effective in working with the legislature, but not possessed of planning skills that were needed by the agency. Unfortunately, neither executive director brought in someone in a secondary role who had complementary skills.

The vice chairman of the original LCDC held that the staff worked very hard and were very dedicated, but were much too young and inexperienced. He noted that he "lost a major battle to be able to recruit more experienced people by paying the director a high salary and setting a comparably high salary scale for professional people below him."[48] The head of the environmental watchdog agency felt in general that a very poor job had been done in staffing the agency, and that staffing quality had ranged from "mediocre to poor." He found this puzzling, since the attraction of Oregon as a landmark experiment in land use should have allowed the agency to recruit experienced and highly competent people.[49] Problems with staffing a new land- and growth-management agency at the state level seem to characterize many of the efforts assessed in this volume. Whether the state agency has had its own staff, or an existing state agency has provided staff, there seems to have been similar complaints: dissatisfaction because the staff people recruited were too young and too inexperienced to handle what was a delicate political and difficult professional task.

Despite funding and staffing problems, some very important things were in fact accomplished in the first 18 months of the commission's existence. Commission Chairman Day saw the admittedly limited funding the first year as not preventing the commission from going to the people all over the state for their ideas about what ought to go into the all-important state goals and guidelines. LCDC staff personnel and commission members held meetings for this purpose in "nearly every community in the state." About 10,000 people participated in workshops, hearings, and other meetings, and 17 advisory committees of technical specialists assisted in the goals and guidelines effort. As Cogan saw it, "The usual bureau-cratic procedures were turned around." Rather than issue arbitrary decisions to which the public would react, the commission tried to get the public's views early on.

By late October 1974, a formal first draft of the goals and guidelines were published in a newspaper tabloid format and widely distributed by direct mail and through public libraries. These were subjected to citizen scrutiny in public hearings throughout the state during the first two weeks of November. By the first week in December, a revised version of the goals and guidelines was given the same wide distribution. After a final public hearing on Decem-ber 13, 1974, and two public markup sessions, the commission adopted the final goals and guidelines on December 27, 1974. The commission was taking additional testimony and making minor revisions at the final hour. In addition to the 10,000 active partici-pants, it was estimated that more than 100,000 Oregonians viewed television programs dealing with the development of the goals and guidelines.[50] One must conclude that Oregon maintained its reputa-tion as being a state in which citizen participation means something more than it does in most other states. Citizens of Oregon seem especially willing to dedicate their time and energy to the considera-tion of major public policy matters.

The goals and guidelines became operative January 1, 1975. The 14 goals initially adopted included the 10 interim goals from senate bill 10, though with changes and elaborations, plus 4 additional goals in the areas of forest lands, energy, citizen involvement, and housing. They ranged from goal 1 of citizen involvement to goal 14 of urbanization. In between these two anchor points were a number of items that would be familiar to any comprehensive planning framework. They included land use planning, of course, and several goals related to natural resources: agricultural lands; forests; open space; scenic and historic areas; natural resources; air, water, and land resources quality; and areas subject to natural disasters and hazards. Goals that were more oriented toward urban quality of life included recreational needs, the economy of the state, housing, public facilities and services, transportation, and the already men-tioned urbanization goal. A reflection of the concerns of the time was represented by the inclusion of energy conservation. Each goal was followed by guidelines with suggested approaches to implementing

the mandatory goals. This mandated framework remained un-
changed until 1976 when four goals pertaining to the Oregon coast
and one for the Willamette Greenway were added.[51] The goals and
guidelines formed the framework for developing a rational and
comprehensive planning and growth-management system for the
state of Oregon. Before examining how effective the goals have been
in Oregon's unique effort, a brief discussion of the most significant
goals is in order.[52]

Of the 19 goals, 5 in particular combine to form the basis for an
impressive set of urban policies and the interface at the urban fringe
with agricultural and other rural areas. The centerpiece of these 5
goals is the urbanization goal, goal 14, which requires the establishment of an urban growth boundary around cities and contiguous
areas. The four closely related goals, which help to define development occurring within the urban growth boundary, are economy
(9), housing (10), public facilities and services (11), and transportation
(12). It has been suggested that sound urban development could not
adequately be dealt with without first pursuing goals 10–12, which
also interact with one another. At the same time, the agricultural
goal (3) is complementary to urbanization—one aim of restricting
urban growth is to protect farmland. At times, however, there may
be conflicts between these two goals which help to define and hold
the boundaries of each.[53] The relationship among these goals are
shown in Figure 6-2.

Figure 6-2. **Policy Framework Diagram**

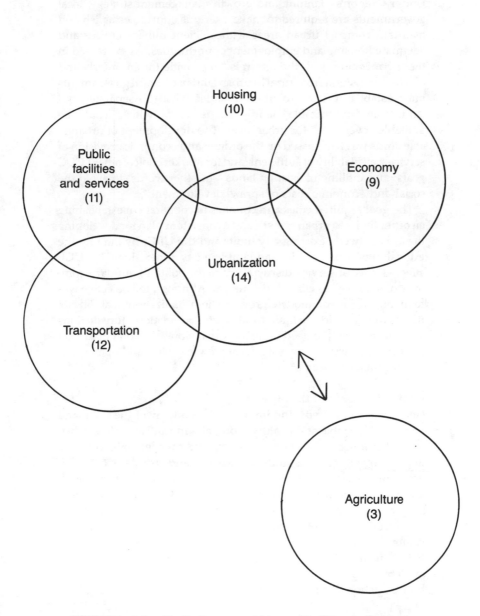

Housing
(10)

Public
facilities
and services
(11)

Economy
(9)

Urbanization
(14)

Transportation
(12)

Agriculture
(3)

SOURCE: John M. DeGrove and Nancy E. Stroud, *Oregon's State Urban Strategy,* prepared for the National Academy of Public Administration (Washington, D.C.: U.S. Government Printing Office and the Department of Housing and Urban Development. HUD-PDR 644, December 1980), p. 17.

Goal 14: Urbanization

Under Oregon's planning and growth-management strategy, local governments are required to make a serious effort to establish and maintain compact urban areas with efficient public services and adequate housing and employment opportunities. As expressed in the urbanization goal, the intent is "to provide for an orderly and efficient transition from rural to urban land use." Local governments must establish urban growth boundaries (UGB) to separate rural land from "urbanizable" land—that is, areas which would be available "over time" for urban uses. The development of urbanizable lands was to be based on the orderly and economic provision of services; availability of sufficient land for market choice; other LCDC goals; and infilling of existing lands—in other words, to avoid the social and economic costs of sprawl development.[54]

The goal required cities and counties to cooperate in establishing an outer limits to urban growth and a consistent plan for developing the area between existing city limits and the UBG. By limiting the extension of urban services and guiding city annexations, the UGB affected special service districts and metropolitan boundary commissions, as well as cities and counties. Although the objective was to manage or accommodate growth, the urbanization goal did not necessarily provide a limit to absolute population. Jurisdictions were to consider the need for urban expansion based on population projections, carrying capacity, local growth policy, and open space and recreational needs.[55]

Goal 9: Economy of the State

Goal 9 was to diversify and improve the economy of the state, and encouraging stable and healthy economies in rural as well as urban areas. Planning jurisdictions were required to meet both economic and urbanization goals and to integrate land use decisions with economic decisions. Economic growth was to be encouraged, particularly "in areas that have underutilized human and natural resource capabilities and want increased growth and activity." Thus, the special needs of distressed areas were to be considered in comprehensive planning. However, economic development was not to be considered in isolation from other considerations such as land availability, pollution control requirements, and the availability of transportation, labor, materials, and—in particular—housing.[56]

Goal 10: Housing

The housing goal, generally, encouraged adequate and mixed housing at affordable prices for Oregon households. It also required an inventory of "buildable lands," those lands in urban and urbanizing areas suitable, available, and necessary for residential use. This requirement complemented the housing needs assessment mandated in goal 14. The availability and costs of public services were key factors in meeting both goals. For each goal, methods required by the LCDC encouraged a compact form of development and higher housing densities. A 1979 clarification of the housing policy stressed the need for local zoning and approval decisions to accommodate low and moderate income housing needs.[57] To disperse low income housing, the guidelines suggested the use of tax incentives, code revisions, land use controls, acquisition, subsidies, and the development of urban facilities and services. To encourage redevelopment, the guidelines suggested using financial incentives and resources to stimulate rehabilitation and to bring dwellings into compliance with building codes.

Goal 11: Public Facilities and Services

This goal was to plan and develop a timely, orderly, and efficient arrangement of public facilities and services to serve as a framework for urban and rural development. LCDC policies did not require a detailed design but rather a strategy for providing key facilities. The strategy was to address the timing and location of services, their means of financing, and the providers of the service. Methods to assist in servicing included tax incentives and disincentives, land use controls, acquisition, code enforcement, and joint development practices. Impact fees have also been suggested by the LCDC. This goal, like the others, would force coordination among planning and service jurisdictions, including special districts.[58]

Goal 12: Transportation

This goal was to provide and encourage a safe, convenient, and economic transportation system. Transportation plans were required to "minimize adverse economic impacts and costs and to facilitate the flow of goods and services so as to strengthen the local and regional economy." Transportation plans had to be intermodal and capable of meeting the needs of the disadvantaged. Transportation guidelines required that area wide transportation studies be submitted to local and regional agencies for approval in light of comprehensive plans. This guideline brought state and federal planning efforts directly in line with local and regional planning. Guidelines also stated that major transportation facilities were to avoid prime agricultural lands and the disruption of farm and urban social units. In this way, both urbanization and rural goals were directly supported.

Goal 3: Agricultural Lands

The goal to preserve and maintain agricultural lands disallows the treatment of these lands as left-over areas available for development, and instead stresses their economic and social value to the state.[59] The goal is based in part on another Oregon statute, "Agricultural Land Use Policy." The goal mandates the designation of exclusive farm use zones (EFU), an approach that had been optional since 1961. Minimum lot sizes within those zones must be of sufficient size to protect existing commercial agriculture, and the land is selected to protect the best soils in the state. Agricultural land can be excepted if it is irrevocably committed to urban or nonfarm rural uses or not reclaimable for farm use. It can also be excepted where there is a compelling need for the land, but such an exception must be justified on a case-by-case basis, with the final decision resting with the commission. Within the zones, all nonfarm development and land divisions must be compatible with the adjacent farm operations, and owners of agricultural land qualify for property and inheritance tax benefits, as well as special assessment benefits.

Implementation Provisions

The policy network described above is made effective through the administrative and legal framework of the legislation. It is this second aspect of the legislation that gives the state policy its implementing force and its national importance. Goals adopted by the LCDC are standards by which comprehensive plans and actions by local governments, special districts, and state agencies are measured, thus assuring consistency between different levels of government. One goal itself was devoted to the central implementing role of local and regional comprehensive plans. This goal, "land use planning," established the planning process and policy framework as a basis for all decisions and actions related to the use of land. Local plans must include implementing mechanisms "consistent with and adequate to carry out the plans," and exceptions in these plans to the statewide goals must be justified according to specific criteria set forth in the goal.

Unlike most comprehensive planning legislation in the nation, Oregon's senate bill 100 established an administrative structure with power to ensure jurisdictional compliance with the goals. The LCDC has the duty to review and accept or reject comprehensive plans and to develop standards to carry out the intent of the law through full implementation of the goals. The commission assists the implementation of goals through grants and technical assistance, and through explanatory "policy papers" that guide the implementing jurisdictions. The 1981 Oregon legislature directed that all such commission policies be adopted by rule if they have statewide impact. The goals adopted by the commission have the force of law. The commission may conduct hearings and issue orders to require regulations, plans, and land use actions to conform to state goals. It is significant, especially in the national perspective, that those powers of the commission have been used; between 1973 and 1979, more than 133 petitions for review were heard by the LCDC under this provision.

In determining goal compliance, the LCDC is assisted by the Land Use Board of Appeals (LUBA) created in 1979. The board consists of a chief hearings officer and two other hearings officers appointed by the governor. It reviews land use decisions of any local or state agency previously heard in the state circuit court, and also recommends orders to the LCDC regarding compliance with statewide planning goals.[60] The board's decisions on land use and the LCDC decisions on goal compliance can be reviewed and enforced by the courts, starting with the court of appeal and ultimately reaching the Oregon supreme court. In the past, Oregon courts have generally supported the legislation, which has generated significant legal as well as administrative review.

The establishment of the Land Use Board of Appeals and its subsequent actions has generated considerable controversy, but has been viewed favorably by most observers. One view is that the quality and speed with which decisions are made has improved drastically under LUBA compared to the performance of the circuit courts. Appeals to LUBA are concerned mainly with procedural matters and above all focus on the adequacy of the record made by the city, county or other agency in applying the standards of senate bill 100. The question asked is: Are the findings of fact and conclusions of law sufficient to justify the decision taken? The answer, especially with regard to county government action, is often "no." The implications of this problem for the future of the land use law will be examined below.

LUBA's relationship with LCDC has been generally good. If a case coming before LUBA involves a goal issue, its action takes the form of a recommendation to LCDC, which still handles goal approval and interpretation matters. LUBA will come up for sunset review in 1983, at which time there will likely be efforts either to abolish it or turn it into a land use court. In the meantime, it is playing an important role in the implementation of the land use law.[61]

Developing and Funding the
Plan Acknowledgment System

A consistent lesson that emerges from almost every state that has adopted some initiative in land and growth management is that accepting new state power in growth management and new mandated requirements on local governments is always made smoother if substantial state dollars accompany the mandates. Oregon has supplied large sums of money to local governments to help them in the admittedly difficult task of complying with the statewide goals. After the program's shaky startup, the budget submitted by the commission to the governor in 1975 was subsequently funded by the legislature in an amount almost equal to the original request. The governor accepted the commission's request for $6.1 million (from state funds and federal grants), but he made substantial and important shifts in how the funds were to be used. The governor increased the funding for local government from $3.3 million to $4.4 million. In acting on the governor's request, the legislature approved a budget of $5.9 million for the 1975–77 period, reducing the state's 50 percent share by about $170,000. The budget passed both house the legislature by a two-thirds majority, indicating, at that point at least, substantial support for the legislation in the Oregon legislature.[62]

Budget notes attached to LCDC's budget made clear that the legislature agreed with the governor's emphasis on local coordination and assistance to local government. Specifically, over 13 professional positions were earmarked for local coordination and proposed positions for training programs and the development of model ordinances were specifically deleted. This reluctance to fund the program more adequately at the state level may have contributed to the slow pace of completing and approving local plans. Recognizing that the commission would receive more local requests than there were funds to disburse, the legislature directed that the dollars be given to jurisdictions which could certify their ability to commit local resources to comprehensive planned development and could reasonably be expected to produce an approved plan.[63] The legislature was determined to keep close tabs on the program. It required the commission to submit its format for contracting with local governments to the Oregon Emergency Board[64] and also required that a schedule of grants be submitted either to the emergency board or to the Joint Committee on Ways and Means should the legislature be in session. Furthermore, the Joint Committee on Land Use was to be given an opportunity to review the proposed grants and give its recommendations to the emergency board or the Ways and Means Committee.

The substantial sum of money earmarked for local planning grants obviously provided a rich opportunity for policy direction and guidance, as well as encouragement for prompt compliance with the goals and guidelines adopted at the beginning of 1975. One of the key issues has been the degree to which the commission has used local grants to set priorities among the goals. Generally, Oregon's land use watchdog agency, 1,000 Friends of Oregon, has been disappointed in the commission's record in this regard. Local governments, by way of contrast, have steadfastly resisted being forced to adopt priorities among the goals. The commission itself has been ambivalent on this issue and has shifted its position to some extent from time to time.

A description of how the process got underway during 1975, provided by a 1,000 Friends of Oregon *Progress Report*, sheds some light on the approach used by the commission. In the absence of extensions, the completed comprehensive plans of 36 Oregon counties and 230 Oregon cities would have been due in the commission's office on January 1, 1976. This deadline was obviously unrealistic, and it was clear that extensions would have to be granted. A central question was what conditions would be attached to these extensions, and how long they would be given for.

During the first two thirds of 1975, the commission spent a substantial amount of time considering what should go into a handbook for local governments to use in preparing their comprehensive plans, and what the groundrules should be in extensions and compliance. The recommendation of 1,000 friends was that grants be given for specific work, projects tied to particular goals, and that the commission should adopt goal priorities for local governments during the two-year funding period. When the commission issued its grant and planning review criteria in the form of a rather lengthy and detailed handbook, its general approach reflected important elements of the 1,000 friends' position, but did not require as close continuing scrutiny as that group would have desired.[65]

The commission's first round of grants and extensions to local governments began on January 5, 1976—the original deadline for completed plans. Twelve local governments received planning assistance totaling $234,732 and one-year planning extensions. The extensions gave some clear indication to other cities and counties as to how the game would work. The LCDC staff had recommended approval of these extensions essentially as requested. However, Chairman L. B. Day held to the hard line that one-year extensions would be sufficient. He also told the planning director in one Oregon county that local governments should focus on the agricultural goal by establishing exclusive farm use zones and on the urban goal by establishing urban growth boundaries.[66] The commission seemed to be agreed on the priority of these two goals. On the other hand, Day repeated a previously announced commission policy that there were no priority rankings among the statewide goals. This inconsistency led to future tension between the commission and people who advocated priority setting among the goals.

The pattern in the first round of grants and extensions was this: a time limit of one year, with a requirement that a revised extension request would have to be made at the end of 1976, and a mandate that all urban areas designate urban growth boundaries and exclusive farm use zoning "as soon as possible." The interpretation of the phrase "as soon as possible" left the degree to which the commission had actually set any priorities among the goals open to question. Certainly environmental groups in Oregon, and especially 1,000 Friends of Oregon, considered the combined use of the urbanization and agricultural goals as the heart of the land use law. Whether these two goals should in effect have number one priority has continued to be a point of controversy between local governments on the one hand and environmental groups on the other, with the state land use agency in the middle.[67]

A local government that had done little or nothing in the way of planning could ask for a temporary (1–6 months) extension during which it would take action to show that it was making satisfactory progress in complying with the LCDC goals. The local government was required to show a work schedule, the adoption of a citizen involvement program, and a list of all federal, state, and local agencies involved in the planning area and how these agencies would be involved in the planning process.[68] An actual planning extension gave additional time for local governments to move toward complying with LCDC goals. The local government was required to present a detailed compliance schedule under which it proposed to meet those goals not already met. Later on they could seek grants to speed up the accomplishment of specific elements of the work program. Local governments could also ask that LCDC recognize its compliance with one or more of the required goals.[69] The initial review of these local government requests was by the county (or, in the Portland area, the Metropolitan Service District). Some state departments in Oregon such as the Department of Environmental Quality and the Department of Transportation also have commented on a local government's request to satisfy itself that any concern of that agency had been fully met in the planning process. This is important because once comprehensive land use plans are adopted by local governments and acknowledged by LCDC, state agencies are required to comply with those plans in their own activities.[70]

By April 1976, the commission had approved 46 temporary extensions and 36 planning extensions; 8 local governments, including 2 counties, had requested compliance acknowledgments; and 35 jurisdictions had received planning grants of almost $1 million. It should be noted that planning grant requests were reviewed by the LCDC staff and a local coordinator and by the citizen involvement and local officials advisory committees. Approved grants were then reviewed by the Joint Legislative Committee on Land Use and authorized by the emergency board. The amount of a grant was tied generally to the size of the local government, and thus ranged from $8,640 for Cascade Lock, a small community of 620, to a grant of almost $190,000 for Multnomah County (Portland), with a population of over 500,000.[71] The 1975 legislature not only provided funds for planning grants; it also made a special allocation of dollars to each county in support of its coordinating responsibility under the law. Grants of $9,000 went to each county for hiring a county coordinator, with some counties pooling their money to employ one person among them.

The commission had 11 field representatives who monitored the compliance schedules of local governments in reviewing their work programs. These field representatives were felt by many observers to be one of the most popular and well-accepted components by local governments of LCDC operations. As one observer put it, they have "abated some of the great opposition at the local level to the Salem bureaucracy."[72] It is true that planning extensions, at least in theory, tied a local government down tightly to a compliance schedule and a developed work program, and involved extensive dealings with the commission. As the same observer noted, this process represented a very active state role which required considerable negotiation and skill on all sides. It is easy to see why some local governments, especially smaller cities, objected to what they considered excessive bureaucratic requirements.[73]

In summing up the early phase of state funding of local programs, as of August 1976, 124 cities and 27 counties had received planning extensions, and LCDC had made 152 grants to 123 cities and 29 counties. The remaining cities in the state had made so little progress that they were not even in a position to request a temporary extension. However, this is a substantial record of accomplishment in a relatively short time in bringing Oregon communities into full compliance with the law. By fall 1976, the state had distributed about $2 million of state and federal dollars in support of planning extensions, all of which required, among other things, a 10 percent local commitment and a work program as noted earlier.[74]

Clearly, the completion of local comprehensive plans that conform with the state goals is the heart of the land- and growth-management system in Oregon. From the perspective of funds channeled to local governments to expedite the process, the environment continued favorable after 1976. For the fiscal year 1978–79, local governments requested about $4.6 million in planning grants and another $655,000 in coordination grants. A little over $3 million in planning and $500,000 in coordination grant dollars were available. In providing the money, the legislature attached a budget note that was a clear signal that the legislature was growing impatient with the continued slow pace of plan development.[75]

The 1979–80 budget request for funds continued the stress on planning funds for local governments. A total of just over $9 million was requested, of which $5.7 million was earmarked for local government planning assistance and plan maintenance grants. Approval of the plan maintenance request would commit the state to continuing financial support for local governments after the commission had accepted their plans. The total request for the 1979–81 biennium was $2.5 million less than the 1977–79 budget, because many cities and counties were expected to have their plans completed and accepted by late 1979 and 1980.[76] The deputy director of LCDC estimated that local governments spent one and a half dollars for every state and federal dollar.

The grants have the potential of being used as a major policy tool to bring the local comprehensive plans into conformance with the state goals, but it is not clear that this has been the case. The issue is whether the annual review of grant performance and the awarding of new grants has been used to further substantive conformance with the goals, or whether the review has simply been an administrative process. A close observer holds that the commission has been weak in this regard.[77] In its 1980 evaluation of the Oregon Coastal Management Program, the federal Office of Coastal Zone Management was sharply critical of the Department of Land Conservation and Development's management of grant funds to local government and demanded that the department's procedures be revised:

> Disbursements of funding should be tied to specific milestones related to development and acknowledgment of local programs which, in turn, are based on the revised schedule (providing a realistic timetable for plan completion). Failure to meet a milestone would be the basis for a finding of unsatisfactory progress and funding termination. This control procedure should be used in concert with DLCD enforcement orders to move the local programs progress toward completion.[78]

These recommendations are tough medicine, and because OCZM is the source of an important part of the grant funds for Oregon's coastal cities and counties, they cannot be lightly pushed aside. Yet, the problem is as much political as programmatic. LCDC and its staff are constantly involved in a balancing act of carrot and stick, persuasion and enforcement approaches. As local plans are completed and monitoring and enforcement become a central focus of LCDC, the problem will become harder, not easier.

It was not until mid-1978 that the commission began to use its power to actually order a local plan to conform to state goals. In mid-1978, "its first enforcement action ever" involved a "county's failure to protect its agricultural land and to meet compliance dates it had agreed to with the commission." After a three-year dispute between the city of Hood River and the county, the commission ordered the approval of the city's proposed urban growth boundary in spite of objections by the county. At the same time, the commission ordered Deschutes County "to adopt measures for the protection of agricultural lands within the county in compliance with goal 3."[79]

Despite the large sums of money channeled to local governments to assist in the development of comprehensive plans that could be acknowledged by LCDC, the progress in achieving the goal of all plans approved has been much slower than anticipated. By 1980 some 18 million dollars in planning assistance and coordination grants had been channeled to local governments, yet only 94 (34 percent) of the 277 cities and counties in the state had approved plans. Money, or its lack, was not the problem. One estimate was that total resources invested in plan development and review over the 1973–80 period, including federal and state government funds and local spending beyond the state grants totaled 75 million dollars.[80] If money could not be blamed, the question of why the plan development and approval process was and continues so slow must be explained in other ways.

The major factors that have delayed completion of the plan development and approval process involve technical, policy and political matters. By March 1982 only 134 (about half) local plans had been acknowledged. Another 84 plans had been reviewed, and 30 local governments—seven years after the goals became effective—had submitted no plan at all.[81] As of July 15, 1982, 147 plans were acknowledged, 22 had never been submitted (4 counties and 18 cities), and of 278 jurisdictions (including a new incorporation) 256 have submitted to LCDC, and 242 have been reviewed. The current estimate is that by July 1983 all except a handful of jurisdictions will be acknowledged. LCDC is stepping up its enforcement order activities to bring the holdouts into line.[82]

The complexity of developing plans that have the force of law and that also must conform to sometimes specific state goals and the policies derived from those goals was greatly underestimated.

Planners, even when they were in place, had little experience with such a process. In many ways the process has been one of "learning by doing," and mistakes were inevitable. The Land Conservation and Development Commission and its supporting department has not been staffed adequately to expedite the development of the policy details to assure compliance with the goals, and at the same time work closely with local governments as they developed their plans so as to maximize chances that once submitted, a plan would be acknowledged. Local plans are almost never acknowledged on first submission, and many have been returned for further work, some more than once. LCDC's staff has in fact developed the policy framework over time and in varying amounts of detail for the several goals. This was often in response to political pressure of one kind or another. Local governments have charged, with some justification, that the rules were changed in the middle of the game, thus delaying the completion of the process. Yet, the legislature early on made clear its desire that most dollars in support of the program be channeled to local governments, leaving LCDC and its department with too few resources to do all the things needed to expedite the process.

Politics as a source of delay in completing the plans has taken several forms. Efforts to repeal or greatly weaken the law in 1976, 1978 and 1982, in the view of some, created a situation in which "many local governments paused in their goal-compliance efforts to see if the laws would survive or if LCDC would be intimidated by a close vote."[83] Constant political pressure on the program, stemming largely from local government resistance to state participation in their affairs, may have caused LCDC to be reluctant to use its enforcement powers in speeding up the process. Whatever the reason, it has not used those powers except on rare occasions. Finally, even if LCDC had marshalled a large staff of wise and wondrous planners skilled in the art of diplomacy, some local governments would have dragged their heels because of fierce opposition to the program.

In a stinging attack on those local governments that by early 1982 had submitted no plans, and on those that submitted plans that clearly violated the goals, Oregon's land use watchdog organization drove home the political resistance point. Eleven counties, five of which had submitted no plans, and six of which had submitted plans "in flagrant violation of the goals," were dubbed the "elusive eleven." In a report to Governor Victor Atiyeh asking that he cause LCDC to issue enforcement orders against the five county holdouts, it was noted that the elusive eleven "have received *$3.6 million in state funds from LCDC for planning and coordination work, and 44* *extensions of time totaling 77 years,* yet none of them has to date adopted a complying comprehensive plan."[84]

The difficulty in bringing the first phase of Oregon's planning and growth-management system to closure by completing the plan development and approval process should not be allowed to obscure the fact that much has been accomplished. By July 1982, 147 plans had been acknowledged, and except for a few diehards, the process should be complete by July 1983. Success stories of productive state-local cooperation abound. Yet, the experience in other states, especially California, suggests that any system which mandates that local governments plan and implement within a state policy framework that includes review and approval at the state level will be fraught with intergovernmental tension. For success, patience, money, and sustained public (political) support must be maintained. Whether or not that can happen in Oregon will be treated in the section on the *Politics of the Future.*

The Implementation Record
for Key Goals

Agriculture.   Goal 3 and Goal 14—the agricultural and urbanization goals—form the very backbone of Oregon's unique land and growth-management system. Goal 3 requires that all land outside the urban growth boundary drawn around every city in Oregon be zoned for exclusive farm use if it falls into soil conservation service soil classes I through IV in western Oregon and I through VI in eastern Oregon. Exceptions are possible, but they can be obtained only if justified in the light of very strict criteria. The statistics to date in the implementation of these twin goals place Oregon far ahead of any other state in protecting important agricultural land. Oregon has about 19.5 million acres of agricultural land. More than 16 million of these acres have been zoned for exclusive farm use, and the total is expected to reach almost 18 million acres when all local plans are completed and acknowledged by the state.[85] Combined with Oregon's agricultural land use policy[86] and use value taxation approach,[87] Oregon is indeed a leader in protecting agricultural land. Furthermore, the 1981 legislative session passed a right-to-farm law, even though most of its components are already found in Oregon law or agency rules.[88]

It is remarkable that with such a record of accomplishment to date, the agricultural goal has emerged in the early 1980s as the center of a storm of controversy that involves the legislature, LCDC, 1,000 Friends of Oregon, and above all Oregon's county governments. How Goal 3 has been developed to date, and what the current controversy is all about, is crucial to any assessment of where

Oregon's land- and growth-management system is, and where it is likely to be going. A key test of the LCDC's commitment to the agricultural and urbanization goals occurred in early 1976 when Marion County, located in the Willamette Valley, made a decision to rezone half of 23,000 acres of prime agricultural land into 3- and 4-acre lots. The land lay outside the Salem urban growth boundary and was at that time almost entirely in farming use. LCDC was petitioned by 1,000 Friends of Oregon to reverse the county's action on the grounds that it violated LCDC's agricultural goal. The county argued that LCDC's appeal authority violated the separation of powers doctrine in the constitution and argued further that 1,000 friends lacked standing in the matter. LCDC ruled that Marion County's action did violate the agricultural goal and that the area would have to be rezoned to exclusive farm use. This particular case was seen by 1,000 Friends of Oregon as a landmark decision in its effort to have local governments, and especially the 89 cities and 7 counties in the Willamette Valley, conform to the urbanization and agricultural goals and thus control urban sprawl and preserve prime agricultural lands.[89] In an important early court case strengthening goal 3, a court of appeals decision held that in a rezoning case land parcels cannot be considered apart from the use of the total unit of which the parcel is a part, in determining if lands are "predominantly" in agriculture. This case, *Meyer* v. *Lord*, also upheld the constitutionality of senate bill 100.[90]

Not all cases have been as supportive of the agricultural goal. For example, in one early 1976 appeal, the LCDC allowed Lane County to apply commercial zoning to parts of a 1,000 piece of agricultural land. The county was granted permission to make an exception to the exclusive farm use zone in areas which the county considered to be "precommitted to nonfarm uses." Although the exceptions would have to be reviewed on a case-by-case basis by the LCDC, proponents of strict enforcement of the agricultural goal feared that it might pave the way to undermining that goal.[91]

The effort to make the agricultural goal a reality has led to continuing state-local strains. For example, Columbia County, located along the Columbia River in northwest Oregon, has expressed "strong opposition to the EFU Zone and zoning in general" since the goals were adopted in 1974.[92] The conflict came to a head at the January 1980 meeting of the LCDC when the LCDC field representative for Columbia County recommended that the commission revoke the unused portion of the state's planning assistance grant provided Columbia County and consider all land outside of mutually adopted urban growth boundaries to fall under provisions of the state's EFU zoning statute.[93]

A busload of Columbia County residents came to the LCDC meeting to argue against the proposed enforcement order, in spite of four years of failure by the county to conform to the agricultural goal. After a long and heated exchange, the commission voted unanimously to direct its staff to prepare a draft enforcement order for review at its February meeting covering all identifiable agricultural lands in the county. The grant funds were to be held in reserve until the next meeting. The case illustrates in classic fashion both the power of the state through the LCDC to force local governments to conform to the goals, and the political reluctance of the commission to bring its ultimate authority to bear. Yet, the authority is there, and it can and has been used, a fact that separates Oregon from most other areas. It may be that the most important impact of the strategy in Oregon to date has been the successful effort to protect prime agricultural land in the Willamette Valley. By 1981 about 1.6 million acres of prime farmland in the valley had been placed in exclusive farm use zones, and when all plans are approved, almost 2 million acres of Oregon's finest agricultural land will be placed in exclusive farm use zones.[94]

The implementation of the goal to protect important farmland in Oregon and its interaction with other LCDC goals, especially housing and urbanization, represent the most extensive effort to convert pious hopes to effective action being undertaken in the nation. Although the executive director of 1,000 Friends of Oregon felt that the commission's failure to give the agricultural and urbanization goals top priority has involved the needless loss of additional farmland in the Willamette Valley,[95] the record to date indicates that Oregon has had more success in protecting agricultural land through a balanced system of planning, land use, and growth-management controls than any other state. The secret appears to be the mandate that exclusive farm use zones be designated. A 1961 law, which authorized but did not require exclusive farm use zones in Oregon that would qualify for sharply reduced property taxes, did not accomplish the desired goal of protecting agricultural land. But this approach, with the agricultural goal of Oregon's land use law, seems to offer great potential for success.

A farmer who served on the LCDC for more than four years noted the importance of the tax policy in responding to the question of whether farmers should be compensated for not being permitted to convert their farmland to urban uses. His reply was that:

> I don't think its practical, and I am not sure that it is fair. We need to remember we have had a special agricultural tax treatment in Oregon since the 1960s. Right now a farmer's tax, where it is under deferral of

EFU, is about 65 percent less, on the average, than in areas where we
have growth and development pressures. In Multnomah County (Portland) the figures show a 73 percent reduction. . . .

The question is, do you use this special tax for speculative purposes or do
you use it for what it was intended—which is to preserve agricultural
land. And it is my feeling, because of the great increase in all classes of
land qualifying for this special treatment, *farmers have been compensated* for
keeping it in an EFU zone.[96]

While the record looks good for the protection of agricultural land
in Oregon, a cloud of considerable proportions has appeared on the
horizon, sufficient in magnitude to threaten the effectiveness of the
agricultural goal and even the entire land- and growth-management
program. The problem involves the willingness and/or ability of
counties to apply the standards for protecting agricultural land that
were derived from goal 3 and which had to be incorporated in their
comprehensive plans before they could be acknowledged by the
state. It has been clear from the beginning that some counties were
determined not to carry out goal 3 in such a way as to be approved by
the state. Five counties have submitted no plan at all, and six others
have submitted plans that fail to protect important agricultural land
as required by goal 3. The problem, however, is far more serious
than bringing a minority of Oregon's counties into line. It involves
the question: Can or will counties who have acknowledged plans
that contain the appropriate standards required by the state apply
the standards in their day-to-day decisions, and if not, what can be
done about it?

Oregon's land- and growth-management watchdog agency
brought the issue into the open early in the 1981 legislative session
by publishing the results of a study done in the last six months of
1980 in which 1,046 actions by 12 county governments were reviewed
which involved applications for residential development in exclusive farm use zones. The data showed that 90 percent of the
applications were approved, and that of these, 81 percent were
illegal. The word *illegal* has a special meaning in the context of the
1,000 friends study: It means that the records examined did not
contain findings of fact and conclusions of law in sufficient detail to
allow a judgment as to whether or not the exception allowing a
nonfarm dwelling in an EFU Zone was or was not justified. The
record of counties in land use board of appeals cases lend credence
to the study's findings. Counties typically lose before LUBA because
of deficiencies in making the record—findings of fact and conclusions of law.[97]

The results of this study raises the spector of a splendid set of state
standards imbedded in local comprehensive plans that are routinely

ignored by county governments that yield to demands for rural sprawl. If such a situation were allowed to continue, not only goal 3 but goal 14 mandating an urban growth boundary would come to have little meaning.

The 1981 legislative session took note of the problem by passing a law requiring that each county "must send its findings to the committee on every decision it makes approving or denying applications to divide land or to place a dwelling in an EFU Zone." The committee referred to was the Joint Legislative Committee on Land Use. In the view of 1,000 friends, the action would "give legislators, farmers and citizens a unique opportunity to evaluate county performance . . . if counties continue to misapply state farmland standards . . . , the legislature will have all the information it needs to reallocate authority over Oregon's farmland."[98] The alarm at county actions was not confined to 1,000 friends. The Oregon Farm Bureau Federation helped draft and supported the reporting action as part of its policy in support of EFU Zones. The state office had been especially active in giving support to the local farm bureau in Klamoth County, where a textbook illustration of county refusal to comply with goal 3 had aroused local farmers to action. The county had zoned 75 percent of the county's farmland for five acre rural development. The area involved amounted to 350,000 acres, including prime potato and livestock land.[99]

In assessing this problem, it is not sufficient simply to ascribe evil motives to county commissioners. The pressure for my little 2 (or 1 or 5 or 10) acres out in the country is very real. Counties, and county commissioners, historically supporters of the program, now find themselves increasingly at odds with the state.[100] As one county person put it, "We've had an uproar since 1979 as people have realized that they couldn't do what they wanted to with their land." As he saw it, local citizens were encouraged to develop their own plan, came up with proposals for residential zoning on rural nonfarm lots, and found that exceptions to the EFU Zone typically would not be allowed. In his view, "There had been no adequate state-local cooperation in the plan making process, so the counties are crying foul."[101] To one 1,000 friends staff member, county commission failure to apply the standards was almost inevitable. Elected to be policymakers, they must play a quasi-judicial role in applying the standards. The solution proposed by 1,000 friends was for counties to allow hearing officers to apply the standards for exceptions to goal 3, with an appeal to LUBA. The county commissioners would be off the hook, but also out of the action.[102] Certainly this proposal will resurface if the evaluation by the Joint Committee on Land Use supports the earlier findings by 1,000 friends. Pressure to "do something about counties" will be increased by a new 1,000 friends study completed in early 1982 in which about 400 county actions involving 5 counties were examined for their substantive compliance with goal 3. About 75 percent of these county actions were found to violate the standards derived from goal 3 and placed in the acknowledged comprehensive plans of the five counties.[103]

The impression should not be left that there is no room for rural residential dwellings outside urban growth boundaries in Oregon. After noting that "the rush for 5 acre rural homesites" is the toughest problem in Goal 3 implementation, the LCDC plan review specialist for agriculture noted that there was 150 to 200,000 acres of rural residential land already approved in the Willamette Valley alone. The lot of record law approved by the 1981 legislature will "open a window" for some rural residential land platted during the period January 1, 1965 and December 1, 1974. A single-family dwelling can be built on such a lot if certain conditions are met. Action to build under this law must be taken by July 1985, and all such approvals must be reported to LCDC and by LCDC to the legislature.[104]

The rural residential problem is essentially one of politics. Many county commissioners have to date seemed unable or unwilling to apply the standards governing the protection of agricultural land. The solution can come in two ways. First, if local citizen groups, including especially the local farm bureau chapter, begin to bring strong pressure on county commissioners to apply the standards, the problem might be solved. Second, decisions on rural residential exception applications could be made at the local level by a hearings examiner with an appeal to LUBA. Some solution is necessary to protect the integrity of the land use law.

Urbanization.   The Oregon Supreme Court's first interpretation of senate bill 100 decided that a city's land use decisions, including annexations, must include sprawl control standards established in LCDC's goals even prior to the adoption of an urban growth boundary. This 1977 case, *Petersen* v. *City of Klamath Falls*,[105] gave impetus to the commission's attempts to establish UGBs. The commission was criticized for being slow to develop policies to guide local governments in drawing their UGBs, even though it published explanations regarding "buildable lands" definitions, public facilities, and growth management. The process itself is undeniably difficult. As the director of the department put it, "The actual drawing of a site-specific growth boundary has quickly pushed the planner-type, philosophical discussions of 'urban form' into the courthouses, city halls, and hearing rooms."[106]

Perhaps the most telling UGB decision that the LCDC has been

required to make involved a 1977 attempt by the Columbia River
Association of Governments (now the Metropolitan Service
District), to include the town of Happy Valley in the Portland area's
UGB. LCDC held that this inclusion would have to be supported by
findings, to "justify including extra, unneeded land as a 'market
surplus' inside the UGB." The commission listed five factors (including the availability of affordable housing) that should be assessed if
such a market surplus concept were to be approved.[107] A revised
UGB was approved by the LCDC in December 1979 for the MSD.

The requirement for drawing on urban growth boundary around
every city in Oregon has gone forward with considerable dispatch
and has not as yet generated as much controversy as might have
been expected. The process calls for negotiations between cities and
counties to agree on the line, based on urban land needs projected to
the year 2000. Population figures used by cities in this process are
subject to LCDC review, and are rejected if they have no basis in
standard population projections for state growth. If cities and
counties cannot agree on a boundary, the matter is taken to LCDC
for resolution. Most observers agree that in spite of efforts to keep
the boundaries tight, LCDC has approved boundaries that are
generous—much too large in the view of some—in light of growth
projections for the state.

The key issues involving the urban growth boundaries for the
future center on the "in-filling" problem. A number of goals bear
directly on this issue—goal 11 (public facilities and services); goal 9
(economy); goal 10 (housing); and goal 12 (transportation). Some
observers feel that the in-filling issue will join or even replace rural
sprawl as the center of controversy in implementing the law during
the 1980s. Two issues are especially difficult, First, the implementation of goal 11—the infrastructure goal—calls for a stable funding
source to finance the water and sewer lines, streets, and other
facilities so as to allow an orderly, phased growth program in developing the land within the boundaries. No such source now exists,
and efforts to pass a real estate transfer tax for Salem, Oregon,
failed. However, there is interest in supporting such a tax for
statewide applications.[108]

Another obstacle in the way of orderly development within
Oregon's UGBs is the state's annexation laws. The logic of urban-
growth boundaries dictates that the city boundaries be extended to
the UGB. The problem is that Oregon has one of the most difficult
annexation laws in the nation. It requires a triple majority: a majority
of the people; a majority of the assessed valuation; and a majority of
the parcels involved. A city or boundary commission can effect
annexation directly, but a very simple initiative procedure can and

typically does negate any such action.[109] In spite of efforts by the League of Cities, the Oregon Association of Homebuilders, 1,000 Friends of Oregon and others, no success has been had in changing the present law. As a league staff attorney put it, "Its been our biggest frustration in life. We're living a lie in our whole urban strategy if we don't put land within the UGB inside the city limits."[110] Like goal 3, major implementation challenges lie ahead for goal 14, many of which are linked to goal 10, the housing goal. As one observer put it, "The key is how you get out to the boundary, not where the boundary is. We don't have our act together to do that."[111]

Housing.   Oregon shares with other states the steadily worsening problem of how to provide affordable housing to low and middle income persons. The state housing division has estimated that housing prices in Oregon increased by about 17 percent in 1977, with only a 7 percent increase in income. One assessment noted that "The *median* cost of a new house in 1977 was over $50,000, a price affordable to fewer than 23 percent of Oregon's households and only 15 percent of its renters."[112] The problem in Oregon, as in other states, is being exacerbated by a shortage of land zoned for multifamily development.[113] There has also been a trend toward zoning for ever larger minimum lot sizes in the Portland metropolitan area, an area that contains 42 percent of the population of the entire state.

Oregon is unique in its attempt to deal with housing problems. As 1,000 Friends of Oregon's executive director puts it:

> " . . . Oregon is the only state to pass laws—senate bill 100 and LCDC's housing goals—which require local officials to improve the quality of local planning and zoning generally, and which specifically require local land use controls to encourage the provision of an adequate supply of affordable housing. . . . The housing goal shows how states can act to fill what now amounts to a huge gap in a nationally critical area of public policy.[114]

In evaluating Oregon's planning and growth-management effort, the importance of the housing goal is hard to overestimate. Can that goal, and other key goals such as the public facilities goal, really come to grips with local government failure to consider housing needs of the entire community? Can a determined LCDC force local governments to avoid action "which frustrates housing availability by restricting needed housing types, or by needlessly adding costs? . . ."[115]

The implementation record in 1978 and 1979 justifies a cautious "yes" answer to these questions, and subsequent action by the 1981 session of the Oregon legislature reinforces that conclusion. In the landmark case of *Seaman* v. *City of Durham*, the city had further decreased by 50 percent an already low density land use pattern in a

257-acre community within the Portland region. Durham's action was appealed by 18 landowners in the city who charged that the reduced density violated goal 10. The commission agreed, and the decision set the framework for the statewide application of policies that would force reluctant local governments to consider the housing needs of not just their own citizens but of the region. LCDC noted that the housing goal:

> . . . clearly says that municipalities . . . are not going to be able to pass the buck to their neighbors on the assumption that some other community will open wide its doors and take in the teachers, police, firemen, clerks, secretaries, and other ordinary folks who can't afford homes in the towns where they work.[116]

LCDC recognized the difficulty of complying with the housing goal, but pointed out: "Just because it won't be easy, however, doesn't mean it can't be done."[117] That it won't be easy is clearly illustrated by LCDC's effort to evolve a policy and criteria to guide local governments in what they must do to comply with goal 10. The so-called St. Helen's Housing Policy adopted by the commission in August 1978 stated that:

> Residential zones need to be consistent with plan policies and map designations. Where a need has been shown for a particular type of housing, it should be permitted outright in some zones, although it may be a conditional use in other zones. Care should be taken to remove vague approval standards from zoning ordinances. In determining compliance with goal 10, an important part of staff analysis will be the amount of vacant buildable land available for each housing type.[118]

The reaction of local governments led LCDC to ask the staff to clarify the August 1978 policy, but the Oregon Business Planning Council, the state homebuilders association, and 1,000 Friends of Oregon all objected to any revisions. These groups maintained that allowing housing needs to be met by conditional-use zoning would again open the door to exclusionary zoning practices by local governments. The executive vice president of the homebuilders association noted that efforts to clarify the policy were causing confusion, with conflicting interpretations abounding, and called on LCDC either to keep the original wording or, "failing that, clarify your clarification."[119] LCDC in July 1979 did adopt a new housing policy, after a number of redrafts and workshops with private groups. The policy retains much of the force of the original policy.[120]

The development of a policy framework for the implementation of the housing goal has been assessed at some length because it illustrates the force of senate bill 100 in changing local government practices in a major policy area. As with other goals, prodded by 1,000 friends and the Oregon homebuilders association, LCDC has provided both precedent in case appeals, and explanatory papers that attempt to further clarify and guide local jurisdictions in plan development. Comparable efforts are now under way in implementing the public facilities (11), and transportation (9), and other LCDC goals.

Some local governments have resisted the imposition of these goals, and are particularly reluctant to take on the responsibility and financial burden of providing low and moderate income housing. As the president of Oregon's State Homebuilders Association saw it, the increased pressure for development inside urban growth boundaries was creating antigrowth movements in some local governments which were willing to accept urban sprawl in the countryside. He pointed up the vital link between the urban growth boundary, agricultural and housing goals:

> It is at this point where goal 10 "housing" becomes the most important of all LCDC goals. Without the requirement of goal 10 for cities and counties to provide for housing commensurate with the needs of Oregonians, growth would be forced to again occur in rural areas. The simple truth is that for agricultural preservation to continue, development must be allowed to proceed in an orderly fashion within urban growth areas. LCDC must begin now to educate the public of the importance of goal 10 and to enforce the goal promptly when local governments unreasonably restrict development in urban areas.[121]

In commenting further on the link between the three goals, he concluded that Oregon had the policy tools:

> . . . to ensure the preservation of adequate amounts of farmland and open space by making a strong commitment to urban development. A strong policy of preventing rural development without an equally strong policy of encouraging urban development will fail. Moratoriums and slow growth policies must fall if goal 10 and goal 3 are to be met.[122]

Analysis of available data, opinions of informed observers, and LCDC plan reviewers all confirm that goals 14 and 10—requiring an urban growth boundary and the application of housing policies, are having the effect of increasing density inside the boundaries. LCDC has concentrated its efforts on larger cities, but smaller jurisdictions ignoring goal 10 do have their plans rejected. The agency has prepared a memo that will be converted into a rule that gives cities guidance on appropriate densities. Generally these guidelines call for average densities of 6, 8, or 10 dwelling units per acre, depending on such things as transportation and other factors. The LCDC goal in the Portland Metropolitan area was for at least 50 percent of the new housing to be multifamily. Multnomah County (Portland) is planning for 60 percent of its new housing to be multifamily.[123]

With the plan acknowledgment process well on its way to completion, the issue of increased density within urban growth boundaries, crucial to meeting Oregon's housing needs, especially for low and moderate income people, will doubtless become more and more controversial. Partly for this reason, the Oregon Association of Homebuilders pushed to win approval of a law at the 1981 legislative session that put LCDC's housing policy in the statute books. Concern that LCDC was not being tough enough in applying the policies, and fear of legal challenges were also a factor in seeking the law. The law defined and required "needed housing, required that local governments regulations be clear and objective, and limited local governments to 180 days for final action on proposals for subdivisions or major petitions inside acknowledged urban growth boundaries." The state housing council, 1,000 Friends of Oregon, and the state homebuilders association joined in drafting and supporting the legislation. 1,000 friends interpreted its passage as a legislative expression of dissatisfaction with LCDC's "weak implementation of the housing goal."[124]

A final issue that has generated great heat but very little light in Oregon involves the impact of urban-growth boundaries on housing costs. Opponents of the program are quick to declare that UGBs are responsible for most if not all of the increase in lot and thus housing costs in Oregon. Others point to the large supply of vacant land within UGBs as "proof" that little or no impact on land and thus housing costs has occurred because of the UGBs. The only systematic effort to assess the impact of UGBs on land/housing costs is being carried out by an economist at Willamette University with a grant from the Weyerhouser Foundation. An earlier study (1976) by the same person found little or no impact on land costs that could be attributed to the UGB. The new study results are not ready, but preliminary figures indicate that in a housing market which saw the average cost of a home in Oregon go from $17,000 to $63,000 in the 1970s largely due to inflation, the UGB impact on land/housing costs is minor. Clearer, more specific and more certain local regulations allowing multifamily and manufactured housing, and a speed up in local government decisions on construction permits, both policies developed under goal 10 and now adopted as part of Oregon law, could more than compensate for any land cost impacts of UGBs.[125]

Goal 9—The Economy of the State. Goal 9 is an example of a goal that has been neglected by the LCDC and concerned interest groups until very recently. It seeks "to diversify and improve the economy of the state" and includes a number of guidelines concerning how to achieve that goal. The present (early 1980s) recession in Oregon associated with the severe decline of the timber industry has caused a renewed interest in goal 9. Governor Atiyeh asked for

$90,000 in special funds from a February 1982 special session of the legislature to allow LCDC and local governments to give more attention in plan development and review of goal 9 objectives. One need is to assure that land zoned for industrial and commercial use is actually available for that purpose. One associated effort that did not pass the legislature would have made a goal 11 change requiring that local plans "include capital improvement budgets for needed services." The board of directors of 1,000 friends has made goal 9 a high priority area and is working with the Oregon Business Planning Council and the Oregon Department of Economic Development "to develop a coordinated effort to review local plans for compliance with goal 9."[126]

The recent development of goal 9 illustrates the fact that not all goals have come in line at the same time, nor have the policies developed in connection with each goal been fleshed out to the same degree. Oregon's land and growth management effort is in that sense evolutionary. Goal 5, natural resources, and goal 4, forestry, have been given increased attention by LCDC and interest groups only in the last two or three years. Other goals still are largely undeveloped, but as time goes by and circumstances change, as with goal 9, their time will come.

Emerging Support and Opposition Groups

The history of senate bill 100's implementation records increasing popular support, sustained support by governors and the legislature, and considerable shift in support and opposition by local governments. As noted elsewhere, counties have become less supportive and cities more supportive of the program. The legislation's importance as an urban strategy is clear particularly in the makeup of the newest coalition of business and environmental interests which support the law's urban-oriented concerns such as housing.

Both Governor McCall and Governor Straub were strong supporters of senate bill 100 and its implementation. Both governors appointed strong commission members, fought a series of state initiatives to repeal the law, and supported substantial budget requests for the program. The record of the third governor to hold office under the law, Victor Atiyeh, is also positive. His appointments to the LCDC are considered in the main to be good ones, and he also opposed repeal initiatives. The new governor is familiar with the operation of the LCDC because of his prior role on the legislative oversight committee and as a member of the senate committee that reported out senate bill 100 in 1973. In a 1979 letter published in the

LCDC newsletter, *Oregon Lands*, Atiyeh expressed strong support for the legislation and land use planning and placed particular emphasis on certain goals. He noted that, "When looking to urban areas, goals 9 (economy of the state) 10 (housing) 11 (public facilities and services) 12 (transportation) 13 (energy conservation) and 14 (urbanization) will assume increased importance." This recognition of priorities has proved important in setting priorities in the law's implementation, as illustrated by Atiyeh's strong support of goal 9.[127]

In 1976 an initiative was mounted which would have repealed senate bill 100 outright. The effort was rejected by the voters, with 57 percent voting against repeal, with the strongest support coming from the 10 Willamette Valley counties whose legislators had strongly supported the original legislation.[128] A 1978 initiative shifted from the repeal approach to one of "drawing the implementation teeth" from the legislation. The initiative would have repealed the power of the state LCDC to review and require changes in local comprehensive plans. The 1978 vote saw some shifts in voter support indicating a broadening of citizen approval of the planning and growth-management effort. Statewide support increased from 57 to 61 percent. Thus it is clear that the implementation effort is gaining strength outside its traditional base of support, the Willamette Valley.[129]

Local government opposition to senate bill 100 seemed to diminish as popular support grew, LCDC continued serious efforts to bring local plans to completion, and the courts consistently upheld the intent of the law. Cities in particular were slow to respond to the law, as the record of litigation indicates. Part of the opposition is explained by jurisdictional jealousy and what local governments typically resent as state intrusion. Neither were local governments impressed with the staff of the Department of Land Conservation and Development, although the good work of field representatives with local governments has mitigated this somewhat. The forceful style of L. B. Day as chairman of the commission also engendered opposition from local governments, especially as his impatience with the cities become apparent. Opposition from cities has quieted in recent years, as indicated by the stance taken by the Oregon League of Cities in the successive initiative attempts. In 1976 the League of Cities remained officially neutral due to conflicting opinions within its membership, though the Association of Oregon Counties opposed the repeal effort. Fifty small-town mayors supported the repeal. In 1978, however, the League of Cities joined the county association in opposing the effort to weaken the law.[130] One very important factor in the decreased opposition is the fact that the legislature has been generous in making available funds to local governments to complete their plans. The funds have indeed been the sugar coating on a sometimes bitter pill.[131]

Counties originally supported the adoption of SB 100, but more recently the burden of implementation has fallen heavily on their shoulders in the form of applying standards involving rural sprawl. As a result, counties individually and as a group have become much more hostile toward SB 100. This hostility caused the board of the Association of Oregon Counties to support repeal of the law in 1982.

Private Sector Support.   The support and opposition of private groups to the state law is one of the most interesting chapters in the study of Oregon's planning and growth management law. The persistence of Oregon's watchdog group, 1,000 Friends of Oregon, has been a primary moving force in the implementation of the law. Organized for this purpose in 1975 with the aid of ex-Governor McCall, 1,000 friends is funded through voluntary contributions from leading state figures, ordinary citizens, and out-of-state support. The organization seems to have existed primarily on willpower, frenzied activity, and the dedication of its director and small staff.

The 1,000 friends has been relentless in offering testimony and in taking administrative and judicial appeals to insure rigorous substantive review of local comprehensive plans by LCDC. From its initial focus on agricultural and environmental goals, the group broadened its concern to include urban goals, particularly housing. In fact, the group has made common cause with builder/developer interests by placing an industry representative on its board of directors and jointly supporting education and lobbying on housing goal implementation.[132]

The post-acknowledgment period in the implementation of SB 100 presents a new challenge for 1,000 friends. The action of the 1981 session of the legislature in setting the framework for the post-acknowledgment period is detailed elsewhere, but of key importance in how 1,000 friends will operate is the provision that plan amendments will be reviewed by LCDC only on appeal, and that to have standing for appeal a written or oral presentation must be made at the local hearing. With an estimated 3,600 such actions per year (an estimate derived from a League of Cities survey), 1,000 friends is challenged to become 10,000 friends and to establish a grassroots organization that can monitor and where needed appeal plan amendments to LCDC where they do not conform to the goals. Such an expansion effort is now underway, with a major focus on involving farmers in the local groups. Since appeals cost money and require legal support, 1,000 friends has organized a cooperating attorneys program that by mid-1982 had enlisted 60 attorneys with a goal of 200. These attorneys are pledged to handle at no cost at least one appeal of a local plan amendment initiated by a local monitoring group or concerned citizen.[133] This group continues as the most successful public interest group in the nation in the land- and growth-management area. It is loved, hated, feared, and respected, and above all, it is dedicated to the full realization of the potential of SB 100.

The Oregon homebuilders association, which believes that "Effective land use planning will benefit our industry greatly," has also been a major factor in the continued implementation of the law. Builders were greatly disappointed by the failure to place emphasis on the housing goal in the early years of implementation.[134] Many members of the association supported the 1976 repeal, in part in order to get a new law with a stronger commitment to housing. When the repeal efforts failed, the 1,000 friends and homebuilders formed a new coalition to press for the full implementation of the housing goal. The association opposed the attempt to weaken the law in 1978 and has continued to work with 1,000 friends and other groups to assure the full implementation of goal 10.

Another important private group, the Oregon Business Planning Council, opposed senate bill 100 and its implementation, but after the second unsuccessful repeal effort in 1978 apparently decided to "join the game" and try to influence the law's implementation. The business council is a consortium including the Association of Oregon Industries, the Association of Oregon Realtors, the Oregon Association of General Contractors, and the Oregon State Homebuilders Association. Originally organized as a temporary organization, in 1982 it was a permanent group in its fourth year of existence. The group supports the full implementation of goal 10, especially higher densities and the elimination of local regulations that handicap the development industry. The group is also especially concerned with the "in-filling" goals such as goal 11 (infrastructure); goal 9 (economy); and goal 12 (transportation).[135]

As the program moves into the post-acknowledgment (implementation) stage, different groups will be impacted—some positively, some negatively—and the groups supporting and opposing the law will change. Key examples to date are both on the negative side. Counties have become much more negative to the program, for reasons discussed elsewhere. As goals 4 (forestry) and 5 (natural resources) have begun to be developed, the Weyerhouser Company, an original strong supporter of the program, has become concerned about its impact on the timber industry. Possible restrictions on forestry practices, including clear cutting, and the possibility that the urban growth boundaries are having a negative impact on the housing industry and thus on the market for timber, have caused Weyerhouser to have second thoughts about its support for SB 100.[136]

Developing the Coastal Program for Oregon

Senate bill 100 authorized LCDC to identify and propose to the legislature for its approval areas of critical state concern. The law also empowered the commission to designate and subsequently require permits for activities of statewide significance. Neither of these parts of the law has been implemented as yet by LCDC, and the failure to do so has been the subject of some controversy and disagreement. Some see the delay as justifiable, given the commission's need to concentrate on local comprehensive plans and the potential value of those plans in identifying critical areas and important state activities.[137] Others object strongly to the failure to use the critical area tool, especially in the coastal zone, and see it as a major policy failure.[138] Still others believe the commission's avoidance of the these two sections was a deliberate strategy to maximize the role of local governments and make the implementation of the law more politically palatable.[139]

The decision by LCDC not to utilize its critical area and activities of statewide significance authority may or may not have been sound, but it did mean that the goal approach would be used in developing Oregon's coastal program as a component of SB 100. In the eyes of some, LCDC's efforts to develop coastal goals got off to a slow and shaky start. Concern was expressed that the goals would be too weak, and LCDC was reminded of the long-term and strong support by Oregon Citizens for Shoreline Management.[140]

The four new coastal goals and guidelines adopted by the commission on December 18, 1976, eliminated some of the feared weaknesses. The goals set minimum standards which local governments would be required to implement for the protection and development of shorelands and ocean resources, beaches and dunes, estuaries, and other wetlands.[141] The effective date was January 1, 1977, and coastal cities and counties had until January 1, 1978 (with extensions, if needed) to incorporate the goals into their comprehensive plans and other local regulations. In the meantime, the coastal goals were to be applied immediately to local land use actions such as subdivision approvals, issuance of building permits, and permits to fill or dredge, in the area within 200 feet of the shoreline or inland from tidal marshes.[142]

In its 1980 evaluation, the Office of Coastal Zone Management criticized the slow pace of Oregon's coastal planning and the lack of a comprehensive monitoring system to assure that permit conditions were met and violations discovered and corrected. The OCZM review held that "It is clear that a significant number of jurisdictions will not be able to comply with the [extended] July 1980 deadline."[143] Only 10 out of 41 coastal cities and counties seemed likely to have approved plans by September 1980.[144] The OCZM report recommended that a reliable system to monitor coastal land use activities be in place by 1981 and called for a formal procedure for local reporting of compliance and enforcement activities as a part of grant performance reports. OCZM held that "LCDC should take a more active role to support other agencies and public interest groups in pursuing litigation or other means to stop or correct violations within the coastal zone."[145]

The coastal program in Oregon adds political and technical complexity to an already difficult planning and administrative system. Coastal Oregon has always been politically isolated from and suspicious of the relatively rich and populous Willamette Valley. Coastal city and county suspicions were confirmed when, in addition to goals 1 through 14, they were given goals 16 through 19 that applied only to the coast. Examples of the content of the coastal goals give a feel for what was involved. In the beaches and dunes goal (goal 18), development was prohibited on the dune barrier parallel to the beach and on areas just behind the dune barrier subject to erosion. In the estuarine resources goal (goal 16) it was required that Oregon's 15 coastal bays be assigned to management classes ranging from preservation to major port center. The coastal shorelines goal (goal 17) aimed at preserving coastal areas for development that required waterfront sites and at protecting life and property from natural disasters and hazards. Goal 19 was concerned with the protection of ocean resources.

One close observer of efforts to implement the coastal goals attributed the long delays partly to the complexity of the issues involved, best illustrated by the estaurine protection goal. No adequate data base was available from which to make policy decisions, and local governments had little or no capacity to address the problem. LCDC contracted with the Federal Fish and Wildlife Service to generate needed estaurine data, and the job was not completed until 1980.[146] Not only were data demands greater on the coast, but the agency coordination demanded was also much greater, involving both federal and state agencies. When this was combined with the strong political opposition to SB 100 that was centered on the coast, it is not surprising that progress has been slow, and the program a considerable source of frustration to the federal Office of Coastal Zone Management.

By July 1982, only 12 of the 42 city and county governments on the coast had acknowledged plans. Twenty-five others had been submitted and were returned to local governments for further work. Only one county, Coos, had submitted no plan at all. There are a number of factors that explain this slow pace, some of which were noted earlier. One observor held that LCDC deserved much of the blame because of its political fear of the "coasties." Money, it was argued, was not the problem, but its distribution was. Too many dollars were passed down to local governments without adequate monitoring for its use and largely wasted by hostile or incompetent local governments. Meanwhile, LCDC did not keep enough money to develop the staff capacity early on to craft the coastal program property.[147]

The best and the worst of using state and federal dollars to move the coastal program along is illustrated by the CREST and the Coos Bay Task Forces. The Columbia River Estuaries Study Task Force, a group of technical experts funded by LCDC, conducted an intensive study aimed at coming up with the data base and policies necessary to implement the estaurine goal. Once completed in draft form the plan was reviewed by state and federal agencies and revised in the light of their responses. This study is regarded as the best done on coastal problems and has given LCDC more confidence in instructing other local governments in what will be required of them. At the other extreme, the Coos Bay Task Force spent about $1 million, the money is gone, and due largely to a recalcitrant city and port district, there are few results and no plans ready for acknowledgment.[148]

The coast has been a difficult area in implementing SB 100, and the 1980–81 federal Office of the Coastal Zone Management evaluation of the Oregon program indicated some progress but continuing problems. With almost $6 million in federal and $1 million in state funds expended since program approval in May 1977, 30 out of 42 coastal jurisdictions did not have approved plans as of early 1981.[149] The DLCD had responded to federal pressure by hiring five plan reviewers on contract with duties only with regard to the coast and had given a commitment to forward local plans promptly to LCDC for review.[150]

Continuing program deficiencies involved the lack of "an effective system of enforcement which would guarantee that local land use actions are executed in compliance with the goals both before and after plan acknowledgment." Noting that DLCD had developed a checklist to assist counties in deciding whether development requests conformed to the goals, the point was made that only one coastal county was using the entire list, two others were using a modified version and producing findings that required conformance to the goals, but other counties on the coast were not doing as well.[151]

Monitoring and enforcing, either directly or through state or local agencies, of the conditions attached to approved permits was another continuing weakness of the program. Furthermore, there was no system in place to "measure cumulative overall physical impacts of the development in the coastal zone." Examples were minor continuing partitioning of agricultural lands in Tillamook County and major goal 3 violations in Coos County.[152]

The federal consistency component of the Oregon program has been working well except for the nationally publicized activities of the Department of the Interior involving Oregon and other west coast states. Oregon has joined California, Washington, Alaska and the Coastal States Organization asking for a Department of Interior consistency determination when the final notice of sale is published. The federal Fish and Wildlife Service, the U.S. Army Corps of Engineers, the Environmental Protection Agency and National Marine Fishery Service were credited with taking a particular interest in the plan development process.[153]

Oregon's coastal program has benefited in some ways from the fact that the program is part of the statewide planning and growth-management effort. Thus all goals apply to the coast, including requirements for the protection of natural resources, agricultural lands, and other matters important to managing coastal lands and waters. However, the addition of four additional coastal goals strengthened the already hostile attitude of many coastal communities toward any kind of state interference in local affairs. A combination of political hostility, the complex data necessary to meet the requirements of the goals, and the reluctance (political) and inability (staff shortages) of LCDC and DLCD to provide technical assistance and close monitoring and enforcement have all combined to cause the coastal program in Oregon to develop slowly and unevenly.

Developing the LCDC State Agency
Coordination Role

The LCDC is specifically empowered by SB 100 to require state agency coordination programs and to "coordinate planning efforts of state agencies to assure conformance with statewide planning goals and compatibility with city and county comprehensive plans," and state agencies are directed to act in accordance with statewide planning goals and guidelines.[154]

Implementation of its state agency coordinating role presents LCDC with a delicate political problem. If it moves too aggressively in requiring state agencies to prepare coordination programs that conform to the goals, it is subject to the change of trying to make itself a superagency. If it is hesitant to assert itself, it is subject to criticism by supporters of the program, and especially by local governments. One of the major incentives for local governments to prepare and gain approval for local comprehensive plans is that once approved state agency actions are required to conform to local plans. If LCDC does not press state agencies to develop coordination programs, the state consistency provision will have little meaning.

The commission has issued a rule requiring agencies to prepare coordination program documents, including an analysis of conformance with state goals, a summary of agency activities, a summary of agency programs to assist local governments, and the agency's coordination programs with local and other state agencies. To varying degrees, state agencies have responded to LCDC requests for the programs. Four of nine key agencies had approved state coordination programs as of April 1979. The housing division of the state Department of Commerce helped to develop goal 10, reviews the housing elements of local comprehensive plans, and has published a housing goal handbook.

State coordination will be a key issue in the post-acknowledgment period for Oregon's land- and growth-management program. The initial survey by LCDC identified 40 of 80 agencies examined that had sufficient identification with the goals to require a coordination program that conforms to the goals. By late 1981, 33 of these agencies had developed coordination programs. The DLCD seems ready to grasp this political nettle, partly because local governments increasingly will pressure them to do so.

The continuing political balancing act for LCDC involved in agency coordination is illustrated by the effort to develop a coordination program with the Department of Agriculture. That department has been described as "not interested in agricultural land protection," concerned only with being a kind of chamber of commerce for agriculture. Since farmers are divided in their attitude toward SB 100, the department's director has resisted developing a coordination agreement. The 1981 legislative session added to the problem by transfering an aquaculture program and the state Soil and Water Conservation Commission to the department. LCDC has a coordination agreement with the SWCC, and the aquaculture program has important land use implications, so presumably the Department of Agriculture will have to take some action.[155]

The governor's special assistant and liaison to LCDC cited as her top priority with LCDC the development of a coordination program with the Department of Agriculture. She noted that the governor appoints the board of agriculture and its director, but is constrained in forcing departmental action by the realities of agricultural politics. It was also pointed out that while the governor supported state agency coordination programs, it was necessary to proceed with caution to avoid raising the super state agency "bugaboo."[156]

There was general agreement that a strong position by LCDC in persuading and in some cases forcing state agencies to develop and observe coordination programs depends above all on equally strong support for that role from the governor's office. The executive director of DLCD places a high priority on reviewing existing coordination programs and where needed developing new ones. He pointed out that the 1981 session of the legislature changed the requirement from "conforming" to "complying" with the goals, presumably a stronger mandate for state agency coordination. A much earlier start on the program would have been preferred, especially in generating credibility with local governments. Yet, state agencies will not be easy to draw into the net, and the state dollars that helped bring local governments along are not available to state agencies.[157] There is a danger that the development of state agency coordination programs will continue to lag behind the rest of SB 100 development efforts. If so, Oregon's landmark program in growth management will not reach its full potential.

The 1981 Legislative Session: Setting the Post-Acknowledgment Framework

The role of the LCDC in the post-acknowledgment period was the subject of much discussion among state agencies, the LCDC, and private groups in the 1979–80 period. At first there seemed to be little consensus or policy direction emerging from those discussions. The Department of Land Conservation and Development in late 1979, however, drafted a policy paper which discussed two major possible activities, technical assistance and oversight in local plan implementation, and the state agency coordination role. The paper suggested that local planning would continue to be assisted with technical assistance and limited grants to small cities and counties, but that in general "implementation functions are a local activity and should be financed locally."[158] However, for particular implementing functions—such as keeping plans current through new studies, continued citizen involvement, and major and minor plan revisions—the department proposed funding through special maintenance and updating grants. The paper foresaw an important role for the LCDC in maintaining goal compliance through annual review of local plan amendments, review of periodically required local plan revisions, and through the appeals process.[159] These several tasks for the commission (LCDC) and the department (DLCD) left an important role for both in the post-acknowledgment period. Others saw the need for some action in the 1981 legislature as an opportunity to eliminate the state program entirely, or at least weaken it by leaving little or no role for the commission or the department in the plan implementation process.

The single most important post-acknowledgment issue before the 1981 Oregon legislature concerned whether, and if so to what degree, LCDC and DLCD would be involved in the plan amendment process once local plans had been acknowledged. Other issues involved efforts to place LCDC housing policies in the statute books, enact measures to better protect agricultural land, and enact a "lot of record" law. Contrary to earlier fears, no serious effort to abolish the program was made. Forces hostile to SB 100, led by certain counties, concentrated their efforts on limiting as much as possible the role of LCDC in approving amendments to acknowledged plans. Oregon's land use watchdog agency, 1,000 friends, strongly supported a requirement that LCDC approve every plan amendment. Many counties supported a position in which there would be no state review of local amendments to the plans, thus making it impossible to enforce state standards over time. The compromise position was an appeals procedure in which all plan changes would be reported to LCDC and to citizens and groups who asked to be put on a list. In this compromise solution, the DLCD itself was responsible for reviewing all decisions and deciding which ones constituted a serious enough departure from state standards (goals) as reflected in the local plans to justify an appeal to the LCDC. An added requirement was imposed in this compromise, objected to very strongly by 1,000 friends, that in order to appeal a local government plan amendment, written or oral objections would have to be filed by any objector, including DLCD, at the local level. Appeals could only be on the basis of objections raised at the local hearing.

All the major interest group actors, except counties, concerned with SB 100 supported a state role at least as strong as the law that finally passed, essentially the compromise position described earlier. For a time the homebuilders supported mandatory review of all plan amendments involving goals 3 (agriculture) and 14 (urban growth boundaries), but later pulled back from this position. L. B. Day, still active in SB 100 matters as a state senator, at first supported the 1,000 friends position for LCDC review of all amendments, but then switched his support to the appeals approach. The League of

Cities strongly supported the provision requiring an appearance at the local hearing in order to appeal, but would not support the minimal to no state role advocated by some counties. The home-builders directed most of their energies to putting LCDC's housing policy into law, and the Association of Oregon Industries, with a divided membership on the general issue of SB 100, did not play an active role in the session.

The Farm Bureau Federation supported some state review of local decisions and concentrated its efforts on passing a special require-ment that counties report all exclusive farm use zone actions to the legislative Joint Committee on Land Use. A long-time staff member for the Association of Oregon Counties, recalling that counties had been strong supporters of the program in the 1973–79 period, felt that the compromise plan review position requiring participation at the local level in order to appeal was a fair balancing between state and local needs.[160] The governor's executive assistant drafted a bill reflecting the compromise statement review appeals procedure that was finally approved, but held it in reserve while the legislative advocates of a stronger or weaker state role fought it out. The Department of Land Conservation and Development and the Commission, much to the disgust of 1,000 friends, played a low key, sometimes invisible role in the legislative actions that meant so much to their future. In the end the department seemed satisfied with the substance of HB 2225, but disappointed at the resources given the agency to carry out its post-acknowledgment duties.[161]

The critical question for the future in Oregon's land and growth management effort is whether some combination of DLCD, 1,000 friends, the farm bureau, Oregon homebuilders, and others can monitor and carry appeals of city and county plan amendments (an estimated 3600 each year) so as to assure the continued application of state standards. In the first six months of the plan amendment review system, 105 plan amendments were reported to DLCD. Of these 19 were commented on, about 10 favorably and 10 unfavorably. In only two cases has there been difficulty in correcting problems to the satisfaction of DLCD. So far, the burden of plan amendment review has not been unmanageable. However, it is too early, with only about half of all plans acknowledged, to generalize about the future.[162] For DLCD, it will be a very tough job with very limited resources. Its budget was cut 10 percent, the same as all other state agencies, by the 1981 legislature. The post-acknowledgment duties of the agency included: (a) review of plan amendments; (b) further development of state agency coordination programs; (c) a full-scale periodic review of each city and county plan to assure continued compliance with state goals, to be made every two to five years; (d) providing staff support to the Joint Committee on Land Use; and (e) converting all LCDC policies to rules. In addition, the department must, by legislative direction, concentrate most of its energies on completing the plan review and acknowledgment process. It seemed an understatement when DLCD's director commented that "We're in poor shape to do all that we need to do."[163]

The passage and importance of the requirement that counties report actions on petitions involving land in EFU Zones (included in HB 2225), the "lot record" law, and SB 4191 making LCDC's housing policies part of Oregon law, have been discussed elsewhere. In addition, the legislature fought down an effort to weaken the state's "fill and removal law" through efforts by 1,000 friends to remove weakening sections from changes made in the law. The legislature also made a number of changes to strengthen the state's laws protecting farmland.[164]

When the dust of battle settled at the close of the 1981 legislative session, there was little reason to despair for the future of Oregon's land- and growth-management system. Once again the program demonstrated that it had the support of the legislature, the governor, and a unique mix of powerful interest groups. The challenge for the future is great. Local actions amending plans will have to be monitored and appealed, DLCD will have to do a very great amount of work with very limited resources, and the coastal program needs close attention to realize its full potential. Yet, none of these problems seem insurmountable, provided Oregon's citizens continue to express their strong support for the program.

The Politics of the Future

Just before the 1981 legislative session convened, some supporters of the program feared that the strong state role that makes the Oregon program of national and even international importance would be substantially weakened if not destroyed. That fear proved to be unjustified. The program came through the legislature with a strong mandate to continue into the future. It did not, however, receive the added resources to carry out the many tasks that must be done— and done well—if the program is to survive and thrive. The critical question is whether future sessions of the Oregon legislature will continue to support the substance of the program and also provide the added resources needed to do the job well. A further question is whether LCDC members will provide the leadership to launch the program into the postacknowledgment era and at the same time see that the remaining plan acknowledgments do not sacrifice speed for quality. Another critical question is whether the governor will provide the strong leadership needed to make the state agency coordination potential a reality.

In trying to predict whether Oregon's program will continue strong into the future or suffer a decline, certain negative and positive factors must be considered. On the negative side, the newly developed hostility of counties and their unwillingness to apply state standards is a threat to its effective implementation. Second, the economic recession, especially severe in Oregon because of the weakness of the timber industry, makes it easier for enemies of the program to place all the blame for Oregon's economic ills at the feet of SB 100.

On the positive side, the unique coalition of interest group support is holding together and in some ways gaining strength. If counties are less supportive of the program, cities are more supportive. Above all, Oregon's watchdog land use group, 1,000 friends, seems ready to rise to the challenge of organizing at the local level all over Oregon to monitor and, where necessary, to support the appeal of local plan amendments that threaten the goals. On a final and optimistic note, the director of 1,000 Friends of Oregon is bullish about future political support for Oregon's land- and growth-management program. Noting that in the spring primaries some of the legislature's leading opponents of SB 100 were defeated, he predicted that the 1983 legislative session would be the strongest since 1973—a decade ago when SB 100 was adopted.[165]

The latest effort to repeal SB 100 in the November 1982 election came at a particularly dangerous time, given the drastic decline of Oregon's timber industry that made the national recession's impact on Oregon especially bad. Opponents of the program, supported by some counties, managed to get enough signatures on petitions to force a November referendum to drastically weaken SB 100. Ballot measure 6 was a bold effort to repeal the key elements of SB 100. It would have abolished the LCDC, repealed the goals, and abolished the land use board of appeals. When the smoke of battle cleared and the votes were in for the November election, the effort to repeal SB 100 failed by a 55–45 vote margin.

The victory was a come-from-behind effort of major proportions. The first poll showed ballot measure 6 carrying by a wide margin— 20 percent. Opponents hammered away at the law, primarily on the grounds that it was the main reason for Oregon's failure to diversify its economic base, especially with regard to attracting high-tech industry. The Association of Oregon Industries, the Oregon Association of Counties (in a close vote of its executive committee), the Association of Oregon Realtors, and some forest products representatives supported repeal of the law. The effort to defeat ballot measure 6 was organized under Citizens to Defend Our Land and was cochaired by the president of Tek-Tronix, the state's largest employer, and by Oregon's largest developer. Others opposing repeal included the League of Cities, the Portland Homebuilders Association, the state AFL-CIO, Hewlett-Packard, and others.

Governor Victor Atiyeh and 1,000 Friends of Oregon played key roles in the effort to defeat ballot measure 6. Atiyeh's Task Force on Land Use held hearings around the state and released a report generally supportive of the law, but also proposing important changes to streamline, simplify, and thus speed up the decision-making process associated with the law. A key recommendation of the task force, and one strongly supported by the governor, involved strengthening the implementation of the economy goal so as to assure the availability of suitable land for industrial development in Oregon.

The effort to defeat repeal was supported at every turn by 1,000 Friends of Oregon, whose staff did critical work in marshaling data to show that SB 100 had provided more, not less, useable industrial land in Oregon, and that the economy goal could be even more important in the future as its standards are made more specific, including the provision of infrastructure needed to make sites useable.

The 1983 legislative session during its first month—mid-January to mid-February 1983—was seen by the executive director of 1,000 Friends of Oregon as the most supportive of SB 100 since the law was passed. Changes in SB 100 that are being proposed—and supported by 1,000 Friends of Oregon include: (1) strengthening the economic goal by making its standards more specific; (2) speeding up decisionmaking all through the process, aimed at a system that will feature one hearing at the local level and one appeal; (3) abolishing LUBA and replacing it with a magistrates system, with magistrates functioning essentially as hearing examiners for the state court of appeals; (4) renewing the requirement that counties report their land use actions in exclusive farm use zones to the Joint Committee on Land Use; and (5) considering ways to allow rural development on certain marginal farm lands in return for even tighter controls on the best farm lands.

The LCDC budget does not seem in any greater danger than any other budget in Oregon, given the state's weak economy. Furthermore, Governor Atiyeh has just appointed two persons to the commission who are strong supporters of the program, have the full confidence of the governor, and thus are capable of giving the program strong leadership. Oregon's growth-management law has come through a "trial by fire" and seems destined to gain strength as the state moves through the 1980s.[166]

7

Colorado: A State-Local Puzzle

The Issue Context

Colorado was one of the first states that attempted to define a state role in land use. Under Republican Governor John A. Love, the legislature in 1970 passed the Colorado Land Use Act and established a Colorado Land Use Commission. In 1971, the legislature made the commission's charge more specific by mandating that it study land use in Colorado and develop proposed legislation to establish a land-management system for the state. The law also provided for the development of a statewide land use plan, but this specific mandate was later changed to require only that a planning program be developed. The original land use commission was a nine-member body appointed by the governor. Until 1974, when a new land use law was passed in Colorado, the land use commission and its staff provided much of the study and effort that went into developing a land-management system for the state.[1]

If one can say that Colorado was moving with apparent vigor and sense of purpose in the early 1970s to strengthen both the state and local roles in land and growth management, the question of why this was so is worth examining. In the first place, Colorado—as with states such as Vermont, Florida, California, Oregon, and Hawaii—was subjected in the 1960s to very substantial population growth pressures. Some negative impacts from these pressures began to be clearly visible in the late 1960s and early 1970s. As one state political leader put it: "Development was tearing up the land, and it is very fragile land. The smog was moving in with a vengeance. Off-road vehicles in the mountains were destroying a lot of our natural areas, and the impacts were visible. The ski industry made this a very attractive second home place."[2] In the face of these negative side effects of growth, Colorado's citizens and its political system began to respond with policy initiatives. To a large degree, their willingness to act was a part of the national environmental movement and

clearly reflected the development of a strong environmental con-
science in the nation.

The growth pressures in Colorado, while perhaps not so dramatic
as those occurring in Florida—as in California at an earlier time—
were still substantial. In the decade of the 1960s, Colorado's
population grew by almost 26 percent, and in the period 1970–76,
grew another 17 percent. By 1980 the population of the state was 2.87
million, an increase of about 30 percent since 1970. According to one
assessment, Colorado's growth rate between 1970–80 was surpassed
by only seven other states.

Such growth pressures might not have had so many visible
negative impacts had the increased population been spread evenly
over the state. However, almost three fourths of Colorado's total
population resides in a 40-mile wide stretch of land that runs north
from Denver to Fort Collins and south from Denver to Colorado
Springs. Although this land area represents less than 2 percent of
the state's total, most of the heavy growth pressures have been
concentrated in this "front range" region. Seven of the high-growth
counties faced difficult environmental problems; these counties
hold large amounts of national forest acreage and yet have been
subjected to intensive demand for recreational and residential use.
One observer has held that: "It is for these seven counties that house
bill 1041 and house bill 1034 [two important initiatives in Colorado
land use law] were enacted, and it is in these counties that the fight
between the environmentalists and the developers will be won or
lost."[3]

Part of the increased support for better land use controls involved
a general increase in citizen activism in general and environmental
activism in particular. Initially, growth in Colorado was welcomed
for producing a number of benefits, including the development of
Denver into a large, sophisticated metropolitan area. However, as
the growth continued, the negative impacts began to be more and
more evident: "increased traffic snarls and air pollution; increased
taxes to subsidize public facilities for new areas; congestion in
mountain recreation areas; scars on the landscape; and increasingly,
lowest common denominator homogeneity of design in the commercial strips and housing tracts of suburban fringe areas."[4]

By the early 1970s, a majority of all Coloradoans were in-migrants,
and many had come to Colorado because of a perceived quality of
life based on clean air, clean water, and an attractive landscape.
When newcomers saw these very attributes deteriorating, they
quickly adopted the last-one-in-syndrome and became concerned
about further growth. It was also at this time that land sales schemes
involving the marketing of thousands of acres of marginal land,

identified as "ranchettes, ranchos, and rancheroonies," began to be seen in Colorado. The obvious abuses of the land involved in these efforts added to the pressure for Colorado to do something to bring its growth under control.[5]

The process of doing something was begun in 1966 when Colorado adopted air and water pollution control statutes. This action was followed in 1967 by the passage of a law establishing a state planning function in the governor's office. In 1968, in a move potentially important to an integrated state/local effort in land and growth management, the state's extremely fragmented administrative structure was reorganized and a governor's cabinet was established that provided for a relatively strong gubernatorial office in Colorado. Part of the rising concern with the negative impacts of growth was a widespread feeling that local governments "really couldn't hack it and that there wasn't much muscle or strength in the whole regional effort."[6] It was in this setting that the 1970 legislation establishing the state land use commission took place.

The initial land use commission has been described as a kind of state planning commission that was charged with providing technical and financial help to local governments to encourage them to engage in the planning process. Perhaps one of its most important functions during the early 1970s was to conduct a good part of the research and involve itself in drafting the legislation that resulted in senate bill 35, a law that required subdivision regulations to be developed in the unincorporated areas of all counties in Colorado. Senate bill 35 also provided a potential state role in land use; should a county fail to carry out its responsibilities for developing the subdivision regulations, the land use commission was empowered to develop them for the counties, and the counties were required to carry out the regulations as though they had drafted them in the first place.[7]

Criteria in senate bill 35 mandated a minimum substantive content for the subdivision regulations including provisions regarding water, sewage, soil, and geologic problems, and the dedication of land, or money in lieu of land, for park and school sites. The law applied only to new subdivisions. An effort to make it applicable to existing subdivisions did not succeed. There also are two major loopholes in the law: (1) it exempts all subdivision of land in parcels of 35 acres or larger, and (2) it also gives the counties the authority to exempt certain subdivisions. The act was largely intended to slow down urban sprawl and leapfrog development on the fringes of urban areas in the front range development area of Colorado. One view was that senate bill 35, along with new health regulations and restrictions on the establishment of special districts, "was responsible for virtually halting the massive sales programs of remote, submarginal lots."[8]

Other assessments, while conceding the benefits of the law, pointed to its failure to deal with problems in subdivisions of 35 acres or more, and to the abuse by some counties of the exemption procedure that allowed a county to declare that a particular subdivision was not within the law's objectives. Furthermore, all efforts to bring cities under the requirements of senate bill 35, both when the law was adopted in 1971 and subsequently, have failed. According to one view, "Cities have resisted strongly using it [senate bill 35] though they have a lot of weak subdivision regulations. The larger cities claim they've already got everything and they don't need to act or be required to act, and this is partly true, but it certainly isn't true with the smaller cities."[9] The land use commission did set up a model subdivision regulation code, and the usual practice was for counties to adopt a code subject to the approval of the land use commission. One observer commented that, "The cities managed to argue themselves out of this mandated regulation by claiming they had subdivision regulations already." In his view, the failure to mandate subdivision regulations for cities "has encouraged developers to play cities off against counties, and developers will play games with a particular city and work out a way in which their land can be annexed by the city to get the zoning that they want from the city government in a kind of prior commitment."[10]

A strong environmental movement in Colorado has expressed itself largely through a "holding company" environmental coalition called the Colorado Open Space Council. This council helped spearhead such actions as the granting of temporary emergency powers to the land use commission in the 1971 law and the successful fight to block the Olympics from being held in Colorado. Such activities contributed to the 1973 attempt to pass a major land use law that would have included a strong state role. When that effort failed, despite the backing of the Republican leadership, a law was passed in 1974 that lodged prime responsibility for land and growth management with local governments and gave only an ambiguous and uncertain mandate to the state to involve itself in the process.

Colorado was the only state among those studied in which partisan politics played a significant role in the adoption or rejection of a land use initiative. Since the failure of the Republicans to rally bipartisan support for a strong land use bill in 1973, the political context for land and growth management has been sharply partisan, with Republicans opposing any suggestion of state control in the area and Democrats supporting a stronger state initiative in the land use field.

In concluding the assessment of the issue setting out of which land- and growth-management initiatives developed in Colorado, it can be said that these issues were very similar to those in a number of other states examined in this study. As in Florida and Hawaii, Colorado's physical environment formed the base for a very important recreational and tourist industry. One of the effective arguments made for strong land and growth management in these three states was that to fail to do so would in the long run, and perhaps in the short run, undermine economic prosperity. For this reason, when the economic recession began in 1974, the advocates of land and growth management in Colorado, Florida, and Hawaii did not find themselves on the defensive as quickly and as completely as their counterparts in some other states.

The Politics of Adoption

In 1973 Republicans were feeling the political heat of the newly developed power of the environmental movement and its apparent ability to threaten any political party that ignored the new status of advocates of environmental and land management. A candid assessment of the situation in which the party found itself in 1973 was given by a leading Republican house member. In her view, Republicans supported land use legislation because: "We were under the gun with regard to a federal land use bill that seemed about to pass." Many Republicans felt that if Colorado did not pass a law, there would be a "federal takeover of our land use." The environmental concern that was sweeping the country and that was being felt in Colorado led to a feeling that if the Colorado legislature did not take action: "We might get something worse from somewhere else." On a more positive and substantive note, this house member did note that Colorado was truly unique in its mineral resources, its reliance on tourists and the recreation industry, and its fragile environment.[11]

A veteran Republican leader and member of the legislature for a decade noted that the politics of land use in Colorado was "briefly bipartisan." When Governor Love, who had occupied the governor's chair for almost a decade, resigned in 1973 and Lieutenant Governor Vanderhoof took his place, Republicans became very nervous about the prospect of losing control of the office of governor and one or more houses of the legislature. Part of their effort to head off such a disaster was to try to pass some kind of land use bill that would prevent Democrats from capitalizing on the issue and bringing defeat to the Republicans.[12] This attempt was also partly in response to the work of the land use commission which, it should be remembered, had been appointed by a Republican governor. The commission had issued an in-depth report at the end of 1972 which recommended a system of land use controls for Colorado and introduced a permitting approach. In any case, the political climate was such that the Republican leadership in the 1973 session of the Colorado legislature did attempt to pass a land use bill that provided a strong state role in land and growth management.[13]

The 1973 Legislative Effort
Senate bill 377, entitled, "State Policies Act of 1973," was a comprehensive package based in part on several land use and environmental bills previously introduced into the legislature. The bill was patterned generally on the approach taken by Florida in adopting its land use legislation. Two prominent Republican senators, Joseph Scheiffelin and John Bermingham, and Democratic representative, Richard Lamm, participated in drafting the bill.[14]

The central questions posed by senate bill 377 were (1) whether the state would have a substantial role in determining land- and growth-management matters (at no time was a direct state administration to the total exclusion of local government ever considered) and (2) whether—with regard to certain limited issues and circumstances—the state rather than local governments would have the final word.

The two houses of the legislature were deeply split on the issue of the state role, as has been the case in every other state analyzed in this volume. The house generally favored land use control with some state authority; the senate emphatically did not. The conference committee could not reach any agreement, and the bill was killed.[15] An in-depth analysis of the effort to pass senate bill 377 concluded that to pass such legislation in the future would require a broad base of political and interest group support, a successful compromise between the degree of state and local authority, and a narrow focus instead of a comprehensive, all-encompassing land use approach.[16]

The 1974 Legislative Effort
With the failure of senate bill 377 in the 1973 session of the legislature, land use proponents quickly organized for a new attempt. They formed a Legislative Council Committee on Land Use, commonly called the interim committee, chaired by Republican Representative Betty Ann Dittemore. A citizen's advisory committee also was established to help the interim committee reach

the essential compromises and to fashion a land use bill that could pass both houses of the Colorado legislature. The advisory committee brought together representatives of a very broad cross section of people, including oil interests, cattlemen, realtors, environmental groups, and others, many of whom had never before worked together.[17]

The interim committee was fairly successful in its effort toward an appropriate compromise between state and local power. Failure to strike such a compromise, it was generally agreed, would mean that either no bill would pass or the bill that did pass would be very limited in terms of any state role. The group also managed to agree on other important goals, including the preservation of agricultural land and the control of urban sprawl—two goals that are the heart of any effort to develop a land- and growth-management system in any state. Furthermore, the committee did successfully maintain, under the leadership of Representative Dittemore, a bipartisan approach to the issue of land use and a legislative strategy. Instead of attempting to design a comprehensive bill, the committee drafted separate bills so that controversial matters could be considered and dealt with separately, and the main land use bill would not rise or fall on these issues.

One important issue on which the interim committee reached a consensus was the need to provide some way of taking into consideration the more-than-local impacts of land use decisions made by local governments. To achieve this end, the legislation proposed by the interim committee, house bill 1041, included the creation of a state land appeals board which would have the power to designate areas and activities of state interest for final approval by the governor. Under this proposal, the land appeals board would have additional powers involving guidelines for administration by local governments, and the right to hear appeals of local government orders granting or denying permits for development. This provision, of course, would have established a significant state role in the process.[18] Regional planning commissions also were authorized to work with local governments and recommend matters of state interest to the state land appeals board.

As the interim committee went about its work, the political winds in Colorado continued to swirl. The leading Democratic contender for governor, Representative Richard Lamm, was a member of the interim committee. Governor Vanderhoof was determined to get some sort of land use bill out of the legislature to strengthen his campaign in the contest with Representative Lamm. Governor Vanderhoof attended the interim committee's first meeting and called their task of drafting land use legislation "The most serious challenge ever before the state." In addition he urged on the committee a bipartisan approach that would hammer out the compromises necessary to get the legislation passed.[19]

The governor made the land use bill his number one priority, placing it on the "governor's call," a special written message to the general assembly outlining policy matters which the governor considers to be of most importance for legislative action. In even numbered years, such as 1974, the Colorado legislature can consider only matters that have been placed on the governor's call. The stage was thus set for the political battle to get the bill through legislature. As one analysis has put it: "The overriding directive for the majority party Republicans was to pass a land use bill. It didn't seem to matter what sort of bill or what the costs just as long as something called land use was passed."[20]

After introduction into the house on January 3, 1974, the legislation was assigned to the house Local Government Committee chaired by Representative Dittemore, a prime sponsor of the legislation. All but one member of the Local Government Committee had also been members of the interim committee. Most people expected the bill to have smooth sailing in the house, and there seemed to be an atmosphere of optimism by Dittemore and other sponsors, both Republicans and Democrats, that the bill could make it through both houses and go to the governor. The prime concern was that the bipartisan effort would fall apart in the face of a conservative senate with a consistent history of opposing land use initiatives, especially those with any element of state control.

To everyone's surprise, the bill ran into trouble in the house almost immediately. A representative of the Colorado State Association of County Commissioners appeared before the committee to oppose the proposed state land appeals board. He took the historic position of counties in Colorado that local government was the appropriate level at which to regulate land use in the state. This opposition was important because the county group in Colorado had a powerful lobby in the legislature, one reported to be well organized and effective in bringing pressure to bear on legislators from county commissions "back home."

Republican Representative Michael L. Strang subsequently proposed an amendment to shift the responsibility for identifying and designating matters of state concern to local government instead of to the state land appeals board, and to shift review functions to the Department of Local Affairs, a state agency long closely identified with Colorado counties. This abrupt change in the compromise between state and local responsibility immediately threw the whole bipartisan effort into jeopardy. In his objection, Representative

Lamm accused Representative Strang of "conspiring with the Association of County Commissioners in proposing the amendment at such a late date."[21]

The votes approving the amendment and sending the bill to the house floor split the committee along party lines, with Democrats on the committee in opposition and Republicans in favor. This show of partisan muscle might well have destroyed the coalition at that point, but the Democrats apparently concluded that the bill still had more good than bad in it, and that they were not in a position to win back a stronger state role on the floor of the house. The Democratic leadership, though objecting strongly to the amendment, worked hard to rebuild support among key Democrats and the house passed the bill by a vote of 50 to 12. The bipartisan atmosphere, however narrow and precarious, was maintained as the bill went to the senate.[22]

At this point, Representatives Strang and Dittemore believed that even the weakened bill would not pass out of the senate committee or the senate as a whole unless strong Republican support could be mobilized. Two key Republican senators, Joseph B. Schieffelin and Joe Shoemaker, were interested in far-reaching amendments generally directed at decreasing further the state's responsibilities. Such groups as the Association of County Commissioners, the Colorado Association for Housing and Building, and the Rocky Mountain Developers Association, although professing support of the bill, also were keenly interested in seeing it amended to lessen the state role. In the face of all this and still convinced that Governor Vanderhoof in particular and the Republican party in general badly needed some kind of land use bill, Strang and Dittemore set about to secure approval of 18 pages of amendments that they thought would make it more acceptable to senate Republicans.[23]

Some of the amendments had to do with administrative streamlining, but others had substantial substantive impacts. In a general way, the amendments tended to delete actions that were mandated on local government as well as on certain state government agencies and to substitute *mays* for most of the *shalls*. By then, Representatives Strang and Dittemore felt that they had made the necessary compromises to secure senate passage of the bill. As another assessment saw it: "They had literally stripped the bill of all remaining state authority. By doing so, they had alienated most of the members of the nonpartisan coalition in the house. But they had satisfied most of the desires of most of the members on the [senate] committee."[24]

Still, assaults on the legislation were not at an end. As a substitute, senators Shoemaker and Schieffelin proposed merely to use the

existing land use commission to channel large sums of money to
local governments for planning. This substitute proposal appeared
to have substantial backing from the Senate Committee on State
Affairs, and the support of the Colorado Association of County
Commissioners. This drastic weakening of the bill led even a key
lobbyist for the Rocky Mountain Land Developers Association to
warn that a deadlock would occur between the house and senate, a
repeat of the senate bill 377 effort of 1973 would take place, and
nothing would pass the legislature.[25] In an attempt to resolve the
deadlock, a closed Republican caucus was held, in possible violation
of the Colorado Sunshine Act, and the governor's representative
made it clear that his position was that house bill 1041 had to remain
intact. The Vanderhoof position was sustained, and the major effort
to completely kill the bill failed. The financial aid approach was
added as a supplement rather than as a substitute.

The bill by now was battered and scarred, but it was still at least
somewhat intact. However, it still had to be reviewed in Senator
Shoemaker's Appropriations Committee. In this committee, the
whole state land appeals board section of the bill was deleted, and
the state role was to be confined to the existing land use commission.
The commissioner's temporary emergency powers were kept, to be
used in extreme cases where the state interest was at stake.[26] Except
for these emergency powers, the role of the state was reduced to one
of providing technical information and assistance and financial help.
Senator Shoemaker was in control of his committee, and the bill
quickly was moved to the floor of the senate. Republican Representative Strang commented that: "One individual came out of the west
like Lochinvar, holding some 20 appropriation bills in his tight little
fist and clobbered the bill. One individual. And he brought the
senate to heel, he brought them to their knees . . ."[27]

At this point, not only had the bipartisan coalition collapsed, but
the Republican party found itself at war internally. The governor
and other Republicans who wanted to have some sort of land use
platform on which to counter the Democrats were almost as
appalled by the Shoemaker assault as were the Democrats. The
battle quickly turned into a kind of rural versus urban, conservative
versus liberal, and, to some extent, Republican versus Democrat,
fight. The Republican party was on center stage as the governor and
his supporters attempted to force some reconsideration of the
Shoemaker triumph.

Although efforts on the floor of the senate to restore some state
role generally failed, a crucial amendment by Schieffelin, which
would allow the land use commission to submit a formal request to a
local government to take action on matters of state interest, did

succeed. When the weakened bill passed the senate, the governor quickly made it clear that he would not sign it and if necessary would call the legislature into a special session in order to get action on an acceptible bill. Representative Dittemore urged the house to kill the bill and let the governor call the special session to take meaningful action on the land use question. Dittemore noted that "to end up with no land use legislation would be disastrous for the Republican party."[28]

In response to the governor's threat, the senate recalled the bill to try again to come up with something satisfactory to all parties. Several amendments, largely minor, did pass. One amendment (in retrospect, of critical importance) gave the land use commission additional authority to seek judicial review if a local government refused to designate an area or activity of state concern or to adopt regulations for permitting. After the senate again passed house bill 1041, a conference committee met very briefly and without making any substantial substantive changes quickly returned the bill to the two houses. Apparently Republicans had decided to take the position that the bill was now satisfactory. By this time, all traces of bipartisan support for land use legislation had disappeared. As one assessment put it, "House Democrats were furious with the outcome. Representatives Lamm, Frank, Gaon, Farley, and others openly denounced the action of the senate. They encouraged the defeat of the bill to allow the legislature another chance to deal with the matter responsibly."[29]

Many Republicans were almost as frustrated as the Democrats, but they were in a different political situation. Representative Strang summed it up by saying: "I think that I will reluctantly support this bill because it is the sole mechanism available to us for any kind of articulation of what the state interest is, and for providing some kind of machinery whereby that state interest as expressed in the bill may be raised by an agency of the state. I think the governor needs this bill." Representative Dittemore, swallowing what must have been a large lump of frustration, called the diluted bill one of the most important laws to come before the general assembly.[30]

The house finally voted for the legislation by a close vote of 31 to 29. The bipartisan coalition had not survived, but Governor Vanderhoof and the Republicans had gotten something that at least they could call a land use bill on which to conduct their campaigns for election. The governor, making the best of the situation, called the bill "a giant step forward for Colorado."[31] The key county lobbyist noted that environmental groups supported a strong bill with a powerful state role, while homebuilders, cattlemen, developers, and utilities would have preferred no bill at all.[32] The governor's chief

aide in the land use area, John Bermingham, noted that the
Colorado Open Space Council and other environmental groups at
the very end brought strong pressure on the administration to
oppose the bill. As he put it: "They were very disappointed in us,
but we felt that even a weak start was better than none."[33] Representative Dittemore stressed that her main goal was to get money to local
governments and to state agencies to help local governments with
their land use plans. She commented that she was "ready to
compromise the strong state role; making that state role weaker
didn't bother me." She saw her role as trying to compromise
between private groups such as developers, ranchers, and the
environmental groups.[34]

A few years later, Republican Senator Bermingham commented
that while Republicans were nervous about their political future in
1973 and 1974 and felt that some land use action was necessary to
protect the party, after 1974 they no longer felt they had to "go along
and support anything in the environmental protection and land use
area in order to hang onto office." Bermingham said: "They've
squeezed me out of the party. I managed to have an impact from the
outside, but now they are trying to go backward."[35] However that
may be, the Republican party has not been conspicuous in its
support of land use or environmental initiatives in Colorado since
1974, if indeed one can say that it was conspicuous in such support at
that time. We examine now exactly what came out of the confused,
contradictory, and abrasive political battles that finally produced
house bill 1041.

The Bill as Adopted

House bill 1041 as it finally was approved[36] seems simple and
straightforward if one reads the legislative summary: "Concerning
land use, and providing for identification, designation, and administration of areas and activities of state interest, and assigning
additional duties to the Colorado Land Use Commission and the
Department of Local Affairs and making appropriations therefor."
The simplicity is obviously misleading, since eight years later there
is still wide disagreement as to exactly what the law provides. There
is still disagreement on whether there really is a state role, especially
to the extent that in any set of circumstances the state can force a
local government to take action against its will.

House bill 1041 in its final form is modeled in some ways on the
American Law Institute's Model Land Development Code. In other
ways, the bill departs drastically from that code by not giving the
state a clear role in the process of identifying and making decisions
on developments of regional impact. In the bill these developments

are called matters of state interest, including activities of state interest and areas of state interest. In each of these two categories, the statute goes to some length in setting legislative criteria for the areas or activities that can and cannot be included. In this regard, it goes considerably beyond the Florida statute and indeed well beyond the American Law Institute's model. As a result of its detailed definitions and other criteria, the statute is also somewhat narrow.[37]

It is clear that the prime responsibility for identifying, regulating, and permitting development in areas and activities of state interest is with local government. Yet, the bill also provides a definite, though sharply limited, role for state government in forcing local government to consider areas or activities of state interest.

The legislative declaration in the bill is certainly far-reaching, holding that "The protection of the utility, value, and future of all lands within the state, including the public domain as well as privately owned land, is a matter of public interest." The declaration goes on to say that "Land use, land use planning, and quality of development are matters in which the state has responsibility for the health, welfare, and safety of the people of the state and for the protection of the environment of the state."[38]

The role of local governments in the legislative declaration is covered by the statement that "Local government shall be encouraged to designate areas and activities of state interest, and, after such designation, shall administer such areas and activities of state interest and promulgate guidelines for the administration thereof." The role of state agencies in this legislative declaration is to "assist local governments to identify, designate, and adopt guidelines for administration of matters of state interest."[39] Thus, despite the broad policy implications in the legislative declaration, the central issue of the allocation of power and authority between local governments and state government is not really addressed. One could conclude that it is entirely the prerogative of local governments whether to designate areas and activities of state interest, and that state agencies have only a supporting role. This interpretation of the bill, though widely held, seems to fall short of identifying fully the potential state role.

Part 2 deals with the four areas of state interest, which include mineral resource areas; natural hazard areas; areas having important historical, natural, or archaeological statewide importance; and areas around key facilities which might have a "material effect upon the facility or on the surrounding community."[40] The criteria for the administration of these areas are spelled out in considerable detail.[41] Article 65.1-203 lists nine activities of state interest, most of which

involve the siting and construction of various facilities such as
domestic water and sewage treatment systems and solid waste
disposal systems, and the siting and development of new communities.

It seems clear on the face of it that legislation giving such authority
to some combination of state and local governments contains many
of the ingredients for a comprehensive land- and growth-management system for a state. Obviously, the authority to control the
location and extent of new water and sewage systems goes a long
way toward establishing growth patterns. This control is especially
significant in Colorado, where water has been described as "the
great equalizer of land use decisionmaking in Colorado . . . Scarcity
of water provides the draconian limits to growth in Colorado's urban
strip, whether it is a drought year or not."[42] The power to intervene
in the siting and development of new communities, depending on
how broadly the power is construed, certainly also has great growth-
management potential. Taken together, the activities and areas of
state interest and the criteria for the administration of regulations
within them seem broad enough to constitute, in the hands of a
determined local government, with varying degrees of participation
by the state, a broad-ranged and powerful tool for managing land
and growth.

One example illustrates the potential for growth management
contained in section 204, spelling out criteria for administering
activities of state interest. The law states: "Major extensions of
domestic water and sewage treatment systems shall be permitted in
those areas where the anticipated growth and development that
may occur as a result of such extension can be accommodated within
the financial and environmental capacity of the area to sustain such
growth and development." Strictly interpreted and administered,
this expression of public policy alone goes far toward constituting a
comprehensive policy base for a growth-management system. Of
course, the fact of the matter is that local governments, except in
very narrowly drawn circumstances, are not required to make any
such designation or activities of state interest unless they choose to
do so.[43]

Part 3 of the law focuses on the levels of government involved and
their function. The agencies required to participate in the designating of matters of state interest are agencies with specialized responsibilities, such as the Colorado Water Conservation Board and the
Colorado Soil Conservation Board, with regard to flood plains; the
state forest service with regard to wildfire hazard areas, and several
others. While the role of the state land use commission is ignored in
this section, it is discussed later in the act.[44]

According to Part 4, if a local government designates either areas or activities of state interest, the guidelines developed in the designation must be consistent with the guidelines developed by the Colorado Land Use Commission, and these guidelines in turn must be consistent with the standards set forth in the act. The designation must spell out "the dangers that would result from uncontrolled development of any such area or uncontrolled conduct of such activity, and the advantages of development of such area or conduct of such activity in a coordinated manner."[45] In adopting its guidelines and regulations, the local governments are empowered to go beyond the minimum criteria in the act and adopt more stringent regulations. In section 403, the state Department of Local Affairs is charged with the coordination and oversight of technical and financial assistance to local governments, and the authority to decide whether and under what circumstances financial or technical assistance would be given to a local government. The act does refer to the bases on which the department is expected to provide this assistance (a showing by the local government of growth pressures and a plan for using the assistance).[46]

The heart of the act so far as any potential state role in the areas and activities of state interest is concerned may be found in sections 406 and 407. These sections go to the question of the role of the land use commission in designations, and the development of guidelines or regulations to control development once a designation is made. Under section 406, a local government that decides to designate a matter of state interest is required to submit its designation order to the commission for review. In turn, the commission is required to notify the local government of any modifications that must be made to comply with the law. The local government can either accept or reject the commission's suggestions. This section, then, seems to leave the commission no recourse for further action except perhaps under the temporary emergency powers provision brought forward from the earlier land use commission legislation. This section, however, does involve a clear mandate for local governments which take designation actions to submit these actions to the land use commission for review and does give the commission the authority to ask local government to change the designation and/or the guidelines if required. At the very least, the land use commission is given an opportunity to attempt directly to persuade local government to go in certain directions.[47]

Section 407 is a more critical matter. If the state is anywhere given in house bill 1041 the power to force local government to do anything under any circumstances, however indirectly, it is under the requirements of section 407. This section gives the land use commission authority to *initiate* identification designation and promulgation of guidelines for matters of state interest. The land use commission is authorized to make a "formal request" to a local government, typically a county, asking that local government to take action in cases the commission considered to be a matter of state interest, either an area or an activity. Furthermore, the local government is then required to publish a notice of public hearing not later than 30 days after the commission's request, hold a hearing within 60 days, and issue its decision in the matter. Section 407 gives the land use commission a powerful bargaining tool, if not a direct grant of power, by virtue of the fact that once the local government receives a formal request from the land use commission, there is a moratorium on development until the designation and guidelines are finally determined. Thus, the Colorado law does provide a means of avoiding a rush of ill-advised and hasty development, if development interests were to try to beat the deadline.[48]

Again, the local government receiving such a request is not required to designate the matter of state interest and adopt the guidelines or regulations under it. It can adopt if it chooses; refuse to adopt if it does not wish to do so. However, in formal request cases, the land use commission has the right, under the act, to seek judicial review of local orders and guidelines in the district court. Furthermore, the moratorium on development continues during such court proceedings, and no development activity can take place "except on such terms and conditions as authorized by the court."[49] The exact extent of this power under the act is a key to the degree to which there is a meaningful state presence in the administration of Colorado's 1974 land use law.

House bill 1041 concludes with part 5, which spells out the procedure by which local governments may grant permits for development in designated areas and activities of state interest. The time frame for permitting generally is aimed at completing the decisionmaking process within 60 days. Local governments are required to approve or deny permits on the basis of their own guidelines and regulations that govern the area or the activity. If the development complies, the permit is to be granted; if it does not, the permit is to be denied. The permitting procedures approach the formal procedures found in a quasi-judicial hearing. The enforcement power again brings the state land use commission into the picture. Persons who ignore the law by failing to get a permit before beginning development "may be enjoined by the Colorado Land Use Commission or the appropriate local government from engaging in such development or conducting such activity." Should a permit be denied, the applicant may seek judicial review in district court.[50]

Under house bill 1041, the Department of Local Affairs is charged with conducting a statewide program encouraging counties and municipalities to prepare a complete and detailed identification and designation of all matters of state interest within each county. Each county wishing to participate is to be given an equal amount of money by the Department of Local Affairs to be spent by the county separately, or through a group of counties or counties and municipalities.[51] An interesting and potentially important section of this provision has to do with the relationship between counties and cities in the matter of carrying out the requirements of house bill 1041.[52] Counties are clearly placed in the crucial position in the matter of implementing house bill 1041's identification and designation requirements at the local level. Municipalities may participate if they wish, but if they do not, the responsibility is taken up by the counties.

A companion measure passed by the 1974 legislative session deserves at least brief mention. House bill 1034, the Local Government Land Use Control Enabling Act of 1974, is in every sense a modern land use enabling statute for local governments. It gives local governments broad authority to plan for and regulate the use of land within their respective jurisdictions, in order to mitigate hazards, protect wildlife, or preserve areas of historic and archaeological importance. It specifically authorizes several innovative land- and growth-management approaches that are just beginning to be tried by local governments around the country. A section authorizing local governments to regulate "the location of activities and developments which may result in significant changes in population density" is a clarion call for growth-management initiatives by local governments in Colorado, and it has in fact been taken up by some of those governments. In providing for "phased development of services and facilities," the intent clearly is to give local governments in Colorado the authority to carry out sequential control of development somewhat along the lines of the so-called Ramapo plan.[53] The act also grants local governments a broad-based exercise of power "to provide planned and orderly use of land and protection of the environment in a manner consistent with constitutional rights."[54] Surely very few states in the nation have given such a specific and at the same time very broad grant of power to local governments to plan for and regulate the use of land at the local level. Although the Colorado legislature was reluctant to grant the state broad powers in the exercise of land use, it showed no hesitation in giving broad powers to local governments for the same purpose.

The Politics of Implementation

An Overview

It is surprisingly difficult to assess the implementation record of
house bill 1041 through the activities of its major vehicles, county
governments at the local level and the land use commission at the
state level. Several key questions about the extent of state authority,
exercised through the land use commission, were not answered
until very recently. Furthermore, local governments have been very
slow to move all the way through the designation process to the
point of requiring development permits within the areas and
activities of state interest described in the law. For both reasons, it is
easy to conclude that the law has had very little impact on land and
growth management in Colorado, and that it might just as well be
forgotten. Such a hasty conclusion would, in the view of this author,
be in error. Despite the limited progress in issuing permits, a great
many other important activities that have taken place must be
assessed before concluding anything about the effectiveness of the
implementation effort. The focus here is on the political context of
the implementation effort and in particular on the relationship
between counties at the local level and the land use commission and
other state agencies at the state level. (See Figure 7-1.)

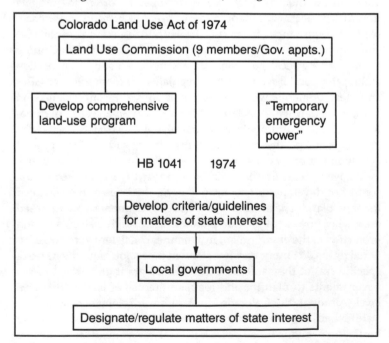

Figure 7-1. **COLORADO: Land-Use Regulation**

In a very real way, 1977 was a critical year for the land use commission in particular and for house bill 1041 in general in Colorado. Resentment by some counties and other participants toward the land use commission reached a boiling point and resulted in a major effort in the legislature to repeal or at least drastically reduce the role of the commission. At this critical juncture, when the land use commission was coming under the strongest political fire of its life, it determined to assert its powers under section 407 to further land and growth management objectives. That new policy direction, however, was short lived. Since 1978, the commission has abandoned its adversarial role and has been stressing coordination and cooperation with local governments. This shift to a less aggressive role can be tied directly to the political context for implementation since the 1978 general elections in Colorado.

Policy Choices in Implementation
In the first three years of implementing house bill 1041, the commission chose to focus heavily on its charge to develop model designation guidelines and regulations in order to assist county governments in carrying out the purposes of the act. The commission had developed expertise in this kind of development and evaluation of model regulations under senate bill 35's requirements in the area of subdivision regulations. This process seems to have gone rather smoothly, and may have influenced the commission's decision to develop guidelines and regulations that clearly went well beyond the minimum requirements of house bill 1041.

The commission could have concentrated instead on using its section 407 power to identify trouble spots within the framework of areas and activities of state interest and then to persuade or formally request local governments to take action. Within this policy option, there was a choice between a passive and a more aggressive approach. The commission could have chosen to simply receive complaints or information from various sources and then in a more or less unsystematic way deal with critical problems as they arose. On the other hand, the commission could have chosen to make more affirmative use of its 407 designation request power by casting it within a broad land- and growth-management framework. In such an approach, broad policy objectives would have been identified, and the commission would have then systematically sought out cases that would fit into and further the policy objectives involved. The commission, for whatever reason, chose to concentrate heavily on model regulations during the 1974–77 period, and confined its action in the "hotspot" category to reacting, somewhat reluctantly

and, in the eyes of many, often belatedly, to problem areas as they
were brought to its attention.

The Commission's Record
in Implementation

In assessing the implementation of house bill 1041, one factor that
must be considered is the adequacy of the funding and the staff
provided for the land use commission. The commission was settled
in the office of the governor, and its staff was not subject to civil
service rules. This gave flexibility in recruitment, but it also added
an element of uncertainty in the staffing situation with regard to
tenure. The funding of the commission was at about the same level
from 1974 to 1977, some $200,000 each year. This supported a small
staff of about eight professionals.

A variety of problems seem to have limited somewhat the capacity
of the commission and its staff to "get its act together" and move in a
deliberate and policy-oriented way beyond the development of
model guidelines and regulations. One commission member felt
that there had been ample dollars spent when one took into consideration all of the funds channeled to counties, but expressed
some doubt that the dollars had been allocated in a way as to provide
the most payoff.[55] Another close observer of the commission and
former staff member noted that in the six years after the land use
commission was established in 1970, there had been five directors,
indicating that the directorship had been a very politicized role.[56]
Another commission member held that "We had only a small staff,
and the issues were large, complex, and tough," in spite of which a
lot of very good staff work was done. Much of the negative criticism
that the staff had come in for was simply the reaction of people who
were "not having things happen the way they wanted them to."[57]
Another view was that "The land use commission has never had
enough staff to analyze the problems thoroughly before they went
after hotspots that have caused the commission so many problems."[58]

It seems fair to say that the appropriation of $200,000 for a
commission of nine members with fairly substantial travel expenses
could not support the kind of staff that would allow commission
initiative over a broad front. The commission had to make some
choices as to where it would concentrate its efforts in the early years.
The land use commission and its staff, in fact, spent a very great
percentage of its time from 1974 to 1977 in developing guidelines and
regulations that went well beyond the minimum required in a
designation action. The commission was careful to point out where

this was the case, and counties were free to follow only the regulations that were required under the act.[59]

One commission member acknowledged that it was perhaps true that the commission had made a strategic error in deciding to concentrate on very elaborate and detailed model regulations that local governments could use selectively instead of developing something very simple and limited. In taking the detailed approach, he said "We really shocked a lot of county attorneys." He said the commission felt that many counties with very small staffs would have a difficult time dealing with the requirements of house bill 1041 if they did not have the benefit of the commission's detailed model regulation work.[60] Thus, to some extent, the commission in an effort to be helpful to counties aroused an alarmed and hostile reaction and created an atmosphere within which some counties were reluctant to move at all to implement house bill 1041.

One of the early commission chairmen noted that it was his position that the commission should have moved immediately in using its section 407 power more aggressively. In making his assessment in 1977, he noted that the commission was belatedly shifting its focus to go after the hotspots, but unfortunately for the commission, the timing was bad.[61] Another commission member concurred that "Too much time was spent on developing model regulations." As an alternative, the commission "should have done some quick stuff, put it out as advisory, and let the rules and regulations be tried instead of trying to perfect them before we started trying to put them into practice."[62]

Whether the land use commission's decision to concentrate on detailed guidelines and regulations was the best approach may not be as important as the fact that this choice postponed any clarification of the commission's full powers under house bill 1041. Had the commission decided in 1974 to try to use its section 407 powers aggressively within the framework of carefully selected land- and growth-management objectives, many questions about the commission's ultimate authority and the general extent of the state role in land management in Colorado probably would have been answered much sooner. On the other hand, given the increasingly hostile attitude of a Republican-controlled legislature to land use in general and the land use commission in particular, such a course of action might have brought the commission much earlier to the point of near death that it was to face in 1977. Before considering the commission's limited exercise of its section 407 powers, we will examine the financial and technical assistance activities under the law, and some crucial administrative problems that were encountered.

Technical and Financial Assistance

In many ways the major thrust of house bill 1041 is focused on providing financial and technical assistance to local governments. The Department of Local Government, through its Division of Planning, has played a major role in dispensing financial assistance. In quantitative terms alone, the dollars provided to local government under house bill 1041 has been impressive. The "long appropriations bill" of 1974, senate bill 468, provided an appropriation of $1,575,000 for a kind of base grant of $25,000 to each of Colorado's counties. In addition, supplementary planning funds in the amount of $500,000 were appropriated for distribution to counties. This relatively generous level of financial assistance for planning in general and land use planning in particular was continued in ensuing years by the Colorado legislature. A summary of appropriations shows that in addition to the first year funds of $25,000 per county and a half-million dollar discretionary fund, the ensuing years saw appropriations as follows: 1975–76, $25,000 per county and a supplementary amount of $200,000; 1976–77, $26,750 per county and $250,000 in supplementary funds; and in 1977–78, $15,000 per county and a $500,000 supplementary amount.[63] Both grants to counties and supplementary planning funds were phased down sharply after 1978, and by 1980 these funds were eliminated.[64] The fixed amount per county appropriation is reserved specifically for "the administration, identification, and regulations of areas and activities."[65] The funds are restricted to counties which are judged to be "actively implementing house bill 1041 objectives for selected areas and activities." Of Colorado's 63 counties, only 5 have failed to comply with the requirement.

One source saw these funds as having made it possible for many counties to establish planning staffs, which in turn substantially improved the professional expertise and increased concern for land use problems in local government. However, it was also noted that the funds had not provided very much in the way of an impetus to local governments to implement the designation of matters of state interest. The funds had failed to achieve this objective "because counties have not had to demonstrate that they have significantly advanced house bill 1041 purposes to qualify for additional funding."[66] A different assessment noted that progress in identifying areas and activities of state interest is one of several criteria used by the Department of Local Affairs in disbursing supplemental funds to both counties and the municipalities.

The legal counsel for the Pueblo County land use administrator and for the Pueblo Regional Planning Commission noted that the land use commission's control of the whole 1041 effort was seriously fragmented by the legislature's assigning fiscal control to the Department of Local Affairs. As he saw it, "that means that the Colorado Land Use Commission, while it may enunciate certain policies and seek to have the same followed by local government, lacks the persuasive tool of control of the purse strings. Since local land use money is controlled by the Department of Local Affairs, the department has the clout to override the policies of the land use commission."[67] The department not only holds the purse strings; its close ties to counties and cities have made it reluctant to force these clients to take any unwelcomed action.

The bottom line is that the land use commission has been unable to use financial assistance as an effective tool for persuading or coercing counties to move aggressively in achieving the goal of identifying matters of state interest under house bill 1041. Thus, a tool that the Land Conservation and Development Commission in Oregon has used to persuade counties to come into conformance with the goals of its land use law, and a tool that the California Coastal Commission has used under the 1976 Coastal Planning and Management Law, has been largely denied to the key land use agency in Colorado. Whether that denial is wise or unwise depends on one's approach and philosophy in land use matters.

A key staff member of the Colorado Association of Counties criticized the state's financial assistance on different grounds. In his view, the equal amount grants to counties were meant to support local efforts to carry out the goals of 1041 in a process sense, and not meant to be used for the substantive aspects of planning, as emphasized by the Division of Planning in the Department of Local Affairs. As he saw it in actual practice on the ground, some counties had used the funds for substantive planning, where they constituted little more than a drop in the bucket in that overall effort. Others had used the funds as he felt they should have been used, by putting them into more effective administration. The more effective administration usually took the form of a strong recommendation to counties that they hire a land use administrator, but the observer, a key participant in the effort to get the law underway, recalled that: "Local planners fought against this, because they wanted to do everything themselves."[68]

The administration of house bill 1041 at the state level has also been fragmented by the bill's provision that, for the purpose of assisting counties in implementing its provisions, field representatives would be under the control of and in fact hired by the Department of Local Affairs, rather than by the land use commission. According to one veteran field representative, the working relationship between field representatives—generally hired from local governments—and the land use commission, though generally good, has varied a great deal, reflecting the constant turnover at both the commission level and staff level of the land use commission. He agreed that there is a potential problem of getting caught in a crossfire between counties and the land use commission, should the commission increase its use of section 407 powers, but said this issue had not been important to date.[69]

Any assessment of the impact of the land use commission on the land- and growth-management process at the local level must take into account the fairly substantial amount of technical assistance and other kinds of activities which the land use commission and its staff have carried out both before and since the law's passage. Of the 49 cases in which the commission was involved between 1973 and 1977, 22 involved technical assistance to local governments, largely to counties. In these cases, counties typically sought the help of the commission in some particular zoning, subdivision regulation, or other kind of growth-management question. The land use commission carried out eight technical reviews and also exercised its temporary emergency powers in six instances to stop development. One land use commission member felt these dual roles of coercion and technical assistance caused considerable problems for the commission. As he put it, "It's been very hard for an agency such as the land use commission to be both a good guy and a bad guy at the same time."[70]

Major Problem Areas in Administration

One of the major difficulties encountered in the early administration of house bill 1041 stemmed from the land use commission's relations with the Department of Local Affairs, particularly its division of planning. One former chairman of the land use commission resigned partly as a protest of his inability to get gubernatorial support to force cooperation from the Department of Local Affairs. He noted that the land use commission "had no cooperation from the Department of Local Affairs, so I called for an appointment with the governor to talk about the problem. He canceled it after giving me an appointment, then he wouldn't reset it, so I quit."[71] As this strong-minded and, according to some, quick-tempered former chairman saw it, the problem was largely that there was a veteran bureaucrat in the Department of Local Affairs who was very opposed to interfering in any way with local government affairs. He noted that the first head of the department was also out of local government, and that "Her biases were that way."[72]

A former staff member of the land use commission cited several reasons why the state agencies had not worked well together in implementing the law. As he saw it, there was a natural desire of each agency to defend its own territory. Furthermore, there was honest confusion over what the law meant. Finally, efforts to educate local government had been weak, partly because the state was not clear itself on what the bill meant.[73] Another observer noted that the division of planning, in its strong focus on local planning, often did not appreciate the broader than local problems that really were a major thrust of house bill 1041. His view was that the planning division tended to shortchange the critical area and regional impact type of land use decisions that did, in fact, have a more than local impact.[74]

The other major problem in administering house bill 1041 has been the land use commission's often strained and abrasive relationship with local government, especially counties. In assessing this relationship, one must start with the fact that Colorado counties by and large have no enthusiasm for any kind of state control over their land- and growth-management decisions. As one commission staff member put it: "What we needed to do and did not do was to sit down with county commissioners and explain the act to them. The field representatives in the division of planning also didn't do that." Every time a county was faced with the prospect of declaring an area or activity of state interest, county commissioners at least pretended to believe that there would be as a result direct state regulation of the activities or areas involved.[75]

Another observer pointed out that the counties were willing to work together on a voluntary basis to carry out the objectives of house bill 1041, but did not want to delegate substantial authority to regional councils. He noted that in fact in a few areas, counties had contracted with councils of government to do some of the work required under the law. According to him, a key problem was that local planners were not inclined to use the appropriate state technical information really needed to carry out the land use law: "The local planners wanted to use the $25,000 initially and the subsequent funds that came later to run out and hire consultants."[76]

For the most part, the responsibility for implementating house bill 1041 was lodged with counties, but a real problem apparently arose from the fact that cities were not mandatory participants in the subdivision regulations required by senate bill 35. Developers were playing off cities against counties, and "The Republicans and their developer friends" would not close the loophole.[77] The situation was helped somewhat by the legislature's passing a law forbidding any new incorporation of cities without the approval of the county within which the incorporation would take place.

According to one member of the land use commission, the root of the difficulties was the very strong tradition of local authority in Colorado. As he describes it, every initiative of a state agency, particularly the land use commission, "creates a kind of crisis in the eyes and minds of the local government people." From his point of view, it had been a mistake for the land use commission to flex its muscles so rarely, since when it did, it really became a big event. He noted further that uncertainties in the law had given county attorneys an opportunity to give what he considered very bad advice to county commissions: "There are many examples of where these attorneys have said that things are illegal when they clearly were not illegal under the act."[78]

In closing this assessment of state/local relations, it is instructive to consider an analysis, by a lawyer who has represented developers in Colorado, of some of the very practical reasons why counties and cities have been reluctant to designate areas and activities of state interest. His assessment was made from the perspective of a developer who finds himself caught in the middle between state and local governments. As the lawyer saw it, most planning staff members and policymakers at the local level were very reluctant to deal with the land use commission with regard to any kind of land use decision, especially in the early stages of decisionmaking. Local government often claimed that the commission seemed to do more harm than good, causing confusion and delays. While admitting that there might be some truth to this, the lawyer also noted that the problem was largely a product of the uncertainties and confusions in the legislation, and the resistance of local government to state control, rather than to any incompetence of the commission or its staff.[79]

Of considerably more significance was the lawyer's view that to expect a local government to seek a designation voluntarily "flies squarely in the face of political reality." The county commission would in effect be bringing down upon itself the requirement to hold a public hearing, and to "say to their constituents that the state boys should come around on this one—possibly even before the said project has been through local planning and zoning procedures."[80] On the other hand, the lawyer noted, if the county later decided that it did not like the proposed project, it was apt to suddenly seek designation. The whole process, as he saw it, created a nightmare situation for the developer, who felt in constant jeopardy in one way or another—from the state level or the local— even after the project was under construction.[81]

Commission's Exercise of
Section 407 Powers

We turn now to a consideration of the commission's limited application of its section 407 power to trouble spots that fell within the areas and activities authorized in the legislation. Between passage of the act to July 1, 1977, the land use commission had used this power to issue only six formal requests for designation hearings to cities or counties. As once source put it, "These few requests have supplied in drama what they have lacked in frequency." A brief review of the circumstances and subject matter of each request will give some feel for the interaction between the land use commission and local governments.

In April 1975, the city of Louisville in Boulder County proposed to annex a 600-acre tract to be developed as the Colorado Technological Center. The land use commission requested the city and Boulder County to designate two areas of state interest (geological hazard and mineral resource areas) and two activities of state interest (new communities and water and sewer systems). The commission went to court in an attempt to enjoin Louisville from annexing the territory until after the designation process was completed. The commission lost this court test of its authority, but after the annexation, the city did hold hearings and designated parts of the tract as a geological hazard area. The land use commission also accepted the city's use of other regulation to meet the commission's concerns.

In another case, the land use commission requested the city of Durango to designate as geologic and flood hazard areas parts of a subdivision which the city had annexed in March 1977. In a consent agreement between the commission, the city of Durango and the developer, the developer agreed to correct the problems, and the city agreed to review and approve the proposed changes. The commission then withdrew its designation request. Here again, the threat of designation was used to force apparently successful negotiation of the issues. The commission issued a second request to the city of Durango which involved flood plain regulation for the Animas River, after the commission learned that the city had revoked its previous flood plain controls. The commission withdrew the designation request after the city council indicated its intention to adopt a comprehensive flood plain regulation that would meet the minimum requirements of house bill 1041. As of August 1977, the city had not adopted a flood plain regulation.[82]

Another designation request came after Routt County residents asked the land use commission to intervene in a proposed development of over 3,000 dwelling units. After lengthy meetings in the county, attended by large numbers of people, the commission determined that the development was exempt from house bill 1041, but did request Routt County to designate the adjoining mountain-side, slated for development as a ski area, as a wildlife habitat. This request aroused considerable county hostility and was withdrawn after Routt County agreed to carry out a natural resource area designation by amending several existing county ordinances.

At its June 1977 meeting, the land use commission requested that Larimer County designate the Big Thompson Canyon, involving the floodway and drywash channels and other parts of the Canyon, as matters of state interest. In the aftermath of the disastrous flood of August 1, 1976, the county had taken considerable action to regulate development in the flood plain, but had subsequently amended its regulations to allow overnight camping as a use by right. On the basis of testimony by the Colorado Geological Survey on the dangers of flooding in the drywash channels, the commission concluded that the county was not regulating these areas so as to meet minimum house bill 1041 criteria. The county commissioners declined the commission's subsequent designation request, but did amend their flood plain zoning regulation to meet in part the commission's objectives. The commission did not take the county to court in the matter.

The picture these six cases present is one in which the land use commission's request to designate, which often has originated from appeals by concerned citizens or groups, has typically been greeted with extreme hostility by local governments. In the face of this hostility, the commission has tended to seek some compromise position which would allow at least partial achievement of its objectives, while at the same time avoiding a final confrontation with the county or city involved. As one assessment put it, "The LUC's efforts under the statute had met with political opposition from development interests and local government partisans. Few groups have rallied behind its program, and the single court test of its authority was a mixed success."[83] Some critics accepted the commission's need to pursue aggressively the exercise of its section 407 power, while others felt that the commission was violating the spirit if not the letter of the law by making any attempts to force local governments to do anything. To one person holding the latter viewpoint, house bill 1041 was a planning bill and not really all that hard to interpret. As Representative Dittemore saw it, the land use commission claimed that the law was confusing because it did not give the commission as strong a state role as it would like to have.[84]

The director of the land use commission who assumed his position in 1977 expressed the view that the section 407 power of the state under house bill 1041 should either be clarified or repealed. In his view, the attempts of the commission to use section 407 "have been a disaster."[85] A land use commission member noted that when the commission had finally begun to use the section 407 power, "It was really too late and it tended to vacillate and take an off again— on again attitude."[86]

A somewhat different critique of the commission's use of its 407 power came from a representative of Colorado Counties, Inc. In his view, the land use commission's tendency to focus on easy case-by-case issues in which the commission "scolds a particular county for doing things incorrectly" had created tense relationships with the counties. He believed a better approach would have been to try to develop general policies and a data base on which action could be taken in a number of counties with regard to a particular issue. For example, instead of zeroing in on the Thompson Canyon flood situation, the commission should have focused on how to handle the general problem of flood plain zoning, laid down certain criteria, and required all counties with flood control problems to go along with them. This view from the county side implies that counties would support a designation request that was cast in this type of broad policy framework.[87] It was not until 1977 that the commission decided to test its authority under section 407 to take a county to court, and if successful, force the county to designate an area or activity and adopt regulations acceptable to the commission. The case in point involved Douglas County, in which the commission had rejected the county's contention that the commission's concerns about growth pressures from Colorado Springs and Denver were being handled satisfactorily under the county's own zoning powers. The chairman of the commission noted that while the commission would press forward with this case, the whole question of what to do if a county refused to designate after being asked to do so was a difficult one. In his view, the land use commission found itself as a custodian "of a bad and unpopular law."[88]

The Douglas County case involved the commission's formal request to the county to designate as a matter of state interest site selection and development of new communities and to subsequently adopt regulations and guidelines appropriate to such designation. On August 2, 1977, the county held a hearing, but at its conclusion issued an order which failed to designate the site selection and development of new communities as a matter of state interest. At its regular monthly meeting of September 23, 1977, the commission heard from its staff and all interested parties, and by unanimous vote agreed to seek judicial review of the defendant's refusal to designate the activity as the commission had requested.

The case presented an opportunity for the commission to begin to address broader land- and growth-management objectives through the pursuit of its section 407 powers. As the commission's brief pointed out, "intense development pressures" could lead to the establishment of major urban centers in the unincorporated areas of Douglas County. The commission saw this kind of urban development as clearly a matter of statewide concern. The judicial review sought by the commission seemed at the time to have historic importance for its future, and the future of the state role in land use in Colorado. As the commission chairman put it: "It's the critical test of the state law, and it will go all the way to the supreme court."[89] However, the Douglas County case was settled out of court, and the key powers question was shifted to the Larimer County "Rawhide case," which eventually went to the Colorado Supreme Court. The court's decision is described later. Thus the Douglas County case served to raise the issue of the land use commission's powers but did not resolve it.[90]

It is difficult to assess the effectiveness of the commission's use of its section 407 power in these cases. In many instances, the commission used the 407 designation to bring about the negotiated settlement with a local government in order to achieve at least some part of what the commission wished to accomplish in a formal request. One must conclude, however, that the section 407 power was not used as frequently nor as effectively as it might have been. A major weakness was the commission's failure to be positive and assertive in the use of the power, and to use it within a broad growth management policy framework, rather than to simply react to individual cases. We turn now to the commission's efforts to move in the direction of a policy framework in 1977 and to get a clearer court definition of its powers under section 407.

The Pawnee Case and the 1977 Legislature: A Time of Crisis

Almost every instance in which the land use commission has requested a county to designate an area or activity of state interest has produced a firestorm of political backlash from local government officials. The Pawnee case differed from the earlier cases only in its direct involvement of several key legislators at a time when the future of the commission and its budget were being considered by the 1977 session of the Colorado legislature. The case involved a Public Service Company of Colorado proposal to establish a 500 megawatt coal-fired electric generating plant in Morgan County near Brush, Colorado. A group of citizens had asked the land use commission to require the county to hold a designation hearing. The commission, after considering the matter in January and reconsidering it in April, decided to request such a designation hearing but to exempt Pawnee unit number one on the grounds that it was a year too late for the commission to make any kind of timely intervention in that particular unit.

The commission, aware that the Morgan County/Pawnee matter would be controversial, had tried very hard to persuade the county to designate the electric generating facility voluntarily. When that effort failed, the series of on again off again actions that followed through to April made the land use commission "look inept, incompetent, and unable to make up its mind." A former staff member felt that the "Pawnee power plant issue destroyed the land use commission."[91] Such a drastic statement justifies some closer analysis of just what did happen in the designation hearings and subsequently in the legislature.

At the January designation hearing of the commission, four legislators (including Representative Betty Ann Dittemore and another Republican representative and two Democrats) appeared before the land use commission to urge it to consider carefully its action in the case on the grounds that it might be exceeding its authority, and that with the legislative session about to start, they ought to act prudently. The attitude, reportedly hostile, of at least two of the legislators caused a very strong reaction from the attorney hired by INFO PLEASE, an ad hoc coalition of ranchers, farmers, and environmentalists. INFO's attorney, both before the commission and in later communications to the press, cited information that the legislators appearing before the land use commission had received political contributions from the Public Service Company; in effect, the attorney accused them of a conflict of interest. The legislators who had testified, especially the two Republican representatives, reacted with great indignation and anger. Partly as a result, Representative Dittemore was one of the sponsors of house bill 1542 in the 1977 legislative session, which would have drastically curtail the authority of the land use commission, placed it under the Department of Local Affairs, and also would have subjected it to a sunset provision in 1979.

Representative Dittemore noted that the lawyer for INFO PLEASE "wrote a scathing attack on me and other legislators who appeared before the land use commission accusing us of being in the pockets of the Public Service Company." With some indignation, Representative Dittemore noted that she received only a $50 campaign contribution from the Public Service Company. At about the same time, there was a proposed development in the city of Durango that involved a flood plain in which the commission also asked the county to make a designation and, as Representative Dittemore put it, "The fireworks began." There was much sentiment at that time for abolishing the land use commission, and in fact Representative Hamlon of Morgan County had introduced such a bill. Representative Dittemore saw her role in the controversy as an effort to act as a mediator and to prevent the complete abolishment of the commission.[92]

The Pawnee case was simply the catalyst that brought to a head the opposition of county elected officials and Republican legislators to the land use commission. As one assessment put it: "After its designation request to Routt County, Durango, and especially to Morgan County, the land use commission came under severe attack by several Colorado legislators because if its failure to act quickly and decisively. It narrowly escaped being abolished or severely curtailed by proposed legislation in the 1977 session."[93] The resentment and hostility of local governments, particularly county elected officials, toward any action that threatened to force them to take unwelcome land- and growth-management actions was also conveyed quickly and efficiently to some key members of the legislature.

Another assessment of the Pawnee affair noted that, "the Pawnee Power Plant controversy was just the sort of red flag insidious, invidious state power that legislators love to rip to shreds for the folks back home."[94] The Pawnee case also increased the concern of the development community over the ability of the land use commission to enter a development issue at almost any point in the process, including well after the development was underway. One attorney with development experience observed that, "the proponents of even stronger land use legislation refused to acknowledge publicly this great power of the land use commission to intimidate developers and indeed put them out of business, which may not be good land use control, but certainly is control."[95]

House bill 1542 did pass the Colorado legislature and was only prevented from becoming law by the governor's veto, which was not overridden in the legislature. Although the land use commission escaped the impact of this bill, the legislature used the appropriation process to force some drastic and potentially far-reaching changes on the commission. The funding for the land use commission was reduced from $200,000 to about $60,000, with the notion that the professional staff of the commission would be reduced from eight to three. The field representatives under the control of the Department of Local Government would continue to be funded as before.[96] This drastic reduction in dollars for the commission forced the governor to place the commission in a much closer relationship with the Department of Local Affairs than had been the case previously.

Reorganizing the Commission:
Charting a New Course

As the land use commission was being threatened by sharp changes in its function, or possible abolishment, the commission was also undergoing an internal policy crisis. In spite of the fact that the commission's use of its section 407 powers in a few highly controversial cases had caused much of its problems with the legislature, the commission determined in a series of meetings in the summer and fall of 1977 to focus in the future on the use of its 407 powers far more extensively than it had in the past. However, the great difference in moving toward this new policy direction was that the use of the 407 designation power would be carried out within the framework of carefully enunciated land and growth management policies, which in turn would be explained at length and in depth in a series of hearings involving the local governments most apt to be affected by the new approach.

This determination by the land use commission seemed politically unrealistic. Furthermore, in the midst of this new policy direction effort, the commission was also undergoing a change to a completely new administrative structure in which it would depend for its staffing largely on the Department of Local Affairs. The political difficulties aside, there was a question whether the commission could function effectively in the future in an administrative and policy sense. The answer depended on whether the commission, in fact, received strong and effective support from the Department of Local Affairs.

The commission's effort to develop a new land- and growth-management framework began to take shape in the form of an in-house memorandum considered by the commission at its July 13, 1977, meeting. This memorandum identified three major areas as new policy goals: natural hazard areas, energy facility siting, and urban sprawl. Within the natural hazard areas, the emphasis would be on flood hazard areas, geologic hazard areas, and wildlife hazard areas, with a maximum effort to notify local government of the commission's emphasis. To prevent urban sprawl, the commission would focus on designation requests regarding the siting and development of new communities and new water and sewage treatment systems.[97]

A follow-up in-house memorandum dated August 19, 1977, further enunciated the intention of the commission to change its approach in exercising its section 407 power. One key statement in the memo held that the commission would conduct designation request meetings in front range counties to determine whether local governments were adequately controlling urban sprawl, energy facility siting, and natural hazard areas. The memo made clear that the whole strategy was based on section 407 of house bill 1041, "since it provides prerogatives under which the commission may fulfill its statutory obligations."

The memo also suggested that the commission might well want to reject claims of local governments that the goals of the act were being met by other kinds of local land use control activities, such as those under senate bill 35. The memo, which was written by a staff member and thus not formal commission policy, nevertheless took a very tough posture on the commission's use of its section 407 powers: "The procedure will remove the notion that trust of local government is part of the commission's statutory obligations under house bill 1041 and will place the emphasis on the regulation of matters of state interest." Thus a kind of challenge was laid down under which, if accepted by the land use commission, the commission would assert itself with a new degree of vigor and aggressiveness and attempt to force local government to come into conformance with the goals of the act even in the face of continuing political controversy.[98] Another memorandum dated August 22, 1977, written by a different commission staff member, confirmed the commission's new policy: "The land use commission work program is an attempt by the land use commission to decide on a positive course, take positions where the law is gray, and use house bill 1041 to accomplish the positive purposes the general assembly has authorized it to do. The time has come and the land use commission is attempting to take the lead to improve Colorado's local land use system."[99]

In assessing the future policy goals, its new chairman in 1977 noted that: "We have worked our way through the model stage and now we're going to have to move into the hotspot areas, the very kind of thing that has gotten us in so much trouble with the legislature." He added: "We're going to change our approach and move into particular cases only within the framework of our new broad land and growth management objectives." He noted that Colorado had not passed energy siting regulations as proposed in the legislature two years before, so it really was the responsibility of the and use commission. He saw urban sprawl as the toughest yet most important policy focus: "It's really a tough one. It's broad; it's trying to stop leapfrog development, and it gets us into really controversial areas."[100]

The year 1977 was a watershed time for the land use commission. In the midst of its deepest political danger, the commission still decided to forge ahead with new, clearer, and tougher policies, using its section 407 powers to maximize the limited but potentially important state role in land and growth management in Colorado. Whether these goals could be achieved depended not only on the commission's sustaining its policy directions but also on the success of its new reliance on the Department of Local Affairs for staff support.

The New Staffing Pattern

From the point of view of the land use commission, the decision by the governor to bring about a much closer link between the commission and the Department of Local Affairs appeared to be a highly negative move. Its relationship with the Department of Local Affairs, and particularly its division of planning, had been strained—filled with suspicion and characterized by little in the way of cooperation. Under the new staffing arrangement, the new deputy director for the Department of Local Affairs served initially as the executive director of the land use commission. He explained at a land use commission meeting that the old approach in which the land use commission's staff members were not civil service employees would be ended, all current staff members would be replaced, and the new staff would have civil service status. Current staff members would be free to apply for the new positions, and two full-time positions would be filled immediately.

The executive director then set out to reassure the commission. He stressed his determination to give the commission the best quality staff work possible, including a fair and impartial analysis of alternatives and recommendations for courses of action. The two full-time staff members would be backed up with the entire resources of the division of planning. Furthermore, the department's field representatives could in fact become the commission's "eyes and ears." In an obvious effort to allay the commission's fears of losing its independence, the executive director said: "We're not out to change, alter, or intimidate the land use commission. That's not our role. We would like to help you broaden the scope of your concern." This was an obvious reference to the commission's concern with setting clear-cut policy goals for the future activities. In a moment of political realism, and perhaps in the understatement of the year, the executive director noted that "The legislature is not firmly in your camp," and went on to stress that he and the staff wanted to help the commission take positions that were defensible and effective. He added that in his view the state had not always been responsive to the needs of the land use commission.[101]

The new deputy director of the department and executive director of the land use commission seemed determined to give the commission the kind of broad-based and in-depth staff support that it would have to have to carry out its new policy strategies in an effective way. There remained, of course, the whole question of the political future of the land use commission. As the executive director put it in his concluding comments to the commission: "If the legislature cuts you out entirely, they have to face the fact that they are also de facto repealing important sections of house bill 1041."[102]

Post-1977 Developments

Since late summer 1977, there have been both positive and negative developments affecting the land use commission's plans for implementing the land- and growth-management law more effectively. Court decisions have been largely negative, the governor's office, faced with the reality of a hostile Republican legislature, has given no strong show of support for a more assertive role by the land use commission, funding has continued to decline to a new low of $11,000 in 1982, and the high hopes of the land use commission for a clearer (and stronger) state role though a more systematic use of the commission's section 407 powers have not materialized. Yet, the land use commission did adopt in June 1978 a statement of policy that clarified when the commission would and would not seek designation of matters of state interest and spelled out its attitude toward alternate methods for complying with house bill 1041 goals. Furthermore, in mid-1979 the governor issued an executive order containing "Colorado's Human Settlement Policies" that constituted a set of growth-management policies of great potential significance to the land use commission. Both of these documents constitute important efforts to place land and growth management in Colorado in a clearer policy framework.

Colorado Supreme Court Decision

It had been expected that the section 407 powers of the land use commission would be clarified by court decisions on the 1977 Douglas County controversy. However, that case did not reach the courts, because a compromise had been achieved through the efforts of a mediator hired by the county.[103] Court clarification of the commission's 407 powers came about instead through the Rawhide case,[104] which did go all the way to the Colorado Supreme Court. The court ruled that the land use commission did have the power to request that local governments designate matters of state interest, but sharply narrowed the right of the commission to take a local government to court to force compliance if it refused to carry through with a designation. The scope of the judicial review would be limited to "questions of illegality or impropriety on the part of local governments."[105]

This narrow ruling meant that the commission could not bring a case to court solely on the substantive issues, as it had tried to do in the Rawhide case. This rendered the review process virtually meaningless to the commission. Nevertheless, the court had upheld the right of the land use commission to formally request a designation of matters of state interest. The commission's having that authority, even absent a meaningful court process to ultimately force a reluctant local government to act, is crucially important. The long-awaited court test of house bill 1041, and especially section 407, constituted a major narrowing of an already limited state role in land and growth management in Colorado.

Commission's 1978 Policy Statement

In its policy statement issued in mid-1978, the commission did not abandon the positions it had embraced in 1977, despite the actions of the 1977 legislature. Nevertheless, the general tone of the document was conciliatory toward local government. Earlier policy drafts had proposed that in most, if not all cases, house bill 1041 requirements should be met by adopting regulations under the land use law. The mid-1978 version stressed the possibility of meeting 1041 standards through the use of regulations adopted by local governments under their own powers. If substitute regulations met the commission's minimum standards, the commission would accept them in all situations except those involving:

1. Site selection of airports.
2. Site selection of arterial highways and interchanges and collector highways.
3. Site selection and construction of major facilities of a public utility.
4. When the "person" to be regulated is a special district or any political subdivision, agency, instrumentality, or corporation of the state.[106]

The thrust of the policy statement was to greatly narrow the substantive concerns that would trigger a commission designation request and set the framework for commission—local government interactions much more focused on cooperation and coordination, rather than an adversarial relationship.

Human Settlement Policies

The reaction to the executive order on human settlement policies which Governor Lamm issued just after the Colorado legislature adjourned in 1979 continues the Colorado tradition of partisan political conflict between a Democratic governor and a Republican legislature. Work on a set of human settlement policies had begun several years earlier. By early 1978, the policies drafted by the division of planning in the Department of Local Affairs were ready for review. The deputy director of the Department of Local Affairs strongly supported early legislative involvement, but he was opposed in this view by senior staff people in the governor's office.[107]

The human settlement policies were to be used as guidelines in reviewing state and federal funding, and as a policy framework for growth-management efforts by state agencies. As expressed in the introduction to the executive order, they were:

> . . . developed to provide direction to the state of Colorado on how to accommodate growth that is projected to occur. The policies are designed in response to the problems of the 1980s: deteriorating air quality, energy scarcity, inflation, waning government resources, changing economic bases. They provide a long-range framework to help gradually reduce our dependence upon consumptive, cost-inefficient life styles.[108]

In discussions continuing into the first half of 1979, the governor's office continued to resist any involvement of the legislature in developing the final version of the policies. The land use commission played a role in reviewing the policies and passed a resolution urging their adoption. The reason for that support is clear. The goals and policies of house bill 1041 are reflected in many of the order's policies, such as encouraging growth in communities with the fiscal and planning capacity to support quality of growth; discouraging development that would adversely effect air, water, wildlife habitats, and important agricultural land; and encouraging compact, contiguous, energy efficient development.[109]

When the governor issued the executive order, it caused a storm of controversy and protest. It apparently struck the legislature as little less than subversive—at best a deliberate effort to usurp the policymaking role of the legislature. As one assessment put it, the legislature "came unglued," and the legislative council protested that the governor was without authority to issue the policies. The 1980 session resulted in a formal resolution by the legislature asking the governor to rescind the policies. "Proviso language" was attached to a number of appropriations bills stating that the human settlement policies were not to have an impact on the spending of the appropriated dollars.[110]

The reaction of the legislature reflected the deep partisan divisions of Colorado's land- and growth-management politics, with Republicans generally opposing a substantial state role. Although Governor Lamm was reelected in November 1978 by a record breaking 60 percent majority, Republicans won larger majorities in both the house and the senate. The sharp political conflict that had focused on the land use commission in 1977 shifted in 1979 and 1980 to the governor and the human settlement policies. The legislature's objection to the policies seemed to focus more on availing itself of an

opportunity to attack the governor than on substantive objections to
the policies themselves. The dispute became so heated that the
governor rescinded the human settlement policies in December
1980, thus reducing the policy framework available to the land use
commission to the commission's own policy statement issued in
1978. The shock waves from the dispute carried over to 1981 when
the joint budget committee reduced the budget of the Department
of Local Affairs by $100,000. This cut and related factors forced the
merger of the division of planning into the division of local
government, with a substantial reduction in personnel. Thus the
capacity of the division of local government to give staff support to
the land use commission was greatly reduced. One staff member
serves part time as the staff administrator to the land use commission. This person also serves as chief planner in the division of local
government, along with two other professionals, the surviving unit
of what was the planning division.[111] Thus the staff support available
to the land use commission has been sharply reduced at the same
time the courts have substantially reduced the powers of the
commission.

Summary Assessment of the Land Use
Commission's Implementation Record

A count of the Colorado counties that had designated areas or
activities of state interest as of June 1977 showed that 16 of the 63
counties had taken such action, 2 counties had designation actions
pending, and another 2 had scheduled hearings for October 1977.
The city of Louisville was the only municipality that had designated
a matter of state interest. Most counties had limited their action to
designating a particular area or activity, but Pitkin County was
reported to have used the designation approach as the foundation
for an "innovative comprehensive land use code." As of July 1977, a
total of only nine permit hearings had been held in five counties.
The only conclusion that can be made about the permitting approach is that it has been relatively ineffective simply because it has
been used in such a limited fashion.[112] The land use commission has
made no designation requests since 1977. The mandatory component of the land use law as reflected in section 407 powers has been
virtually eliminated through a combination of court rulings, local
government resistence, and legislative hostility.[113]

Has Governor Lamm given as much support as he might have to
the land use commission in its efforts to implement house bill 1041?
The answer seems to be "yes and no." One observer explained that
the governor had "got burned pretty badly" in a political fight over
interstate highway I-470 and in battles over several other environ-

mental issues. This observer also pointed out that the governor had
to moderate his support of the commission in order to avoid being
tagged with a "no-growth, anti-business" image.[114] It is interesting
to note that other governors (Askew of Florida and Ariyoshi of
Hawaii) who have taken substantial initiatives in the land- and
growth-management field have had to contend with the same image
problem.

The governor's support of the land use commission was probably
limited as much as any other one thing by the political climate of the
times. The sustained and strong opposition to any state role in land
and growth management by the legislature left the governor very
little opportunity to give greater support to the land use commission. In an interview with the author before the 1978 election, the
governor made it clear that he intended to stick to his environmental
and land use goals in the 1978 campaign, and that the election results
would have a great deal to do with what could happen in the future.
That election's split decision between the governor and the legislature cut off his ability to initiate new legislation to strengthen the
state role in land and growth management in Colorado.

The negative aspects of the effort to implement house bill 1041
should not obscure the fact that some good things have been done.
The commission's model guidelines and regulations have in fact
been used by many counties, and some counties have welcomed the
commission's assistance in attempting to strengthen their own land-
and growth-management initiatives.[115] Furthermore, the commission's hotspot actions under its section 407 powers have highlighted
key land- and growth-management problems and focused public
attention on them. The very substantial amounts of money and the
technical assistance given to local governments under house bill 1041
certainly have strengthened local land and growth management to
some extent.

Perhaps the fairest assessment of the implementation of the law
was made by one participant observer when he said: "From a state
level perspective, house bill 1041 has neither been a rousing success
nor a resounding failure." Other assessments have been substantially more positive, and many have been substantially more
negative, but this judgment seems to be the best that can be made at
the present time.[116] With the benefit of hindsight, it is clear that
house bill 1041, as finally passed, was not as weak as many
disappointed land use proponents perceived it to be in 1974. The
land use commission, under the law, could have developed a
framework for using section 407 powers to deal systematically with
growth-management problems, as it belatedly tried to do in 1978. If
the commission had adopted the policy early on, instead of singling

out a few counties, it might have avoided stirring up so much local hostility. In the actual course of events, it was the political climate and negative rulings by the courts, not the provisions of the law, that did most to weaken Colorado's progress toward effective growth management.

The Land Use Commission: New Roles in an Uncertain Future

By 1982 the legislative appropriation for the land use commission had been reduced to a token $11,000, it had no staff of its own, and little or no capacity to exercise a mandatory role in land and growth management in Colorado. Still, the commission had available persuasion and cooperative approaches with local government to carry out the still considerable powers of house bill 1041. The significance of these roles should not be underestimated. While it is far from the mandatory state role that legislative Democrats and the governor would prefer, it is still a role of considerable importance. The power of the commission to request that a local government designate a matter of state interest does force a public hearing on important land- and growth-management issues. Certainly this can have an impact on local government behavior, although the commission has not used this authority since 1977.

The potential of using land use commission powers in cooperation with local government is illustrated by a recent series of actions taken in early 1982 in Wells County. Faced by extensive conversion of marginal range lands to wheat farming by absentee owners, the county by unanimous action of the county commission asked the land use commission to utilize its temporary emergency powers to halt the conversion of the class III and VII soils to wheat farming to give the county time to adopt regulations controlling such activity. The land use commission responded by issuing a cease and desist order that halted land conversion, giving the county time to place its ordinance into effect.[117] Other counties have worked with the land use commission to utilize house bill 1041 and related powers in the past, and it is reasonable to assume that more will do so in the future. The new roles of the land use commission are focused on persuasion and cooperation with local government, but they are still important to managing growth in Colorado.

The Politics of the Future

The politics of land and growth management in Colorado is more clearly a partisan political party matter than in any other state analyzed in this study. Since the early 1970's, the division has been sharply along Republican-Democratic party lines, with Republicans being generally hostile to a strong state role in any land use effort, and Democrats supporting as strong a state role as they feel can be defended, given the political makeup of the legislature and the general attitude toward land and growth management in the state. The land use commission seemed in jeopardy in Colorado at the beginning of 1978, and subsequent developments have combined to force the land use commission into a much more passive role. The 1978 elections seemed crucial in determining whether the land use commission itself would survive, or if it survived, whether it would be allowed to play any kind of role in making a significant state presence felt in Colorado's land and growth management. Many counties, powerful in the Colorado legislature, were "gunning" for house bill 1041 and for the land use commission. Few counties were giving either the commission or the law any major support. One veteran observer of land and growth management in Colorado in 1977 expressed his doubt that the commission could get another appropriation from the legislature and subsequent events proved him almost correct. As he put it, "The land use bill has few friends left either in the legislature or at the local level."[118] Even Governor Lamm's impressive 1978 victory did not result in a stronger role for the land use commission, or for a significant state presence in land and growth management because in the same election Republicans opposed to a stronger state role strengthened their hold on the house and the senate.

Governor Lamm's reelection in 1978 might have protected the land use commission from being abolished, but Republican victories in the house and senate gave the governor little opportunity to strengthen the role of the state through proposing programs to the legislature. Discussing his views of house bill 1041 before the 1978 election, the governor held: "I believe in it, and I'm going to stick to it, in spite of the fact that for the moment it doesn't look very popular politically."[119] Other Democrats expressed confidence that there was much more support for an environment-, land-, growth-management effort in Colorado than Republicans believed.[120] Yet, when the November 1978 votes were counted, Lamm was faced with the legislature even more hostile to an important state role in land and growth management than ever before. The governor's strategy then became one of strengthening the role of the state through his own executive authority. Both as a result of court action and the approach of new commission members appointed by the governor, the land use commission moderated substantially its intention to use its section 407 powers aggressively. The commission has not been the object of the legislature's outrage over the human settlements policies. Nevertheless, the price the commission is paying for even continued minimal support in the legislature is to restrict the state role in implementing house bill 1041. The Colorado Supreme Court decision in the Rawhide case at the end of 1979 made that approach a virtual necessity.

What then can we say about the future of land and growth management in Colorado? First, the land use commission has been reduced to largely coordinating and persuasion roles in land and growth management. Second, sharp partisan political conflict, into which the land use commission may yet be pulled once again, will continue between Democratic Governor Lamm and the Republican legislature. The land use commission must continue to search for ways to maximize its ability to represent state interests in local land- and growth-management decisions relying largely on voluntary cooperation by local governments.

There are some positive things that can be said. The 1978 policy paper adopted by the land use commission does set a clearer state policy framework for land and growth management at both the state and local levels. Furthermore, the continued authority of the land use commission to request designation action by a local government can be used by a willing local participant to strengthen its own land- and growth-management efforts under house bill 1041. Yet, one must conclude that Colorado, which started with the least clear state role of any of the states in this study, has not managed to strengthen or clarify that role over the last eight years and the prospects for the future are at best uncertain. Governor Lamm was a candidate for reelection in November 1982, and he again was a strong winner. The legislature, however, remained firmly in the hands of the Republicans, so that the partisan makeup did not change substantially. As a result, the political climate within which the land use commission must function will remain the same as the state moves deeper into the 1980s.

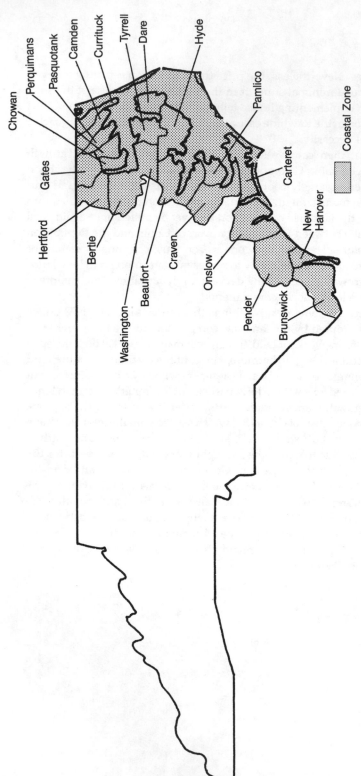

Coastal Zone

Chowan
Perquimans
Pasquotank
Camden
Currituck
Tyrrell
Dare
Hyde
Pamlico
Carteret
New Hanover
Gates
Hertford
Bertie
Washington
Beaufort
Craven
Onslow
Pender
Brunswick

North Carolina

8

North Carolina: Combining the Local and State Roles

The Issue Context

As a southern state, North Carolina might have been expected to be reluctant to take land- and growth-management initiatives. To understand why it actually undertook bold and far-reaching action in this area, one must consider the fact that although North Carolina is not a state at the top of the national growth curve, it has experienced considerable growth pressure in recent years. The state has been sharing the growth surge in the Sun Belt that has been well documented in recent growth assessments.[1] For example, North Carolina's population grew from 4.5 million in 1960 to over 5 million by 1970—an 11.5 percent increase. From 1970 to 1980, the population grew by 14.9 percent to a total of 5.8 million. In North Carolina, the areas in which this growth has aroused the most concern have been in the mountain and coastal aras.

In interviews with key participants in North Carolina's land use initiative about the perceived problems that led to state action, there was a considerable degree of consensus. To explain the need for better managing the state's coastal resources, several reasons were repeatedly cited: the protection of sand dunes (particularly in the light of the damage from hurricanes which in recent years have destroyed dunes and their vegetation), the impact of unwise development on prime shell fishing areas through water pollution, the feeling that marshes needed to be protected for a variety of reasons, and other factors.

One state government official noted that the coast had been the focus of the problem, and that a considerable portion of that problem grew out of second home development, leading to water pollution and other environmental problems. One view held that there was a major problem in the loss of important agricultural land to urban development, but felt that the correction of that problem should have been entrusted to the Department of Agriculture. Still another assessment reinforced the view that "The main concern was for the environment on the coast and to a lesser degree for the environment in the mountains." The focus of concern was seen as second home developments in the mountains and second homes and extractive industries on the coast. Still another assessment put the focus on bad development on the coast which resulted in the destruction of the beaches. The negative impact of urban sprawl in the Piedmont and, in general, a growing perception of the destruction of natural systems, especially on the coast, were also cited as major contributing forces to North Carolina's actions.[2]

One factor repeatedly cited as a prime, if not the prime, mover in causing North Carolina to adopt the 1974 Coastal Area Management Act (CAMA) was the federal Coastal Zone Management Program, particularly the state/federal consistency section of that law. One observer noted that the argument was used with great effectiveness throughout North Carolina, and especially in the legislature, that there was a unique chance to get a lot of federal permitting powers delegated back to state and local levels. He went so far as to say that if the federal government backed out of the program and kept its permitting and other kinds of control tightly in its own hands, then the North Carolina law could well be repealed, "because the legislature is still to some extent rural dominated."[3] Another observer noted that "The whole movement was helped along greatly by the national concern for the coast." He pointed out that there was considerable agreement that if North Carolina "did not get its act together," the federal government would take over even more control than it already had. He noted that this dimension of the argument also was a key point used to support the coastal area legislation that was eventually passed.[4]

One detailed analysis of development pressures in three coastal area counties sheds considerable light on the nature of the economy in the coastal counties and the kinds of developments that were arousing concern at about the time the Coastal Area Management Act was introduced in the North Carolina legislature. Most coastal counties in North Carolina still are relatively thinly populated, and many are predominantly rural. Farming is a major activity for local residents, and forest holdings, which tend to be very large, constituted the major land use in all three of the counties. Commercial fishing is of some importance, and the low and flat topography in these coastal counties inevitably produced some of the environmental concerns, in that it demanded dredging and filling for both development and farming. The kinds of developments that were producing environmental concerns, and no doubt contributed to the general atmosphere of support for the legislation, were illustrated by a large Weyerhauser pulp mill, and by a large, relatively new phosphate-mining operation in one of the counties, with another planned, both on the banks of a river.[5]

New development in the more urbanized of the three counties involved two large projects, a 1,000-acre first home development on half-acre lots, and a 2,000-acre development lying in a floodplain and largely on swampy land. It was intended primarily for second home recreation development, but, after passing through successive owners and finally coming to rest in the hands of Westinghouse, very little construction had taken place and only a few homes were occupied, mainly by retired persons. Septic tanks and other problems involved in attempts to develop low, swampy land had been of some concern in this case. In the third county analyzed, a popular tourist and summer vacation area, an accumulation of rather small scale tourist facilities and condominiums, including many mobile home parks, had produced increasing concern about water pollution and other problems. There were also some large projects in this county, including a retirement community on the intracoastal waterway and a defunct development in the western portion of the county. Commercial fishing was important in the county, and both environmentalists and fishermen had expressed increasing concern about the pollution of oyster beds and other fishing areas that apparently stemmed from the recreation developments and mobile homes.

Finally, another kind of development on the coast that had led to considerable concern for the environment and certainly was a part of the issue setting that led to the consideration and approval of the Coastal Area Management Act involved corporate farming, that is, farming on a very large scale. One example involved the purchase by an Italian firm of 45,000 acres to raise beef cattle, soy beans, and corn at about the time the Coastal Area Management Act was being considered by the legislature. One tricounty area included a corporate farm of 375,000 acres. Some of the potential problems associated with this large-scale agriculture involve land drainage, pesticides and fertilizer runoff problems, and animal wastes. Such problems fall within the category of "nonpoint source pollution" as distinguished from such "point" sources as industrial and municipal wastewater and sewage outlets. Rural "nonpoint" pollution has been very difficult for states and local governments to come to grips with.

In the particular case of the Italian firm's farm, the land was only a few feet above sea level, and extensive drainage and reclamation were required before it could be used. Its drainage canals connected directly into saltwaters, and there had been continuing complaints

of resulting damage to shellfish areas. While efforts were being
made to correct the problem, including the use of settling ponds,
this corporate farm was a focus of continuing concern, especially in
view of the fact that this large corporate farming approach seems to
be spreading in some areas of the North Carolina coast.

The whole development question along the coast, of course,
brings into focus the classic trade-off problem in which an area
which has long been economically depressed and has strong forces
supporting economic growth finds that growth challenged because
of its negative impact on environmental values. The residents of the
coast by and large seemed to be strongly committed to economic
growth in order to improve the standard of living of the area. At the
same time, some of the environmental costs of this development
were being recognized, especially in one of the three counties
involved in the case study. This concern already had been reflected
in a number of new state programs that were approved prior to the
passage of the Coastal Area Management Act.[6]

Among the early attempts to deal with the environmental costs of
development, the most significant was a dredge and fill statute
passed in 1969. This law, coupled with other recently enacted laws
regarding water withdrawal and use permits, wastewater discharge
permits, well construction permits, dam building, mine restoration,
and sedimentation permits, comprised substantial statutory authority in the area of environmental management. The important
forestry industry was strongly affected by permit requirements
involving wastewater, air pollution discharge, and water use permits, and the impact of the water permits was felt especially by pulp
and paper plants, since they were heavy users of water.

The dredge and fill law was administered by the Division of
Marine Fisheries and the Department of Natural and Economic
Resources, which in 1976 was the main environmental control
agency at the state level in North Carolina. A regional office located
on the coast was responsible for educating local developers on what
the dredge and fill requirements were and for funneling permits
along with the regional office recommendation for final action at the
state capitol. While the law was adopted in 1969, it did not become
fully effective until 1972. Most developers other than small farmers
were required to file dredge and fill permits with both the state and
the U.S. Army Corps of Engineers. Smaller farmers and developers
seemed to be more resentful, as evidenced in one study, of these
regulations, while larger developers and corporate agriculture
seemed satisfied with the state enforcement, although resentful of
the federal permitting activity. Small farmers particularly seemed to
resent what they considered to be unjustified intrusion on their
private property rights.[7]

A potentially important law, the state Sedimentation Control Law of 1973, had been rendered largely inoperative, both because farming operations were exempt and because local governments had been very reluctant to adopt a law that met the state standards. Furthermore, the North Carolina Department of Natural and Economic Resources staffing to implement the law, which was supposed to happen in the absence of local government activity, had involved only one regional engineer. Prior to the passage of the Coastal Area Management Act in 1974, local governments in the coastal area were not very active in land use and environmental control programs. As one study put it, local governments "had clearly taken a back seat to the state in developing programs to influence mining, corporate farming, forestry, and recreational and urban development" taking place in the coastal area.[8] A general reluctance to undertake land-management programs was true of all coastal counties with the exception of Currituck and Dare counties in the northernmost section of the state that had been subjected to particularly intense recreational growth and development pressures.

A survey of land use regulations in coastal North Carolina counties ranged from high regulation (those with zoning, subdivision regulations, and other controls); medium regulations (those with no zoning but with subdivision regulations and some other regulations in force); low regulations (those with neither zoning nor subdivision controls, and only limited other controls and regulations); and little or no regulation (those with neither zoning, subdivision regulations, nor other controls). One county had absolutely no controls of any kind. The generalization would apply with almost equal force to many of the cities in the coastal zone, although more would be apt to have some limited local land use control tools. Because the Coastal Area Management Act focused special importance on county governments, this particular assessment was especially concerned with that level.[9]

In a summary assessment of the issue context of the passage of a major land- and growth-management initiative by the state of North Carolina, a number of important factors can be identified. First, the chance to avoid the specter of increasing federal regulation and even to recapture for the state and local levels some permitting authority being exercised by the federal level was of prime importance in persuading the North Carolina legislature to pass a land-management law. Second, concern about the negative impacts of ill-advised or poorly planned development, including agricultural and forestry development, had been quietly growing to the point where further action seemed called for. Finally, a new governor and his administration were ready to work to pass land use regulation for the state.

The Politics of Adoption

The passage of North Carolina's far-reaching land use law is unique among the states examined in this volume in that there was no general outcry of public concern about the issue. As one key participant put it, "There was no great public outrising, no great grassroots movement of citizen groups, and in fact the principal impetus to do something in the way of adopting a land-management bill in North Carolina was from within the government."[10] That point of view was confirmed from a number of other sources in the course of the interviews. That is not to say, of course, that there were not concerns among citizen groups and others about land use and environmental problems, but they did not play the key role that they played in states such as California and Oregon.

The origins of the 1974 legislation can be traced to the 1969 session of the North Carolina General Assembly. That session not only passed the landmark dredge and fill law, but also mandated a study of coastal problems in North Carolina by the commissioner of Commercial and Sports Fisheries, with the ultimate purpose of preparing a comprehensive and enforceable plan for the state's coastal area.[11] An interim product of this effort was the adoption in 1971 of a Coastal Wetlands Act which authorized rule-making procedures to regulate land development in coastal marshes subject to salt tidal influences. A number of other environmental laws were enacted in 1971, and a new blue ribbon study panel was established to respond to various drafts of a coastal management bill then being developed. The committee's official name was the Comprehensive Estuarine Plan Blue Ribbon Committee. The 25 members, appointed by the commissioner of Commercial and Sports Fisheries, ranged from state government officials to environmental scientists and industry representatives.

The blue ribbon committee received, evaluated, and made revisions to a series of drafts over the period July 1972 to the point where a proposed coastal management bill was delivered to the newly installed Holshouser administration in January 1973. The state government dominance of the early drafting process had resulted in proposals that were very much focused at the state level and largely left local government out of the process entirely. In a general way, the rewriting in succeeding drafts involved finding a way to bring local governments into the process. By 1973, this approach had the backing of key legislators and the Republican governor. By contrast, environmental groups wanted to hold out for a stronger state role, "because they had the historic and longstanding mistrust for local government that so many environmental groups have.[12]

The committee delivered a draft of a coastal bill to the Holshouser administration in January 1973, and the bill was introduced in that session, mainly in order to meet the deadline set in the 1969 coastal study law. However, hearings held in April 1973 revealed strong local opposition to the bill, and legislative proponents and the governor quickly agreed that the major push should be delayed until 1974. Coastal legislators took the classical position that the legislature should "hold it off, we are really not ready, maybe we could support it some other year."[13] A mountain area management act had also been hastily drafted for the 1973 legislative session at the insistence of Governor Holshouser. Under his pressure, a key member of the Department of Natural and Environmental Resources (DNER) took the very carefully and intensively prepared Coastal Area Management Act and "more or less substituted mountain for coast."[14]

Prior to the opening of the 1974 session, proponents of both bills decided to hold a new series of hearings in the hope of defusing local opposition. A joint senate-house committee took the proposed legislation on a road-show and traveled to five of the principal coastal area cities and to four principal mountain area cities. This special joint committee was cochaired by the key legislative sponsors in each house of the North Carolina General Assembly— Senator William Staton, chairman of the Senate Committee on Natural and Economic Resources, and Representative Willis Whichard, chairman of the House Committee on Air and Water Resources. All sides agreed that this unique legislative approach was "a highly successful venture in popular democracy,"[15] as Whichard later described it:

> These hearings proved to be a highly successful venture in popular democracy, which built support for the bill, and furnished a convincing response to the contention that interested citizens in local governments had not been adequately consulted on the bill.[16]

In addition to confirming the desire for more local control, the hearings revealed a surprising amount of general support for some kind of legislation on the coast and, to some extent, in the mountain area. During this period, the members of the joint interim committee and state government staff working on the bill visited several states, including Florida, Maine, and Vermont, to get further ideas on how those states had handled their land use initiatives. All of this culminated in a rather extensive rewriting of the 1973 bill, to put a much stronger emphasis on the involvement of local government in the planning and management system. The new version provided for additional nominees by local governments to the proposed coastal commission, and shifted some powers from state cabinet departments to that commission, which would be, in effect, a regional commission. The joint committee introduced the redrafted bill on the second day of the 1974 session. Committee hearings were begun immediately in both senate and house. Since key legislators had been so heavily involved in the development of the bill, they did not have to spend time becoming familiar with it, but could plunge immediately into trying to get it through the legislature.

Although a deluge of amendments were proposed at one time or another, the bill that finally emerged was very close to the version introduced. The decision to entitle the act the Coastal Area Management Act rather than the Coastal Zone Management Act apparently stemmed from an observation, made by a member of the staff of the Department of Administration reflecting the view of the governor, that zoning was a dirty word, and it would be better not to use it in the title of the act.[17] The strategy for passing the Coastal Zone Management Act in 1974 was probably much more carefully worked out than is usually the case in efforts to enact major and controversial legislative proposals. The two key committee chairmen, Staton and Whichard, were not only thoroughly familiar with the bill but were strongly committed to getting it through the legislature. Although they were both Piedmont Democrats, reflecting the Democratic control of the general assembly, they had worked very closely with incoming Republican Governor Holshouser's administration, so that there was no problem with regard to party conflict.

The game plan, as described by Milton Heath, was to move first to pass the coastal bill, then the mountain bill, and only then push the third bill in the land use package, the land policy council legislation. The plan was generally followed, but time ran out on the mountain bill, and opponents pushed the land policy council bill in the senate ahead of the coastal area bill, perhaps in the hope that they could persuade the general assembly that "The toothless land policy legislation made the coastal bill unnecessary."[18] However, the house Committee on Water and Air Resources held the land policy bill captive until the house completed work on the coastal area bill. Originally, the plan was to move the coastal area bill first to the floor of the senate and then in the house. With some backing and filling, this approach was carried out. It was also agreed that both committees would work on the bill simultaneously and thus would be in a position to move quickly to get the bill to the floor as soon as the second committee to act was ready to move. Thus, a unique close relationship developed during the course of legislative consideration of the bill between the two committees, chaired by a relatively new legislator in the house and a veteran legislator in the senate.

The speaker of the house took no formal stand on the bill, but on several occasions he used his power as speaker to delay the bill until problems he felt were important were fully considered. On the other hand, he did not use his power to shunt the bill aside completely. The presiding officer of the senate, Lieutenant Governor Jim Hunt, a Democrat, was a strong supporter of the bill, and he worked closely with the Republican governor to assure passage of the legislation.[19]

In summing up the politics of adoption, one can say, as then representative, later senator and judge, Whichard did say, that it was a product of "a vigorous and extensive bipartisan effort by both the executive and legislative branches. The governor could and did deliver approximately one half of the total votes needed in each house to pass the bill. Senator Staton and I then had the task of rounding up only the remaining one half."[20] The key role of the governor was constantly attested to in interviews with major participants and was further supported by Heath's detailed description of how the legislation was finally passed. Generally speaking, the governor was able to "pull the strings on 35 or so representatives in the house and 12 or 14 senators" when the chips were down and the votes were needed for the bill. The coalition that put it over was a solid Republican block and a group of urban Democrats, most from the Piedmont area of North Carolina, who were able to overcome the fairly solid opposition of eastern North Carolina Democrats, the very area at which the regulation was directed.[21]

There were several heroes in the passage of the bill, and there was a surprising consensus on who the heroes were—the leaders of the respective committees in the house and the senate, Governor Holshouser, Lieutenant Governor Hunt, and also the secretary of the Department of Natural and Economic Resources. An appointee of Governor Holshouser, the secretary was himself a large-scale developer, and he enjoyed the strong confidence and support of many Democrats. This team worked together with a surprising lack of friction and with great effectiveness in staving off efforts to kill the bill, and in pulling it through a number of crises that seemed to threaten its life. As Heath has put it, "the enactment of North Carolina's Coastal Area Management Act was an object lesson in legislative persistence."[22]

The coastal area bill was finally approved by the house after 20 of the more than 50 amendments had been accepted. Then it went to the senate, which had earlier approved the bill by a healthy margin, but which now called for a conference committee. With the general assembly only a few days from adjournment, reference to a conference committee would have meant sure defeat. The bill's supporters (including Senator Staton, Governor Holshouser, and

Lieutenant Governor Hunt) rallied their forces and finally managed to successfully move to reconsider the bill. Some "45 minutes and 8 amendments later," the effort to stave off its adoption was abandoned, and the bill passed by a voice vote.[23] North Carolina thus became the second southern state to take major action in the land- and growth-management field.

Milton Heath, a close participant observer from preliminary stages to the final act in the drama, has left an amazingly complete and clear account of the legislative history of the 1974 Coastal Area Management Act. Some of the highlights of his account, involving positions taken by major lobby groups, and the compromises worked out to meet their objective, are noted later. The first wave of lobbying was led by the League of Municipalities and the North Carolina Association of Realtors. The league was successful in clarifying and strengthening the role of cities in the planning and permitting sections of the law, and in pushing for the enlargement of the Coastal Resources Advisory Council to add four members representing the coastal area cities. Once these changes were negotiated, the league held to its bargain to support the bill, albeit without very much enthusiasm. Representatives of the banking interests tried to hold out for one more hearing, which they may well have hoped would cause the bill not to clear the legislature at all during the 1974 session.

The caucus of coastal area legislators quickly came to their central concern, which was a stronger voice for cities and counties in the selection of the Coastal Resources Commission. After much tense negotiating, a compromise was struck in which 12 of the 15 members of the commission would be named by the governor from a panel of nominees presented to him by the cities and counties. Only three appointments would be made by the governor alone.[24]

Another major issue was the boundary question, in which the challenge was to stave off efforts by individual legislators to exclude "their" counties from the area to be included in the legislation. All such efforts were beaten back, but not without a great deal of time and effort. At one point, Dr. Arthur Cooper, the assistant secretary of the Department of Natural and Economic Resources and scientific advisor to the legislature on the bill, took a position in the well of the House with maps to explain the definition of the coastal area. This unusual maneuver required suspension of the rules, and it is credited with allaying the fears of some house members about the impact of the law in their localities. Finally, the legislature decided to allow the governor to name the affected counties according to criteria approved by the legislature. The essence of the criteria was that all counties bordering on the Atlantic Ocean or on saltwater sounds would be included; thus, there are 20 North Carolina counties in the coastal zone.[25] The debate reached a "rhetorical peak" when one representative from a coastal county detailed his disagreement with any approach of setting boundaries that involved the extent of sea water encroachment. The legislator noted that, "If there were any saltwater at this point," he was "sure that he would know about it. His dog had been drinking water out of the river there all its life," he said, "and would certainly have complained if it was salty."[26]

In original drafts in 1972 and 1973, planning for the coastal area would have been done by one or another state agency. One of the major revisions in 1974—a reflection of the hearings—was to place the planning responsibility in the hands of local governments, with state review to ensure compliance with its standards and guidelines. An earlier draft of the bill had placed the responsibility for designating areas of environmental concern in the hands of the secretary of the Department of Natural and Economic Resources, but the 1974 bill assigned that power to the Coastal Resources Commission.[27]

There was considerable debate about the permitting requirements in an area of environmental concern. Heath reported that, "as the word got around that the coastal bill might be for real," a number of special interests came forward to press their particular case. Each group typically attempted to get some sort of exemption from the law, or at least some sort of adjustment that would lessen the law's impact on them. The utility companies, for example, succeeded in getting some relief in allowing them to upgrade as well as maintain and repair existing rights-of-way, and several other similar exemptions.[28] A compromise that satisfied both the utilities and cochairmen Staton and Whichard was that if the state utilities commission actually exercised jurisdiction over the siting of generation and transmission facilities, the Coastal Resources Commission would not assert its own jurisdiction. Thus, the utilities would be subject to only one site control process, not to the dual regulation they feared. The proliferation of permitting requirements is one that threads its way through not only the adoption of legislation in North Carolina, but also has come to the fore in the implementation process, and the same can be said of many other states across the nation. Once the compromise was worked out, the utilities ceased their opposition to the legislation.[29]

Since agriculture and forestry are of particular importance in a still strongly rural North Carolina, the question of what to do about them in the Coastal Area Management Act was of key importance. At the insistence of the North Carolina Farm Bureau Federation and other agricultural interests, agriculture and forestry activities were exempted from the category of developments in the bill, and during the house floor debate an effort was made to eliminate both prime agricultural and prime forestry lands as areas eligible for area of environmental concern designation. In order to at least preserve forestry, Representative Whichard moved for a division on the amendment. Prime agricultural land was deleted 64-to-38, and prime forestry land retained by 68-to-36. It should be noted that this does not mean that farmland is completely exempt from control under the act, because, according to another provision, renewable resource areas can be designated as areas of environmental concern where uncontrolled development "could jeopardize future water, food or fiber requirements of more than local concern." The degree to which this provision is used will only be determined as the act is implemented and interpreted in the courts.[30]

One group that expressed great concern about the bill was developers, especially those interested in large second home or resort projects. For the most part the developers tried to clarify and simplify the permitting process so as to avoid undue delays. However, developers centered in one coastal county made a major last minute effort to defeat the bill. This effort included a large mailing highly critical of the bill, an open letter to all mayors and chairmen of boards of county commissioners in the coastal area, and other similar efforts, including attempting to amend the bill to death on the floor of the house. However, the bill survived these concerted efforts and moved on to passage.[31]

In an effort to make it clear that the bill was not aimed at the very ordinary activities of citizens of North Carolina, the commission was given the power to exempt certain minor maintenance and improvements on the basis of minimal prospect of any environmental damage, and local governments were given the option of issuing other smaller scale permits.[32] With regard to the "takings issue," of special concern to the speaker of the house, the legislature finally concluded that the courts must decide whether a particular regulatory action involved a taking of property rights. The speaker was more or less satisfied by a procedure that would speed up the judicial review process.[33]

Provisions of the Act
The Coastal Area Management Act, article 7, general statutes 113A, North Carolina, passed by the 1974 legislature was a unique blend of local government and state responsibilities in both the planning and regulation areas. (See Figure 8-1.) In the planning portion of the act, local governments, primarily counties, carry out the preparation of local plans within the framework of state policies, and with a limited

state review of the substance of the local plans. In the area of regulation, the state, through the Coastal Resources Commission, has a direct permitting role in areas of environmental concern. Local governments were given a role in nominating areas of environmental concern and the option of doing the permitting for minor projects.

The justification for having a major new law on the planning and management of North Carolina's coastal land and waters was included in an early section of the law:

> In recent years the coastal area has been subjected to increasing pressures which are the result of often conflicting needs of a society expanding in industrial development, in population, and in the recreational aspirations of its citizens. Unless these pressures are controlled by coordinated management, the very features of the coast which make it economically, aesthetically, and ecologically rich will be destroyed. The General Assembly, therefore, finds that an immediate and pressing need exists to establish a comprehensive plan for the protection, preservation, orderly development, and management of the coastal area of North Carolina.[34]

The act then spelled out the fundamental goals for the program, which serve as the orienting framework for the Coastal Resources Commission and local governments in developing more detailed administrative rules and regulations:

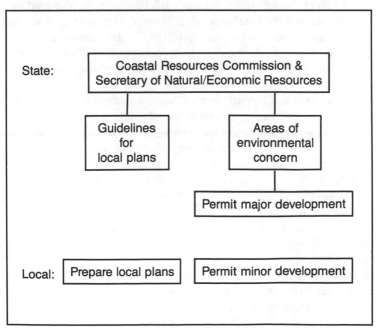

Figure 8-1. **Coastal Area Management Act of 1974**

1. To provide a management system capable of preserving and managing the natural ecological conditions of the estuarine system, the barrier dune system, and the beaches, so as to safeguard and perpetuate their natural productivity an their biological, economical, and aesthetic values.
2. To ensure that the development or preservation of the land and water resources of the coastal area proceeds in a manner consistent with the capability of the land and water for development, use, or preservation based on ecological considerations.
3. To ensure the orderly and balanced use and preservation of our coastal resources on behalf of the people of North Carolina and the nation.
4. To establish policies, guidelines, and standards for seven subsidiary goals.[35]

The act went on to establish the Coastal Resources Commission, the main rulemaking and regulatory body, and a Coastal Resources Advisory Council, designed to bring closer contact between the coastal region being regulated and those doing the regulating. The Coastal Resources Commission consists of 15 members appointed by the governor, 12 of whom are nominees of local governments, for four-year terms. The Coastal Resources Advisory Council consists of not more than 47 members, some by virtue of holding another office, with others appointed by boards of county commissioners and lead regional agencies in the several coastal districts.[36]

Part two of the act mandated that a land use plan be prepared for each county in the coastal area, such plans to be consistent with the goals of the act and with state guidelines to be drawn up by the Coastal Resources Commission. Technical assistance for the Coastal Resources Commission in carrying out this and its other tasks was to come mainly from the Department of Natural and Economic Resources and the Department of Administration. Counties were mandated to prepare a timetable for adopting the land use plan within 120 days after the law went into effect. A city could choose to make a plan, if the commission ruled that the city had the professional and the legal capacity required.

Once the land use plans were approved by the Coastal Resources Commission, the act provided that no permit could be issued in areas of environmental concern that was not consistent with the land use plan for the county involved or the state guidelines. In places not designated as areas of environmental concern, the Coastal Resources Commission could point out ordinances and regulations of local governments that were not consistent with the land use plans, but changes were not mandated as they were in areas of environmental concern. The secretary of Natural and Economic Resources was authorized to make grants to local governments to assist them in developing or carrying out their land use plans.[37]

Part 3 charged the commission with designating by rule areas of environmental concern in such places as coastal wetlands, estuarine waters, and areas involving renewable resources where "uncontrolled or incompatible development" might result in long-range environmental or other damage (for example, watersheds and aquifers, areas with severe pollution problems, and prime agricultural or forest land). Also eligible are fragile or historic sites, and other areas containing environmental or natural resources of more than local significance such as national and scenic river systems, wildlife refuges, and virgin forest stands. The act also singled out areas involving tidal waters or navigable waters in which the public might have a right of access, and natural hazard areas, including sand dunes along the outer banks, ocean and estuarine beaches and shorelines, and floodways and floodplains. Finally, the act provided for the designation of an area of environmental concern when key facilities would have an impact on the area. *Key facilities* were defined as major public facilities, such as airports or highways, and major private facilities such as power complexes. In other states that have taken land use action, such a category might be called developments of regional impact or some similar term.

Interim areas of environmental concern could be designated at the discretion of the commission, which was required to hold subsequent hearings in five coastal cities. Once established as permanent, such areas were to be reviewed at least biennially, new areas could be designated, and designated areas could be deleted, but only if a finding was made that the condition that led to the original designation had been "substantially altered."[38]

Part 4 spelled out the procedures under which the state and local governments would jointly carry out the permitting that would be done within areas of environmental concern. Once the areas of environmental concern were established, all development would require a permit unless exempted by the act or by the Coastal Resources Commission within the framework of the statutory standards. Major developments were required to obtain permits from the Coastal Resources Commission, with a major development defined as a project: (1) requiring permission from a number of state agencies; (2) occupying a land or water area in excess of 20 acres; (3) involving drilling or excavating natural resources; or (4) involving a structure or structures on a single parcel whose ground area was 60,000 square feet or more. Minor developments included all those requiring a permit not classified as major and could be permitted by local governments under rules developed by the Coastal Resources Commission. The commission was authorized to take back the authority for minor permitting if local governments were not implementing the program in accordance with the law or adopted rules.

The act listed eight major grounds for denial of permits, authorized the inclusion of conditions that would have to be met in carrying out the project, and provided for variances under certain hardship conditions. If local governments or the secretary of Natural and Economic Resources failed to act on a minor permit application within 30 days, or a major permit application within 90 days, the permit was to be automatically issued. Quasi-judicial proceedings were required in hearings involving permits.[39]

The attorney general was charged with acting as attorney for the Coastal Resources Commission, with initiating actions in the name of the commission, and was responsible for representing the commission in the hearing of an appeal or a review of any order of the commission. Injunctive relief and penalties were provided, with each violation carrying a fine of not less than $100 nor more than $1,000, imprisonment of not more than 60 days, or both. Failing to secure a permit could result in a fine of not more than $1,000, as could failing to file required data or to allow the commission or its representatives to inspect premises to determine conformance with the rules of the act. Willful failure to follow the provisions of the act could result in a penalty of up to $1,000 for each separate violation after the first assessment.[40]

The Politics of Implementation

In assessing the implementation phase of any land- and growth-management effort in the United States, there is always the twin problem of the short time span of most of these efforts, and the fact that most were brought into being coincident with a major economic recession that swept the nation. The task here is somewhat simpler, in that our focus is on examining the movement of political forces over the eight years that the implementation process has gone forward. In North Carolina, the permitting process was not put into place until April 1978. By then, all of the preliminary planning at the local government level and the identification of areas of environmental concern by the state government had taken place. As a framework for gauging the politics of implementation, a quick sketch of these developments will be helpful.[41]

The Planning Process and Interim
Selection of Areas of Environmental Concern
All of the coastal area's 20 counties and 33 of its municipalities initially elected to do their own planning. A substantial number of

cities did elect to have the planning done by the county within which they were located. The planning guidelines, the crucial first step that would provide the framework for local governments, were adopted by the Coastal Resources Commission on January 27, 1975. In developing the guidelines, the commission began an effort which it has continued throughout the entire implementation period of involving local government to the maximum extent possible. The guidelines were refined a number of times, on the basis of consultation with local governments, regional planning agencies, and other state departments involved in the coastal zone. The November 1975 deadline for plan completion was extended by six months by an amendment to the Coastal Area Management Act adopted by the 1975 legislature.

The commission's guidelines focused on the general process and the substance of plan development, with only a limited amount of time spent attempting to set the particular form they might take. Cooper outlined five key substantive areas in which the guidelines required treatment by local plans. Those elements were (1) development of goals, objectives, policies, and standards for the community's growth; (2) data regarding population and economic trends and factors; (3) identification of areas which represented valuable resources, environmentally sensitive areas, and areas which were culturally valuable; (4) a land classification plan reflecting the desired short-term urbanization patterns for new development; and (5) recommended interim areas of environmental concern with applicable development standards. In an effort to promote meaningful citizen participation, each local government was required to develop a nontechnical summary or synopsis of its plan that could be widely used in a citizen education effort.

In January 1975, the Department of Natural and Economic Resources prepared planning grants for the calendar year, drawn from state funds and from North Carolina's federal coastal zone planning dollars. Local governments were given the option of using their planning assistance in several ways. Twelve local governments chose to have the planning done by their own planning department and receive dollars directly from the state. Two local governments decided to have their planning done by the multicounty planning agency, 12 decided to have their planning done by a private consulting firm, and 27 decided to have their planning done by the field office personnel of the Department of Natural and Economic Resources, local planning and management services section. Additional grants were provided in June 1975 to support public participation efforts and to fund the extended planning grant period provided for by the 1975 legislature. In all, more than $1 million was provided to local governments for land use planning, which constituted about two thirds of all monies spent for coastal management by North Carolina in the fiscal years 1975 to 1976.

The Coastal Resources Commission asked local governments in the North Carolina coastal area to submit draft copies of their plans by November 1975. The plans were scrutinized by a technical review staff team drawn from 23 state agencies, the North Carolina League of Municipalities, and the North Carolina Association of County Commissioners, and by the support staff for the Coastal Resources Commission. Several federal agencies also provided comments. On the basis of the review, the commission gave local governments suggestions about how deficiencies could be overcome.

By February 1976, the Coastal Resources Commission was ready to begin work on the all-important matter of the designation of interim areas of environmental concern. It had earlier solicited recommendations from local governments on the selection of these areas and the kinds of development standards that should be applied. It is interesting to note that local governments' suggestions for areas of environmental concern were substantially more extensive than the Coastal Resources Commission had in mind. In the beginning, there was also substantial disagreement between the Coastal Resources Commission and the Department of Natural and Economic Resources as to the scope of the areas to be designated. For instance, in his first interim proposal, the secretary of the Department of Natural and Economic Resources recommended the designation of all of the Outer Banks as an interim area of environmental concern. Adverse reaction to this and other proposed designations by the secretary was voiced by local citizens at required public hearings. The matter was resolved by making substantial reductions in the designated areas. By Spring 1976 a compromise was reached in which interim areas of environmental concern were agreed on and taken to public hearings in six locations within the coastal area. On May 20, 1976, the interim areas were designated and the regulations went into effect August 1, 1976. No permits were required for development in the interim areas, but notice to the Coastal Resources Commission was required before development could begin.[42]

Ultimately all but one of the 20 coastal counties and 34 cities had their plans approved in the 1975–76 period. This first round of plans focused on getting a planning process and an adequate data base in place, since many communities were starting from nothing.[43] Such things as existing land use and water and sewer capacity were stressed, and each plan was required to use the land classification system developed by the Land Policy Council. This system required that land be divided into developed, transition, community, rural, or conservation categories, with a possibility of subdividing in each category. More than $550,000 in planning grants was used in this effort, most of which was channeled to cities and counties for the planning effort. After a final public hearing, the plans were adopted at the local level and certified by the Coastal Resources Commission as consistent with the goals of the Coastal Area Management Act (CAMA) and the guidelines developed by the commission.[44]

The Coastal Resources Commission held a major conference with each local government on their land use plans, focusing on key problem areas, such as septic tank pollution. By May 21, 1976, the commission had received final local plans for review and approval from 51 of the 53 coastal communities that were developing plans, and the last two were later completed. All of these plans were found acceptable, with only minor changes required to bring them fully into compliance. In July 1976, members of the Coastal Resources Commission and the Advisory Council broke up into small teams to visit each coastal locality to discuss the commission's comments on the plans and to remind local governments that they would have future opportunities of participating in the coastal area management program. These visits were assessed by one observer as very successful.[45]

Carteret County and Indian Beach (located in Carteret County), the only two coastal localities that failed to submit final plans, indicated their determination not to do so in the future. Carteret County's Republican County Commission had initially been in favor of the Coastal Area Management Act, apparently in response to the strong environmental movement in the county. However, when commission members encountered a political reaction against land use controls and environmental concerns in their 1976 re-election campaigns, they reversed their position. Successful Democratic candidates in later elections were more supportive of the Coastal Area Management Act.[46]

Carteret County attempted to have the law struck down in the courts, but the state supreme court, in the fall of 1978, upheld the law's constitutionality.[47] On the first allegation that CAMA was prohibited by the North Carolina Constitution because it made an arbitrary distinction between the coast and the rest of the state, the court ruled for the law on the grounds that "It is reasonably adapted to the special needs of the coastal region and does not exclude from its coverage areas that clearly should have been covered.[48] The court also rejected the claim that the law constituted an improper delegation of legislative authority by its failure to provide sufficient direction to the agency in adopting policies for the coast. The court found that both procedural and substantive standards in the law were adequate. An allegation that the state planning guidelines were not authorized by the act was also rejected. Finally an attack on the law based on the taking issue and illegal search and seizure was also rejected on the grounds the plaintiffs had not been actually subjected to either.

With the backing of the court decision, the state set about preparing a plan for the county and for Indian Beach.[49] With these two exceptions, the first round of plan making and area of environmental concern work was complete by the March 1978 deadline. By January 1979, the Coastal Resources Commission had begun to reevaluate the local land use plans in order to develop new guidelines for the required 1980–81 revisions. The agenda called for interviews with local, state, and federal agencies, and with coastal area residents. The new guidelines were scheduled for adoption by mid-1979.[50]

At the Coastal Resources Commission meeting in February 1979, a report giving an initial evaluation of the local land use plans was presented to the commission. The report showed that most first round plans "had addressed the issues of commercial and industrial development, recreation, and regional water and sewer systems," with lesser emphasis given to resource production areas, "such as highly productive agricultural and forestry land." Local government priorities regarding areas of environmental concern had received very little attention, and urban growth patterns were treated only in communities subject to heavy growth pressures.

Acting on the report and other data, the Coastal Resources Commission in March 1979 set public hearings on proposed changes in the guidelines and announced a schedule for required updating of all local plans by August 31, 1981. The proposed changes reflected the concerns expressed in earlier commission discussions that clearer, more specific policies with an implementation system was needed. Local policies were required regarding:

(1) The protection of hazardous or fragile natural resource areas (including areas of environmental concern); (2) the management of productive resource areas, such as land and water areas important for agriculture, forestry, mining, fisheries, and tourism; (3) [and] the type of industrial growth and urban development the community desires and how that development will be serviced.

For each of these topics, the plan is to define the issue in the community, discuss the alternatives for addressing the issue, set forth the community's policies on the issue, and explain how the policies will be implemented.[51]

The need for continued strong citizen participation was emphasized, as was the importance of updating the data base for the plans.

Finally, local governments were encouraged to refine the five-part land use classification system by using subclassifications. To make the whole package more palatable to local governments, the availability of grants from the Department of Natural Resources and Community Development was stressed, grants that could be used both for updating plans and other planning and management needs.[52]

The new local land use plan guidelines were approved essentially as described earlier at the July 18, 1979 meeting of the Coastal Resources Commission. Proposals for 34 plan updates and the preparation of 4 new plans had already been received by the NRCDs Office of Coastal Management, with the remaining plans scheduled for updating in 1980–81.[53] The 1979–80 state grants to update local land use plans were awarded in October, with almost $430,000 distributed to 48 coastal cities and counties.[54] By April 1980 it was clear that 30 of the 35 land use plans scheduled for updating during 1979–80 were on schedule. The Coastal Resources Advisory Council recommended special meetings with the 5 local governments that were experiencing problems, and as a result 4 of the 5 were able to make changes allowing them to come close to meeting the September 1980 deadline.[55]

Over the period 1980–81, 68 local governments—20 counties and 48 municipalities—completed and had certified land use plans that met guidelines that were considerably more specific and covered a broader range of topics than those used for the 1975–76 plan making effort. Over the two-year update, some $650,000 was expended by local governments and the CRC in review activities, with most of that sum going in grants to the 68 local governments to support their planning efforts. While the guidelines were more specific for the 1980–81 update, they still left a great amount of leeway for local governments to make policy choices. A prime state objective was to require local governments to make those policy choices in a clear and precise way. As a result, the second round planning process involved elected officials, special interest groups, and citizens in general much more heavily than the first round effort. A large amount of controversy was engendered by this process, and it brought into focus new challenges to balance economic development and environmental protection values as proposals for large-scale peat mining and coal facilities were considered. For the most part the professional planning staffs and the elected officials performed well. The second round plans were much stronger in at least two important ways: they addressed the issue of whether, and if so how, the particular community wanted to grow; and they linked the regulatory component of the coastal program—areas of environmental concern—much more closely to the planning effort.[56]

The availability of federal funds were an important component of this success story. Over the period 1978–82, federal funding totaled over $5.7 million with a state total of $1.5 million. These dollars made it possible to give substantial support to local governments in their planning process. The state, through the Office of Coastal Management and the Coastal Resources Commission, has managed to strike a good balance between persuading and mandating local government compliance with state criteria. As the local governments have become more familiar with the program, the substantive content for specificity of the state criteria have been strengthened without rupturing state-local harmony.

An important aspect of the state-local cooperative effort to strengthen local planning has been the close relationship between planning and permitting. Since almost all coastal cities and counties opted to issue minor permits in areas of environmental concern, and that option required the development of a state-approved program, the opportunity for linking the planning and regulatory effort was at hand. The new guidelines for updating the local land use plans were in part a function of experience gained in the area of environmental concern permitting program. In this regard the North Carolina effort is similar to that of California.

In assessing the planning effort, the conclusion by Heath and Moseley tells the story:

> The counties, cities, and towns of the coastal area have grasped firmly the planning opportunities offered by CAMA, and the CAMA objective of strengthening local planning programs is very much on target. Notably, this has been accomplished with a minimum of local-state friction or disagreement. Only once did the CRC find it necessary to exercise its statutory option of adopting a land-classification plan for a county that did not adopt its own plan. The success of CAMA's local planning aspect has helped earn for North Carolina a national reputation for productive state-local collaboration in coastal management.[57]

Implementing the Regulatory Component of CAMA

The final stage in the initial implementation of North Carolina's Coastal Area Management Act—the permitting process within areas of environmental concern—was completed in early 1978. The selection of these areas had gotten underway immediately upon the designation of the interim areas, but was slowed somewhat by difficulties in gathering sufficient technical data and accurate legal information. By January 1977 the Coastal Resources Commission staff had completed their recommendations, guided in part by data from notices of development received under the interim area reporting requirement. The Coastal Resources Commission, the Coastal Advisory Commission, and staff discussed the proposed areas of environmental concern with local governments during February and March 1977. Local government reactions, as well as state and federal agency comments, resulted in a refinement of the proposals and public hearings on them in each of the 20 coastal counties affected. Finally, 13 areas of environmental concern were formally designated by the Coastal Resources Commission on June 22, 1977.[58] A summary view of these designations noted that:

> All of the above mentioned AECs combine to create a zone that includes all estuarine waters and coastal wetlands and a narrow buffer zone around them. This zone is the area where strictest regulation is deemed necessary, and therefore where the most thorough regulatory process (the CAMA permit letting process) will be applied to practically all development.[59]

Permission for major developments within these areas are issued from the state level by the Office of Coastal Management, Department of Natural Resources and Community Development, with a right of appeal to the Coastal Resources Commission. Local governments, with the approval of the commission, can exercise the option of permitting minor developments. To date, 19 of 20 counties and 38 municipalities in the coastal area, which have taken this option, have had implementation and enforcement plans approved by the Coastal Resources Commission and have named local permitting officers. Before approving these plans, the Coastal Resources Commission evaluated such factors as the locality's zoning and subdivision regulations, 201 waste water facility plans, sand dune and shoreline protection ordinances, and flood hazard regulations.[60] In August 1977 the Coastal Resources Commission prepared a model local implementation plan and enabling ordinance to help these local governments, and staff of the Department of Natural and Economic Resources was available to give further assistance, including training local permitting officers.

The date for the permitting system for both minor and major developments to become effective was March 1, 1978. During the first four months of the program, 355 applications for minor development permits were processed, including 66 in the estuarine shoreline areas, and 289 in ocean hazard areas. Of this total, 352 applications were approved and 3 were denied or conditioned. Of the 78 major development permits applied for, 50 were approved, 5 were denied or contested, 19 were exempted, and four were "on hold."[61]

The practice in other states of approving almost all permits, but attaching conditions to assure protection of environmental and other values, was being followed in North Carolina, as the following quote suggests:

> ... Permits are commonly approved with conditions relating to bulkhead alignment or placement of fill material; protection of salt marsh or aquatic species; sedimentation control; water quality . . . ; and specific conditions related to projects.[62]

The designation of areas of environmental concern was focused during the period 1978 to mid-1980 on two of the six categories set forth in the act: Estuarine Shorelines and Ocean Hazard Areas. (See Figure 8-2.) Estuarine shorelines "are those nonocean shorelines that are especially vulnerable to erosion, flooding, or other adverse effects of wind and water and are intimately connected to the estuary. The Estuarine Shoreline AEC extends landward 75 feet from the mean water level." Ocean hazard areas "include beaches, frontal dunes, inlet lands, and other areas in which geologic, vegetative, and soil conditions indicate a possibility of excessive erosion or flood damage."[63] The latest federal assessment of the North Carolina coastal program noted that areas of environmental concern included "all navigable waters in the coastal area, coastal wetlands, a 75-foot strip along estuarine waters, an ocean erodible area 100 to 600 feet wide, inlet hazard areas, high hazard flood areas, and public water supply areas."[64]

The great majority of all AEC designations were in these two categories, with a few public water supply designations. During the first half of 1980 some interest seemed to be developing for designations in "areas containing fragile coastal natural and cultural resources" and for the implementation of the key facilities provision of the act.[65]

In the midst of its efforts to bring the planning and regulatory arms of CAMA fully into operation, the North Carolina program passed another milestone—approval by the federal Office of Coastal Zone Management. With that approval, the state could qualify for operating funds, enjoy the federal consistency benefits provided for under the federal Coastal Zone Management law, and qualify for other federal benefits under the law, such as section 308, the Coastal Energy Impact Assistance Program. The state submitted its application in 1977 and received approval in September 1978. North Carolina thus became the first southern state to gain such approval and one of the first in the east.[66]

After several months experience with issuing permits in Ocean Hazard and Estuarine System AECs, the Coastal Resources Commission, through its environmental committee, began an intensive examination of the originally adopted AEC standards. In December 1978, the committee distributed a draft of proposed changes to coastal advisory council members, technical experts, special interest groups, and federal, state, and local officials. After reviewing their comments, the commission held nine public hearings during March 1979. Estuarine system changes involved "specific construction standards for navigational channels, canals, boat basins, marinas, docks and piers, and bulkheads."[67] Standards for building and maintaining drainage ditches were clarified, and special requirements where septic tank setback rules could not be met were established. For ocean hazard AECs, the ocean erodible area was "defined as that area subject to damage from annual erosion within 30 years and/or erosion in a 100-year storm." The construction line related to ocean dunes was clarified and a requirement for conformance with federal flood insurance regulations and state building codes was added.[68]

The new standards were adopted by the Coastal Resources Commission at its April 1979 meeting with an effective date of June 1, 1979. The chairman of CRC stated that "Our study . . . led us to preparing more specific standards that would protect our resources more effectively and equitably."[69] State dredge and fill law standards were included in the regulations for reasons noted later, and archaeological and historic sites were added as categories of the fragile coastal natural and cultural resource AECs. In February 1979, the commission also adopted policy guidelines on "shoreline erosion, shorefront access, and energy facility siting," all policies with a direct impact on the permitting activities in AECs.[70]

The North Carolina Office of Coastal Management reported that for 1978–79—the first full year of permitting activity—170 major development permits were processed, almost all within the estuarine shoreline category. Almost 800 minor development permits were processed, with city permitting officers dividing their work about equally between estuarine shoreline and ocean hazard areas. County permits were mostly in the estuarine shoreline area. Of the 166 major permits acted on, 4 were denied, while 14 minor permits were denied.[71] For the 1979–80 year, 140 major permit applications were received, including dredge and fill permits, of which 8 were denied. Minor permit applications totaled 714, of which 15 were denied. Thus the number of permits acted on, both major and minor, declined slightly in the second year.[72] More important than the number of permits was the evidence that standards for guiding their issuance were improving, and the second round update of local land use plans was tying the AEC and planning guidelines more closely together.

A Coastal Resources Commission report dated June 4, 1982, contained a summary of major and minor permits issued over the

18-month period from July 1, 1980 to January 1, 1982 for major permits and from June 1, 1980 to November 30, 1981 for minor permits. During this period, 322 of 335 major permit applications were issued, for a denial percentage of only 3.88 percent. The report attributed the high approval rate to a "cooperative approach between applicant and staff in developing projects which meet the needs of both the applicant and the public." Assignment of Coastal Management field staff in four locations in the coastal zone made it possible for applicants to confer at length with staff about changes needed to make projects acceptable. It is also true that many of the permits were issued with important conditions attached. During the June 1, 1980 to November 30, 1981 period 1,227 minor permits were processed, of which 1,203 were approved and 24 (less than 2 percent) denied. Of the 27 permits (major and minor) denied, 17 were appealed to the Coastal Resources Commission, with most withdrawn or settled before final CRC action or appeal to the courts.[73]

In any regulatory system where large numbers of permits are approved with important conditions attached, monitoring and enforcement becomes critical to the success of the program. North Carolina does a better job in this area than any other state analyzed in this book. The monitoring and enforcement program was strengthened in early 1981 by the addition of field personnel that allowed assignment of monitoring and enforcement specialists to three of the four OCM field offices. All permit areas along the coast are surveyed by air once each month. Each major development project is visited before, during, and after construction. A new civil penalties schedule involving fines of $100 to $1,000 per violation and using a restoration requirement has been very effective.[74]

The Coastal Resources Commission and its support staff, the Office of Coastal Management, have taken the initiative in conducting in-depth studies and developing new policy initiatives concerning a number of problem areas on the coast. The whole problem of ocean front lots that are unsuitable for development is one example. These studies form the basis of changes in planning guidelines as well as new rules that govern the permitting process. Inlet hazard areas and the development of new standards to govern construction in such areas is one example. In this case, the CRC adopted new rules that placed stricter limits on construction in inlet hazard areas. In addition, the area of environmental concern boundaries in such areas have been expanded, although extensive boundary changes have not taken place. Similar studies which have resulted in guideline and rule changes involve marina and canal standards.[75]

Proposals to expand substantially the export of coal from North Carolina ports and the mining of peat have raised issues of major facility siting that impact both the permitting and the planning process. The Coastal Energy Impact Program (CEIP) studies have provided a data base from which both local governments and the state coastal program can guide such efforts more effectively.[76]

Finally, the CRC and the office of coastal management have engaged in perhaps the most ambitious postdisaster planning effort undertaken by any state. The Coastal Resources Commission set up a special task force to develop policies that would guide action after hurricanes hit the barrier islands along the coast. The task force has met with the Federal Emergency Management Agency (FEMA) and relevant state agencies and then made site visits to the towns of Sanibel in Florida and Gulf Shores in Alabama. In the latter case, they found a classic example of how not to handle postdisaster problems: build everything back the way it was and wait for it to be destroyed again. The study will include permit standards, capital investment policies, local ordinances, and the impact of CRC standards on the problem. The ultimate aim of the study is to provide the data and generate the public understanding of the problem that will allow new state guidelines that will mandate postdisaster planning as part of local government plan updates, and thus to implement a set of planning and regulatory measures that will assure postdisaster actions that will avoid setting the stage for a repeat of the problem at the next severe storm.[77]

The consistency provision of the federal law was a key in securing approval of North Carolina's coastal program, and many observers have expressed the view that if the federal government failed to honor the consistency provision of the law it might lead to the repeal of the statute. Whether or not that is so, it is a happy circumstance for the law that the consistency provision is working very well in North Carolina. During the period from January 1 to September 30, 1981, the Office of Coastal Management coordinated the review for consistency with the North Carolina Coastal Management Plan "30 federal projects, 175 licenses and permits, 4 OCS plans, and 111 federal assistance applications." Four permits and two federal assistance applications were found inconsistent. A satisfactory resolution of the issues were worked out in some cases, and in others the final solution is still being debated.

A major dispute which arose in 1981 involved proposed leases by the U.S. Department of the Interior for oil and gas exploration just off the Carolina coast 13 miles east of Cape Lookout, near Morehead City. When persuasion failed to move the Interior Department, the

state brought suit, a compromise held briefly, the issue surfaced
again in early 1982 when interior again proposed to offer the leases,
and the whole problem was headed back to the courts when
Secretary Watt withdrew the lease plan.[78] Happily this case is the
exception rather than the rule in applying the consistency standards
in North Carolina. The 13 federal agencies involved are becoming
much more active in the consistency effort, and consideration for
and cooperation with the state is increasing steadily. The federal
Office of Coastal Zone Management summed it up by saying that:

> Overall, federal agencies involved in North Carolina are starting their
> consultations with the OCM earlier in the project development stage. A
> part of this success is due to the positive and unrelenting effort of the
> OCM [state] to make federal consistency work as the Congress intended
> in agreeing to let those states having approved coastal management
> programs exercise consistency review over federal and federally assisted
> projects in coastal areas.[79]

Subsequent Legislation

One way of gauging the political strength of CAMA is to review the
subsequent amendments and other relevant legislation. Most of the
amendments have their major impact on the regulatory component
of the law. A 1975 amendment allowed additional time for completing local plans and for getting the permitting system in place. In 1977
two bills effecting CAMA were introduced, but neither passed. One
which would have abolished the program did not receive serious
support. The other, also unsuccessful, would have amended the law
to incorporate Coastal Resources Commission proposals growing
out of three years experience with administering the act.

The first important statutory changes affecting the coastal program were approved in 1979, all aimed at consolidating, simplifying,
and coordinating the permitting process in the coastal zone. The
Coastal Resources Commission was substituted for the Marine
Fisheries Commission as the issuing authority for dredge and fill
permits and coastal wetlands orders, a major move for regulatory
consolidation. The law also authorized the CRC to delegate its
power to issue permits to the Department of Natural Resources and
Community Development, so that full commission hearings for all
permits was not required. This move was important in allowing CRC
to achieve its goal of shortening the average time required to get
action on a permit from the original 85 days to 50 days.[80] Another act
repealed the state's earlier sand dune protection law on the grounds
that it was made redundent by CAMA (chapter 141), and a third act
ended CRC review of the pesticide permits issued by the pesticide
board (chapter 299).[81] The legislative move to consolidate and
simplify permitting was supported by the CRC, which also took the

lead in merging five federal and state permit application forms into one.

A major breakthrough in permit consolidation came in January 1981 when the U.S. Army Corps of Engineers and officials responsible for the state coastal program reached agreement eliminating the necessity for project applicants to seek separate Corps 404 and Section 10 permits. The procedure, hailed as "the first of its kind in the nation between a state and the U.S. Army Corps of Engineers," involves corps issuance of a general permit for most corps permitting requirements on the basis of approval by the state under CAMA and dredge and fill requirements. About 80 percent of all corps permits required under 404 and Section 12 are covered. An estimated 7 to 14 days will be cut from permit processing time, and applicants will contact only one person for CAMA major development, dredge and fill and corps permits.[82] An additional step in permit consolidation took place in the spring of 1982 when the Office of Coastal Management and the North Carolina Division of Environmental Management reached agreement to merge "401" water quality certification with CAMA major permits. This action brings to five the number of formerly separate state and federal permit requirements that have been consolidated in areas of environmental concern into one application. In effect, the CAMA major permit is all the applicant needs to satisfy the requirements of all five regulatory programs.[83] No bills to repeal CAMA were filed in 1979, and a proposal to limit its ability to control agricultural drainage did not emerge from committee.[84]

The 1981 legislative session was of major importance to CAMA and its future. The legislature authorized two groups to conduct special reviews of CAMA, repealed the sunset provision that had been a part of the law since its adoption, rejected a move that would have eliminated CAMA funding, and passed and funded a beach access law that also had important implications for the "unbuildable lot" issue. Other minor changes were made involving the definition of development as it applies to the replacement of structures subject to CAMA permit requirements, and concerning an adjustment to the appeals procedures under the law.

The first committee authorized to review CAMA placed it among about 60 other state agencies to be reviewed by the legislative committee on agency review. That group reached a preliminary decision in spring 1982 to recommend continuing CAMA with several technical amendments supported by the coastal agency. In addition, the legislative research commission was authorized to assess CAMA's "rules and regulations" and file any interim report in the 1982 session, a final report in the 1983 session, or both. This study was sponsored by a senator not friendly to CAMA. Its 12 members were drawn from the house and senate equally, with house members generally supportive and senate members generally opposed. The group met in January 1982 and postponed further meeting until it could hold hearings on the coast, which would require additional funds.

Environmental groups, local governments and others have rallied to the support of CAMA in the face of a perceived threat of adverse action by the legislature. Environmentalists formed a political action committee with its first priority opposition to any weakening of CAMA. A number of local governments have sent resolutions opposing any weakening of the law.[85]

The beach access statute passed by the 1981 session did several things supportive of the coastal program. It placed into the statute books important language about the hazardous nature of ocean front development that should support the effort to prevent construction on oceanfront lots which constitute a danger to life and property and also cost the public large sums in efforts to reconstruct damaged or destroyed structures. Second, the law is supported by a million dollar appropriation in the state's capital budget to implement the program, with priority to be given to purchasing lots unsuitable for permanent structures. The Office of Coastal Management and the Coastal Resources Commission have moved quickly to implement the law. The April 23, 1982 Coastal Resources Commission Report noted that access projects had been approved for four communities. The June 4, 1982, report noted that the program was "coming along very well," and that more than $3.5 million in requests from local governments for beach access projects had been received. The program came at a time when the OCM and CRC were struggling to find a way to allow limited use of upwards of a 1,000 lots where the commission's tough setback rules had prohibited any structure of any kind. Prior to the beach access law the commission had moved to allow limited use of some lots in the form of nonpermanent structures, and also to allow permanent structures on some of the lots where certain stringent conditions could be met. These initiatives still left perhaps 500 lots that could not be used, and the beach access law will help in dealing with charges of a taking and/or demands for compensation.[86]

The 1981 legislative session had both positive and negative potential for CAMA. The critical question is whether supporters of the program can fight off efforts to damage or destroy it through legislative action. That question will be treated further in the concluding section on the *politics of the future*.

Summary Assessment of the
Implementation Phase

In assessing the implementation of the Coastal Area Management Act in North Carolina to date, the positive aspects seem to far outweigh those that are negative. The deadlines established in the act were met, and mandated programs, including land use plans in all the coastal cities and counties, have been carried out at a level that, while somewhat uneven, is generally good. The second round of plan review in 1980–81 put the focus on a qualitative strengthening of local land use plans. Further, the program met a key test of the act during 1977 and 1978 when the process moved to the full implementation stage with the final designation of areas of environmental concern and the issuing of permits by both the state (for major developments) and local governments (for minor developments). Strong efforts have been made on all sides to work out a reasonable partnership between the state and local governments in this effort. Without question, the existence of a Coastal Resources Commission that is strongly influenced by local government, as well as a coastal advisory group that has as its main function the communication of local government attitudes to the Coastal Resources Commission, have both been very positive factors in the implementation program to date. The permitting effort has been strengthened by legislation assigning responsibility for dredge and fill responsibilities to the coastal program, by the continued refinement and strengthening of areas of environmental concern guidelines, and by other permit consolidation and coordination efforts.

What appeared to be a serious problem of resistance by local governments seems to have moderated substantially. The problems with regard to staffing have been largely overcome by the development of a well-staffed Office of Coastal Management in the Department of Natural Resources and Community Development. Although some environmentalists doubtless would prefer a direct state implementation of the whole program, they are strongly supportive of the program. The federal consistency provision seems to be working well from the viewpoint of state and local officials. Certainly a continuing effort needs to be made to bring local governments into the implementation effort in every way possible. Continued funding for planning and implementation work has helped greatly in strengthening local planning capacity and in making the program acceptable to local governments.

A 1980 evaluation coauthored by a continuing observer and participant in the development and implementation of the Coastal Area Management Act concluded that:

1. The Coastal Resources Commission has kept abreast of a demanding administrative schedule and has maintained a balanced, middle-ground philosophy of coastal land management—neither delighting its friends nor distressing its foes.
2. The CAMA experiment in local-state cooperation has been an effective vehicle for intergovernmental coordination. In particular, the political wisdom of CAMA's provisions for local involvement in various phases of the program has been vindicated.
3. CAMA's objective of strengthening local land use planning progams has been achieved with substantial help from federal subsidies.
4. CAMA has passed its first major legal test in court, has withstood early political attacks, and has even begun to pick up legislative support for needed amendments.
5. Although it has not been possible to consolidate all federal and state coastal permits into one, the number of required permits has been reduced and the application process for remaining permits has been streamlined.
6. CAMA has not been accepted as a model for land use management in other regions of the state or as a model for statewide local policy.[89]

This assessment is consistent with that of the author: on balance, the program is alive, well, and moving forward.

The Land Policy Council

North Carolina's Land Policy Act of 1974 established a statewide Land Policy Council and charged it with the initiative for developing a general land use planning program at the state government level. The bill contained no permit authority, nor did it require local governments to take any particular actions until further consideration could be made of the council's recommendations by the legislature. The Land Policy Council was required to conduct analyses of existing state laws related to land use, prepare a system of data retrieval for the state, prepare guidelines for identification of areas of environmental concern, examine the state tax structure with respect to land, and prepare a state land use policy. The act also spelled out the basic framework for the state land use policy and required the state to develop a uniform system of land classification. This act passed the general assembly without a dissenting vote on April 11, 1974.

The council was assisted by a 24 member advisory board, the advisory committee on land policy, appointed by the governor. Half of the membership were municipal and county officials, and the rest represented a wide range of interests and geographical areas in the state selected by the governor.

The Land Policy Council itself was composed of state officials and legislators, plus a representative of the League of Municipalities and a representative of the County Commissioners Association. The council was originally staffed by the Department of Administration and later by the Department of Natural Resources and Economic Development.

The Land Policy Council made a substantial number of important recommendations in its December 1976 final report to the governor. The heart of its proposals was a land classification system for local governments in North Carolina. The council described the system as one "for accomplishing general, coarse-grained land resource planning," perhaps to avoid the implication that it was proposing any kind of state-imposed zoning. The five classification categories developed by the council were identical to the classification scheme used in developing local land use plans in the coastal zone:

1. Developed—existing urban areas.
2. Transition—land suitable for urban development needed to accommodate urban growth over the ensuing ten years.
3. Community—clustered rural development.
4. Rural—lands used for agriculture, forestry, mineral extraction, and other low intensity uses.
5. Conservation—significant, limited, and/or irreplaceable natural, recreational, productive or scenic resources.

The assignment of land to the various classes was based on such factors as the existing characteristics of land, the projected future demand for land needed for development, the ability of local government to provide services, and compatibility with existing federal, state, and local plans and policies.[88]

The council's land classification recommendation, which Senator Willis Whichard introduced into the legislature as part of a 1977 land use bill, was in fact a mandatory land use planning requirement for local government. There were state standards, and a countywide plan had to be worked out, including an implementation element. The key focus was on the county, although municipalities were given a right to participate if they chose to do so, but county and municipal plans had to be compatible.[89] The legislation did not provide for new regulatory authority, but it did propose the establishment of a statewide Land Resources Commission charged with monitoring large-scale developments in areas of environmental concern, reviewing proposed key facilities, and recommending needed legislation with regard to areas of environmental concern to the 1979 general assembly. This latter recommendation reflected the feeling of the Land Policy Council that it might be appropriate to extend the state's permitting authority from the coastal zone to the remainder of the state, when the political climate became favorable.

In addition to a 32-member Land Resources Commission, the law would have set up four district committees, three of which were to be composed of local officials. The district committees and their membership illustrate yet again the strong pressure in North Carolina for giving local governments a major role in any state initiative in the land use area. The fourth district, in a provision to be a link to the Coastal Area Management Act, was to consist of six members designated from the Coastal Resources Commission. The district committees were to have the responsibility for reviewing and certifying local land classification plans.[90]

The proposed law did not get a friendly reception. The hostile reaction was probably best summed up by a representative of the Department of Agriculture, who no doubt expressed the feeling of many others: "There are people in state government behind the scenes who are misleading the Land Policy Council as to what is going on. It is really a statewide zoning scheme, yet they are told over and over that planning is not zoning." It is interesting to note that this issue of what a statewide land use plan would be, and particularly whether it would be state zoning, came into focus in North Carolina in much the same way it did in Vermont. In any event, the political climate for passing the proposed new land use initiative in North Carolina was not right in 1977. Senator Whichard, recognizing that he could not mobilize sufficient support, made no serious effort to push his bill.[91] The Land Policy Council and its advisory group continued in existence until the 1981 session of the North Carolina Legislature abolished it. Thus ended for the short run future the effort to extend the successful experience of the Coastal Area Management Act to the remainder of the state.[92]

The Politics of the Future

Few persons, friend or foe, who watched the struggle to pass the Coastal Area Management Act in 1973 and 1974 would have predicted that eight years later the act would not only survive, but actually gain political strength and support in the period 1974–82. Yet, few today would deny that just such a development has occurred. With the benefit of hindsight, the reasons for this political success story seem reasonably clear. In a sense the local government people who fought for a meaningful role in the process sowed the seeds of their own support for the program by their very involvement in it. Many of the 47 members of the Coastal Resources Advisory Council have become firm supporters of the program. The 15 members of the Coastal Resources Commission have by most testimony been dedicated and hardworking individuals who typically came from a local government setting. The first vice chairman of the commission, a former county commissioner and developer, spent may long hours promoting and organizing the work of the commission.

The state, through the Coastal Resources Commission and the state agencies that have staffed it, has seldom made the mistake of going too far too fast, and when it has, seems to have been able to pull back, regroup, and press forward again. The first set of local land use plans doubtless left much to be desired in both a procedural and substantive sense, but the second round plans developed in the 1980–81 period were substantially better. The geographical extent of areas of environmental concern were minimal in the first round of designations. Now the standards are being tightened, new categories for designations are being added, and modest boundary extensions are being made. All of this is possible because many hundreds of hours have been spent in public hearings and informal meetings educating local elected officials and others about the program, and much of the educating has been done by local officials who themselves hold positions of responsibility in the program. Furthermore, the consistency provision of the federal Coastal Zone Management Act has begun to have real meaning for North Carolina. The U.S. Corps of Engineers has delegated part of its section 404 permitting authority to the state. In addition, since early 1979 corps' section 10 permits, U.S. Coast Guard Bridge permits, and all federal assistance projects related to the coast and outer continental shelf exploration plans were being reviewed for consistency with the state program. These reviews are being seen as meaningful, and this is a powerful political plus for the coastal planning and management program in North Carolina.

With a firm base of local support developing for the coastal management program and with a governor who is strongly committed to it, legislative foes have pulled in their horns, and the political future for the program looks bright. These are pitfalls to be sure. The 1979 legislature mandated a study of the impact of the Coastal Area Management Act on land use and land values, with a view to determining whether the impact of regulations demanded compensation to landowners in order to be fair. Thus the compensable regulation question has raised its head in North Carolina just as it has in virtually every other state examined in this book. The study concluded that the CAMA program, when considered alone, was having no major impact on land values when the entire coastal area was considered. This may or may not put the matter to rest. The issue of unbuildable oceanfront lots seems headed for a reasonable solution, as discussed earlier in the chapter.

The 1981 legislative session illustrated both the broadened base of support for the program and the continued hostility to it. The unsuccessful effort to end state funding for the program, and the successful effort to set up a legislative study which included in its membership legislators hostile to the program testify to the continued opposition to CAMA in important places. On the positive side, many local government officials in the coastal zone have rallied to CAMA's support, and a newly formed environmental political action group promises added support from that sector.

One of the major sources of political strength for CAMA has been the strong support from the office of the governor that the program has had from the beginning. Republican Governor James Holshouser was instrumental in getting the law passed in 1974. The lieutenant governor at that time, James B. Hunt, has served as governor during the eight-year history of the program and been a strong and consistent supporter of the effort. Enemies of the program know that if they lead an assault on the coastal program, they will have to confront the governor as well. With Governor Hunt's term ending in 1984, that strong support from the governor's chair may be in question. None of the candidates at mid-summer 1982 were identified as strong supporters of the program.[93]

Another source of danger to the program lies in the funding issue. On the assumption that federal funding will be phased out, the Office of Coastal Management is asking for funds in the 1983 fiscal year and beyond to make up a substantial part of the federal funds that will be lost. It is anticipated that Governor Hunt will support the appropriation, but approval in the general assembly is questionable. It may hinge on whether the nation and North Carolina have recovered from the recession by the time the decision has to be made. The whole problem could be resolved and the program supported more strongly than ever if North Carolina Congressman Walter Jones' OCS revenue sharing bill passes Congress and is approved by President Reagan. Prospects for approval seem good in the house, but doubtful in the senate. Whether the administration will raise token or strong opposition to the bill is not yet clear.[94]

There are serious problems for the program to be sure, but none seem so large as to threaten its continued existence. The Office of Coastal Management is well staffed and is working well with both the Coastal Resources Commission and coastal local governments. If political support can be maintained as qualitative improvements are made in the program, North Carolina will continue as a major success story of national significance, demonstrating a truly effective state-local partnership in land and growth management for the coast. What has not happened, and does not appear on the horizon in the near future, is the extension of this coastal success story to the rest of the state.

9

Land and Growth Management in the States: A Comparative Assessment

While each of the seven states examined in this volume differs in its governmental structure, its political, cultural and economic history, and the nature and degree of its growth problems, there are several threads that can be traced through the recent history of all seven of the states. These links will be analyzed in terms of the major analytical categories used in this study. In addition, special attention will be given to three other matters that deserve highlighting in this final chapter. One is the impact on the federal system of the land- and growth-management initiatives taken by these seven states. This analysis will focus especially on changing state/local relationships that have come about as a result of new state initiatives in the area. An analysis will be made of the evolving relationship between the regulatory process and the development of meaningful plans that are used in the decisionmaking process, and the impact of that new relationship on planners and planning. Finally, a special assessment will be made of the most dramatic weakness that threads its way through all the programs: the failure to fund and put in place an effective monitoring and enforcement program.

The Issue Context: The Environmental Roots Reassessed

The issues that led to land- and growth-management actions in the seven case studies were all centered in environmentally related problems, and the drive for action was often spearheaded by environmental groups. The point can be illustrated by reviewing briefly the issue context in the states analyzed earlier.

California   In California, heavy growth pressures on an 1,100-mile long coastline increasingly brought to the forefront a wide variety of environmental problems including air and water pollution and the destruction of natural terrain. Perhaps the most import factor of all in mobilizing public support for some control over development—in a state where 85 percent of the population lives an hour's drive from the shore—was the blocking of public access to the beach. Led by the Sierra Club, the strongest of the state environmental groups, efforts were made during the early 1970s to bring about the adoption by the legislature of a special planning and management program for the coast. These efforts were spearheaded by a coalition of environmental groups that succeeded in broadening its base of support beyond the original environmental circle in an organization called the California Coastal Alliance. The alliance was able to take the issue directly to the citizens of California when attempts in 1970, 1971, and 1972 failed to pass a coastal planning and management law in the California legislature. The positive voter response was a resounding victory for the environmental coalition. California is a clear case of the environmental base of the land- and growth-management movement, both in terms of the issues themselves and the groups and individuals that led the fight for new policy initiatives.

Colorado   In Colorado, the growth pressures brought about by the increasingly popular second home developments in the mountains and the strong population pressures on the front-range urban growth centers began to produce negative impacts that were of increasing concern to environmental groups in Colorado during the 1960s and the early 1970s. These groups took the lead in spearheading a major land management legislative effort in 1973, which was not successful, and succeeded in gaining the 1974 passage of a somewhat weaker state land and growth management law. The concerns that motivated the action in Colorado were clearly environmental in nature, especially with regard to second home development in the mountains and other areas of Colorado. Furthermore, increasing urban pressures along the front range raised important issues with regard to water supply. Air pollution had become a problem of great concern to environmental groups, especially in the Denver metropolitan region. Thus, all three of the major components of the natural systems in Colorado seemed to environmental groups or other groups and citizens in the state to be coming under severe pressure as the population growth of the state increased. It was widely perceived in Colorado, especially after the decision to cancel the Winter Olympics there, that environmental concerns were a major issue with the citizens of the state, and environmental groups found themselves operating from a position of considerable strength that seemed destined to lead to much stronger legislation than was finally adopted. In any event, the issue base from which the land- and growth-management initiatives occurred was environmental in nature, and the leadership role was taken by an environmental coalition to secure passage through the Colorado legislature.

Florida   In Florida, one can again see the environmental base of the issues that came to a head in the late 1960s and early 1970s and led to the adoption of a major package of land and water management legislation by the 1972 legislature. No other state examined in this study was subject to so severe population growth pressures over such an extended time as Florida in the post-World War II period. Those pressures resulted in damage to Florida's land and water resources that became increasingly evident and of increasing concern during the 1960s and into the 1970s. Environmental groups moved from a position of relative unimportance to one of major significance in Florida politics when they took the lead in pinpointing the environmental abuses that were taking place; the widespread pollution of water; the destruction of natural dune systems along the beaches; the blocking of public access to the beaches; and a variety of other environmental damages that grew from unplanned and uncoordinated development in response to heavy growth pressures. A series of major environmental events, such as the effort to establish a large jetport in the Everglades west of Miami and the issue of a cross-state barge canal further north on the peninsula, established a base from which environmental groups were able to test their political wings and find that they could indeed wield important political power in the state. At the same time, as was the case in many other states, they were able to broaden their base and bring many more people and groups into their organization. The Audubon Society took the lead in Florida and quickly became the catalyst for more concerted action. Thus, we see in Florida a repeat of the pattern in California and in Colorado in which heavy growth pressures highlighted various environmental problems which were taken up by organized environmental groups who gained political strength and broadened public support as they championed legislation to meet the problems brought forth by the growth pressures.

Oregon   In Oregon, the picture is somewhat less clear with regard to the role of environmental groups in mobilizing the forces to act on the emerging problem brought about by heavy growth pressures, especially in the Willamette Valley. While there were some organized environmental groups in Oregon that responded to the increasingly serious problems of urban encroachment on valuable farmland and open space, as well as severe water pollution problems in the major rivers of the state, the movement in Oregon was more a broad-based citizen effort than one confined to any particular environmental group. Leadership to mobilize that broad-based support for legislative action came from the governor and from individual legislators. Although environmental groups played a less definitive role in the drive for better growth management, Oregon citizens displayed a unique degree of willingness to participate in the process and to support a comprehensive growth-management system.

Hawaii   In the other three states—Hawaii, North Carolina, and Vermont—the problems and issues also evolved from the need to protect the natural systems of the state from what were perceived as severe growth pressures, but the initial force came not so much from environmental groups as from the executive and/or legislative branches of government.

In Hawaii, adoption of a major land use law in 1961 preceded the development of a strong environmental movement in the United States. The adoption of that law was not at all a response to perceived environmental problems, but was pushed by new political factions that saw a need to bring more democracy to land holdings in Hawaii and to protect the islands' major source of income in 1961, agriculture. Over time, however, the Hawaii initiative took many of the same policy directions as land- and growth-management legislation later adopted in other states, and that modification and redirection was partly the result of the growth of environmental forces in Hawaii. However, the environmental movement has never gained the strength in Hawaii that it has in most of the mainland states treated in this volume.

North Carolina   In North Carolina, the growth pressures developed in much the same pattern as in other states, with particular reference to second home development and commercial and industrial enterprises along the coast. It was out of concern for the destruction of valuable fisheries, wetlands, and other land and water resources in North Carolina's coast—concern articulated largely by state agency personnel—that the policy initiatives proposed by the governor and approved by the legislature emerged. Environmental groups were not a key factor in this development, and indeed no strong, well-organized environmental force was present in the state when the pressure for action developed in the early 1970s. In North Carolina, the leadership came from a number of scientists, most of whom were in state government, and from key political figures. Again, we can say that the issues that were perceived that led to an important initiative in land and growth management were based on a concern for the environment—for the natural systems of the state. But here, as in Hawaii, and Oregon, the leadership role came not from environmental groups but from the state itself.

Vermont   In Vermont, a state renowned for its conservatism and its devotion to individual freedom, the adoption of strong land- and growth-management legislation was an event that broke with the state's characteristic patterns of public policy initiatives. The growth pressures that led to this historic break were a function of the construction of the interstate highway system that brought large metropolitan areas, such as New York and Boston, into the easy commuting distance of the environmentally fragile southern Vermont slopes. These areas began to come under heavy growth pressure from second home developers, and a large proposed development brought to a head the fears of conservative Vermont native residents that their treasured way of life would be overrun by an invasion from out of state—an invasion that cared little for the protection of their land, water, and air resources. As a result, the citizens of southern Vermont appealed to the conservative Republican governor of the state, and he responded by strongly supporting adoption of land- and growth-management legislation. Thus, in Vermont we see a pattern where growth pressures were producing negative environmental consequences with which the state was ill-prepared to cope. In this sense, Vermont is similar to the other states examined in this study. In responding to that perceived crisis, however, Vermont fits with Hawaii and North Carolina, and to some extent Oregon, in that environmental groups were not of crucial importance in the policy initiatives that led to the adoption of the state's new land- and growth-management law in 1970.

In this review of the issue context of land- and growth-management initiatives, we see a pattern in which the substantive issues that formed the basis of state action was in every case except Hawaii rooted in concern for the environment. However, when we come to identifying the major sources of support for moving from the issue identification to the political action stage, we see contrasting patterns in which three of the states saw environmental forces clearly take the lead in achieving action as well as identifying the issues, with a fourth state developing the leadership from a more broad-based citizen concern. In that state, and in the other three, the leadership for action to respond to the identified environmental concerns did not come from environmental groups themselves but from other sources, primarily state government.

It is clear, then, that a concern about the environmental impacts from growth pressures formed the issue basis from which states moved to adopt land- and growth-management legislation. In several cases, environmental groups took the lead in bringing about action from the perceived issue base, and in the process matured and expanded their strength politically. In other cases where environmental groups were not the driving force, they have developed some importance since adoption of the legislation, such as in Oregon with the establishment of the 1,000 Friends of Oregon. A key question about the future of the land- and growth-management movement lies in whether these environmental forces can demonstrate the capacity to change with the times and continue to play a leadership role in mobilizing support for the adoption of new and the implementation of existing land- and growth-management laws. This question will be explored in its comparative dimensions later in the chapter.

The Politics of Adoption

With the exception of California, all states in the study adopted land- and growth-management laws through the regular legislative process. In California, failure to pass a law through the legislature in three successive years led environmental groups to go directly to the people in the form of an initiative, and voters responded by putting a strong coastal planning and management law on the books.

A number of generalizations can be made about the legislative action that led to the adoption of the laws in the several states studied. First, except in the case of Colorado, the adoption of land- and growth-management legislation was not a partisan political issue. It tended to be both supported and opposed by Democrats and Republicans. There were some important geographic patterns of support and opposition, especially in Oregon, but they did not fall neatly along political lines. In Colorado, while the Republican governor and some legislative leaders initially supported a strong land-management law, the issue in the 1974 legislature assumed clear partisan political dimensions, with Republicans supporting either no law or a very weak law and Democrats supporting a strong law. The Republican governor continued to support at least some sort of land- and growth-management legislation, but he had great difficulty in bringing legislative leaders in his party along with him. A second generalization that holds in all cases except California is that the proposed laws enjoyed strong support from the governor's office, which was typically complemented by strong legislative leadership in one or both houses.

With regard to sources of support and opposition in the attempt to adopt new legislation, the opposition forces often but not always included developer and real estate interests, as well as other private sector groups such as utility companies. Local governments tended to oppose any new initiatives unless they played an important role in the implementation process that was envisaged by the legislation. Environmental groups were the single greatest source of support for the adoption of new legislation, often backed up by such broad-based citizen groups as the League of Women Voters.

The seven states analyzed can be grouped into three categories with regard to the *politics of adoption.* Hawaii and Vermont represent cases in which the legislation was proposed from a broad base of support, was strongly supported by the governor, and passed by the legislature with little or no change and a minimum of political controversy. In the case of Hawaii, there was some resistance in the senate, but it was overcome without great difficulty. In the case of Vermont, the widespread support for the bill among the people of the state, and a careful lobbying job by the governor before the legislature convened, resulted in the passage with little or no debate.

In the case of Florida, Oregon, North Carolina, and Colorado, the picture was much different. Major compromises were necessary in order to allow the legislation to survive the political rapids in the legislature. In three of these states (Oregon, North Carolina, and Colorado), a pattern emerged in which the initial legislative proposals largely bypassed local government because most environmental groups did not trust local government to do an effective job of planning and management to meet the perceived problems. Thus, the initial legislation in Oregon gave a state agency, the Land Conservation and Development Commission, substantial permitting powers in areas of critical state concern, and local governments were bypassed to some extent by assigning the integrative local planning effort to regional agencies. Both of these proposals were strongly opposed by both cities and counties in Oregon, and as a result were stricken from the bill. The pattern in Oregon can be identified in several other states in which environmental groups were able to bring about proposed legislation that involved a strong, direct regulatory role for the state and/or regional levels. In the heat of the legislative battle, local governments often made common cause with private interests opposed to any legislation to force a much stronger role for local government in the implementation process.

The original laws drafted in North Carolina in 1973 envisaged a strong, direct state and regional regulatory role, with a minimum role for local government. In statewide hearings held between the 1973 and 1974 legislative sessions, the primary source of opposition to the proposed legislation came from local governments and others who pressed for a much larger role for local government in the implementation process. This effort was successful in North Carolina, and a sharply scaled-down state role and a substantially strengthened local role for coastal counties and cities was the result. In the case of Colorado, the pattern is clearest of all. In 1973, a bill passed the house with a strong state policy framework and direct state action provisions. In the further consideration of the legislation in the 1974 legislative session, local governments and their allies from the legislature and in the private sector were successful in so substantially weakening the state role that some would question whether there is any meaningful state role in the Colorado law.

Only in Florida was such a local versus state issue not a factor. In Florida, where the proposed law followed the American Law Institute's state land development code model, the underlying philosophy was to leave almost all land- and growth-management decisions in the hands of local governments, with the state and regional levels entering the picture only to assure consideration of the more than local impact of land and growth management decisions. Local governments in Florida were neutral in the political battle that raged over whether or not to pass the state Land Management Act in 1972. The opponents were the state home-builders association, most of the state's large developers (with one conspicuous exception), a number of utility interests, and other private sector groups. Support came from environmental groups, especially the Audubon Society, from the League of Women Voters, and from very strong leadership by the governor and by key legislators. In California, one sees a picture in which environmental groups found it necessary to bypass the legislative process completely and go directly to the people. As a result, the environmental groups were able to put into place their preferred position of direct state and regional regulatory authority that largely bypassed local government. Even here, a self-destruct provision in the law meant that the legislature would have to reconsider and attempt to adopt a law four years later.

The most important generalizations that can be made about the *politics of adoption* in the states is that in the great majority of cases environmental groups played an important role in bringing about the adoption of the legislation. However, in most cases, their preferred position of having a direct, strong state and regional regulatory role did not survive the heat of the political battle. Compromises were agreed to which resulted in a much stronger position for local governments in the implementation process. The other major generalization is that strong and sustained gubernatorial support was typically present and obviously necessary to bring about successful passage of the law. One reason California could not pass the legislation in the early 1970s is that Governor Reagan did not support it. In all other states that considered legislation, the governor was a strong supporter of the effort.

The Politics of Implementation

The assessment of the *politics of implementation* does not include an effort to make firm judgments about how effective the implementation of the land- and growth-management laws have been in meeting the goals set out in those laws. Our effort has been to assess the adequacy of continued support from key areas that helped bring about the passage of the legislation in the first place; on efforts to amend the legislation either to strengthen or weaken it; and on the general evolvement of support or opposition for the implementation effort among key interest groups. In short, was adequate political support in all its dimensions sustained in the implementation effort?

Governor's Role
The role of the governor was important in the *politics of adoption* in every state except California, and the chief executive has continued to be an important factor in the *politics of implementation*. In a general way, it can be said that governors in all the states who remained in office in the implementation effort have continued to be strongly supportive of that effort, and that in every case new governors elected during the implementation period have also continued to be supportive. Only in California has a new governor (1982) been elected to office who ran on a platform of opposition to the land- and growth-management legislation or who, once elected, attempted to dismantle or weaken the implementation effort. Generally speaking, governors have been alert to oppose efforts to weaken the legislation by amendment and have supported adequate appropriations to carry out the implementation process.

In Hawaii, Governor John Burns supported the adoption of the original land use law in 1961, and his successors including the current Governor George Ariyoshi have strongly supported the legislation. Ariyoshi has attempted to strengthen the state framework through the establishment of a clear set of state policies and generally has been able to secure adequate appropriations for the implementation of the law.

In California, Governor Reagan did not support the adoption of the coastal planning and management effort in 1970, 1971, and 1972, but his successor Governor Jerry Brown did support the adoption of the coastal planning and management law in 1976 and has continued to be supportive of the implementation of the legislation since that time. Governor Brown sought appropriations for the implementation process, and funding was adequate with the exception of funds for monitoring and enforcement.

However, in November 1982, Republican George Deukmejian upset the Democratic candidate Thomas Bradley. Part of Deukmejian's platform was a pledge to repeal the state's coastal management law. It is unlikely that he will be successful in repealing the law because of strong support for it by Democratic majorities in the legislature, but the governor's lack of support will make continued effective implementation of the law more difficult.

In Oregon, three governors have served since the passage of the pioneering land- and growth-management legislation in 1973. Republican Governor Tom McCall's passionate espousal was a critical factor in the original passage of the Oregon land use law. His Democratic successor, Governor Bob Straub was also quite supportive of the law, and in spite of apprehensions on the part of supporters of the legislation, Republican Governor Atiyeh has also proven to be supportive of the implementation effort. Both Governor McCall and Governor Straub strongly opposed efforts in 1976 and again in 1978 to repeal or to greatly weaken the land- and growth-management legislation adopted in 1973, and Governor Atiyeh was equally strong in his opposition to the repeal effort in 1982. All three governors successfully sought large appropriations in the legislature for the implementation of the legislation, the bulk of which has been passed through to local governments to complete their comprehensive plans.

In Colorado, Governor Love supported a much stronger bill than was actually adopted in 1973, as did Governor Richard Lamm from his house post in 1973. Upon election to the chief executive post, Lamm has continued to be strongly supportive of the legislation, and in fact would support a much stronger state role in Colorado if the votes could be martialed in the legislature. Governor Lamm sought and until 1978 obtained adequate funding for a staff for the state land use commission. The legislature since then has forced a different staffing pattern by drastically cutting funds that can be used by the land use commission, but Lamm has continued his support for implementation of the legislation.

In the case of Vermont, three governors—Davis, Salmon and Snelling—have served since the land- and growth-management legislation was adopted in 1970, and all have been supportive of the effective implementation of the law. Each governor has also been supportive of adequate funding for the implementation of the legislation. In North Carolina, Republican Governor James Holshouser strongly supported the adoption of the legislation and took the lead in providing Republican minority votes in the house and senate to secure its passage. His successor, then lieutenant governor, James Hunt, has also been supportive of the implementation of the Coastal Planning and Management Law passed in 1974. In Florida, Governor Reubin Askew was a driving force in passing the original legislation, and he continued to be supportive in the implementation stages, both by seeking appropriations and by making it known that any crippling or debilitating amendment would be vetoed. His successor, Governor Bob Graham, was the key legislator from his base in the state senate who brought about the passage of the land- and growth-management legislation in 1972. As governor, he has continued to be strongly supportive and took the lead along with Governor Askew in bringing about readoption of the area of critical state concern component of the law in 1979. Governor Graham then supported another strengthening amendment to the development of regional impact process which successfully passed the legislature in 1980. Thus, the record finds only one case in which a governor has attempted to weaken or repeal the land and growth management legislation, and generally governors have been supportive in the implementation effort.

Legislative Role
The securing of adequate appropriations for the implementation efforts is of course closely tied to the approach and the attitude of the governor. In a general way, gubernatorial support has gone along with legislative support of the implementation effort in the form of refusal to adopt crippling amendments and in appropriating adequate funds for the implementation effort. Only in Colorado was a major effort mounted in 1977 and succeeding years in the legislature to substantially weaken and if possible to abolish the land use law adopted in 1974. In that case, Governor Richard Lamm vetoed legislation that would have been especially harmful to the continued implementation of the law. Lamm used his executive authority to help make up for the shortfall in appropriations brought about by the legislative hostility. In Hawaii the legislature has generally followed the governor's lead in supporting the legislation, and in California the situation moved from one in which the governor was

not supportive of the coastal planning and management law to one in which Governor Brown has been supportive of the legislation, and now back to one in which Governor Deukmejian is hostile to the law.

In the case of Oregon, where major efforts to repeal the 1973 land- and growth-management legislation was mounted through the initiative process, the legislature has continued to be supportive of the law as evidenced above all by its willingness to approve very substantial appropriations for its implementation. In Vermont, no serious effort has been made to repeal the components of the land- and growth-management legislation adopted in 1970, 1972, and 1973. The final phase envisaged when the law was adopted in 1970, a so-called land use law, has never been brought to completion in the face of increasing hostility by many groups in Vermont. However, there have been no serious efforts to weaken or repeal those components of the land- and growth-management system that were enacted, and many observers of the Vermont experience feel that a minimal if not ideal state policy framework exists for carrying out an effective program even in the absence of the third stage land use plan.

In North Carolina, there have been rumblings from time to time of an intent to repeal the coastal planning and management legisla- tion, but strong gubernatorial support has headed off this threat even had it had serious political backing. A hostile minority in the legislature has discouraged any attempt to extend the coastal planning and management model to the mountain region or the Piedmont. Early hopes that this would follow the initial implemen- tation effort in the coastal area have not come to fruition. The legislature has been generally supportive in terms of funding and otherwise in supporting what has been a very effective implementa- tion record. In Florida, both the legislature and its leadership have continued to be generally supportive of the implementation effort. While there have been quite a few amendments to the Florida law, as a result of adverse court rulings and for other reasons, the amend- ments on balance have not been weakening and in some ways have actually strengthened the potential effectiveness of the legislation. While there has been some discussion of repealing one section or another of the law, no serious political effort to do so has been mounted.

Bureaucratic Adequacy

Another crucial factor in the implementation effort might be sum- med up as bureaucratic adequacy—the funding and staff quality of the implementing agencies and the cooperation received from other state agencies. Here, the record is generally positive. In each of the states involved the majority view was that a lack of funding had not been a serious impediment to the effective implementation of the law. However, a strong minority view held in Hawaii, North Carolina, and Florida was that there needed to be a more substantial appropriation of funds for the key agency responsible for implementing the law. Also, particularly in the case of Hawaii, the key agency's dependence on another state agency for its major staffing was seen to be a negative factor. In six of the seven states, funding was seen as inadequate for monitoring, enforcement, and evaluation efforts. This problem has emerged as an increasingly serious one as the implementation efforts have developed over the last decade.

In the area of staff quality, the general complaint in every state was not so much that technical competence was missing but that all too often young, inexperienced, "fresh-faced planners," who did not really understand the development process and did not have adequate experience and familiarity with the problems involved in land and growth management, were put into key positions prematurely. Some held that this was caused in part by not making a strong fight for higher salaries, which would have allowed the agencies to hire more experienced people from the very first. Many states have worked themselves out of this problem over time as the experience factor has been gained through "on-the-job training."

In the matter of cooperation from other state agencies, the record is mixed. There has been a good deal of the to be expected hostility and unwillingness to cooperate where that cooperation meant that other agencies had to surrender any of their prerogatives. This problem can be seen in clear focus as the implementation effort in Oregon nears the point where state agencies will be drawn into and in some ways made subject to the goals of the Land Conservation and Development Commission, the state's agency responsible for implementing the legislation.

Major Interest Group Positions
In the area of major interest groups and their attitude toward the land- and growth-management program adopted in their state, one sees a very interesting and potentially significant pattern in which the implementation effort has in some cases attracted new supporters and made supporters out of old enemies as the process has moved forward. This has been especially true with regard to the attitude of local governments and of homebuilders and developers,

as the major groups directly concerned with such legislation. The states where such changes are most evident are California, Oregon, and Florida. In California, the 1976 law made a fundamental change in the role of local governments in the implementation process, and in fact placed the prime responsibility for carrying out the law in the hands of 68 coastal cities and counties. This meant that the very strong direct regulatory role of the state and regional coastal commissions would be sharply curtailed, with the role of local governments sharply increased. Thus, cities strongly supported the legislation, and while counties never fully supported it, they certainly were less hostile to the coastal program.

In the case of Oregon, the state homebuilders association has in recent years made common cause with Oregon's watchdog group, 1,000 Friends of Oregon, to support the key goals of housing, agriculture, urban growth boundary establishment, and most recently economic development in the implementation of the law. This has brought about a powerful coalition that puts the Oregon implementation effort in a uniquely strong position, the culmination of a number of repeated expressions of support for the law by Oregon's citizens. In the case of Florida, again a coalition of homebuilders, local governments, and environmentalists in 1979 and 1980 supported successful efforts to amend the Land Management Act. There was no such coalition when the original legislation was passed in 1972, and thus one can say that political support for land- and growth-management legislation in Florida has grown stronger during the implementation period.

Predictions that the land- and growth-management initiatives adopted in the early 1970s would soon lose their political support and fade from the scene have not proven to be accurate. On the contrary, powerful interest groups that opposed the initial legislation in a number of states now have shifted their position and are in support of the essential thrust of the land- and growth-management program. In some cases, the change in attitude has been due to the success of these interest groups in shifting the direction of the implementation effort in ways more acceptable to them. However, the new acceptance is also due in considerable part to a recognition of the general public support for the land- and growth-management legislation. In view of this broad-based support, many former opponents have concluded that the laws were there to stay and the most practical thing to do was to support the legislation and attempt to make it serve their purposes to the extent possible. This seems especially true of private-sector groups in Florida and Oregon.

The State/Local Impact of Land and
Growth Management Initiatives

The environmentalists who backed most of the original land- and growth-management initiatives were determined if possible to avoid placing major implementation responsibility in the hands of local governments. Had this model been adopted in even a majority of the states analyzed in this study, a much more drastic impact on state/local relations would have come about than has in fact occurred. As we have seen, the initial legislation, strongly influenced by environmental interests, often proposed a direct state and/or regional regulatory role to implement the new legislation. Typically, in the heat of the battle to pass the legislation, compromises were made that took away some of the direct state and regional authority and placed it in the hands of local government. Only in California, where the legislature failed to pass the law and environmental groups went directly to the people, was it possible to put on the books a law that left the implementation process largely in the hands of special state and regional agencies set up for that purpose, thus effectively bypassing local governments. The more general pattern was one in which there was a substantial sharing of implementation authority between the state and local levels.

In the seven states involved in this study, the generalization can be made that on balance both state and local governments have increased their authority and responsibility in the land- and growth-management area. However, it is true that states, by asserting a strong state and regional interest in land- and growth-management decisions, which previously had been left entirely to local governments, have assumed a new role, and a role that puts them in a position to exercise some degree of policy control over local government activities in this area. In the case of Florida, where it was agreed from the beginning that local governments would keep most of the decisionmaking responsibility, it is also true that, in those areas of more-than-local impact, state and regional agencies do have an important role and one that ultimately can result in an overriding of local government action.

In the new California law adopted in 1976, local coastal programs developed by local governments must be reviewed and approved by the state coastal commission with the assistance of the regional commissions so long as they existed. Thus, even here where there has been the clearest reassertion of local government responsibility, it by no means took the state back to the days when local governments were virtually free to make—or not to make—any kind of land- and growth-management decisions without any interference from the regional or state level, regardless of the impact beyond the boundaries of local government. In the case of Oregon, we see again a clear example of substantial strengthening of the state role vis à vis local government in land- and growth-management decisions. Even though the bulk of the implementation of the law will be carried out by local governments, it is carried out within the framework of goals developed by the key state land- and growth-management agency. That agency has the authority to review and approve the adequacy of local comprehensive plans as to whether they reflect the goals and implementing policies laid out by the state agency. In the case of North Carolina, while coastal cities and especially counties have a major part of the responsibility for planning and implementing the coastal management legislation, the state retains a direct permitting role in areas of environmental concern and has an important review authority over the county and city plans mandated by the legislation. In Colorado, the controversy that has raged since 1974 over the implementation of the state's land use law has centered on the degree to which the state policies should be binding on local governments. A 1979 court case sharply limited the extent of the state role, and even the modest state authority left continues to be the subject of controversy.

In Hawaii, the implementation effort has been marked by the continuing struggle for power between the state on the one hand and the four counties of Hawaii on the other. Starting from a very centralized state government framework, counties have succeeded over time in asserting a stronger role in implementing Hawaii's land- and growth-management efforts. Some would say that there is now a stalemate between the state and counties as to who is to be responsible for what in the implementation effort, with a resulting inability to achieve state goals and objectives. Finally, in the case of Vermont, the state/local relationships are unique; a lay-citizen regional board is set up to handle most of the implementation effort with an appeal available to a state environmental board appointed by the governor. Here local governments have in fact been largely bypassed, and the system seems to work well for the peculiar political environment in Vermont. No serious effort to date has been made to change it. Local governments, however, can have a greater role in the implementation effort if they adopt local land use ordinances, and the trend is for them to do so.

The land- and growth-management initiatives in the states analyzed in this study have brought about some important changes in the nature of state/local relationships in all of those states. The general change has been to assert for the first time in an effective way a state and regional concern and interest in land- and growth-management decisions that were formerly left entirely to local governments. It is not surprising, therefore, that local governments have often objected to these changes. The interesting thing is that the political dynamics of the adoption of most of these laws was such that many local governments felt fortunate to be "dealt into the game" at all, in the face of original legislative proposals that excluded them altogether. In any event, as these laws have been carried out, local governments by and large have accommodated themselves to the new state role, and states have exercised considerable restraint in asserting their new authority and responsibility. In these seven states, at least, there is a new balance of power in which states have assumed substantially greater responsibility in land and growth management than was the case before the adoption of these laws. The potential for further development along these lines in bringing about important changes in the federal system is obvious.

At a time when there is a great amount of uncertainty and soul-searching about the respective roles of the national, state, substate, and local levels in the federal system, the impact of growth-management initiatives by states can be an important factor in the continued evolution of the federal system in the 1980s and beyond. States that reassert their authority in land and growth management also assume new responsibilities vis à vis their local and regional governments. Along with mandatory local and regional planning within state goals and policies, states have typically offered new financial and technical assistance to the regional and local levels. The level of that financial and technical help has been uneven, but it has been substantial in California and North Carolina, and even more so in Oregon. The combined impact of policy directives and financial and technical assistance is to create a new web of relationships among the state, regional, and local levels in which all levels assume added responsibility in land and growth management, with the state playing the lead and integrative role.

A lead role for states in turn calls for them to put their own house in order in articulating an integrated policy framework that must be followed by the regional and local levels. State agencies whose policies and regulations can have a strong impact on growth patterns, but who have historically gone their separate ways, begin to be pulled into the policy framework. Such a pattern is evolving in Oregon and North Carolina and may evolve in the implementation of the state plan in Hawaii. In Florida, the governor's office staff has recommended some form of development cabinet aimed at bringing together departments such as transportation, commerce, environmental regulation, and community affairs to develop and implement an integrated set of growth-management policies for the state.

The notion that state agencies will actually move in the direction of coordinated behavior to further a clear and well-understood set of state goals and policies is no less than revolutionary.[1] If current trends in this direction continue, it will have a major impact on the relationship between states and their regional and local levels. That changed relationship may be viewed as a mixed blessing by local governments. Although added financial and technical assistance may be welcome, and a more coherent focusing of state resources on local problems a refreshing change, the vehicle for that focusing, an integrated state policy framework, also will bring greater state influence over and even control of local governments.

The efforts of states to integrate their growth-management systems can and already is beginning to affect the relationship between states and the federal government. Encouraged by the consistency provisions of the federal Coastal Zone Management Act, several states have begun to press for the coordination of federal land-, water-, and growth-management programs through and with the state's own integrated policy framework. The evidence of success in this regard is limited, but the potential can be seen in California, Oregon and especially North Carolina as the federal consistency provisions of the Coastal Zone Management Act is put to the test.

As the federal system in the United States continues to evolve, the role of the state clearly can become more important if such developments continue and are strengthened. A state that develops a clear and coordinated set of goals and policies is in a unique position to expand its authority and influence substantially vis à vis the local and national government levels. Land- and growth-management programs that further the development of integrated policy frameworks thus become important change agents in the allocation of authority and responsibility in the federal system.

The New Planning: Merging Planning, Regulation, and Service Delivery

In theory, all regulatory and service delivery programs should move forward within the framework of policies that flow from carefully developed and constantly evolving plans. Historically, however, planning in the United States has been largely divorced from regulation, and all too often from the decisionmaking process in general. The gulf between theory and practice in this regard has been well-documented. Our concern is with the degree to which land- and growth-management initiatives and related efforts have had an impact on planning and its relationship to the regulatory and service delivery systems that are—or should be—the implementation tools of the planning process. The data suggest that the impact has been substantial.

The status of planning in every state included in this book has been substantially altered by the adoption of a state land- and growth-management system. First, either as part of the key state legislation or in companion bills, the development of local and/or regional plans has been made mandatory in all the states assessed except Vermont, and the plans themselves have often been given new legal status. In Florida local governments must develop comprehensive plans that have the force of law, and implementation mechanisms such as zoning and subdivision regulations must conform with the plan. The 1980 legislature mandated the development of comprehensive regional policy plans subject to review and approval by the governor, and the whole system is moving toward "review and approval" rather than the current "review and comment" system for local comprehensive plans. In Oregon, mandated local comprehensive plans must reflect the state goals and the policies that flow from them. The local plans must be approved by a state agency and once approved must be conformed to by all actors in the growth-management process, including special districts, state agencies, and to the extent possible federal agencies. All local government implementing actions must conform to the comprehensive plan. In North Carolina, local land use plans must be developed by the coastal counties and towns, they must reflect state policies, and they must be approved by a state agency. In Hawaii, local and state functional plans must reflect the policies contained in the state plan approved by the 1978 legislature. In California, required local coastal programs must reflect the state policies articulated by the legislature and fleshed out by the state coastal commission. They are subject to review and approval at the regional and state level, and all implementing mechanisms must conform to them. In Colorado, the land use commission has some impact on the development of required local plans, and in Vermont, the policies imbedded in act 250 are increasingly affecting the development of town plans, although such plans are not yet mandated.

All of this adds up to a vast change in the way plans are made and their impact once put in place. The days of fancy plans being developed every five or ten years and then placed on the shelf are giving way in these and other states to plans that are linked both to state and regional policies and the local implementation process. Planners who long dwelt in a world of comfortable irrelevance now finds themselves in the midst of the give and take of the political process. Some may welcome it, others may deplore it, but all are faced with its reality. In the real world, the niceties of design become less important than an understanding of the policy and administrative process.

The content of plans that emerge from this process has been improved, in the view of this writer, by the link to the regulatory process. The regulatory process, in turn, has been given a new policy direction and a capacity for positive growth management that is always lacking when permitting goes forward on an ad hoc, case-by-case basis. The positive impact of the permitting experience on planning and vice versa is clearest in California and North Carolina, but it is also emerging in Hawaii and Vermont. In the case of Oregon, the potential for such interaction is present in the system established by senate bill 100, but it has not yet developed to any significant degree. In Florida efforts now under way by the governor's office would draw the permitting process into the orbit of an integrated policy framework, while in Colorado the weakness of the state initiative to date has not allowed any significant development in that direction. In California, proposition 20 made a close link between planning and permitting a necessity by assigning the responsibility for both activities to the regional and state coastal commissions. The result was that important policy issues identified in the process of permit hearings were incorporated in the coastal plan, and the shaping of the plan, even before its approval by the legislature in 1976, began to give policy direction to the permitting process.

In North Carolina, the development of guidelines for permitting in areas of environmental concern has had an important impact on the closely related guidelines spelled out by the state agency to guide the development of the second round revision and approval of local land use plans. In a general way, the experience of the permitting process adds reality and specificity to the planning process, while the planning process gives policy direction and coherence to the permitting process. Furthermore, the development of an integrated set of policies provides the framework within which the coordination and simplification of the permitting process can and should take place, as the experience of North Carolina suggests.

Monitoring and Enforcement

A common characteristic of all of the seven land- and growth-management systems analyzed in this book has been the existence of some kind of state permit as a key element in the implementation process, and/or the requirement that local government decisions conform to state standards when a local government issues a permit or development order. In the case of the Colorado program, where the mandatory components of the law have been substantially eroded by a combination of legislative actions and court decisions, the permitting effort has been minor. A second characteristic common to our states is that almost all permits are approved, but often with major conditions attached whose enforcement is vital to the achievement of the goals of the laws. Monitoring and enforcement received little attention in the stress of passing and getting in place the new laws. As the implementation efforts have matured, the lack of an effective monitoring and enforcement component in the system has emerged as the Achilles heel in the implementation of the growth-management systems analyzed here.

In some states, such as Oregon and Florida, the problem has been documented in detail. In others it lurks as a ticking time bomb in the eyes of program administrators who readily admit the lack of time and money for an effective monitoring and enforcement system. In Oregon, a study of more than 1,000 actions by counties showed that over 80 percent failed to conform to state procedural standards. A follow-up study of over 400 county actions showed that some 70 percent failed to conform to state substantive standards that had been incorporated into state approved local plans. The monitoring effort was carried out by a public interest group—1,000 Friends of Oregon—not by the state agency that developed the state standards and approved the local plans. That agency's resources were not adequate to support a comprehensive monitoring and enforcement effort, yet in the absence of such an effort there is no assurance that state goals will be met.

In Florida, recent evaluations of the actions of local governments in the Florida Keys Area of Critical State Concern have shown a consistent pattern of failure to apply required state standards in approving major development orders. The state land planning agency has not used its power to appeal these local actions to the state land and water adjudicatory commission for reversal, at least in part because it has lacked the resources for a monitoring and enforcement effort. In Vermont, where, several thousand permits have been issued, many with major conditions attached, there are virtually no resources for a monitoring and enforcement effort. In California, where over 50,000 permits have been issued over the past decade, many with major conditions, a monitoring and enforcement system has only recently begun to be developed. Hawaii's efforts in monitoring and enforcement of county actions in coastal zone special management areas have been strongly criticized by the federal Office of Coastal Zone Management. Only in North Carolina has a monitoring and enforcement effort been mounted that seems able to address the problem of assuring that permit conditions are adhered to, and the scale of that effort is much smaller than in a state such as California. In its evaluation of state coastal programs, the federal Office of Coastal Zone Management has been critical at one time or another of all the monitoring and enforcement efforts of coastal programs analyzed here, and has made strengthening such efforts one of its highest priorities.

The problem is not beyond solution. It calls for the commitment of funds necessary to put in place effective follow-up programs. In Florida, regional agencies can and should be used more effectively to assure that state standards are actually applied. A state capacity to "blow the whistle" on local governments that cannot or will not enforce state standards is a must. State fiscal support to local governments for strong monitoring and enforcement programs is a key. Greater legislative and executive sensitivity to the issue is necessary if adequate resources are to be secured. Public interest groups must be ready to take action comparable to 1,000 Friends of Oregon's assessment of county actions to force attention to the problem. For state land- and growth-management programs to have real meaning, a strong monitoring and enforcement program must be put on line.

The Politics of the Future

The question that must be asked about the land- and growth-management initiatives that have been examined in this volume is whether they represent a temporary phenomenon that came about because of the great environmental concerns that swept the nation in the 1960s and reached their peak in the early 1970s, and in particular whether land- and growth-management initiatives can survive in the more difficult economic, energy, and antibureaucratic atmosphere of the 1980s. In short, will the early initiatives fade away and be replaced on the policy agenda by other concerns.

Certainly the political context has changed sharply since the early 1970s when most of the land- and growth-management initiatives examined in this volume were adopted. The first hurdle was a severe recession in 1974 and 1975 that presented special difficulties for the housing and development industry of the nation. Adding to the difficulties have been the widespread disillusionment with government in general—partly as an aftermath of Watergate—and government regulation in particular, the anxieties brought about by the energy crisis, and the economic problems enveloping the country as it moved into the 1980s. All these phenomena might be interpreted to mean that the environmental movement was a passing fad, and that new policy initiatives would not emerge and earlier efforts would actually be dismantled in the face of a hostile political environment. Many observers in the mid-to-late 1970s reached what seems to this writer the hasty conclusion that such a gloomy prognosis either already had become or soon would become a reality.

The record does not support any such drastic conclusion. First, the implementation record of the policy initiatives examined in this volume generally has been good, and it continues to be so as the decade of the 1980s opens. Second, efforts to weaken or repeal the laws adopted have not succeeded, and indeed there is substantial evidence that support has grown in some states for the originally adopted land- and growth-management initiatives. The state of Oregon offers an excellent example of this growth in support. Two major efforts to either repeal or drastically weaken the law were put on the ballot through a citizens initiative in Oregon in 1976 and in 1978. In both cases, the effort to repeal or weaken the law was soundly defeated, and the 1978 effort was even more conclusive (61 percent of a heavy voter turnout supporting the full implementation of the law) than the 1976 vote. Thus, in Oregon, one can say that public support has been tested and has been found growing for the full implementation of that state's land- and growth-management initiatives.[2]

Where court decisions or other factors have required the passage of new legislation, the assumption that "It could only have been done in the environmental euphoria of the early 1970s" has proven not to be accurate. In Florida, the test arose when the courts ruled that the area of critical state concern component of Florida's land-management legislation constituted an improper delegation of legislative authority to the executive, thus making it necessary to revise and reenact a major section of the law. The success of that effort in the 1979 legislature revealed for the first time a new political coalition in support of land- and growth-management initiatives in Florida. Unlike 1972, when only environmental and citizen groups supported the policy initiative, a coalition of environmental groups, local governments, and the homebuilding and development industry joined to support the passage of the 1979 legislation. That coalition continued its support in important new legislative initiatives in 1980 involving both the Land Management Act and regional planning councils. A similar coalition has developed in Oregon, and there are some signs of its development in California.

In California, the 1972 initiative that resulted in the original coastal planning and management legislation required that a new law be adopted by the 1976 legislature if the entire program was not to be eliminated. The legislature did in fact for the first time in California history adopt a comprehensive coastal planning and management law. The environmental groups made common cause with developers and other components of the private sector, a major factor in the passage of the legislation. Thus, we see a situation in which political support for land- and growth-management initiatives is far from fading away. On the contrary, the political support for these programs has now extended well beyond environmental groups to include some private sector groups that were strongly opposed to such initiatives in the late 1960s and the early 1970s.

Another indication that political support for land- and growth-management initiatives has not eroded in any substantial way may be seen in the evolvement of the coastal planning and management program within the framework of the federal legislation. The federal Coastal Zone Management Act can be seen as a national land use law focused on the coastal states. A critical test of that law is now occurring as the 35 states and territories that participated in the planning phase decide whether to move on to the implementation phase. By mid-1982, 19 states had approved programs, and the number was expected to reach 25 by January 1983. Thus, the prediction that most states would drop out of the coastal zone management program at this stage has not proven to be accurate. The implementation of this program involves the central issue that is equally important in noncoastal land- and growth-management programs—the allocation of authority and responsibility among the various levels of government. This push and pull as to the appropriate role of state, substate, regional, and local government will continue to be a major policy issue. The distribution of authority will require much delicate compromise as coastal programs unfold, but it is going forward. In the late 1970s, the federally framed state coastal planning and management program was not the only evidence of the continued vitality of the land- and growth-management movement emanating from the top level in the federal system. The Environmental Protection Agency at that time was gradually moving toward a greater concern for the land- and growth-management impact of its air and water regulatory programs.[3] That initiative, it is true, has not been carried forward by the Reagan administration.

It would not be realistic to assume that continued political support for land- and growth-management initiatives will be automatically forthcoming in the 1980s or that it will be easy to expand these initiatives. There is a need to reassess the question: Can land- and growth-management initiatives command significant political support in the 1980s to both sustain those policy initiatives already taken and to make it possible for additional policies to be adopted? The answer can be given as "yes, but." The narrowly based environmental groups of the 1960s, often accused of being strident and even hysterical, have in many cases matured as their political base has broadened and they have become actively involved in rather than only critics of the policymaking process. This process of political maturation and the attraction of new allies can be most clearly seen in the case states of California, Oregon, and Florida.

In California, after three successive years of failing to get a coastal planning and management program through the legislature, environmental groups formed a broad-based coalition, the California Coastal Alliance, and went directly to the people to bring about the adoption of a law with a strong state and regional orientation. However, the very same environmental groups wrote into that initiative the requirement that the legislature readdress the issue in 1976. In the meantime, environmental groups took the initiative in negotiating with developer, utility, and other private sector and local government groups to come to some sort of agreement on a bill that could garner support in the 1976 session of the California legislature. The local government and private sector groups had developed a willingness to come to the negotiating table in the light of the success of the environmentally sponsored initiative in 1972. However, the key ingredient in the successful formation of a coalition of support for the 1976 legislation was the leadership of the California Coastal Alliance. Thus we see in California clear evidence of the maturing of environmental groups as major actors in the political process.

In Oregon, the key environmental/public interest group in that state, 1,000 Friends of Oregon, has in the last two years worked closely with the state's homebuilders association and other private sector groups in a new coalition to support the full implementation of Oregon's land- and growth-management legislation. The *quid pro quo* here seems to be that the homebuilders will support the protection of agriculture, forests, and open space land at and beyond the urban fringe in exchange for strong environmental support for raising densities within urban growth boundaries to allow homebuilders to construct the housing needed to accommodate Oregon's population growth. In any event, the coalition has been formed and seems to be working. In Florida, the necessity to amend the land- and growth-management initiative in the 1979 and 1980 sessions of the legislature revealed a coalition that had in fact been maturing over the years since the adoption of the law in 1972. Here again, the key actors are environmental groups and the state homebuilders association, with large developer groups, who operate partly within and partly outside the homebuilders association, joining the coalition. The private sector groups seem now to appreciate the value of a well-defined and fairly implemented land- and growth-management program, operating within a state policy framework, and prefer such a program to dealing with what they often see as irrational or unreasonable behavior by local governments that attempt to limit or stop growth at the local level. Furthermore, a state policy framework that drives the decisionmaking process has the capacity to force the coordination of duplicatory and even contradictory regulations and programs. Such action can go far toward achieving what many parts of the private sector want most out of government: timeliness and certainty in government decisions about development. In any event, the Florida coalition is in place and seems to be working and was joined in the 1979 and 1980 sessions of the legislature by local governments. This makes a powerful group which seems to bode well for the future of land- and growth-management initiatives in Florida.

What we see, then, is continuing political support for policy and program initiatives that are much broader than the narrow environmental concerns that often spurred their adoption, but that support continues to include environmental interests. Several key ingredients are necessary to maintain the new coalition and to give it added strength in the 1980s. State officials and private sector groups have shown an increasing awareness that unless natural systems are protected from unwise development, the economy as well as the environment will suffer. But, the need for sensible tradeoffs in the economic versus environment arena must be faced by both environmental and economic development advocates. If environmentalists allow this issue to be defined so that environmental protection means economic decline and loss of jobs, then they will not be able to build an effective political coalition with the private sector. The approach taken by the governors of Florida, both Askew and the present Governor Graham, seems the proper one to support an environmental/developer/homebuilders coalition. As they define the issue, environmental and economic values do not need to conflict. People of goodwill can negotiate reasonable compromises that will allow both the protection of important natural systems and the development of a healthy economy.

Finally, the meaning of the term *growth policies* or *growth management* must be expanded from a focus on urban fringe to include the central city and the rural countryside. The issue of central city development and redevelopment must be seen as the reverse side of the protection of important agricultural, forest, and open space land. These new definitions of land and growth management can be seen in their early development stages in enough states such as Oregon to offer hope that they will take firm root elsewhere. If they do, the prospects for the successful implementation of current programs and the adoption of new policies in the decade of the 1980s can be viewed as cautiously optimistic.

Notes

Chapter One. Introduction

1. *Growth management*, as it is used in this book, is a broader term than *land management*. It includes all elements typically encompassed by comprehensive plans, including the economic, social, and physical aspects of growth management. The major expression of growth policy and management to date in the United States has been through new initiatives in the land-management area. But as the implementation in some of the programs examined in this study matures, the multifaced initiatives are clearly beginning to take the form of a policy effort much broader than what we usually identify as land management.

2. Fred Bosselman and David Callies, *The Quiet Revolution in Land Use Control* (Washington, D.C.: U.S. Government Printing Office, 1971); and William K. Riley, ed., *Task Force Report, The Use of Land: A Citizen's Guide to Urban Growth* (New York: Thomas Crowell Company) are only two of the many publications illustrating the new mood in land and growth management.

3. One such study was Florida Defenders of the Environment, *Environment and Florida Voters*, Workpaper no. 7 (Gainesville, Florida: Urban and Regional Development Center, University of Florida, 1974). Another such study, one of a series by the Gallop Poll Organization, reported on by George Gallop at the National Conference on Managed Growth held in Chicago on September 16, 1973, also supported the proposition that the strength of the environmental, and more broadly the quality of life, movement was very great. A more recent study by Robert Cameron Mitchell of Resources for the Future, in conjunction with Roper and Cantril Research, Appendix A, "Public Opinion on Environmental Issues," The 11th Annual Report of the Council on Environmental Quality, *Environmental Quality—1980* (Washington, D.C.: U.S. Government Printing Office, 1980), pp. 401–23, confirmed the continued strong support for environmental matters by citizens of the country. Polling results as late as 1981 showed that American support for clean air and water is holding firm even in the current economic crisis.

4. Council of State Governments, *Land: State Alternatives for Planning and Management, A Task Force Report* (Lexington, Kentucky: Council of State Governments, 1975).

5. 12 U.S. Code, § 3122 (1070).

6. 16 U.S. Code, § 1451–64 (Supp. 5, 1975).

7. 33 U.S. Code, § 1251–1376 (Supp. 5, 1975).

8. 42 U.S. Code, § 1857 (1970 and Supp. 5, 1975).

9. 42 U.S. Code, § 4901–18 (Supp. 5, 1975).

10. For a more detailed report on local government initiatives in the land

and management area, see Randall W. Scott, David J. Brower and Dallas D. Minor, eds., *Management and Control of Growth: Issues, Techniques, Problems, and Trends*, Vol. 2 (Washington, D.C.: Urban Land Institute, 1975), chapters 10 and 11. The Urban Land Institute's four volume series on growth management remains the most comprehensive treatment of the subject. For a full discussion of some legal issues involving land and growth management, see Fred Bosselman, David Callies, and John Banta, *The Taking Issue* (Washington, D.C.: U.S. Government Printing Office, 1973).

11. For a provocative discussion of the taking issue, see Donald G. Hagman and Dean J. Misczynski, *Windfalls for Wipeouts* (Chicago: American Society of Planning Officials, 1977).

Chapter Two. Hawaii:
First, Different, and Changing

1. U.S. Department of Commerce, National Oceanic and Atmospheric Administration, Office of Coastal Zone Management, *State of Hawaii: Coastal Management Program and Draft Environmental Impact Statement* (Honolulu: Department of Planning and Economic Development, 1978), p. 3.

2. *State of Hawaii*, p. 145.

3. Ibid.

4. Ibid., pp. 3 and 147. Certainly not all caucasians in Hawaii are descended from missionaries, Calvinist or otherwise. Merchants, seamen, and others also form part of the caucasian base of the islands.

5. Ibid., pp. 146–47. See also Phyllis Myers, *Zoning Hawaii: An Analysis of the Passage and Implementation of Hawaii's Land Classification Law* (Washington, D.C.: The Conservation Foundation, 1976), pp. 15–17.

6. Myers, *Zoning Hawaii*, p. 19; and Robert H. Horwitz and Judith B. Finn, "Public Land Policy in Hawaii: Major Landowners," Legislative Reference Bureau, report no. 3 (Honolulu: University of Hawaii, 1967), p. 3.

7. Interview with Tats Fujimoto, director, Land Planning Division, Department of Planning and Economic Development, on April 27, 1977.

8. Interviews with Tom Dinell and Kem Lowry, University of Hawaii, Honolulu, on April 27, 1977.

9. Interview with Mayor Elmer Cravalho, Kahului, Maui, on April 29, 1977.

10. Interview with Ray Suefuji, former planning director of the island of Hawaii and in 1977 a legislative aide in the area of planning in the Hawaii legislature, Honolulu, on April 25, 1977.

11. Interview with Myron "Pinky" Thompson, trustee of the Bishop Estate and former chairman, Hawaii Land Use Commission, on April 26, 1977.

12. *1957 Hawaii Session Laws*, act 35.

13. *1957 Hawaii Session Laws*, act 234.

14. *1957 Hawaii Session Laws*, act 150.

15. The quote came from Robert Wenkum, "Kauai and Park County of Hawaii," p. 131, as quoted in *State Planning in Hawaii: A Primer*, rev. ed (Honolulu, Hawaii: League of Women Voters, 1975), p. 5.

16. *1961 Hawaii Session Laws*, act 187.

17. Interview with Mayor Elmer Cravalho, on April 29, 1977. See also Myers, *Zoning Hawaii*, p. 20 for Gill's role. Gill was Democratic party chairman at the time.

18. Interview with Ray Suefuji, on April 25, 1977.

19. Myers, *Zoning Hawaii*, p. 21.

20. Ibid., pp. 21–22.

21. The description of the land use law is taken from the law itself and from a very excellent League of Women Voters of Hawaii publication, *Facts and Issues: Hawaii's Land Use Law*, which summarized the law and also assessed its implementation.

22. *Hawaii Revised Statutes* § 205–2(1) (1977).

23. *Hawaii Revised Statutes* § 205–2(3) (1977).

24. *Hawaii Revised Statutes* § 205–5(b) (1977).

25. *Hawaii Revised Statutes* § 205–2(2) (1977).

26. *1961 Hawaii Session Laws*, act 187, § 15.

27. Ibid., § 6 sets out the criteria for boundary changes.

28. *1963 Hawaii Session Laws*, act 205.

29. Myers, *Zoning Hawaii*, pp. 64–65.

30. Myers, *Zoning Hawaii*, pp. 22–23.

31. Interview with Tom Dinell and Kem Lowry on April 27, 1977.

32. Myers, *Zoning Hawaii*, p. 23.

33. Interview with Myron Thompson on April 26, 1977. The commission was in a state of considerable flux during its first year because of the failure of the senate to confirm the governor's appointments to the commission.

34. Interview with Eddie Tangen, chairman, Land Use Commission, on April 28, 1977.

35. Interview with Carol Whitesell, Land Use commissioner, Honolulu, Hawaii, on April 27, 1977.

36. Ibid.

37. The problem in North Carolina has been overcome by establishing a strong coastal management staff within the Department of Natural Resources and Community Development.

38. Interview with Hideto Kono, director, Hawaii Department of Planning and Economic Development, April 27, 1977.

39. *Facts and Issues*, p. 7; and Daniel R. Mandelker, *Environmental and Land Use Controls Legislation* (Washington, D.C.: Urban Land Institute, 1976), pp. 276–77.

40. Mandelker, *Environmental and Land Use Controls Legislation*, p. 277.

41. Ibid.

42. Carol Whitesell (letter to the author, July 9, 1979) reported that the big developers "strongly object to incremental districting on the basis that they can't get financing if they don't have assurance of the proper classification.

43. Mandelker, *Environmental and Land Controls Legislation*, p. 277.

44. Carol Whitesell (letter to the author, on July 9, 1979).

45. Myers, *Zoning Hawaii*, p. 36.

46. Ibid., pp. 37–39.

47. Telephone interview with Carol Whitesell, on June 14, 1982.

48. The assessment of the commission was based on an amalgam of interviews with three members or former members of the commission and other close observers of the commission's work.

49. *Town v. Land Use Commission*, 55 Haw. 538.524 P.2d 84 (1974).

50. Hawaii Land Use Commission, *Report to the People: Second Five Year District Boundaries and Regulations Review*, February 1975, pp. 10–11, and interviews with Tats Fujimoto on April 27, 1977, and Eddie Tangen on April 28, 1977.

51. 1975 Hawaii Session Laws, act 193, §1.

52. Hawaii Revised Statutes, §205–1 (1977).

53. Hawaii Revised Statutes, §205–16.1 (1977).

54. Some of the policies were restatements of policies contained in the original law; others placed land use commission regulations in the statutes; and others were entirely new.

55. Hawaii Revised Statutes, §205–16.1(5) (1977).

56. Hawaii Revised Statutes, §205–4(h) (1957). The time frame for decisionmaking was changed to "not more than 180 days" in a 1976 amendment to the law.

57. Hawaii Revised Statutes, §205–16.1 (1977).

58. *State Planning in Hawaii*, p. 7.

59. Hawaii Revised Statutes, §205–1 (1977).

60. Mandelker has included a good discussion of the revision of the land use law and the implications of the movement from quasi-legislative to quasi-judicial in his chapter on Hawaii in *Environmental and Land Use Controls Legislation*, pp. 303–11.

61. Interview with John McConnell, former counsel assigned to the Land Use Commission, and deputy director, Department of Regulatory Agencies, Honolulu, Hawaii, on April 25, 1977.

62. Interview with Tats Fujimoto on April 27, 1977.

63. Ibid.; and interview with Susum Ono, executive assistant to the governor, Honolulu, Hawaii, April 25, 1977.

64. Interview with Gary Caulfield, special assistant to the governor, Honolulu, Hawaii, on April 25, 1977. This unified system also has a negative side in that the state position may be skewed to support a unified position not supportive of sound land and growth management policies. The staff assigned to the commission makes no independent evaluation to guard against such a problem.

65. Ibid.

66. U.S. Office of Coastal Zone Management, *Evaluation Findings for the Hawaii Coastal Zone Management Program for the Period from June 1980 through June 1981*, p. 8, and Interview with Carol Whitesell on March 22, 1982.

67. Interview with Gary Caulfield on April 25, 1977.

68. Carol Whitesell, panel presentation on land use in Hawaii, American Society for Public Administration annual meeting, Honolulu, Hawaii, on March 24, 1982.

69. As quoted in Myers, *Zoning Hawaii*, p. 34.

70. Ibid., pp. 34–36.

71. Mandelker, *Environmental and Land Control Legislation*, pp. 272–75, 284–94.

72. Land Use Commission, *Report to the People*, February 1975, pp. 23–25.

73. Myers, *Zoning Hawaii*, p. 41.

74. *Honolulu Star Bulletin*, December 21, 1974.

75. *Hawaii. Act 100* (1979).

76. Hawaii, Department of Planning and Economic Development, *The Hawaii State Plan* (Honolulu, Hawaii: 1978), p. 26.

77. Ibid., p. 45.

78. *Honolulu Star Bulletin*, June 5, 1978, editorial page.

79. Telephone interview with Carol Whitesell on June 14, 1982.

80. For a good recent assessment of the status of the "big four" in Hawaii's economy—tourism, defense, sugar, and pineapples—see *Hawaii: Coastal*

Management Program and Draft Environmental Impact Statement, pp. 147–56. By 1982 the sugar industry was in a crisis brought about by increased operating costs and low sugar prices and was calling on the state for major subsidies to allow its survival.

81. Ibid., pp. 153–54 for a good discussion of the prospects for pineapple, sugar, and diversified agriculture, and interview with "Pinky" Thompson on April 26, 1977.

82. Interview with Mayor Elmer Cravalho on April 29, 1977.

83. Ibid.

84. Interview with Fred Trotter, executive of the Campbell Estate, Honolulu, Hawaii, on April 26, 1977, and Act 175 (1973).

85. Interview with Fred Trotter on April 26, 1977.

86. *Facts and Issues*, p. 5.

87. Ibid., pp. 5–6.

88. Hawaii, *Constitution*, art. XI, § 3.

89. Hawaii, Department of Agriculture, "A State Functional Plan Technical Reference Document Prepared In Accordance with Chapter 226, Hawaii Revised Statutes," *State Agricultural Plan*, September 1981, pp. I–2.

90. David Callies, professor of Law, University of Hawaii, panel presentation to American Society for Public Administration annual meeting in Honolulu, Hawaii on land use in Hawaii, on March 24, 1982.

91. Telephone interview with Carol Whitesell on June 14, 1982.

92. "A State Functional Plan," *State Agricultural Plan*, pp. II–91, 104.

93. Ibid., pp. II–103.

94. Ibid., pp. II–115, 116.

95. Ibid., pp. II–118, 120.

96. See Myers, *Zoning Hawaii*, pp. 79–87; and Mandelker, *Environmental and Land Use Controls Legislation*, pp. 288–91.

97. This analysis by Thomas P. Gill was reported by Jerry Tune in an article on Housing costs, in *Honolulu Star-Bulletin*, August 24, 1971, cited in *Facts and Issues*, p. 7.

98. Ibid., p. 8.

99. Hawaii, *Act 207*, (1977).

100. Mandelker, *Environmental and Land Use Controls Legislation*, p. 289.

101. Interview with Gary Caulfield on April 25, 1977.

102. Interview with Mayor Elmer Cravalho, April 29, 1977.

103. League of Women Voters of Hawaii, *Conservation and Hawaii's Conservation Districts* (Honolulu: 1802 Keeaumoku Street, 1972), p. 5.

104. Ibid., pp. 5–7.

105. Ibid., pp. 11–12.

106. Interview with Eddie Tangen on April 28, 1977.

107. Interview with Carol Whitesell on April 30, 1977.

108. League of Women Voters of Hawaii, *Conservation and Hawaii's Conservation Districts*, p. 13.

109. Hawaii, Department of Land and Natural Resources, Regulation No. 4, May 25, 1978, 14 pp. (mimeographed).

110. Interview with Ray Suefuji on April 25, 1977.

111. Interview with Hideto Kono on April 27, 1977.

112. Interview with Carol Whitesell on April 27, 1977.

113. Interview with Eddie Tangen on April 28, 1977.

114. Interview with Mayor Elmer Cravalho on April 27, 1977.

115. Interview with Toshio Ishikawa, Maui planning director; Zuke

Matsui, deputy director; and Jeff Chang, senior planner, on April 29, 1977.

116. Interview with George Akahane, Honolulu City Council member, Honolulu, Hawaii, April 28, 1977.

117. Interview with Robert Way, Honolulu planning director, on April 27, 1977.

118. Interview with George Akahane on April 27, 1977.

119. As reported in *Facts and Issues*, p. 8.

120. Mike McElroy, panel director, Department of Land Utilization, City/County of Honolulu, presentation to the American Society of Public Administration annual meeting on Land Use in Hawaii, Honolulu, Hawaii, on March 24, 1982.

121. *Hawaii Coastal Management Program*, pp. 3–4.

122. Ibid., pp. 19–20.

123. Ibid., pp. 233–34. Act 188 is included in full, pp. 233–37.

124. Ibid., p. 233.

125. Ibid., p. 234.

126. Ibid.

127. U.S. Department of Commerce, *Evaluation Findings for the Hawaii Coastal Zone Management Program for the Period from June 1980 through June 1981*.

128. Ibid., p. 12.

129. Ibid., pp. 12–13.

130. Ibid., pp. 5–6.

131. Ibid., pp. 6–7.

132. Ibid., p. 8.

133. Ibid., pp. 12–13.

134. Brian Thornton, "Rebirth of Life of the Land," *Hawaii Observer*, April 21, 1977.

135. Ibid.

136. Interview with Carol Whitesell on April 30, 1977.

137. *Facts and Issues*, p. 9.

138. Ibid.

139. Interview with Carol Whitesell on April 30, 1977.

140. Carol Whitesell (letter to the author, July 9, 1979).

141. Interview with Doug Meller, private consultant and citizen activist, Honolulu, Hawaii, on April 25, 1977.

142. Ibid.

143. U.S. Department of Commerce, *Evaluation Findings for the Hawaii Coastal Zone Management Program for the Period from June 1979 through June 1980*, Draft Copy, September 9, 1980, pp. 20–21.

144. League of Women Voters of Hawaii, *State Planning in Hawaii*, p. 15.

145. *Facts and Issues*, p. 5.

146. Interviews with Tom Dinell and Kem Lowry on April 27, 1977.

147. Interview with Susum Ono on April 25, 1977.

148. Interview with Dr. Hubert Kimura, Department of Finance, governor's office, April 25, 1977.

149. Carol B. Whitesell (letter to the author, July 9, 1979).

150. *Boca Raton* (Florida) *News*, June 19, 1978.

151. Interview with Fred Trotter on April 26, 1977.

152. See *Hawaii's Agricultural Lands: An Essential Resource We Must Protect*, pamphlet prepared by the office of the lieutenant governor, March 1982.

Chapter Three. Vermont:
The Struggle to Meld Permitting and Planning

1. Phyllis Myers, *So Goes Vermont* (Washington, D.C.: Conservation Foundation, 1974), pp. 9–10.

2. Ibid., p. 10; see also Robert G. Healy, *Land Use and the States*, 1st ed. (Baltimore, Md.: Johns Hopkins University Press, 1979), pp. 36–38; and David G. Heeter, "Almost Getting It Together in Vermont," in Daniel R. Mandelker *Environmental and Land Use Controls Legislation*, ed. (Washington, D.C.: Urban Land Institute, 1976), pp. 325–27.

3. Interview with Jonathan Brownell, attorney and advisor on land use to Vermont governors from Gibbs through Snelling on October 21, 1976.

4. See Healy, *Land Use and the States*, pp. 36–38.

5. Interview with Seward Weber, executive director, Vermont Natural Resources Council, Montpelier, Vermont, on October 21, 1976.

6. Heeter, "Almost Getting It Together in Vermont," pp. 325–26.

7. Ibid., pp. 326–27, and p. 327, note 7.

8. Interview with Jonathan Brownell on October 21, 1976.

9. Ibid.; and Heeter, "Vermont Experience," p. 329.

10. Myers, *So Goes Vermont*, p. 11.

11. As quoted in ibid., p. 12.

12. From the Gibb Commission report as reported in ibid.

13. Interview with Jonathan Brownell, October 21, 1976.

14. Ibid.

15. Heeter, "Almost Getting It Together," p. 330, notes 14 and 15.

16. Ibid., p. 331.

17. Ibid.

18. Ibid.

19. Ibid., pp. 332–35, and *Vermont Statutes Annotated*, 6001 (3).

20. *Vermont Statutes Annotated*, 6086 (a) (1)–(10).

21. Healy, *Land Use and the States*, pp. 47–48.

22. Ibid., pp. 48–50.

23. Robert K. Reis, "Vermont's Act 250: Reflections on the First Decade and Recommendations for the Second," (South Royalton, Vermont: Vermont Law School, 1980), pp. 14–15 and appendix, p. 34.

24. Ibid., pp. 34–35.

25. Interview with Jonathan Brownell on October 21, 1976.

26. Interview with Arthur Hogan, executive director, Chittendon Regional Planning Commission, Burlington, October 22, 1976, and telephone interview with Jan Eastman, state environmental board executive officer, Montpelier, on June 3, 1982.

27. Interview with Schyler Jackson on October 22, 1976. Jackson served at different times as head of the environmental board and the environmental agency.

28. Heeter, "Almost Getting It Together," p. 379. See also Robert G. Healy and John S. Rosenberg, *Land Use and the States*, 2d ed. (Baltimore, Md.: Johns Hopkins University Press, 1979), p. 56 for a more recent appraisal of the review committee's effectiveness.

29. See Healy and Rosenberg, *Land Use and the States*, pp. 58–73.

30. Telephone interview with Jan Eastman on June 3, 1982.

31. Heeter, "Almost Getting It Together," p. 371.

32. Heeter, "Almost Getting It Together," pp. 372–73.

33. Telephone interview with Jan Eastman on June 3, 1982.

34. Heeter, "Almost Getting It Together," p. 377.

35. The examples of efforts to deal with the reaction against needless bureaucratic complexity have been taken from Heeter, "Almost Getting It Together," pp. 377–78.

36. Interview with Arthur Hogan on October 22, 1976.

37. Telephone interview with Jan Eastman on June 3, 1982.

38. Heeter, "Almost Getting It Together," p. 342.

39. Ibid., p. 344.

40. Ibid.

41. Ibid., p. 347.

42. Ibid., p. 348; and Healy, *Land Use and the States*, p. 48.

43. Interview with Jonathan Brownell on October 21, 1976. Brownell and Wilson were both members of the Vermont Natural Resources Council's Environmental Protection Information Center, which assumed responsibility for getting information to the public on act 250 during the 1970–73 period. Wilson was a director of state planning under Governor Phil Hoff. During the early 1970s, Brownell was chairman of the Republican state committee's environmental section and Wilson held the same position for the Democrats. Thus they were in a unique position to work with outgoing Governor Davis and incoming Governor Salmon.

44. Ibid.

45. Ibid.

46. Interview with Schyler Jackson on October 22, 1976. It should be made clear that the Vermont Natural Resources Council had no part in preparing the maps or any other material it sent out. The material was furnished to the council by the state.

47. Interview with Jonathan Brownell on October 21, 1976.

48. Heeter, "Almost Getting It Together," p. 349, especially note 89.

49. Ibid., pp. 350–51; and interviews with Jonathan Brownell and Schyler Jackson.

50. Heeter, "Almost Getting It Together," p. 351.

51. For a good brief discussion of the Land Capability and Development Plan, see Healy and Rosenberg, *Land Use and the States*, p. 59–61, 72–74.

52. Healy, *Land Use and the States*, pp. 48–49.

53. Healy and Rosenberg, *Land Use and the States*, p. 62.

54. Ibid., pp. 62–63.

55. Heeter, "Almost Getting It Together," pp. 358–64.

56. Ibid.

57. Healy and Rosenberg, *Land Use and the States*, p. 63.

58. Ibid.; and interview with Jonathan Brownell on October 21, 1976.

59. Heeter, "Almost Getting It Together," p. 368.

60. Interview with Henry Carse, dairy farmer and legislator, Burlington, October 22, 1976.

61. Interview with Jonathan Brownell, October 21, 1976.

62. Heeter, "Almost Getting It Together," pp. 368–69.

63. Ibid., pp. 369–70.

64. Interview with Henry Carse on October 22, 1976.

65. Ibid.

66. Ibid.

67. Vermont, H.B. 383 (1975).

68. Interview with Henry Carse on October 22, 1976.

69. Ibid.; Healy and Rosenberg, *Land Use and the States*, p. 65; and Heeter, "Almost Getting It Together," p. 370.

70. Ibid.

71. Vermont, District Environmental Commission, no. 4, re: Pyramid Company of Burlington, Findings of Fact, Conclusions of Law, and Order Denying Land Use Permit, pp. 1–3.

72. Ibid., p. 39.

73. Ibid., pp. 41–48.

74. Ibid., p. 48. The planning commission in successive meetings had held that the mall conformed, then that it did not conform, and finally, again, that it was in conformance with the plan.

75. Ibid., p. 55.

76. Letter to the author from Jonathan Brownell, December 12, 1978.

77. Telephone interview with Jonathan Brownell on August 22, 1980.

78. Ibid.

79. Interview wih Jonathan Brownell on October 21, 1976.

80. Telephone interview with Jonathan Brownell on August 22, 1980.

81. Ibid.

82. Reis, "Vermont's Act 250," p. 4, 5, 8.

83. See Reis, "Vermont's Act 250," for a critical but hopeful assessment of act 250's first years. Reis argues strongly that a state land use plan with maps is necessary to complete the law as a positive growth-management system. In addition, Gov. Snelling was reelected.

84. Vermont continues to struggle with the issue. An effort to gut the capital gains tax on land failed in 1979. A law establishing a use value tax on productive land/farm and forest has proved so complicated that it has not yet been implemented. The issue remains on Vermont's growth policy agenda for the 1980s.

Chapter Four. Florida:
Harmonizing Growth and the Environment

1. John M. DeGrove, *Approaches to Water Resource Development in Central and South Florida, 1845–1957*, Studies in Public Administration no. 17 (Gainesville, Florida: Public Administration Clearing Service of the University of Florida, 1958).

2. Ibid. Luther J. Carter, *The Florida Experience: Land and Water Policy in a Growth State* (Baltimore: The Johns Hopkins Press, 1974), pp. 57–66 is an excellent and revealing analysis of the historic development of land and water policy in Florida leading up to the events of the late '60s and early '70s in which the whole approach to growth shifted, and Florida became committed to attempting to better manage its explosive growth forces. A recent book by Nelson Manfred Blake, *Land into Water—Water into Land* (Tallahassee: University Presses of Florida, 1980), is the best treatment of the history of Florida's water management efforts.

3. For a detailed description of these events see Carter, *Florida Experience*, pp. 66–73; Blake, *Land into Water*, pp. 88, 89; and DeGrove, *Approaches to Water Resource Development*, pp. 14–17.

4. Carter, *Florida Experience*, pp. 71–73; DeGrove, "The Central and Southern Florida Flood Control Project: A Study in Intergovernmental Cooperation and Public Administration" (Ph.D. diss., University of North Carolina at Chapel Hill, 1958), pp. 61; DeGrove, *Approaches to Water Resource*

Development, p. 50; and Blake, *Land into Water*, pp. 176–82.

5. Reubin O D. Askew, governor, State of Florida, *1977 Economic Report of the Governor* (Tallahassee, Florida: Governor's Office, August 1977), pp. 31, 40, 41, and Executive Office of the Governor, Office of Planning and Budgeting, *Florida's Decade of the Eighties*, July 1981, p. 1.

6. *Florida's Decade of the Eighties*, pp. 1–2.

7. D. Robert Graham, "A Quiet Revolution: Florida's Future on Trial," *The Florida Naturalist* 45: 5 (October 1972), pp. 146–47.

8. The complex story of how and why the White House intervened in the canal controversy and why President Nixon took the unprecedented action of stopping construction of the canal is developed in detail by Carter in *Florida Experience*, chapter 9. Legislation was introduced into Congress in the spring of 1983 to deauthorize the canal and bring a complete end to the project.

9. Carter, *Florida Experience*, pp. 107–24. Water for the park has reemerged as an issue in 1983 in the form of a demand by park officials and environmentalists that water be delivered to the park more consistent with the historic natural sheet flow.

10. Ibid., chapter 7.

11. Graham, "Quiet Revolution," pp. 146–47.

12. Interview with Wade Hopping, Tallahassee attorney and developer/lobbyist on April 7, 1978.

13. Interview with Jay Landers, environmental assistant to Governor Askew, secretary of the Department of Environmental Regulation, director of the Department of Natural Resources, now a Tallahassee attorney on April 7, 1978.

14. Interview with Bob Rhodes, Tallahassee, Florida, April 5, 1978. Rhodes was formerly chief of the Florida Bureau of Land Planning.

15. Remarks of Governor Reubin O D. Askew to the Governor's Conference on Water Management in South Florida, Miami Beach, Florida, on September 22, 1971. The author served as chairman of the conference and later as chairman of the task force that drafted implementing legislation.

16. Central and Southern Florida Flood Control District, "Statement to Governor Reubin O D. Askew from the Governor's Conference on Water Management in South Florida," *Water Management Bulletin* 5: 3 (December–January 1971–72): 4.

17. Ibid., pp. 4–5.

18. This is taken from the author's personal notes on the task force organization, and James W. May, "The Florida Environmental Land and Water Management Act of 1972: Planning and the State Legislative Policy–making Process," (Master's thesis, Florida State University, 1974). May's thesis is by far the best recounting of the work of the task force and the subsequent effort to pass major land- and water-management legislation in 1972. This account of the task force work and the effort to put the resulting bills through the legislature will draw heavily on this source.

19. Gilbert S. Finnell, Jr., was a law professor at Florida State University and had a special interest and expertise in environmental management.

20. The task force through the governor's office retained one of the practitioner/scholars who had been one of the drafters of the Model State Land Development Code. Fred P. Bosselman proved to be an invaluable resource to the task force in its effort to draft complex legislation in a short time frame.

21. Gilbert S. Finnell, Jr., "Saving Paradise: The Florida Environmental Land and Water Management Act of 1972." *Urban Law Annual*, no. 103 (1973): 116.

22. Charlton W. Tebeau, *A History of Florida* (Miami: The University of Miami Press, 1971), p. 289.

23. For a more detailed assessment of the changes brought to Florida's state and local governments by reapportionment, see John M. DeGrove, "Florida's Governmental Structure: Perspectives and Prospects" (Research paper available through the FAU-FIU Joint Center for Environmental and Urban Problems, 1515 West Commercial Boulevard, Fort Lauderdale, Florida). See also Manning J. Dauer, "Florida the Different State," in *The Changing Politics of the South* ed: William Havard (Louisiana: Louisiana University Press, 1972). While the grant of home rule power to local governments was a positive factor in strengthening the capacity of local governments to develop a comprehensive growth-management system, including but not confined to the components of the land management act, it has probably increased the resistance of local governments to that part of Chapter 380 involving the overruling of local governments by the Land and Water Adjudicatory Commission, as illustrated by local government reaction to the Estech case discussed elsewhere in this chapter.

24. Unpublished listing of environmental legislation, courtesy of Wade Hopping, Tallahassee attorney.

25. Interview with Ray Sittig, executive director, League of Cities, Tallahassee, Florida, on April 6, 1978; see also Carter, *Florida Experience*, chapter 2.

26. Interview with Wade Hopping on April 7, 1978.

27. Governor's opening address to the 1972 session of the Florida legislature, *House Journal*, February 1, 1972, p. 14.

28. Author's notes on the task force and follow-up legislative activity on land use legislation, November 1971–February 1972.

29. Ibid.

30. Graham's statement as quoted in May, "Florida Environmental Land and Water Management Act of 1972," p. 45.

31. Ibid., p. 52.

32. Ibid., p. 55.

33. Phyllis Myers, *Slow Start in Paradise* (Washington, D.C.: The Conservation Foundation, 1974), p. 15.

34. Interview with Ray Sittig on April 6, 1978.

35. Ibid.

36. Interview with Wade Hopping on April 7, 1978.

37. Interview with Governor Reubin Askew on June 10, 1978.

38. For a fuller discussion of the details of the Water Resources Act and the experience in attempts to implement the act through 1977, see John M. DeGrove, "How Florida Manages Its Water Resources," *Business and Economic Dimensions*, 16: 1 (University of Florida, Gainesville, Florida: Bureau of Economic and Business Research, 1980), pp. 4–9.

39. Interview with Governor Reubin Askew on June 10, 1978.

40. Carter, *Florida Experience*, p. 135.

41. Interview with Bob Rhodes on April 5, 1978.

42. *Fla. Stat.* §380.05(2).

43. *Fla. Stat.* §380.05(16).

44. *Fla. Stat.* §380.05(17).

45. Ibid., §380.06(2).

46. Ibid., §380.06(2)(a).

47. *Fla. Stat.* §380.06(8)(a–f).

48. *Fla. Stat.* §380.06(11)(a–c).

49. *Fla. Stat.* §380.07.

50. Ibid., §380.09.

51. Ibid., §380.09(5)(d).

52. Ibid., §380.09(9).

53. There are no reliable data on what proportion of the total development effort is affected by chapter 380, especially if indirect impacts are considered. Such data are being sought by the second Environmental Land Management Study Committee, appointed by Governor Graham in 1983.

54. American Institute of Planners, *Newsletter,* January 1977.

55. Robert M. Rhodes, "Florida's Environmental Land and Water Management Act," American Institute of Planners, *Newsletter,* January 1974, p. 8.

56. Interview with Jim May, head, Bureau of Land and Water Management, Tallahassee, Florida, on April 5, 1978.

57. Ibid.

58. Ibid.

59. *Fla. Stat.* §380.06(2)(b)(6).

60. *Fla. Stat.* §380.06(4)(a–c).

61. *Fla. Stat.,* §380.06(20)(b).

62. *Cross Key Waterways* v. *Askew,* 351 So. 2d 1062 (Fla. 1st District Ct. App. 1977); *Askew* v. *Cross Key Waterways,* (Florida Supreme Court, No. 52,251 and 52,252, November 22, 1978); and Nancy E. Stroud, "Areas of Critical State Concern: Legislative Options Following the Cross Key Decision," *Florida Environmental and Urban Issues* 6: 4 (April 1979); 4, 5.

63. For a full discussion of the pros, cons, and implications of the Cross Key decision, see Gilbert L. Finnell, Jr., "Coastal Land Management in Florida," American Bar Foundation, *Research Journal* 1980: 2 (Spring); 349–57.

64. For the Resource Planning and Management Committee provision, including required state agency and local government membership, see *Fla. Stat.,* 380.045(1)(2), 1981. For the general changes, see F. S. 380.05, 1–21. For the specific redesignation of the Green Swamp and related changes, see 380.0551. For the keys, including the city of Key West, see 380.0552. See also Stroud, "Areas of Critical State Concern," pp. 4–6, 15; and Nancy E. Stroud, "Legislative Action on Natural Resource Management," *Florida Environmental and Urban Issues* 7:1 (October 1979): 2–3.

65. Florida, Governor's Task Force on Resource Management, Section Three, *Final Report to Bob Graham of the Resource Management Task Force,* vol. 1, *Recommendations,* "Improvements in the Developments of Regional Impact Process," January 1980, pp. 23–30.

66. Florida, Governor's Task Force on Resource Management, Committee Three, "The Development of Regional Impact Process and Comprehensive Planning."

67. Nancy E. Stroud, "Regionalism Reaffirmed: The 1980 Florida Regional Planning Council Act." *Florida Environmental and Urban Issues* 8: 1 (October 1980): 19.

68. Ibid., p. 2.

69. The 1974 legislature did in fact subsequently approve a growth policy that went a long way toward meeting the recommendations of the Florida 2000 Conference. For the full text of the Florida 2000 Conference, see "A

Statement to Reubin O D. Askew, governor, state of Florida, the Office of the Governor, Florida 2000: Governor's Conference on Growth and the Environment," Tallahassee, October 1973.

70. Local Government Comprehensive Planning Act of 1975: Chapter 75–257, Laws of Florida (ss. 163.3161–163.3211, F.S., 1975); Robert A. Catlin, "Comprehensive Planning in Hillsborough County," *Florida Environmental and Urban Issues* 6: 2 (December 1978): 1, 5, 17; John Sidor, Jr., "Local Government Comprehensive Planning Act: Three Years Later," *Florida Environmental and Urban Issues* 6: 1 (October 1978): 4–7, 11–12; Alan S. Gold, "Dade County's Comprehensive Development Master Plan: What the Courts Have to Say," *Florida Environmental and Urban Issues* 5: 3 (February 1978): 1–3, 12, 13; Helge Swanson, "The Florida State Comprehensive Plan: An Overview," *Florida Environmental and Urban Issues* 5: 5 (June 1978): 9–14; Unidentified member of Governor Askew's staff, "The Florida Comprehensive Plan: Part II," *Florida Environmental and Urban Issues* 5: 6 (August 1978): 9, 21; Daniel W. O'Connell, "Status Report: Local Government Comprehensive Planning Act of 1975," *Florida Environmental and Urban Issues* 4: 3 (February 1977): 8–11; Ernest R. Bartley, "Local Government Comprehensive Planning Act of 1975," *Florida Environmental and Urban Issues* 3: 1 (October 1975): 1–2, 13–15.

71. John M. DeGrove, "Administrative Systems for Water Management in Florida," p. 10 (paper prepared for presentation at the Southeast Conference on Legal and Administrative Systems for Water Allocations, April 29–30, 1978, at Virginia Polytechnic Institute and State University), and Jeanne M. DeQuinne and Joseph M. Thomas, "Environmental Reorganization," *Florida Environmental and Urban Issues* 1: 4 (April 1975): 1–2, 14–16.

72. "The Water Management Constitutional Amendment, Pro and Con," *Florida Environmental and Urban Issues* 3: 3 (February 1976): 8, 9; see also *Fla. Const.* art. VII, § 9.

73. Interview with Governor Reubin O D. Askew on June 10, 1978.

74. 1973 *Fla. Laws.* 73–131.

75. Florida, Department of Administration, Division of State Planning, Bureau of Land Planning, *Final Report and Recommendations for the Big Cypress Area of Critical State Concern to the State of Florida Administration Commission*, October 1973, p. 12 (hereafter cited as *Big Cypress Report*).

76. *Big Cypress Report*, pp. 2–3, and Carter, *Florida Experience*, pp. 249–51.

77. Carter, *Florida Experience*, pp. 249–51, and *Big Cypress Report*, pp. 2 and 3.

78. Myers, *A Slow Start in Paradise*, as quoted from the *Immokalee Bulletin*, September 6, 1973, p. 23.

79. Carter, *Florida Experience*, pp. 254–57.

80. Ibid.

81. Interview with Governor Reubin O D. Askew on June 10, 1978.

82. Florida, Department of Administration, Division of State Planning, Bureau of Land Planning, *Final Report and Recommendations for the Proposed Green Swamp Area of Critical State Concern: Lake and Polk Counties, Florida*, June 1974, p. 23.

83. Ibid., pp. 37–40.

84. Stephen Fox, "Florida Areas of Critical State Concern: An Update," *Florida Environmental and Urban Issues* 5: 4 (April 1978): 7.

85. Florida, Department of Administration, Division of State Planning, Bureau of Land and Water Management, *Final Report and Recommendations*

for the Proposed Florida Keys Area of Critical State Concern, December 1974, pp. 2, 8 (hereafter cited as *Florida Keys Report*).

86. *Florida Keys Report*, pp. 33–39.

87. Ibid., pp. 42–45.

88. Ibid., pp. 45–46.

89. Ibid., pp. 46.

90. Author's notes on the designation hearing. The administration commission designated the Florida Keys as an area of critical state concern on April 15, 1975.

91. Dr. Nino J. Spagna, letter to the author, August 2, 1978.

92. Telephone interview with Jim May on July 7, 1982.

93. F.S., Section 380.0552(4). See also Department of Veterans and Community Affairs, "Recommendation Concerning the Green Swamp Area of Critical State Concern" (Tallahassee, Florida: Department of Veterans and Community Affairs, June 1982), p. 1.

94. Florida, Department of Legal Affairs, Office of the Attorney General, Letter to the Honorable Joan Heggen, Secretary, Department of Veteran and Community Affairs, *Re: areas of critical state concern*, March 25, 1982.

95. Letter charge from Florida Governor Bob Graham to chairman, Green Swamp Planning and Management Committee, September 29, 1981.

96. DVCA, *Recommendation Concerning The Green Swamp Area of Critical State Concern*, pp. 1–2.

97. Ibid., p. 2.

98. Interview with Ted Forsgren, Critical Areas Unit, Bureau of Land and Water Management, Division of State Planning, Tallahassee, Florida, April 5, 1978, and with Governor Reubin O D. Askew on June 10, 1978.

99. Personal communication from Kermit Lewin to the author on August 3, 1978.

100. Personal communication from William L. Keefer to the author on August 5, 1978.

101. Interview with Jim May on May 13, 1982.

102. *Fla. Stat.* § 380.045 (2).

103. The Florida Keys Resource Planning and Management Committee, *Florida Keys Area of Critical State Concern: An Assessment of the Comprehensive Plans and Critical Area Regulations, with Recommendations*, February 1982, Introduction pp. 1–2, and *A Review of the Comprehensive Plans and Critical Area Regulations by the T.A.C.*, January 1982.

104. Florida Department of Veterans and Community Affairs, *Recommendations Concerning the Florida Keys Area of Critical State Concern* to the administration commission, undated, p. 2.

105. Ibid, p. 7.

105A. Florida Administration Commission, *Agenda: Florida Keys Area of Critical State Concern*, June 29, 1982, p. 1.

105B. Ibid., p. 2.

106. City of Key West, Ordinances 76–8 and 76–112. The Florida Land and Water Adjudicatory Commission denied the appeal of Ordinance 76–9 on November 29, 1977.

107. At a meeting of the administration commission August 3, 1982, the state land planning agency reported that it would immediately place one full-time person in each of Monroe County's three suboffices concerned with planning, zoning and development for monitoring and enforcement and technical assistance purposes. However, this action will be for two to

four weeks. Lack of staff prevents any permanent assignment of such staff in the field.

108. Florida, Sixteenth Judicial Circuit, *Final Report of the Grand Jury*, Fall Term, 1981, p. 2–3.

109. Ibid., pp. 5–6.

110. Ibid., pp. 11–12.

111. Major development in Monroe County includes: (1) a subdivision or plat of 5 acres or more of land and/or water; (2) a zoning change of 5 acres or more of land and/or water area; a planned unit development of 5 acres or more of land and/or water area; (4) buildings in excess of 45 feet; (5) a development involving 10 or more units per acre density or a total of 50 or more dwelling units; (6) any nonresidential activity involving 5 acres or more of land and/or water area. Any other activity can be designated a major development if it is judged to fall within a series of additional criteria which are essentially judgmental rather than quantitative in character. See Florida Keys Resource Planning and Management Committee, *An Assessment of Local Governments' Implementation of Land Use Regulations*, June 18, 1982, pp. 27–29.

112. Ibid., pp. 30–32.

113. Ibid., pp. 32–34.

114. Ibid., p. 39.

115. Ibid., p. 53.

116. Ibid., p. 59.

117. Telephone interviews with Jim May, on July 7, 1982 and July 15, 1982, and personal interview on July 23, 1982; and author's notes as a participant in the 1981 effort. Acting on the recommendation of his Environmental Land Management Study Committee, Governor Graham has included in his fiscal 1983 budget about $800,000 and 13 new positions to strengthen the State Land Planning Agency.

118. Letters dated October 26, 1981; January 19, 1982; January 20, 1982 and June 22, 1982 from the state land planning agency, all addressed to the Monroe County Building, Planning and Zoning Department except the January 20 letter, addressed to the "Mayor, Monroe County."

119. Charlotte Harbor Resource Planning and Management Committee, *Charlotte Harbor Management Plan*, adopted June 5, 1981, available through the Department of Community Affairs, Tallahassee, Florida; see also Division of State Planning, Bureau of Land and Water Management, *Charlotte Harbor: A Florida Resource* (Tallahassee, Florida, 1978).

120. Ibid., objective 15.

121. *Resolution of Charlotte Harbor Resource Planning and Management Committee*, December 11, 1981, p. 1.

122. Ibid.

123. Ibid., p. 2.

124. Interview with Jim May on July 15, 1982. Subsequent developments in Lee County involving the appointment by the governor of two new county commissioners have resulted in the county's adopting the required regulations.

125. Interview with Jim May on July 15, 1982. All 11 counties subsequently adopted the required regulations.

126. Florida, Department of Administration, Division of State Planning, Bureau of Land and Water Management, *Developments of Regional Impact Summary of the First Five Years*, 1979, and data supplied by Department of

Community Affairs, Division of Local Resource Management, Bureau of Land and Water Management.

127. Developments of regional impact are defined in the Florida Administrative Code, ch. 27F–2.01 through .12, formerly Rule 22F–2.01 through .12. Rule numbers and abbreviated definitions are *27F–2.01, Airports*. Any new airport, new runway or runway extension as defined in the Federal Airport and Airway Development Act of 1970; *2.02, Attractions and Recreational Facilities*. Sports arenas, stadiums, race tracks, tourist attractions and similar facilities with parking for 2,500 or more cars or seats for more than 10,000, with lower numbers for serial performance facilities; *2.03, Electrical Generating Facilities and Transmission Lines*. Any steam electrical generating facility of greater than 100 megawatts and any electrical transmission line with a capacity greater than 230 kilovolts that crosses a county line; *2.04, Hospitals*. 600 beds or more or where designed to serve more than one county. *2.05, Industrial Plants and Industrial Parks*. Parking for more than 1,500 motor vehicles or greater than one square mile. *2.06, Mining Operations*. Area greater than 100 acres or water consumption of more than 3,000,000 gallons per day; *2.07, Office Parks*. Occupies more than 30 acres of land, or involves more than 300,000 square feet of gross floor area; *2.08, Petroleum Storage Facilities*. Facility within 1,000 feet of a navigable waterway with a storage capacity of over 50,000 barrels and any other facility with a storage capacity of over 200,000 barrels; *2.09, Port Facilities*. Any water port except those designed primarily for watercraft used exclusively for sport or pleasure with fewer than 100 slips; *2.10, Residential Developments*. A DRI is triggered according to a sliding scale where the higher the population of a county, the greater the number of units required to trigger a DRI, ranging from 250 dwelling units in counties with a population of less than 25,000 to 3,000,000 dwelling units in counties of over 500,000 population. *2.11, Schools*. Any public or private post-secondary educational campus planned for more than 3,000 full-time equivalent students; *2.12, Shopping Centers*. Any wholesale or retail business establishment occupying more than 40 acres or encompassing more than 400,000 square feet, or providing parking spaces for more than 2,500 cars.

128. *Developments of Regional Impact Summary.*

129. Ibid., pp. 13–15, and data furnished by the Bureau of Land and Water Management.

130. Ibid., pp. 15–16, 18.

131. Ibid., p. 17, and data furnished by the Bureau of Land and Water Management.

132. Ibid., pp. 17–19.

133. For a discussion of the issue and the cases involved, see Thomas G. Pelham, *State Land Use Planning and Regulation*, (Lexington, Mass.: D.C. Heath and Co., 1979), pp. 54–56.

134. The governor's office is sponsoring an effort to develop a set of resource (growth) management policies that will serve as the first component of the complete integrated policy system.

135. For another evaluation of the effectiveness of DRI process, see Healy and Rosenberg, *Land Use and the States*, pp. 144–65; and Thomas G. Pelham, *State Land-Use Planning and Regulation* (Lexington, Mass.: D.C. Heath & Co., Lexington Books, 1979), pp. 26–63.

136. Pelham, *State Land Use Planning and Regulation*, pp. 26–63.

137. Ibid.

138. Daniel H. Dennison, "The DRI Process: A Developer's View," *Florida Environmental and Urban Issues* 3: 2 (December 1975): 9. For a response to this article, see James W. May, "The DRI Process: A State View," *Florida Environmental and Urban Issues* 3: 4 (April 1976): 11.

139. *General Development Corporation* v. *Division of State Planning*, Fla. App., 353 So. 2d, pp. 1207–08. Rule 22F2 has been changed to Rule 27F2. 1–12.

140. Interview with Jim May, April 5, 1978.

141. Data supplied by the Bureau of Land and Water Management.

142. *Graham* v. *Estuary Properties, Inc.*, 399 So. 2d 1374 (Sla. 1981). For a discussion of the First District Court of Appeal decision, see Finnell, "Coastal Land Management," pp. 387–93. Professor Finnell urged the Florida Supreme Court to reverse the district court decision.

143. Florida League of Cities, "Florida League of Cities Survey," Tallahassee, Florida, 1974.

144. *Florida Municipal Record*, April 1978, pp. 10–11. See also Daniel W. O'Connell, "Status Report: Local Government Comprehensive Planning Act of 1975," *Florida Environmental and Urban Issues* 4: 3 (February 1977): 8–11. Latest data from the Bureau of Land and Water Management, courtesy of Bob Kessler in telephone interview on August 24, 1982. By May 1983, all but one county had plans in place.

145. For a summary of early activities by the Central and Southern Florida Flood Control District in reviewing DRIs, see "Report to the Governing Board on DRI Activities and DRI Procedures," Resource Planning Department, November 1974.

146. Jon M. Ausman, "Chapter 380 Mandated Actors, Actor Interactions, Roles and Relationships in Southeast Florida: Six Studies" (Masters thesis, Florida Atlantic University, available through the FAU-FIU Joint Center for Environmental and Urban Problems, 1976), pp. 45–51.

147. Ibid.

148. The South Florida Regional Planning Council was fortunate to have the former chairman of the Environmental Land Management Study Committee as its legal counsel during this period.

149. Broward County, Florida, *Resolution Amending Development Order of April 8, 1976 Relating to the Entire Arvida Corporation, Indian Trace Development of Regional Impact*, undated, p. 4.

150. Ibid., p. 4–5.

151. Lee O. Stepanchak, "The DRI Process: A Study of Local Government Response in Broward County" (Masters thesis, Florida Atlantic University, available through the FAU-FIU Joint Center for Environmental and Urban Problems, 1515 West Commercial Boulevard, Fort Lauderdale, Florida, March 1976). Also, George Griffith, Jr., "Planning Without Regulations: Troubled Path of the DRI Regional Development Condition," (Masters thesis, Florida Atlantic University, also available from the FAU-FIU Joint Center, December 1974), p. 77.

152. The governor's Task Force on Resource Management recommended and the legislature accepted a change in section 6, chapter 380 strengthening the monitoring and oversight function. The responsibility of local government in monitoring approved development conditions was clarified. In addition, annual reports were required by the developer of a DRI to be submitted to the affected local, regional, and state agencies. Failure to submit such a report would result in the temporary suspension of the

development order. See *Florida Environmental and Urban Issues*, Nancy E. Stroud, "The Second Generation Legislation for Developments of Regional Impact," 8:1 (October 1980): 3, 10–14.

153. Gary L. Rawlinson, Jr., "Dade County's Development Impact Committee," *Florida Environmental and Urban Issues* 4: 5 (June 1977): 13.

154. Ibid., pp. 14–15.

155. Interview with Jay Landers on April 5, 1978.

156. Interview with Governor Reubin O D. Askew on June 10, 1978.

157. Interview with Reubin O D. Askew on June 10, 1978.

158. The governor's Resource Management Task Force recommended such a move in its final report in 1980.

159. Nancy E. Stroud, "The Second Generation Legislation for Developments of Regional Impact, *Florida Environmental and Urban Issues* 8: 1 (October 1980): 3, 10–14; and Stroud, "Regionalism Reaffirmed: The 1980 Florida Regional Planning Council Act," *Florida Environmental and Urban Issues* 8: 1 (October 1980): 2–3, 19–23.

160. Florida Department of Community Affairs, *Florida Keys Area of Critical State Concern*, February 1, 1983. Available from the Department of Community Affairs.

Chapter Five. California:
Planning and Managing the Coast

1. California Council for Environmental and Economic Balance, *An Economic Profile of the California Coastal Zone* (San Francisco: 215 Market Street, Suite 930, July 1975), pp. 2–9.

2. Janet Adams, "Proposition 20: A Citizen's Campaign," *Syracuse Law Review* 24: 3 (Summer 1973): 1019–20.

3. Ibid., pp. 1019–21.

4. Ibid., pp. 1021–22.

5. Robert G. Healy, *Land Use and the States* (Baltimore, Md.: Johns Hopkins University Press, 1976), pp. 64–69. See also Robert G. Healy and John S. Rosenberg, *Land Use and the States*, 2d ed. (Baltimore, Md.: Johns Hopkins University Press, 1979), pp. 80–85. The population of California in 1970 was 19,971,000. By 1980, it had increased to 23,510,000 for a percentage increase in the decade of 17.7 percent.

6. Interviews with Janet Adams, head, California Coastal Alliance, on November 29, 1976, and Larry Moss, director, Planning and Conservation League, on December 3, 1976. For a further discussion of problems that led to far-reaching action to plan and manage California's coast, see Peter M. ·Douglas and Joseph E. Petrillo, "California's Coast: The Struggle Today—A Plan for Tomorrow," Florida State University *Law Review* 4: 2 (April 1976): 179–84; and Adams, "Proposition 20," pp. 1022–23.

7. Adams, "Proposition 20," pp. 1024–25. For a description of the unsuccessful legislative struggle and the initiative campaign, see William T. Duddleson, "How the Citizens of California Secured Their Coastal Management Program," in *Protecting The Golden Shore: Lessons From The California Coastal Commissions* edited by Robert G. Healy (Washington, D.C.: The Conservation Foundation, 1978), pp. 1–15.

8. Ibid., pp. 1028–29.

9. Ibid., pp. 1027–28.

10. Ibid., pp. 1030–31.

11. Ibid., pp. 1031–32, and interview with Janet Adams on November 29, 1976.

12. Interview with Janet Adams, on November 29, 1976.

13. Janet Adams, "Proposition 20," pp. 1034–36.

14. Ibid., p. 1033.

15. Ibid., p. 1037.

16. Ibid., pp. 1038–40.

17. Janet Adams, "Proposition 20," p. 1036, note 34.

18. Ibid., p. 1041.

19. Interview with Larry Moss on December 3, 1976. See also Healy and Rosenberg, *Land Use and the States*, pp. 87–89.

20. *California Public Resources Code.* Division 18, § 27200 California Coastal Zone Conservation Commission (West Supp. 1973).

21. Ibid., Chapter 3, Article 1, § 27201.

22. Ibid., Chapter 4, Article 2, § 27320.

23. Ibid., Chapter 4, Article 1, § 27302.

24. Ibid., Chapter 2, § 27100.

25. Ibid., Chapter 4, Article 2, § 27320.

26. Ibid., Chapter 5, Article 1, § 27402.

27. Ibid., Chapter 5, Artice 1, §§ 27400, 27401, 27402.

28. Ibid., Chapter 5, Article 1, §§ 27400 & 27401.

29. Ibid, § 4.

30. Douglas and Petrillo, "California's Coast," p. 188.

31. Ibid.

32. Ibid., pp. 189–90.

33. Ibid., p. 190.

34. See Douglas and Petrillo, "California's Coast," for a good treatment of the content of the 1972 Coastal Act, especially pp. 184–91. See Adams, "Proposition 20," pp. 1043–46, for a summary of the content of the 1972 law. See Healy and Rosenberg, *Land Use and the States*, pp. 85–89, for comments on the passage and content of proposition 20. Data in the earlier sections were also taken from interviews by the author with Janet Adams, Peter Douglas, and Norbert Dahl. Douglas at the time of the interview was a member of the legislative staff of Assemblyman Charles Warren (D., LA), chairman of the Assembly Select Committee on Coastal Resources. For a complete text of the California Coastal Zone Conservation Act of 1972, see California Coastal Zone Conservation Commission, *California Coastal Plan*, December 1975, appendix IV, pp. 431–34.

35. There is some evidence that the longer the coastal program stayed in existence, the more problems developed with other state agencies. See John S. Banta, "The Coastal Commissions and State Agencies: Conflict and Cooperation," pp. 98–131, in Healy, *Protecting the Golden Shore* (Washington, D.C.: The Conservation Foundation, 1978) and the treatment of the problem in the post-1976 period later in this chapter.

36. Douglas and Petrillo, "California's Coast," part 1, pp. 195–99.

37. It is interesting to note that this broad approval with the liberal use of conditions approach has also been used in almost every other state that has gone into the permitting side of managing land. Certainly this is true in Vermont and Florida, both of which have a substantial implementation record involving different types of permitting activity.

38. Interview with Joseph Petrillo, former head, Permit Division, Coastal

Commission, Sacramento, California, December 2, 1976.

39. Ibid.; see also Healy and Rosenberg, *Land Use and the States*, p. 90.

40. Interview with Joe Petrillo on December 2, 1976.

41. Ibid.

42. Ibid.

43. Interview with Janet Adams on November 29, 1976.

44. Interview with Mike Fischer, executive director, North Central Regional Commission, Sacramento, California, on December 2 and 3, 1976.

45. California Coastal Commission, *Coastal News* 4: 4 (June/July 1981): 2.

46. Ibid., and telephone interview with Mike Fischer, executive director, California Coastal Commission, July 7, 1982.

47. Interview with Norbert Dahl, Sierra Club coordinator, on December 3, 1976.

48. Interview with Larry Moss on December 3, 1976.

49. As will be detailed later, the state coastal commission proposed legislation approved by the 1979 legislature that exempts many of these single family projects.

50. Douglas and Petrillo, "California's Coast: The Struggle Today—A Plan for Tomorrow," part II, Florida State University *Law Review* 4:3 (October 1976): 177.

51. Ibid.

52. For a more extensive discussion of the question of the grandfather clause, see Douglas and Petrillo, "California's Coast," part I, pp. 203–5, and Healy and Rosenberg, *Land Use and the States*, pp. 90–91.

53. Douglas and Petrillo, "California's Coast," pp. 205–6.

54. Ibid. pp. 209–11, and Healy, *Land Use and the States*, p. 76.

55. Douglas and Petrillo, "California's Coast," p. 211. For a discussion of the effectiveness of citizen appeals to bring "recalcitrant" local governments and regional commissions into line with the goals of the act, see Duddleson, "How Citizens Secured Coastal Programs," pp. 30–32.

56. Douglas and Petrillo, "California's Coast," pp. 211–12.

57. Ibid., p. 213 and 217.

58. Ibid., p. 218; and Healy and Rosenberg, *Land Use and the States*, pp. 91–93.

59. Douglas and Petrillo, "California's Coast," part I, pp. 218–20.

60. Healy and Rosenberg, *Land Use and the States*, pp. 93–106.

61. Douglas and Petrillo, "California's Coast," part I, p. 223. (The further development of this policy in the post-1976 period will be developed later.)

62. Ibid., pp. 220–22. (The further development of the agricultural land protection policy in the post-1976 period will be assessed later.)

63. Ibid., pp. 222–23. See also Healy and Rosenberg, *Land Use and the States*, pp. 93–97. (Important new initiatives in this area taken in 1979 will be treated later.)

64. Douglas and Petrillo, "California's Coast," part I, pp. 226–27.

65. Ibid., pp. 228–29.

66. For a further assessment of the impact of proposition 20, especially the permitting process over the 1973–76 period, see Douglas and Petrillo, "California's Coast," part II, vol. 4: 3 (October 19, 1976): 329–41, for evaluations of such things as the concept of property rights, attitudes about the use of coastal resources, the impact of property values, the economic effects of proposition 20, and social equity and public use issues. In a general way, the conclusions were that effects on property values were mixed, with

increases in the value of developed property and undeveloped property in urban areas, and some at least temporary negative impacts on the value of undeveloped property in nonurban areas. It was also noted that the economic impacts of proposition 20 were almost impossible to separate from the economic impacts that came from a number of other sources. See also Healy and Rosenberg, *Land Use and the States*, pp. 89–106, for assessments including, in addition to those already cited, density and growth, the natural environment, and energy and the coastline. For an extended discussion of the economic property rights and land values, see Healy, "An Economic Interpretation of the California Coastal Commissions," pp. 133–75, in *Protecting the Golden Shore: Lessons from the California Coastal Commissions*, ed. by Robert G. Healy (Washington, D.C.: The Conservation Foundation, 1978).

67. Donald M. Pach, "The Coastal Plan and the Property Owner," in *The California Coastal Plan: A Critique* (San Francisco: Institute for Contemporary Studies, 1976), p. 139.

68. For a review of the regulation effort under proposition 20, see Duddleson, "How Citizens Secured Their Coastal Program," pp. 21–32. See also Healy, "The Role of the Permit System in the California Coastal Strategy," in Healy, *Protecting the Golden Shore:*, pp. 67–95, for a thoughtful discussion of the impact of the permitting process on the development of the coastal plan in the 1973–1975 period.

69. *California Coastal Plan*, December 1975, p. 4.

70. Ibid. See also Healy and Rosenberg, *Land Use and the States*, pp. 107–11.

71. *California Coastal Plan*, p. 68.

72. The 11 elements were marine environment, coastal land environment, coastal appearance and design, coastal development, energy, transportation, public access to the coast, recreation, education and scientific use, restoration of coastal resources,and public acquisition of coastal land.

73. *California Coastal Plan*, pp. 84–89.

74. Ibid., pp. 91–138.

75. Ibid., pp. 209–10. The continuing controversy over Sea Ranch was discussed earlier.

76. Ibid., pp. 209–10. The California Coastal Plan in its entirety constitutes almost 450 pages of double-columned detailed text and maps. It is a remarkably comprehensive and detailed document worthy of careful study by anyone interested in land use and growth management approaches. Its significance is by no means confined to coastal areas, since many of the findings of fact, policies and implementation techniques would be equally applicable to inland areas. The plan is available from the California Coastal Commission, 1514 Market Street, Second Floor, San Francisco, California 94102. For an assessment of the planning process under proposition 20, see Duddleson, "How Citizens Secured Coastal Programs," pp. 32–45.

77. Interview with Janet Adams on November 29, 1976.

78. Ibid.

79. Interview with Norbert Dahl on December 3, 1976.

80. Interview with Bob Testa, staff director of the California Senate Natural Resources and Wildlife Committee, on December 2, 1976.

81. Ibid.

82. Ibid.

83. Ibid.

84. Ibid., and interview with Peter Douglas on December 2, 1976.

85. Interview with Peter Douglas on December 2, 1976.

86. Interview with Norbert Dahl on December 3, 1976.

87. Ibid.

88. Ibid.

89. Interview with Bob Testa on December 2, 1976.

90. California Research, *State Coastal Report*, Sacramento, California: 1024 Tenth Street, Suite 300, August–September 1976, p. 2. For an excellent review and evaluation of the California Coastal Act of 1976 see Gilbert L. Finnell, "Coastal Land Management In California," *American Bar Foundation Research Journal* 1978: 4 (Fall): 717–33.

91. Interview with Janet Adams on November 29, 1976.

92. Ibid.

93. California Research, *State Coastal Report*, August–September 1976, p. 2.

94. U.S., Department of Commerce, National Oceanic and Atmospheric Administration, Office of Coastal Zone Management, *California Coastal Management Program and Final Environmental Impact Statement*, appendix II, "State Coastal Conservancy Act of 1976" (Washington, D.C.: Department of Commerce, NOAA, OCZM, 1977), pp. 2–1 through 2–8.

95. California Coastal Commission, "Local Coastal Program Manual: Supplement No. 1," appendix B (September 30, 1977), pp. B–3.

96. California Coastal Commission, *Coastal News* 1: 7 (October 1978): 5.

97. Stanley Scott, "Coastal Planning in California: A Progress Report," *Public Affairs Report*, a bulletin of the Institute of Governmental Studies, University of California, Berkeley 19: 3–4 (June–August 1978): 9, and "Local Coastal Program Manual: Supplement No. 1," appendix B, pp. B–1 and B–2.

98. Interview with Janet Adams on November 29, 1976.

99. Ibid.

100. Interview with Bob Testa on December 2, 1976.

101. Interview with Norbert Dahl on December 3, 1976.

102. Interview with Larry Moss on December 3, 1976.

103. Interview with Mike Fischer on December 2 and 3, 1976.

104. Ibid. For a detailed discussion of the relationships between the Coastal Commission and other state agencies, see John S. Banta, "Coastal Commissions and State Agencies," pp. 97–131. The discussion covers the period 1973–76.

105. Interview with Mike Peevey, executive director of the California Council for Environmental and Economic Balance, November 29, 1976.

106. Ibid.

107. Ibid.

108. Interview with Tim Leslie, land use specialist, California County Supervisor's Association, Sacramento, California, on December 3, 1976.

109. Ibid.

110. Ibid.

111. It is reprinted in *California Coastal Management Program*, appendix I, "The California Coastal Act of 1976," pp. 1–38.

112. *Cal. Pub. Res. Code.* Division 20, §§ 30000–30001.2.

113. Ibid., § 30001.5.

114. Ibid., ch. 4 §§ 30300–30302.

115. Ibid., §§ 30400–30404.

116. Ibid., Chapter 6, Article 1, §§ 30500–30504; Article 2, §§ 30510–30522;

Chapter 7, Article 1, §§ 30600–30611; Article 2, §§ 20620–20626. This summary of the content of the law was taken from the law as reproduced in the *Combined State of California Coastal Management Program (Segment) and Final Environmental Impact Statement* (United States, Department of Commerce, Office of Coastal Zone Management, National Oceanic and Atmospheric Administration, and the California Coastal Commission, August 1977).

117. Ibid., §§ 30500–30502.

118. Ibid., § 30502–5.

119. Ibid., § 30602.

120. Ibid., §§ 30603 and 30604(d).

121. Ibid., § 30610.

122. Ibid., § 30610.5.

123. California Coastal Commission, *Public Hearing Draft of Interpretative Guidelines for Coastal Planning and Permits* (San Francisco, California: 1540 Market Street, February 11, 1977).

124. California Coastal Commission, *Interpretative Guidelines*, adopted May 3, 1977.

125. California Coastal Commission *Local Coastal Program Regulations*, adopted May 17, 1977.

126. California Coastal Commission, *Coastal News* 1: 1 (December 1977): 1.

127. *Coastal News* 1: 2 (January 1978): 3.

128. *Coastal News* 1: 5 (July 1978): 4–5.

129. *Coastal News* 1: 6 (September 1978): 3.

130. *Coastal News* 1: 7 (October 1978): 5.

131. *Coastal News* 2: 1 (January/February 1979): 3.

132. Healy and Rosenberg, *Land Use and the States*, pp. 114–16. See Finnell, "Coastal Land Management in California," for an assessment of the LCP approach and problems that were apt to emerge, pp. 734–38.

133. Scott, "Coastal Planning in California," p. 4.

134. Ibid., pp. 2–5. See also Healy and Rosenberg, *Land Use and the States*, pp. 116–19.

135. *Coastal News* 3: 1 (January/February 1980): 6.

136. Ibid.

137. Ibid., p. 8.

138. *Coastal News* 2: 5 (June 1979): 3. It is interesting to note that Sea Ranch was the subject of one of the hearings.

139. Ibid., p. 3.

140. *Coastal News* 2: 10 (November 1979): 1.

141. Ibid., 3: 2 (March/April 1980): 5.

142. Ibid., p. 2.

143. Ibid., pp. 4–5.

144. *Coastal News* 3: 1 (January/February 1980): 3.

145. Ibid.

146. Ibid.

147. *Coastal News* 2: 4 (May 1979): 3.

148. *Coastal News* 4: 2 (March 1981): 2.

149. *Coastal News* 4: 5 (August 1981): 4–5.

150. *Coastal News* 4: 7 (November/December 1981): 5.

151. Telephone interview with Mike Fischer on June 24, 1982.

152. *Coastal News* 4: 7 (November/December 1981): 4, and telephone

interview with Mike Fischer on June 24, 1982 and July 7, 1982.

153. *Coastal News* 3: 2 (March/April 1980): 5.

154. *Coastal News* 3: 1 (January/February 1980): 3.

155. *Coastal News* 4: 4 (June/July 1981): 2, and telephone interview with Mike Fischer on July 7, 1982.

156. U.S. Office of Coastal Zone Management, *Evaluation Findings for the California Coastal Zone Management Program for the Period from September 1980 to November 1981*, pp. 15–16.

157. Ibid.

158. See *Coastal News* 3: 6 (October/November 1980) for *Joint Staff Report, California Coastal Commission/State Coastal Conservancy, Standards and Recommendations for Coastal Access*, and *Coastal News* 4: 1 (January 1981), for a progress report on implementing the program.

159. OCZM, Evaluation Findings, California Coastal Program, September 1980–November 1981, p. 16.

160. Telephone interview with Mike Fischer on July 7, 1982.

161. *Coastal News* 4: 6 (September/October 1981), and telephone interview with Mike Fischer on July 7, 1982.

162. See *Coastal News* 4: 4 (June/July 1981): 7, for a report on legislation midway in the session.

163. *Coastal News* 4: 7 (November/December 1981): 4.

164. Telephone interview with Mike Fischer on July 7, 1982.

165. *Coastal News* 4: 7 (November/December 1981): 4. The interpretation of the impact of the changes are the author's.

166. Ibid., and OCZM, *Evaluation Findings, California Coastal Management*, September 1980–November 1981, p. 2.

167. Telephone interview with Mike Fischer on July 7, 1982.

168. See Healy and Rosenberg, *Land Use and the States*, pp. 119–20.

169. Telephone interview with Mike Fischer on July 7, 1982.

170. Ibid.

Chapter Six. Oregon:
A Blend of State and Local Initiatives

1. Interview with Steve Schell, former member, Land Conservation and Development Commission, Portland Oregon, September 7, 1976.

2. Charles E. Little, *The New Oregon Trail: An Account of the Development and Passage of State Land-Use Legislation in Oregon* (Washington, D.C.: The Conservation Foundation, 1974), p. 11.

3. Ibid.

4. Interview with Henry Richmond, executive director, 1,000 Friends of Oregon, Portland, Oregon, September 9, 1976.

5. Little, *New Oregon Trail*, p. 13.

6. Ibid., p. 12.

7. Interview with Bill Young, director, Division of Intergovernmental Relations, Office of the Governor, Salem, Oregon, September 8, 1976. Young was later director, Oregon Department of Environmental Quality.

8. As quoted in Little, *New Oregon Trail*, p. 7.

9. *Or. Rev. Stat.* § 459.810 (1971).

10. *Or. Rev. Stat.* § 366.514 (1971).

11. Or. *Const.* art. XI-H created through House Joint Resolution no. 14,

1969, and adopted by the people. Enacted in *Or. Rev. Stat.*—468.197, et seq. (1969), May 26, 1970.

12. *Or. Rev. Stat.* 390.605, et seq. (1967).

13. *Or. Rev. Stat.* § 377.705, et seq. (1971). These laws are summarized in Little, *New Oregon Trail*, p. 8.

14. Interviews with Steve Schell on September 7, 1976. For the Scenic Rivers bill, see *Or. Rev. Stat.* § 390.805, et seq. (1971).

15. *Or. Rev. Stat.* § 215.515.

16. Interview with Jerry Orrick, executive director, Association of Oregon Counties, Salem, Oregon, September 8, 1976.

17. Interview with Hector Macpherson, former state senator and agriculturalist, on September 8, 1976, and with Steven Bauer, assistant executive director, Oregon League of Cities, on August 4, 1976.

18. *Or. Rev. Stat.*, § 191.110–180.

19. This account of the drafting and redrafting process is based on interviews with Hector Macpherson, L. B. Day, and Steve Schell.

20. Little, *New Oregon Trail*, pp. 19–20.

21. Interview with Steve Schell on September 7, 1976.

22. Interview with Bill Young on September 8, 1976.

23. Interviews with Jerry Orrick and Don Jones, executive director, League of Oregon Cities, on September 8, 1976.

24. Interview with William Moshofsky, vice president, Georgia-Pacific, on September 9, 1976.

25. Interview by Jim Coke with Fred VanNatta, executive officer, Oregon State Homebuilders Association, on August 4, 1976.

26. Little, *New Oregon Trail*, p. 16.

27. Ibid., p. 17.

28. *Or. Rev. Stat.*, § 197. See also *Oregon Land Use Legislation*, vol. 1: *Analysis*, senate bill 100, p. 100–8, prepared by the Local Government Relations Division, executive department and the Oregon State University Extension Service, 1974. This publication, along with volume 2: *Enacted Bills* which contains the actual legislation including senate bill 100 that was passed by the Oregon legislature in 1973 that had a bearing on land use, constitutes an invaluable documentary source in tracing the development of land use initiatives in Oregon.

29. Senate bill 769 was passed during the 1973 session and provided for a regional mechanism to act as the local integrative unit for the Portland metropolitan area.

30. The Metropolitan Service District is the nation's first regional agency with a directly elected governing board. It was authorized by the legislature (*Or. Laws*, ch 665) in 1977 and subsequently approved by the voters.

31. See senate bill 570 (1977), and senate bill 435 (1978).

32. *Or. Rev. Stat.*, §§ 197.325 and 197.330.

33. *Or. Rev. Stat.*, §§ 197.125, 197.130, 197.135.

34. *Or. Rev. Stat.*, § 197.160.

35. Ibid., §§ 197.705–197.795. As noted earlier, CRAG was replaced by the Metropolitan Service District in 1978.

36. Ibid., § 197.190.

37. *Oregon Land Use Legislation*, vol. 1, pp. 100–12 and 100–13. See also *Or. Rev. Stat.* §§ 197.225–197.285. A 1977 amendment to the law defined guidelines by statute.

38. Ibid.

39. *Or. Rev. Stat.*, §§ 197.040–197.060. One view is that the LCDC will address the critical area and activities of statewide significance issues after the process of preparing and acknowledging comprehensive plans is completed.

40. Ibid., § 197.300.

41. Ibid., § 197.080.

42. Arnold Cogan, "Oregon . . . Took Giant Steps Toward Sound State Land Use Planning," *AIP Newsletter*, July 1975, p. 9.

43. Ibid.

44. Interview with Henry Richmond on September 9, 1976.

45. Interview with Hector Macpherson on September 8, 1976.

46. Interview with Bill Young on September 8, 1976.

47. Interview with L. B. Day on September 8, 1976.

48. Interview with Steve Schell on September 7, 1976.

49. Interview with Henry Richmond on September 9, 1976.

50. Cogan, "Oregon," p. 9; and U.S. Department of Commerce, National Oceanic and Atmospheric Administration, Office of Coastal Zone Management, *Oregon Coastal Management Program of 1976*, p. 391 (Oregon Land Conservation and Development Commission, 1175 Court St. N.E., Salem, OR 97310, financed through a Program Development Grant under the Coastal Zone Management Act of 1972, administered by the Office of Coastal Zone Management); and undated summary of *Or. Rev. Stat.*, § 197, p. 4, furnished to the author by the LCDC staff.

51. A complete text of all goals and guidelines, 1 through 19, is found in Oregon, Land Conservation and Development Commission, *Statewide Planning Goals and Guidelines*, n.d.

52. The following elaboration of certain LCDC goals is adapted from John M. DeGrove and Nancy E. Stroud, *Oregon's State Urban Strategy*, prepared for the National Academy of Public Administration (Washington, D.C.: U.S. Government Printing Office and the Department of Housing and Urban Development, HUD-PDR 644, December 1980).

53. Interview with Dale Blanton, plan review specialist, Department of Land Conservation and Development, on August 8, 1979.

54. For a detailed discussion of LCDC acknowledgement policies regarding goal 14, see W. J. Kvorsten, executive director, Department of Land Conservation and Development, unpublished memorandum to city and county officials, planning staffs and local coordinators re: detailed discussion of LCDC acknowledgement policies regarding goal 14, February 16, 1979, noting LCDC concurrence with parts of a February 2, 1979 memorandum, Kvorsten to the commission.

55. For a further discussion of population projection issues, see Oregon Department of Land Conservation and Development, "Population Projection Issues: Briefing Paper," n.d. See also Oregon, Department of Land Conservation and Development, memorandum, June 21, 1979.

56. Oregon, Land Conservation and Development Commission, draft memorandum, "Common Questions on Urban Development," June 20, 1979, pp. 6–13.

57. Oregon, Land Conservation and Development Commission, "Housing Policy," adopted July 12, 1979.

58. For a full discussion of the LCDC policies that guide the implementation of goal 11, see LCDC draft memorandum "Common Questions on Urban Development," June 20, 1979, pp. 3–6.

59. For a full discussion of policies guiding the implementation of the agricultural goal, see Oregon, Land Conservation and Development Commission, memorandum, "Common Questions about Goal 3—Agricultural Land," n.d.

60. Oregon legislative assembly, 1979 regular session, Senate bill 435, June 28, 1978.

61. Interviews with Henry Richmond on October 21, 1981, and Mike Reynolds, chief hearing officer, LUBA, Salem, Oregon, October 23, 1981.

62. Oregon, Land Conservation and Development Commission, staff, *Summary of Or. Rev. Stat., chapter 197*, n.d., pp. 5–6.

63. Ibid.

64. The emergency board is an executive group that acts on certain matters when the legislature is not in session.

65. 1,000 Friends of Oregon, *Progress Report*, Fall 1975. This detailed handbook produced a very negative reaction from some local governments, especially smaller cities.

66. 1,000 Friends of Oregon, *Newsletter* 1: 4 (January 1976): 5.

67. Ibid.

68. 1,000 Friends of Oregon, *Newsletter* 1: 7 (April 1976): 6.

69. Ibid.

70. Ibid. In several other places in Oregon, cities and counties have voluntarily agreed that councils of governments would be local coordinating bodies.

71. Ibid.

72. Interview by Jim Coke with LCDC field representative, James Knight, on August 4, 1976.

73. Ibid.

74. Ibid.

75. Oregon, Department of Land Conservation and Development, Newsletter, *Oregon Lands* 1: 1 (May 1978): 4.

76. Oregon, Department of Land Conservation and Development, Newsletter, *Oregon Lands* 1: 4 (August 1978): 1, 5.

77. Interview with Henry Richmond on September 9, 1976.

78. U.S. Department of Commerce, Office of Coastal Zone Management, "Draft Evaluation Findings for the Oregon Coastal Management Program Covering the Period from March 1979 through March 1980" (Washington, D.C.: Department of Commerce, Office of Coastal Zone Management of the National Oceanic and Atmospheric Administration, 1980) p. 16.

79. Oregon, Department of Land Conservation and Development, Newsletter, *Oregon Lands* 1: 3 (July 1978): 7, and 1: 2 (June 1978): 1.

80. Interview with Jim Ross, then deputy director, now director, Department of Land Conservation and Development, on August 8, 1979. The $75 million is based on the assumption that for every dollar of grants to local governments, substantial additional dollars were expended by state and even federal agencies, and by local governments themselves.

81. 1,000 Friends of Oregon, *Newsletter*, Spring 1982, p. 10. By June 1982 the figure has changed to 145 plans acknowledged. Telephone interview with Henry Richmond, on June 21, 1982.

82. Telephone interview, Jim Ross on July 1, 1982.

83. 1,000 Friends of Oregon, *Newsletter*, Spring 1982, p. 10.

84. Ibid., p. 3. Governor Atiyeh declined to take the action recommended by 1,000 Friends of Oregon.

85. Special Report to First Annual National Agricultural Lands Conference: February 8–10, 1981, *Oregon's Agricultural Lands Protection Program,* prepared by DLCD and 1,000 Friends of Oregon, pp. 1–2.

86. *Or. Rev. Stat.* § 215.243.

87. *Or. Rev. Stat.* § 308.345–308.960.

88. See 1,000 Friends of Oregon, *Newsletter* (Spring 1981): 4.

89. 1,000 Friends of Oregon, *Progress Report,* April 1976, p. 2. *1,000 Friends of Oregon* v. *Marion County,* LCDC No. 75–006 (1977).

90. *Meyer* v. *Lord,* 37, Or. App. 59, 586 P. 2d 367 (1978).

91. 1,000 Friends of Oregon, *Newsletter* 1: 8 (May 1976): 1–2.

92. Oregon, Department of Land Conservation and Development, Newsletter, *Oregon Lands* 2: 1 (January 1979): 4.

93. Ibid.

94. Oregon, Department of Land Conservation and Development, Newsletter, *Oregon Lands* 1: 3 (July 1978): 1–7; and Special Report to the National Agricultural Lands Conference, *Oregon's Agricultural Lands Protection Program,* p. 4.

95. Interview with Henry Richmond on September 9, 1976.

96. Oregon, Department of Land Conservation and Development, Newsletter, *Oregon Lands* 1: 3 (July 1978): 3.

97. 1,000 Friends of Oregon, *Newsletter* (Winter 1981–82): 1, and personal interviews with Richard P. Benner, staff attorney, 1,000 Friends of Oregon, October 27, 1981, and with Henry Richmond on October 21, 1981.

98. 1,000 Friends of Oregon, *Newsletter* (September 1981): 4.

99. Interview with Scott Ashcom, Oregon Farm Bureau Federation, on October 27, 1981, and 1,000 Friends of Oregon, *Newsletter* (Spring 1982): 3.

100. Two close observers of the program mainly concerned with the role of the cities pinpointed the counties problems with applying the standards. One noted that "counties are not used to saying 'no', while cities are. Counties are now taking the lead to bring the program down." The other observer noted that "the brunt of the program has fallen on the counties, and it is producing recall efforts against county commissioners all over the state." Interviews with Burton Weast, director, Portland Homebuilders Association, October 27, 1981, and with Mike Houston, staff attorney, Oregon League of Cities, on October 28, 1981.

101. Interview with Gordon Fultz, staff member, Association of Oregon Counties, on October 28, 1981.

102. Interview with Richard P. Benner, 1,000 Friends staff attorney, on October 27, 1981.

103. Telephone interview with Henry Richmond on June 21, 1982.

104. 1,000 Friends, *Newsletter* (September 1981): 5, and interview with Ron Eber, plan review specialist, DLCD, on October 26, 1981. No estimate of how many rural dwellings might be approved under this law was available.

105. *Peterson* v. *City Klamath Falls,* 279 Or. 249,566 P.2d 1193 (1977).

106. Oregon, Department of Land Conservation and Development, Newsletter, *Oregon Lands* 1: 7 (November 1978): 2.

107. *Fujimoto* v. *City of Happy Valley/CRAG.*

108. Interview with Russ Beaton, economist, Willamette University, Salem, Oregon, October 29, 1981.

109. Interview with League of Cities staff attorney, Mike Houston on October 28 and 29, 1981.

110. Ibid.

111. Interview with Russ Beaton on October 29, 1981.

112. Henry R. Richmond, "Housing Costs and Local Control," 1000 Friends of Oregon, *Newsletter* 3:9 (June 1978):1.

113. Ibid.

114. Ibid.

115. Ibid.

116. *Seaman* v. *City of Durham*, Land Conservation and Development Commission, case no. 77-025. Case summary in the files of 1,000 Friends of Oregon, 400 Dekum, 519 S.W. 3rd, Portland, Oregon 97204; and Jack Kartez, "Housing Oregonians Requires Tough Decisions," Department of Land Conservation and Development, Newsletter, *Oregon Lands* vol. 1, no. 4 (August 1978): 3.

117. Ibid.

118. Oregon, Department of Land Conservation and Development, W. J. Kvarsten, director, Memorandum to the Land Conservation and Development Commission, "Subject: Item 4–5, LCDC Housing Policy," (300448/6346) July 3, 1979, p. 1.

119. Fred Van Natta, executive vice president, Oregon State Homebuilders Association, letter to Departent of Land Conservation and development director, W. J. Kvarsten, March 11, 1979 (in LCDC files).

120. Oregon, Land Conservation and Development Commission, "Housing Policy," July 3, 1979, p. 1.

121. Dale C. DeParpport, "Goal 10 and the Protection of Farmland," Department of Land Conservation and Development, Newsletter, *Oregon Lands* 1: 4 (August 1978): 4.

122. Ibid.

123. Interview with Greg Winteroud, DLCD housing and urban development specialist and Goal 10 plan reviewer, and DLCD Newsletter, *Oregon Lands* 3: 4 (April 1980): 2. Persons interviewed from the homebuilders and League of Cities agreed that densities were increasing.

124. Interviews with Greg Winteroud and Burton Weast, Portland Homebuilders, and 1,000 Friends *Newsletter* (September 1981): 6.

125. Interview with Russ Beaton on October 27 and 29, 1981.

126. 1,000 Friends of Oregon, *Newsletter* (Spring 1982): 1–2.

127. Oregon, Department of Land Conservation and Development, *Oregon Lands* 2: 11 (November 1979): 4.

128. 1,000 Friends of Oregon, *Newsletter* 4: 2 (November 1978): 1–4.

129. Ibid. A petition to force yet another vote on S B 100 in November 1982 received enough signatures to force an election. The aim is about the same as the 1978 effort: A shift in the state role from mandatory to advisory.

130. Interviews with Don Jones on January 21, 1980, and Jerry Orrick, September 8, 1976, and Oregon, Department of Land Conservation and Development, in-house memorandum, "Land Use Memorandum." January 1976.

131. Interview with Mike Houston on August 7, 1979 for the importance of dollars in bringing compliance by local governments.

132. The record of 1,000 Friends of Oregon is documented in its *Newsletters* and *Progress Reports* from 1975 to date. Its effectiveness is attested to in part by the opposition it has engendered, especially at the local government level. See testimony of Martin Crampton, Multnomah County planning director, at LCDC meetings, August 9, 1979, Salem, Oregon. In Crampton's eyes, 1,000 Friends had helped make the process unduly legalistic. For examples of the increasing interest by 1,000 Friends in the housing goal, see *Newsletter* 3: 8 (May 1978): 1; and 3: 9 (June 1978): 1–8.

133. 1,000 Friends *Newsletter,* (Winter 1981–82) and telephone interview with Henry Richmond on June 21, 1982.

134. Oregon State Homebuilders Association, statement adopted August 19, 1976.

135. Interview with Kathy Keene, staff director, Oregon Business Planning Council, Salem, Oregon, October 23, 1981.

136. Interviews with Claire Puchy, DLCD, plan review specialist, Salem, Oregon, October 23, 1981, and Lloyd Chapman, LDCD, plan review specialist, Salem, Oregon, October 29, 1981.

137. Interview with Henry Richmond on September 9, 1976.

138. Interview with Steve Schell on September 7, 1976. Schell felt strongly that it was "a mistake to put all our eggs in a comprehensive planning basket," but he was not successful in persuading LCDC to his viewpoint.

139. Interview with Bill Young on September 8, 1976.

140. 1,000 Friends of Oregon, *Progress Report,* Fall 1976.

141. 1,000 Friends of Oregon, *Newsletter* 2: 4 (January 1977), and see also Oregon, Land Conservation and Development Commission, Department of Land Conservation and Development, *Oregon Coastal Management Program,* 1976, pp. 179–216, for a full text of the goals and guidelines applying to the coast.

142. *Oregon Coastal Management Program,* pp. 182–83, 195–96.

143. U.S. Department of Commerce, Office of Coastal Zone Management, "Draft Evaluation," March 1979 through March 1980, p. 13.

144. Ibid., pp. 13–15.

145. Ibid., pp. 16–20.

146. Interview with Richard Benner on October 27, 1981.

147. Interview with Richard Benner on October 27, 1981. It is true that LCDC asked for more staff in the early days of the program and did not receive support from either the governor or the legislature, doubtless discouraging them from seeking added staff.

148. Interviews with Richard Benner on October 27, 1981, and Dick Mathews, DLCD plan review specialist, Salem, Oregon, October 23, 1981.

149. U.S. Department of Commerce, National Oceanic and Atmospheric Administration, Office of Coastal Zone Management, "Performance Review of Oregon Coastal Management for the Period from April 1980 through February 1981" (Washington, D.C.: Office of Coastal Zone Management, 1981), p. 1.

150. Ibid., p. 5.

151. Ibid., p. 10.

152. Ibid.

153. Ibid., p. 8.

154. See senate bill 100, part I, § 1 (2) and part II, § 11 (6).

155. Interview with Jim Claypool, state agency coordination specialist, DLCD, Salem, on October 22, 1981, and with Leonard Kunzman, director, Department of Agriculture, on October 26, 1981.

156. Interview with Pat Amadeo, special assistant to the governor, on October 26, 1981.

157. Interview with Jim Ross on October 22, 1981.

158. Oregon, Department of Land Conservation and Development, "Post-Acknowledgement Policy Draft," DLCD files, n.d.

159. Ibid.

160. Interview with Gordon Fultz, staff member, Association of Oregon Counties, October 28, 1981.

161. For a full detailing of all the major actions by the 1981 legislature, see 1,000 Friends of Oregon, *Newsletter* (September 1981). The assessment is drawn from interviews with representatives of 1,000 Friends, the governor's office, the Oregon League of Cities, the Oregon Association of Counties, the Oregon Business Council, and DLCD.

162. Telephone interview with Jim Ross on July 1, 1982.

163. Interview with Jim Ross on October 22, 1981.

164. 1,000 Friends, *Newsletter* (September 1981).

165. Telephone interview with Henry Richmond on June 21, 1982.

166. Telephone interview with Henry Richmond, on February 22, 1983; and Terry D. Morgan, "Oregon's Land Use Laws Upheld," *Land Use Law,* January 1983, p. 3.

Chapter Seven. Colorado:
A State-Local Puzzle

1. John R. Bermingham, chairman, Colorado Land Use Commission, "Colorado Land Use Laws," June 1975, unpublished, p. 5, available in the files of the Colorado Land Use Commission.

2. Interview with John R. Bermingham, former state senator, former governor's assistant, and former chairman, Colorado Land Use Commission, Denver, Colorado, October 25, 1977. Bermingham was an advocate for a strong state role in land use.

3. Christopher J. Warner, "Of Growth Controls, Wilderness and the Urban Strip," *The Colorado Lawyer, Land Use, A Special Symposium* 6: 10 (October 1977): 1734–35.

4. Kirk Wickersham, Jr., "Land Use Management in Colorado: Past, Present and Future," *The Colorado Lawyer* 6: 10 (October 1977): 1779–80.

5. Ibid., p. 1780.

6. Interview with Lee Woolsey, former deputy director, Department of Local Affairs, and director, Colorado Land Use Commission, Denver, October 27, 1977.

7. Wickersham, "Land Use Management," p. 1781. The power of the state to intervene has not been used.

8. Ibid.

9. Interview with Lee Woolsey on October 27, 1977. For a further assessment of senate bill 35, see Colorado, Senate Committee on Wildlife, Parks, Natural Resources and Energy, "Committee Memorandum," March 13, 1976, p. 4.

10. Interview with J. K. Smith, assistant director, Colorado Counties, Inc., Denver, Colorado, October 25, 1977.

11. Interview with Representative Betty Ann Dittemore, Colorado house, October 26, 1977.

12. Interview with John Bermingham on October 25, 1977. The nervousness of the Republicans was well founded, since in the subsequent 1974 elections Republicans did in fact lose the governorship and the house and only maintained control of the senate by a very narrow margin.

13. John R. Bermingham, "Colorado Land Use Laws," p. 5.

14. This description of senate bill 377 is based in part on the author's interviews with John Bermingham and others but is taken in large measure

from an excellent masters thesis analyzing the effort to pass a land use law in both 1973 and 1974. See Gary K. Fisher, "A Political Analysis of the Enactment of HB 1041" (Masters thesis, Colorado State University, Fort Collins, Colorado, 1975).

15. Gary Fisher, "Political Analysis," pp. 14–15.

16. Ibid., pp. 15–16.

17. Interview with John Bermingham on October 25, 1977.

18. A detailed explanation of the interim committee's proposed bill is given in Fisher, "Political Analysis," p. 24.

19. Bob Ewegan, "Coalition Confident Land Proposal Will Pass in House," *Denver Post*, March 3, 1974, quoted in Fisher, "Political Analysis," p. 27.

20. Fisher, "Political Analysis," p. 28.

21. Quote taken from tapes of House Local Government Committee consideration of HB 1041, February 4, 1974, discussion of Strang Amendment by Lamm, as reported in Fisher, "Political Analysis," p. 30.

22. The political maneuvering at this point is reported in Fisher, "Political Analysis," pp. 31–32, and is taken in part from Ewegan, "Coalition Confident," and from James Monoghan, "Legislature's Land Use Remedy is Fog of Confusion," *The Rocky Mountain News, Trend Magazine*, June 30, 1974.

23. Fisher, "Political Analysis," p. 35.

24. Ibid.

25. Ibid., p. 37.

26. Ibid., p. 40.

27. Colorado State Legislature, House Land Use Committee, tapes of the floor debate on H.B. 1041, 49th General Assembly, Representative Strang speaking to Senate Amendments to H.B. 1041, April 24, 1974, as reported in Fisher, "Political Analysis," p. 40.

28. Bob Ewegan, "Battlelines Drawn on Land Use Issue," *Denver Post*, April 19, 1974, as cited in Fisher, "Political Analysis," p. 44.

29. Fisher, "Political Analysis," p. 46.

30. Tapes of house floor debate on house bill 1041, Concurrence Debate, April 24, 1974, as reported in Fisher, "Political Analysis," p. 47.

31. Fisher, "Political Analysis," p. 47.

32. Interview with J. K. Smith on October 25, 1977.

33. Interview with John Bermingham on October 25, 1977.

34. Interview with Representative Betty Ann Dittemore on October 26, 1977.

35. Interview with John Bermingham on October 25, 1977.

36. For a detailed but relatively brief assessment of the provisions of house bill 1041, see John A. Bermingham, "1974 Land Use Legislation in Colorado," *Denver Law Journal* 51: 4 (1974): 492; and Michael D. White and Raymond L. Petros, "Land Use Legislation: HB 1034 and HB 1041," *Colorado Lawyer* 6: 10 (October 1977); and Daniel R. Mandelker, *Environmental and Land Use Control Legislation* (Washington, D.C.: Urban Land Institute, 1976), pp. 117–22.

37. In the light of Florida's difficulties, examined in an earlier chapter, with the issue of the unconstitutional delegation of legislative authority, this may have been a wise approach.

38. *Colo. Rev. Stat.* (1973) house bill 1041 (1974) hereafter house bill 1041 or "C.R.S. 1973 (1975 Cum. Supp.), § 24–65–101 et seq."

39. Ibid., C.R.S. 1973 (1975 Cum. Supp.) § 24–65.1–101(2)(b)(c).

40. Ibid., C.R.S. 1973 (1975 Cum. Supp.), § 24–65.1–202.

41. Ibid., C.R.S. 1973 (1975 Cum. Supp.), § 24–65.1–201.

42. Warner, "Of Growth Controls," p. 1744.

43. Ibid., C.R.S. 1973 (1975 Cum. Supp.), § 24–65.1–204.

44. Ibid., C.R.S. 1973 (1975 Cum. Supp.), §§ 24–65.1–301 and 24–65.1–302.

45. Ibid., C.R.S. 1973 (1975 Cum. Supp.), § 24–65.1–401(2)(b).

46. Ibid., C.R.S. 1973 (1975 Cum. Supp.), § 24–65.1–403.

47. Ibid., C.R.S. 1973 (1975 Cum. Supp.), § 24–65.1–406.

48. C.R.S. 1973 (1975 Cum. Supp.), § 24–65.1–404 and § 24–65.1–407.

49. C.R.S. 1973 (1975 Cum. Supp.), § 24–65.1–407(c).

50. C.R.S. 1973 (1975 Cum. Supp.), § 24–65.1–501.

51. C.R.S. 1973 (1975 Cum. Supp.), § 24–32–111.

52. Ibid.

53. Michael D. White and Raymond L. Petros, "Land Use Legislation: house bill 1034 and house bill 1041," *Colorado Lawyer*, 6: 10 (October 1977): 1691–94.

54. Ibid., p. 1694.

55. Interview with Fred Saunderman, land use commission member, Colorado Springs, October 29, 1977.

56. Interview with Gary Fisher, former staff member, Colorado Land Use Commission, on October 27, 1977.

57. Interview with Buie Sewell, former member, Colorado Land Use Commission, and Head, State Energy Conservation Office, on October 27, 1977.

58. Interview with Lee Woolsey on October 27, 1977.

59. Interview with J. K. Smith on October 25, 1977.

60. Interview with Fred Sauderman on October 29, 1977.

61. Interview with John Bermingham on October 25, 1977.

62. Interview with Buie Sewell on October 27, 1977.

63. Interview with Gene Fisher, Denver, Colorado, on October 28, 1977.

64. Telephone interview with Steve Ellis, staff administrator to the Colorado Land Use Commission and Chief Planner, Division of Local Government, Colorado Department of Local Affairs, June 1, 1982.

65. Long Appropriations Act, as enacted by Senate Bill 581 in 1977, as quoted in White and Petros, "Land Use Legislation," p. 1698.

66. Ibid.

67. Alan N. Jenson, "Colorado's Land Use Law as Seen by a Country Lawyer," *Colorado Lawyer* 6: 10 (October 1977): 1772–73.

68. Interview with J. K. Smith on October 25, 1977.

69. Interview with Charlie Foster, former field representative and coordinator of field representatives, Division of Planning, Department of Local Affairs, Denver, Colorado, October 28, 1977.

70. Interview with Fred Saunderman on October 28, 1977.

71. Interview with John Bermingham on October 25, 1977.

72. Ibid.

73. Interview with Gary Fisher on October 27, 1977.

74. Interview with J. K. Smith on October 25, 1977.

75. Interview with Gary Fisher on October 27, 1977.

76. Ibid.

77. Interview with John Bermingham on October 25, 1977.

78. Interview with Fred Saunderman on October 28, 1977.

79. R. James Nicholson, "Of Land Use Legislation, Developers, Uncertainty and Things," *The Colorado Lawyer* 6: 10 (October 1977): 1760–61.

80. Ibid.

81. Ibid.

82. The details of these six cases were taken from White and Petros, "Land Use Legislation: house bill 1034 and house bill 1041," p. 1706, and James L. Kurtz-Phelan, "HB 1041: A Step Toward Responsible and Accountable Land Use Decisions," *The Colorado Lawyer* 6: 10 (October 1977), notes 20, 21, 22, 23, 24, and 26. See also in-house memorandum, "LUC Cases: 1973–present," March 23, 1977, Colorado Land Use Commission. This memorandum also contains an extensive listing of matters in which the commission has given technical assistance, carried out technical reviews and otherwise been of assistance to local governments beyond the use of its formal 407 and temporary emergency review powers.

83. Kurtz-Phelan, "Step Toward Responsible Land Use Decisions," pp. 1723–24.

84. Interview with Representative Betty Ann Dittemore on October 26, 1977.

85. Interview with Lee Woolsey on October 27, 1977.

86. Interview with Fred Saunderman on October 29, 1977.

87. Interview with J. K. Smith on October 25, 1977.

88. Interview with Gene Fisher, chairman, Colorado Land Use Commission, on October 28, 1977.

89. Ibid.

90. The data for this description of the Douglas County case come from the verified complaint of the state land use commission to the District Court in and for the county, Colorado Land Use Commission, plaintiff, versus the Douglas County Board of County Commissioners. See also letter from the assistant attorney general to the county attorney of Douglas County, dated October 11, 1977, all available in the files of the state land use commission.

91. Interviews with J. K. Smith on October 25, 1977, and Gary Fisher, October 27, 1977.

92. Interview with Representative Betty Ann Dittemore on October 26, 1977.

93. White and Petros, "Land Use Legislation," pp. 1706–07.

94. Warner, "Of Growth Controls," p. 1737.

95. Nicholson, "Of Land Use Legislation," p. 1763.

96. Colorado, *Appropriations Act*, ch. 1, *Colo. Sess. Laws*, SB 525, 52nd General Assembly, 1st regular session, p. 61. The Land Use Commission appropriation is $61,164 from the general fund (2.0 FTE).

97. Colorado State Land Use Commission, in-house memorandum, "Land Use Commission Work Program: Fiscal 1977–78," July 13, 1977.

98. Ibid., August 19, 1977, "Procedures for Work Program."

99. Ibid., August 22, 1977, "LUC Work Program and Related Topics."

100. Interview with Gene Fisher on October 28, 1977.

101. Presentation by Lee Woolsey, executive director, at Colorado Land Use Commission meeting on October 28, 1977.

102. Ibid.

103. Telephone interview with Lee Woolsey on July 31, 1980, and with Ted Rodenbeck, staff member, senior planner, Division of Planning, Colorado Department of Local Affairs, August 11, 1980.

104. *Colorado Land Use Commission v. The Board of County Commissioners of*

the County of Larimer, et al., in the Supreme Court of Colorado, no. 79SA47, December 17, 1979.

105. Ibid., p. 8–9.

106. Colorado Land Use Commission, "Statement of Policy Regarding Local Regulation of Matters of State Interest, June 16, 1978," unnumbered, third page.

107. Telephone interview with Lee Woolsey on July 31, 1980.

108. Colorado, Division of State Planning *Colorado Human Settlement Policies,* July 20, 1979, p. 1.

109. For a more complete statement of the content of the ten policies, see ibid., pp. 2–3 and the narrative supplement statements that follow.

110. Telephone interviews with Lee Woolsey and with Ted Rodenbeck on July 31, 1980 and August 11, 1980.

111. Telephone interview with Steve Ellis on June 1, 1982.

112. White and Petros, "Land Use Legislation," pp. 1706–08.

113. Telephone interview with Steve Ellis on June 1, 1982.

114. Interview with Gary Fisher on October 27, 1977.

115. Jensen, "Colorado's Land Use Law," pp.1771–77.

116. Kurtz-Phelan, "Step Toward Responsible Land Use Decisions," p. 1719.

117. Telephone interview with Steve Ellis on June 1, 1982.

118. Interview with J. K. Smith on October 25, 1977.

119. Interview with Governor Richard Lamm on October 27, 1977.

120. Interview with Gene Fisher on October 28, 1977.

Chapter Eight. North Carolina: Combining the Local and State Roles

1. Southern Growth Policies Board, The Commission on the Future of the South, "The Future of the South," *Report of the Commission on the Future of the South to the Southern Growth Policies Board* (Research Triangle Park, North Carolina: Southern Growth Policies Board, 1974), pp. 21–29.

2. Interviews with James Harrington, former state secretary of natural and economic resources; Dr. Arthur Cooper, forestry department, North Carolina State University, former assistant secretary of the Department of Natural and Economic Resources, now a member of the Coastal Resources Commission; Durwood Laughinghouse, special assistant for environmental affairs to the commissioner of agriculture; Jonathan Howes, director, Center for Regional and Urban Studies and chairman, Advisory Committee to the Land Policy Council; and Bruce Lentz, secretary, Department of Administration, over the period August 2–4, 1976.

3. Interview with James Harrington on August 2, 1976.

4. Interview with Dr. Arthur Cooper on August 3, 1976.

5. Elizabeth H. Haskell, *Land Use Organizations for North Carolina,* (Raleigh, N.C.: North Carolina Land Policy Council, March 1, 1976), pp. 171–72.

6. Ibid., pp. 171–75.

7. Ibid., pp. 177–78.

8. Ibid., p. 179.

9. Ibid., pp. 176–82.

10. Interview with Dr. Arthur Cooper on August 3, 1976.

11. Milton S. Heath, Jr., "A Legislative History of the Coastal Area Management Act," *North Carolina Law Review* 53 (December 1974): 345.

12. Ibid.

13. Ibid.

14. Ibid.

15. Interview with Willis Whichard, member, North Carolina house, now member of the senate on July 22, 1976.

16. Willis P. Whichard, remarks to the Rotary Club, Durham, North Carolina, on June 9, 1975, pp. 3–4.

17. Heath, "Legislative History," p. 350.

18. Ibid., p. 360.

19. Ibid., pp. 360–62.

20. Whichard, Rotary Club speech, on June 9, 1975.

21. Interview with James Harrington on August 2, 1976.

22. Heath, "Legislative History," p. 397.

23. Ibid., pp. 397–98.

24. Ibid., pp. 365–67.

25. Ibid., pp. 370–71.

26. Ibid., p. 371, note 74.

27. Ibid., p. 381.

28. Ibid., pp. 384–86.

29. Ibid., pp. 386–87.

30. Ibid., pp. 387–89.

31. Ibid., pp. 389–92.

32. Ibid., pp. 392–93.

33. Ibid., pp. 393–97.

34. *N.C. Gen. Stat.* Article 7, Coastal Area Management Act, §§ 113A–102.

35. Ibid., § 113A–102(b)(1–4).

36. Ibid., §§ 113A–104 and 113A–105.

37. Ibid., part two, Planning Process, §§ 113A–106 through 113A–105.

38. Ibid., part three, Areas of Environmental Concern, §§ 113A–113, 114, and 115.

39. Ibid., §§ 113A–116 through 113A–122.

40. Ibid., part four, Permit Letting and Enforcement, §§ 113A–116 through 113A–126.

41. This framework is taken largely from an interview with Arthur W. Cooper and from the U.S. Department of Commerce, National Oceanic and Atmospheric Administration, Office of Coastal Zone Management, "Draft Environmental Impact Statement and Proposed Coastal Management Program for the State of North Carolina," prepared by the Office of Coastal Zone Management, National Oceanic and Atmospheric Administration, Department of Commerce, Washington, D.C. and the North Carolina Coastal Management Program, Department of Natural Resources and Community Development, Raleigh, N.C., 1978, Vol. II: "Appendices," pp. 245–47.

42. "Draft Environmental Impact Statement and Proposed Coastal Zone Management Program for the State of North Carolina," Vol. I, pp. 31–32, and Vol. II, pp. 315–16.

43. In 1974 only four counties and seven cities had land use plans. See Bill Finger and Barry Jacobs, "Coastal Management: A Planning Beachhead in North Carolina," *N C Insight* 5: 1 (May 1982): 3.

44. North Carolina, *Coastal Resources Commission Report*, April 23, 1982, attachment, "Coastal Management Update: Progress in Planning for the Coastal Area," unnumbered, first page, available from the Office of Coastal Management, Department of Natural Resources and Community Development, Raleigh, N.C. See also Finger and Jacobs, "Coastal Management," pp. 2–3.

45. Draft Environmental Impact Statement and Proposed Coastal Zone Management Program for the state of North Carolina," Vol. I, pp. 22–25.

46. Interview with Dr. Arthur Cooper on June 14, 1979.

47. *Adams v. Department of Natural and Economic Resources*, 295 N.C. 683, 279 SE 2nd 402 (1978).

48. Milton S. Heath, Jr. and Allen C. Moseley, "The Coastal Area Management Act." *Popular Government* 45: 4 (Spring 1980): 3.

49. "Draft Environmental Impact Statement and Proposed Coastal Zone Management Program for the State of North Carolina," Vol. II, pp. 245–47.

50. *Coastal Management News* 2: 5 (January 1976): 6.

51. *Coastal Management News* 2: 7 (March 1979), p. 1.

52. Ibid., pp. 4–6.

53. *Coastal Management News* 2: 3 (July 1979): 1.

54. *Coastal Management News* 3: 2 (October 1979): 3, 6.

55. Ibid.; see also U.S. Office of Coastal Zone Management, *Final Evaluation Findings for the North Carolina Coastal Management Program: March 1981–January 1982* (Washington, D.C.: Office of Coastal Zone Management, 1982), p. 1.

56. Telephone interview with David Owens, assistant director, Office of Coastal Management, N.C. Department of Natural Resources and Community Development, on June 7, 1982. See also "Coastal Management Update: Progress in Planning," pp. 1–2, and Heath and Moseley, "Coastal Area Management Act."

57. Heath and Moseley, "Coastal Area Management Act" p. 2.

58. "Draft Environmental Impact Statement and Proposed Coastal Zone Management Program for the State of North Carolina," Vol. I, pp. 32–34.

59. Ibid., p. 127. The selection of these areas was very conservative given the scope of the CAMA authority. It focused only on those areas of environmental concern peculiar to the coast, partly in an effort to guard against a court challenge of the constitutionality of the law on equal protection grounds. For a detailed description of the areas of environmental concern and the regulations involved, see chapter 5, and also Vol. II, pp. 87–127, including maps of areas of environmental concern in each county.

60. Ibid., Vol. II, pp. 244–47. See also Heath and Moseley, "Coastal Area Management Act," p. 2, and *Final Evaluation North Carolina Coastal Management Program: March 1981–January 1982*, p. 3.

61. *Coastal Management News* 1: 6 (April 1978): 5, and 2: 1 (August 1978): 3.

62. *Coastal Management News* 2: 3 (October–November 1978): 1, 2.

63. Charles D. Liner, *The Impact of State Regulation of Coastal Land in North Carolina* (University of North Carolina at Chapel Hill, Institute of Government, May 1980), p. 18.

64. *Final Evaluation North Carolina Coastal Management Program: March 1981–January 1982*, p. 3.

65. *Coastal Management News* 2: 10 (July 1979): 3, and 3: 1 (August–September 1979): 3.

66. For the proposal submitted to the U.S. Department of Commerce,

National Oceanic and Atmospheric Administration, Office of Coastal Zone Management, see "Draft Environmental Impact Statement and Proposed Coastal Zone Management Program for the State of North Carolina," Vols. I and II.

67. *Coastal Management News*, 2: 6 (February 1979): 1.

68. Ibid.

69. *Coastal Management News*, 2: 8 (April–May 1979): 1.

70. *Coastal Management News*, 2: 6 (February 1979): 3.

71. *Coastal Management News* 2: 8 (April–May 1979): 5–6.

72. *Coastal Management News* 3: 5 (April–May 1980): 4–5.

73. North Carolina, *Coastal Resources Commission Report*, June 4, 1982, Appended summary, "Coastal Management Permits," available from the Office of Coastal Management, Department of Natural Resources and Community Development, Raleigh, North Carolina.

74. *Final Evaluation North Carolina Coastal Management Program: March 1981–January 1982*, pp. 6–7.

75. *Coastal Management News* 4: 4 (May–June 1981): 1–2; *Final Evaluation North Carolina Coastal Management Program: March 1981–January 1982*, p. 9, 12; and telephone interview with David Owens on June 7, 1982.

76. *Final Evaluation North Carolina Coastal Management Program: March 1981–January 1982*, p. 11.

77. Ibid., p. 10–11.

78. Finger and Jacobs, "Coastal Management," pp. 7–8.

79. *Final Evaluation North Carolina Coastal Management Program: March 1981–January 1982*, pp. 16–17.

80. Heath and Moseley, "Coastal Area Management Act," p. 3.

81. Ibid.

82. *Coastal Management News* 4: 3 (March–April 1981): 1, 4. See also *Final Evaluation North Carolina Coastal Program March 1981–January 1982*, p. 15.

83. Finger and Jacobs, "Coastal Management," p. 7, and *Coastal Resources Commission Report*, April 23, 1982, p. 1.

84. *Coastal Management News* 2: 10 (July 1979): 4.

85. Finger and Jacobs, "Coastal Management," pp. 12–13, and telephone interview with David Owens on June 7, 1982.

86. For a detailed description of the setback rules adopted in 1978 and 1979 and amended in February and June 1981, see *Final Evaluation North Carolina Coastal Management Program: March 1981–January 1982*, pp. 9–10.

87. Heath and Moseley, "Coastal Area Management Act," p. 1.

88. North Carolina: Office of State Planning, Land Policy Council, Final Report: *A Land Resources Program for North Carolina* (Raleigh, N.C.: Land Policy Council, Office of State Planning, December 1976), pp. 4–1, 4–2.

89. Interview with Jonathan Howes on August 4, 1976, and follow-up interview, 1980.

90. North Carolina, Senate, DRS 8566, "Outline of Main Features of State Land Resources Act," courtesy of Senator Willis Whichard, n.d.

91. Interview with Senator Willis Whichard on July 14, 1977.

92. Telephone interview with Jonathan Howes on June 7, 1982.

93. Telephone interviews with Jonathan Howes and David Owens on June 7, 1982.

94. Telephone interview with David Owens on June 7, 1982.

Chapter Nine. Land and Growth Management in the States: A Comparative Assessment

1. A further articulation of this movement can be seen in the development by a number of states of state urban strategies, themselves typically an outgrowth of land- and growth-management initiatives. See Charles R. Warren, *The States and Urban Strategies: A Comparative Analysis* (Washington, D.C.: National Academy of Public Administration, September 1980).

2. The law was tested anew in November 1982 in the midst of the state's worst recession since the 1930s. The vote on whether to convert the state program to an advisory status failed by a 55 to 45 percent margin.

3. U.S. Environmental Protection Agency, National Research Council, Committee on Environmental Decision Making, "Decision Making in the Environmental Protection Agency: A Report to the U.S. Environmental Protection Agency from the Committee on Environmental Decision Making, Commission on Natural Resources, National Research Council" (Washington, D.C.: National Academy of Sciences, 1977). The Reagan administration effort to phase out funding for the coastal program by 1984 will test the capacity—political, fiscal, and otherwise—of states to continue the programs. Early indications are that they will not be abandoned.

Index